D1198775

The Zend-avesta

THE

SACRED BOOKS OF THE EAST

TRANSLATED

BY VARIOUS ORIENTAL SCHOLARS

AND EDITED BY

F. MAX MÜLLER

VOL. IV

Oxford

AT THE CLARENDON PRESS

1880

[*All rights reserved*]

5021
.798
pt. 1
v.4

THE ZEND-AVESTA

PART I

THE VENDÎDÂD

TRANSLATED BY

JAMES DARMESTETER

Oxford

AT THE CLARENDON PRESS

1880

[*All rights reserved*]

CONTENTS.

INTRODUCTION.

TRANSLATION OF THE VENDÎDÂD.

INTRODUCTION.

CHAPTER I.

THE DISCOVERY OF THE ZEND-AVESTA.

THE Zend-Avesta is the sacred book of the Parsis, that is to say, of the few remaining followers of that religion which reigned over Persia at the time when the second successor of Mohammed overthrew the Sassanian dynasty [1], and which has been called Dualism, or Mazdeism, or Magism, or Zoroastrianism, or Fire-worship, according as its main tenet, or its supreme God [2], or its priests, or its supposed founder, or its apparent object of worship has been most kept in view. In less than a century after their defeat, nearly all the conquered people were brought over to the faith of their new rulers, either by force, or policy, or the attractive power of a simpler form of creed. But many of those who clung to the faith of their fathers, went and sought abroad for a new home, where they might freely worship their old gods, say their old prayers, and perform their old rites. That home they found at last among the tolerant Hindus, on the western coast of India and in the peninsula of Guzerat [3]. There they throve and there they live still, while the ranks of their co-religionists in Persia are daily thinning and dwindling away [4].

As the Parsis are the ruins of a people, so are their

---

[1] At the battle of Nihâvand (642 A. C.)   [2] Ahura Mazda.

[3] They settled first at Sangân, not far from Damân ; thence they spread over Surat, Nowsâri, Broach, and Kambay ; and within the last two centuries they have settled at Bombay, which now contains the bulk of the Parsi people, nearly 150,000 souls.

[4] A century ago, it is said, they still numbered nearly 100,000 souls; but there now remain no more than 8000 or 9000 souls, scattered in Yezd and the surrounding villages (Dosabhoy Framjee, The Parsees).

sacred books the ruins of a religion. There has been no
other great belief in the world that ever left such poor and
meagre monuments of its past splendour. Yet great is the
value which that small book, the Avesta, and the belief of
that scanty people, the Parsis, have in the eyes of the his-
torian and theologist, as they present to us the last reflex
of the ideas which prevailed in Iran during the five centuries which preceded and the seven which followed the
birth of Christ, a period which gave to the world the Gospels, the Talmud, and the Qur'ân. Persia, it is known, had
much influence on each of the movements which produced,
or proceeded from, those three books; she lent much to
the first heresiarchs, much to the Rabbis, much to Mohammed. By help of the Parsi religion and the Avesta, we are
enabled to go back to the very heart of that most mo-
mentous period in the history of religious thought, which
saw the blending of the Aryan mind with the Semitic, and
thus opened the second stage of Aryan thought.

Inquiries into the religion of ancient Persia began long
ago, and it was the old foe of Persia, the Greek, who first
studied it. Aristotle[1], Hermippus[2], and many others[3]
wrote of it in books of which, unfortunately, nothing more
than a few fragments or merely the titles have come down
to us. We find much valuable information about it, scattered in the accounts of historians and travellers, extending
over ten centuries, from Herodotus down to Agathias and
Procopius. It was never more eagerly studied than in the
first centuries of the Christian era; but that study had no
longer anything of the disinterested and almost scientific
character it had in earlier times. Religious and philosophic
sects, in search of new dogmas, eagerly received whatever
came to them bearing the name of Zoroaster. As Xanthus
the Lydian, who is said to have lived before Herodotus,
had mentioned Zoroastrian Λόγια[4], there came to light, in
those later times, scores of oracles, styled Λόγια τοῦ Ζωροάσ-

---

[1] Diogenes Laertius, Prooemium 8.
[2] Pliny, Hist. Nat. XXX, 1, 2. Cf. infra, III, 11.
[3] Dinon, Theopompus, Hermodorus, Heraclides Cumanus.
[4] See Nicolaus Damazcenus, Didot, Fragm. Hist. III, 409.

τρου, or 'Oracula Chaldaïca sive Magica,' the work of Neo-
Platonists who were but very remote disciples of the Median
sage. As his name had become the very emblem of wisdom,
they would cover with it the latest inventions of their ever-
deepening theosophy. Zoroaster and Plato were treated
as if they had been philosophers of the same school, and
Hierocles expounded their doctrines in the same book.
Proclus collected seventy Tetrads of Zoroaster and wrote
commentaries on them[1]; but we need hardly say that
Zoroaster commented on by Proclus was nothing more or
less than Proclus commented on by Proclus. Prodicus the
Gnostic had secret books of Zoroaster[2]; and upon the
whole it may be said that in the first centuries of Christianity, the religion of Persia was more studied and
less understood than it had ever been before. The real
object aimed at, in studying the old religion, was to form a
new one.

Throughout the Middle Ages nothing was known of
Mazdeism but the name of its founder, who from a Magus
was converted into a magician and master of the hidden
sciences. It was not until the Renaissance that real inquiry was resumed. The first step was to collect all the
information that could be gathered from Greek and Roman
writers. That task was undertaken and successfully completed by Barnabé Brisson[3]. A nearer approach to the
original source was made in the following century by
Italian, English, and French travellers in Asia. Pietro
della Valle, Henry Lord, Mandelslo, Ovington, Chardin,
Gabriel du Chinon, and Tavernier found Zoroaster's last
followers in Persia and India, and made known their existence, their manners, and the main features of their belief to
Europe. Gabriel du Chinon saw their books and recognised that they were not all written in the same language,
their original holy writ being no longer understood except

---

[1] Fabricius, Graeca Bibliotheca, fourth ed. p. 309 seq.
[2] Clemens Alexandrinus, Stromata I. Cf. infra, III, 11, and Porphyrius, de vita Plotini, § 16.
[3] 'De regio Persarum principatu libri tres,' Paris, 1590. The second book is devoted to the religion and manners of the ancient Persians.

by means of translations and commentaries in another tongue.

In the year 1700, a professor at Oxford, Thomas Hyde, the greatest Orientalist of his time in Europe, made the first systematic attempt to restore the history of the old Persian religion by combining the accounts of the Mohammedan writers with 'the true and genuine monuments of ancient Persia[1].' Unfortunately the so-called genuine monuments of ancient Persia were nothing more than recent compilations referring to the last stage of Parsîism. But notwithstanding this defect, which could hardly be avoided then, and notwithstanding its still worse fault, a strange want of critical acumen[2], the book of Thomas Hyde was the first complete and true picture of modern Parsîism, and it made inquiry into its history the order of the day. A warm appeal made by him to the zeal of travellers, to seek for and procure at any price the sacred books of the Parsis, did not remain ineffectual, and from that time scholars bethought themselves of studying Parsîism in its own home.

Eighteen years later, a countryman of Hyde, George Boucher, received from the Parsis in Surat a copy of the Vendîdâd Sâdah, which was brought to England in 1723 by Richard Cobbe. But the old manuscript was a sealed book, and the most that could then be made of it was to hang it by an iron chain to the wall of the Bodleian Library, as a curiosity to be shown to foreigners. A few years later, a Scotchman, named Fraser, went to Surat, with the view of obtaining from the Parsis, not only their books, but also a knowledge of their contents. He was not very successful in the first undertaking, and utterly failed in the second.

In 1754 a young man, twenty years old, Anquetil Duperron, a scholar of the Ecole des Langues Orientales in Paris, happened to see a facsimile of four leaves of the

---

[1] 'Veterum Persarum et Parthorum et Medorum religionis historia,' Oxford, 1700.

[2] Thus he recognised in Abraham the first lawgiver of ancient Persia, in Magism a Sabean corruption of the primeval faith, and in Zoroaster a reformer, who had learnt the forgotten truth from the exiled Jews in Babylon.

Oxford Vendîdâd, which had been sent from England, a few years before, to Etienne Fourmont, the Orientalist. He determined at once to give to France both the books of Zoroaster and the first European translation of them. Impatient to set off, without waiting for a mission from the government which had been promised to him, he enlisted as a private soldier in the service of the French East India Company; he embarked at Lorient on the 24th of February 1755, and after three years of endless adventures and dangers through the whole breadth of Hindustan, at the very time when war was raging between France and England, he arrived at last in Surat, where he stayed among the Parsis for three years more. Here began another struggle, not less hard, but more decisive, against that mistrust and ill-will of the Parsis which had disheartened Fraser; but he came out of it victorious, and succeeded at last in winning from the Parsis both their books and their knowledge. He came back to Paris on the 14th of March 1764, and deposited on the following day at the Bibliothèque Royale the whole of the Zend-Avesta and copies of most of the traditional books. He spent ten years in studying the material he had collected, and published in 1771 the first European translation of the Zend-Avesta[1].

A violent dispute broke out at once, as half the learned world denied the authenticity of the Avesta, which it pronounced a forgery. It was the future founder of the Royal Asiatic Society, William Jones, a young Oxonian then, who opened the war. He had been wounded to the quick by the scornful tone adopted by Anquetil towards Hyde and a few other English scholars: the Zend-Avesta suffered for the fault of its introducer, Zoroaster for Anquetil. In a pamphlet written in French[2], with a verve and in a style which showed him to be a good disciple of Voltaire, W. Jones pointed out, and dwelt upon, the oddities and

---

[1] 'Zend-Avesta, ouvrage de Zoroastre, contenant les Idées Théologiques, Physiques et Morales de ce Législateur. . . . Traduit en François sur l'Original Zend.' Par M. Anquetil Du Perron, 3 vols. in 4°, Paris, 1771.

[2] 'Lettre à M. A*** du P***, dans laquelle est compris l'examen de sa traduction des livres attribués à Zoroastre.'

absurdities with which the so-called sacred books of Zoroaster teemed. It is true that Anquetil had given full scope
to satire by the style he had adopted : he cared very little
for literary elegance, and did not mind writing Zend and
Persian in French ; so the new and strange ideas he had to
express looked stranger still in the outlandish garb he gave
them. Yet it was less the style than the ideas that
shocked the contemporary of Voltaire[1]. His main argument was that books, full of such silly tales, of laws and
rules so absurd, of descriptions of gods and demons so
grotesque, could not be the work of a sage like Zoroaster,
nor the code of a religion so much celebrated for its simpli-
city, wisdom, and purity. His conclusion was that the
Avesta was a rhapsody of some modern Guebre. In fact
the only thing in which Jones succeeded was to prove in a
decisive manner that the ancient Persians were not equal
to the lumières of the eighteenth century, and that the
authors of the Avesta had not read the Encyclopédie.

Jones's censure was echoed in England by Sir John
Chardin and Richardson, in Germany by Meiners. Richardson tried to give a scientific character to the attacks of
Jones by founding them on philological grounds[2]. That
the Avesta was a fabrication of modern times was shown,
he argued, by the number of Arabic words he fancied he
found both in the Zend and Pahlavi dialects, as no Arabic
element was introduced into the Persian idioms earlier than
the seventh century ; also by the harsh texture of the
Zend, contrasted with the rare euphony of the Persian ;
and, lastly, by the radical difference between the Zend
and Persian, both in words and grammar. To these objec-
tions, drawn from the form, he added another derived from
the uncommon stupidity of the matter.

In Germany, Meiners, to the charges brought against the
new found books, added another of a new and unexpected
kind, namely, that they spoke of ideas unheard of before,
and made known new things. 'Pray, who would dare

---

[1] Cf. the article on Zoroaster in the Dictionnaire philosophique.
[2] 'A Dissertation on the Languages, Literature, and Manners of Eastern
Nations,' Oxford, 1777.

ascribe to Zoroaster books in which are found numberless names of trees, animals, men, and demons unknown to the ancient Persians; in which are invoked an incredible number of pure animals and other things, which, as appears from the silence of ancient writers, were never known, or at least never worshipped, in Persia? What Greek ever spoke of Hom, of Jemshîd, and of such other personages as the fabricators of that rhapsody exalt with every kind of praise, as divine heroes [1]?' Yet, in the midst of his Ciceronian nonsense, Meiners inadvertently made a remark which, if correctly interpreted, might have led to important discoveries. He noticed that many points of resemblance are to be found between the ideas of the Parsis and those of the Brahmans and Musulmans. He saw in this a proof that Parsîism is a medley of Brahmanical and Musulman tales. Modern scholarship, starting from the same point, came to that twofold conclusion, that, on the one hand, Parsîism was one of the elements out of which Mohammed formed his religion, and, on the other hand, that the old religions of India and Persia flowed from a common source. ' Not only does the author of that rubbish tell the same tales of numberless demons of either sex as the Indian priests do, but he also prescribes the same remedies in order to drive them away, and to balk their attempts.' In these words there was something like the germ of comparative mythology; seldom has a man approached the truth so closely and then departed from it so widely.

Anquetil and the Avesta found an eager champion in the person of Kleuker, professor in the University of Riga. As soon as the French version of the Avesta appeared, he published a German translation of it, and also of Anquetil's historical dissertations [2]. Then, in a series of dissertations of his own [3], he vindicated the authenticity of the Zend books. Anquetil had already tried to show, in a memoir

---

[1] 'De Zoroastris vita, institutis, doctrina et libris,' in the Novi Commentarii Societatis Regiae, Goettingen, 1778-1779.

[2] 'Zend-Avesta . . . nach dem Franzoesischen des Herrn Anquetil Du Perron,' 3 vols. in 4°, 1776.

[3] 'Anhang zum Zend-Avesta,' 2 vols. in 4°, 1781.

on Plutarch, that the data of the Avesta fully agree with
the account of the Magian religion given in the treatise on
'Isis and Osiris.' Kleuker enlarged the circle of comparison
to the whole of ancient literature. He tried also to appeal
to internal evidence, an attempt in which he was less successful. The strength of his defence was seldom greater
than the strength of the attack. Meiners had pointed out
the mythical identity of the Mount Alborg of the Parsis
with the Mount Meru of the Hindus, as a proof that the
Parsis had borrowed their mythology from the Hindus:
the conclusion was incorrect, but the remark itself was not
so. Kleuker fancied that he could remove the difficulty by
stating that Mount Alborg is a real mountain, nay, a doubly
real mountain, since there are two mountains of that name,
the one in Persia, the other in Armenia, whereas Mount
Meru is only to be found in Fairyland. Seldom were worse
arguments used in the service of a good cause. Meiners
had said that the name of the Parsi demons was of Indian
origin, as both languages knew them by the Latin name
'Deus.' This was an incorrect statement, and yet an important observation. The word which means 'a demon' in
Persia means quite the contrary in India, and that radical
difference is just a proof of the two systems being independent of one another. Kleuker pointed out the incorrectness
of the statement; but, being unable to account for the identity of the words, he flatly denied it.

Kleuker was more successful in the field of philology: he
showed, as Anquetil had done, that Zend has no Arabic elements in it, and that Pahlavi itself, which is more modern than
Zend, does not contain any Arabic, but only Semitic words
of the Aramean dialect, which are easily accounted for by
the close relations of Persia with Aramean lands in the time
of the Sassanian kings. He showed, lastly, that Arabic words
appear only in the very books which Parsi tradition itself
considers modern.

Another stanch upholder of the Avesta was the numis-
matologist Tychsen, who, having begun to read the book
with a prejudice against its authenticity, quitted it with
a conviction to the contrary. 'There is nothing in it,' he

writes, 'but what befits remote ages, and a man philo-
sophising in the infancy of the world. Such traces of a
recent period as they fancy to have found in it, are either
due to misunderstandings, or belong to its later portions.
On the whole there is a marvellous accordance between the
Zend-Avesta and the accounts of the ancients with regard
to the doctrine and institutions of Zoroaster. Plutarch
agrees so well with the Zend books that I think no one
will deny the close resemblance of doctrines and identity
of origin. Add to all this the incontrovertible argument to
be drawn from the language, the antiquity of which is established by the fact that it was necessary to translate a part
of the Zend books into Pahlavi, a language which was
growing obsolete as early as the time of the Sassanides.
Lastly, it cannot be denied that Zoroaster left books, which
were, through centuries, the groundwork of the Magic religion, and which were preserved by the Magi, as shown by a
series of documents from the time of Hermippus. Therefore I am unable to see why we should not trust the Magi
of our days when they ascribe to Zoroaster those traditional
books of their ancestors, in which nothing is found to indicate fraud or a modern hand[1].'

Two years afterwards, in 1793, was published in Paris a
book which, without directly dealing with the Avesta, was
the first step taken to make its authenticity incontrovertible.
It was the masterly memoir by Sylvestre de Sacy, in which
the Pahlavi inscriptions of the first Sassanides were deciphered for the first time and in a decisive manner. De
Sacy, in his researches, had chiefly relied on the Pahlavi
lexicon published by Anquetil, whose work vindicated itself
thus—better than by heaping up arguments—by promoting
discoveries. The Pahlavi inscriptions gave the key, as is
well known, to the Persian cuneiform inscriptions, which
were in return to put beyond all doubt the genuineness
of the Zend language.

Tychsen, in an appendix to his Commentaries, pointed

---

[1] 'Commentatio prior observationes historico-criticas de Zoroastre ejusque
scriptis et placitis exhibens.' Goettingen, in the Novi Comment. Soc. Reg. 1791.

to the importance of the new discovery : ' This,' he writes,
' is a proof that the Pahlavi was used during the reign of
the Sassanides, for it was from them that these inscriptions emanated, as it was by them—nay, by the first of
them, Ardeshîr Bâbagân—that the doctrine of Zoroaster
was revived. One can now understand why the Zend books
were translated into Pahlavi. Here, too, everything agrees,
and speaks loudly for their antiquity and genuineness.'

About the same time Sir William Jones, then president
of the Royal Asiatic Society, which he had just founded,
resumed in a discourse delivered before that Society the same
question he had solved in such an off-hand manner twenty
years before. He was no longer the man to say, ' Sied-il à un
homme né dans ce siècle de s'infatuer de fables indiennes?'
and although he had still a spite against Anquetil, he spoke
of him with more reserve than in 1771. However, his
judgment on the Avesta itself was not altered on the
whole, although, as he himself declared, he had not thought
it necessary to study the text. But a glance at the Zend
glossary published by Anquetil suggested to him a remark
which makes Sir William Jones, in spite of himself, the
creator of the comparative grammar of Sanskrit and Zend.
' When I perused the Zend glossary,' he writes, ' I was
inexpressibly surprised to find that six or seven words in ten
are pure Sanscrit, and even some of their inflexions formed
by the rules of the Vyácaran[1], as yushmácam, the geni-
tive plural of yushmad. Now M. Anquetil most certainly,
and the Persian compiler most probably, had no knowledge
of Sanscrit, and could not, therefore, have invented a list of
Sanscrit words ; it is, therefore, an authentic list of Zend
words, which has been preserved in books or by tradition ;
it follows that the language of the Zend was at least a dialect of the Sanscrit, approaching perhaps as nearly to it as
the Prácrit, or other popular idioms, which we know to have
been spoken in India two thousand years ago[2].' This conclusion, that Zend is a Sanskrit dialect, was incorrect, the
connection assumed being too close ; but it was a great

---

[1] The Sanskrit Grammar.   [2] Asiatic Researches, II, § 3.

thing that the near relationship of the two languages should have been brought to light.

In 1798 Father Paulo de St. Barthélemy further developed Jones's remark in an essay on the antiquity of the Zend language[1]. He showed its affinity with the Sanskrit by a list of such Zend and Sanskrit words as were least likely to be borrowed, viz. those that designate the degrees of relationship, the limbs of the body, and the most general and essential ideas. Another list, intended to show, on a special topic, how closely connected the two languages are, contains eighteen words taken from the liturgic language used in India and Persia. This list was not very happily drawn up, as out of the eighteen instances there is not a single one that stands inquiry; yet it was a happy idea, and one which has not even yet yielded all that it promised. His conclusions were that in a far remote antiquity Sanskrit was spoken in Persia and Media, that it gave birth to the Zend language, and that the Zend-Avesta is authentic: ' Were it but a recent compilation,' he writes, ' as Jones asserts, how is it that the oldest rites of the Parsis, that the old inscriptions of the Persians, the accounts of the Zoroastrian religion in the classical writers, the liturgic prayers of the Parsis, and, lastly, even their books do not reveal the pure Sanskrit, as written in the land wherein the Parsis live, but a mixed language, which is as different from the other dialects of India as French is from Italian?' This amounted, in fact, to saying that the Zend is not derived from the Sanskrit, but that both are derived from another and older language. The Carmelite had a dim notion of that truth, but, as he failed to express it distinctly, it was lost for years, and had to be re-discovered.

The first twenty-five years of this century were void of results, but the old and sterile discussions as to the authenticity of the texts continued in England. In 1808 John Leyden regarded Zend as a Prakrit dialect, parallel to Pali; Pali being identical with the Magadhi dialect and Zend with the

---

[1] ' De antiquitate et affinitate linguae samscredamicae et germanicae,' Rome, 1798.

Sauraseni[1]. In the eyes of Erskine Zend was a Sanskrit
dialect, imported from India by the founders of Mazdeism,
but never spoken in Persia[2]. His main argument was that
Zend is not mentioned among the seven dialects which
were current in ancient Persia according to the Farhang-i
Jehangiri[3], and that Pahlavi and Persian exhibit no close
relationship with Zend.

In Germany, Meiners had found no followers. The
theologians appealed to the Avesta in their polemics[4],
and Rhode sketched the religious history of Persia after
the translations of Anquetil[5].

Erskine's essay provoked a decisive answer[6] from Emmanuel Rask, one of the most gifted minds in the new
school of philology, who had the honour of being a pre-
cursor of both Grimm and Burnouf. He showed that the
list of the Jehangiri referred to an epoch later than that to
which Zend must have belonged, and to parts of Persia
different from those where it must have been spoken; he
showed further that modern Persian is not derived from
Zend, but from a dialect closely connected with it; and,
lastly, he showed what was still more important, that Zend
was not derived from Sanskrit. As to the system of its
sounds, Zend approaches Persian rather than Sanskrit;
and as to its grammatical forms, if they often remind one
of Sanskrit, they also often remind one of Greek and Latin,
and frequently have a special character of their own. Rask
also gave the paradigm of three Zend nouns, belonging to
different declensions, as well as the right pronunciation of
the Zend letters, several of which had been incorrectly
given by Anquetil. This was the first essay on Zend
grammar, and it was a masterly one.

<hr/>

[1] Asiatic Researches, X.　　　　　[2] Ibid. X.

[3] A large Persian dictionary compiled in India in the reign of Jehangir.

[4] 'Erlauterungen zum Neuen Testament aus einer neueröffneten Morgenländ-
i-chen Quelle, 'Ἰδοὺ μάγοι ἀπὸ ἀνατολῶν,' Riga, 1775.

[5] 'Die Heilige Sage ... des Zend-Volks,' Francfort, 1820.

[6] 'Ueber das Alter und die Echtheit der Zend-Sprache und des Zend Avesta'
(übersetzt von F. H. von der Hagen), Berlin, 1826. Remarks on the Zend
Language and the Zend-Avesta (Transactions of the Bombay branch of the
Royal Asiatic Society, III, 524).

The essay published in 1831 by Peter von Bohlen on the origin of the Zend language threw the matter forty years back. According to him, Zend is a Prakrit dialect, as it had been pronounced by Jones, Leyden, and Erskine. His mistake consisted in taking Anquetil's transcriptions of the words, which are often so incorrect as to make them look like corrupted forms when compared with Sanskrit. And, what was worse, he took the proper names in their modern Parsi forms, which often led him to comparisons that would have appalled Ménage. Thus Ahriman became a Sanskrit word ariman, which would have meant 'the fiend;' yet Bohlen might have seen in Anquetil's work itself that Ahriman is nothing but the modern form of Angra Mainyu, words which hardly remind one of the Sanskrit ariman. Again, the angel Vohu-manô, or 'good thought,' was reduced, by means of the Parsi form Bahman, to the Sanskrit bâhuman, 'a long-armed god.'

At last came Burnouf. From the time when Anquetil had published his translation, that is to say, during seventy years, no real progress had been made in knowledge of the Avesta texts. The notion that Zend and Sanskrit are two kindred languages was the only new idea that had been acquired, but no practical advantage for the interpretation of the texts had resulted from it. Anquetil's translation was still the only guide, and as the doubts about the authenticity of the texts grew fainter, the authority of the translation became greater, the trust reposed in the Avesta being reflected on to the work of its interpreter. The Parsis had been the teachers of Anquetil; and who could ever understand the holy writ of the Parsis better than the Parsis themselves? There was no one who even tried to read the texts by the light of Anquetil's translation, to obtain a direct understanding of them.

About 1825 Eugène Burnouf was engaged in a course of researches on the geographical extent of the Aryan languages in India. After he had defined the limits which divide the races speaking Aryan languages from the native non-brahmanical tribes in the south, he wanted to know if a similar boundary had ever existed in the north-west; and if it is outside of India that the origin of the Indian languages and civilisation is to be sought for. He was thus led to study the languages of Persia, and, first of all, the oldest of them, the Zend. But as he tried to read the texts by help of Anquetil's translation, he was surprised to find that this was not the clue he had expected. He saw that two causes had misled Anquetil: on the one hand, his teachers, the Parsi dasturs, either knew little themselves or taught him imperfectly, not only the Zend, but even the Pahlavi intended to explain the meaning of the Zend ; so that the tradition on which his work rested, being incorrect in itself, corrupted it from the very beginning ; on the other hand, as Sanskrit was unknown to him and comparative grammar did not as yet exist, he could not supply the defects of tradition by their aid. Burnouf, laying aside tradition as found in Anquetil's translation, consulted it as found in a much older and purer form, in a Sanskrit translation of the Yasna made in the fifteenth century by the Parsi Neriosengh in accordance with the old Pahlavi version. The information given by Neriosengh he tested, and either confirmed or corrected, by a comparison of parallel passages and by the help of comparative grammar, which had just been founded by Bopp, and applied by him successfully to the explanation of Zend forms. Thus he succeeded in tracing the general outlines of the Zend lexicon and in fixing its grammatical forms, and founded the only correct method of interpreting the Avesta. He also gave the first notions of a comparative mythology of the Avesta and the Veda, by showing the identity of the Vedic Yama with the Avesta Yima, and of Traitâna with Thraêtaona and Ferîdûn. Thus he made his 'Commentaire sur le Yasna' a marvellous and unparalleled model of critical insight and steady good sense, equally opposed to the narrowness of mind which clings to matters of fact without rising to their cause and connecting them with the series of associated phenomena, and to the wild and uncontrolled spirit of comparison, which, by comparing everything, confounds everything. Never sacrificing either tradition to comparison or comparison to tradition, he knew how to pass from the one to the other, and was so enabled both to discover facts and to explain them.

At the same time the ancient Persian inscriptions at Persepolis and Behistun were deciphered by Burnouf in Paris, by Lassen in Bonn, and by Sir Henry Rawlinson in Persia. Thus was revealed the existence, at the time of the first Achæmenian kings, of a language closely connected with that of the Avesta, and the last doubts as to the authenticity of the Zend books were at length removed. It would have required more than an ordinary amount of scepticism to look still upon the Zend as an artificial language, of foreign importation, without root in the land where it was written, and in the conscience of the people for whom it was written, at the moment when a twin language, bearing a striking likeness to it in nearly every feature, was suddenly making itself heard from the mouth of Darius, and speaking from the very tomb of the first Achæmenian king. That unexpected voice silenced all controversies, and the last echoes of the loud discussion which had been opened in 1771 died away unheeded [1].

CHAPTER II.

THE INTERPRETATION OF THE ZEND-AVESTA.

THE peace did not last long, and a year after the death of Burnouf a new controversy broke out, which still continues, the battle of the methods, that is, the dispute between those who, to interpret the Avesta, rely chiefly or exclusively on tradition, and those who rely only on comparison with the Vedas. The cause of the rupture was the rapid progress made in the knowledge of the Vedic language and literature: the deeper one penetrated into that oldest form of Indian words and thoughts, the more striking appeared its close affinity with the Avesta words and thoughts. Many a mysterious line in the

---

[1] The attacks of John Romer ('Zend: Is it an Original Language?' London, 1855) called forth a refutation only in Bombay (Dhanjibai Framji, 'On the Origin and the Authenticity of the Aryan Family of Languages, the Zend-Avesta and the Huzvarash,' 1861).

Avesta received an unlooked-for light from the poems of
the Indian *Ri*shis, and the long-forgotten past and the
origin of many gods and heroes, whom the Parsi worships
and extols without knowing who they were and whence
they came, were suddenly revealed by the Vedas. Em-
boldened by its bright discoveries, the comparative method
took pity on its slower and less brilliant rival, which was
then making its first attempts to unravel the Pahlavi traditional books. Is it worth while, said the Vedic scholars[1], to
try slowly and painfully to extract the secret of the old
book from that uncouth literature? Nay, is there any hope
that its secret is there? Translating the Avesta in accordance with the Pahlavi is not translating the Avesta, but only
translating the Pahlavi version, which, wherever it has been
deciphered, is found to wander strangely from the true
meaning of the original text. Tradition, as a rule, is wont
to enforce the ideas of its own ages into the books of past
ages. From the time when the Avesta was written to the
time when it was translated, many ideas had undergone
great changes : such ideas, tradition must needs either mis-
understand or not understand at all, and tradition is always
either new sense or nonsense. The key to the Avesta is
not the Pahlavi, but the Veda. The Avesta and the Veda
are two echoes of one and the same voice, the reflex of one
and the same thought : the Vedas, therefore, are both the
best lexicon and the best commentary to the Avesta.

The traditional school[2] replied that translating Zend by
means of Sanskrit and the Avesta by means of the Vedas,
because Zend and the Avesta are closely related to Sanskrit and the Vedas, is forgetting that relationship is not
identity, and that what interests the Zend scholar is not to
know how far Zend agrees with Sanskrit, but what it is in
itself : what he seeks for in the Avesta, is the Avesta, not
the Veda. Both the Vedic language and the Vedas are
quite unable to teach us what became in Persia of those
elements, which are common to the two systems, a thing
which tradition alone can teach us. By the comparative

---

[1] Roth, Benfey, Haug. Cf. Revue Critique, 1877, II, 81.   [2] Spiegel, Justi.

method, the Zend meregha, which means 'a bird,' would
assume the meaning of 'gazelle' to accord with the Sanskrit m*r*iga; ratu, 'a part of the day,' would be extended
to 'a season' out of regard for *r*itu; mainyu, 'a spirit,' and
dahyu, 'a province,' would be degraded to 'anger' and to
'a set of thieves,' and 'the demons,' the Daêvas, would
ascend from their dwelling in hell up to heaven, to meet
their philological brothers, the Indian Devas. The traditional method, as it starts from matters of facts, moves
always in the field of reality; the comparative method
starts from an hypothesis, moves in a vacuum, and builds
up a fanciful religion and a fanciful language.

Such being the methods of the two schools, it often happened that a passage, translated by two scholars, one of
each school, took so different an aspect that a layman
would have been quite unable to suspect that it was one
and the same passage he had read twice. Yet the di-
vergence between the two methods is more apparent than
real, and proceeds from an imperfect notion of the field in
which each of them ought to work. They ought not to
oppose, but assist one another, as they are not intended to
instruct us about the same kind of facts, but about two
kinds of facts quite different and independent. No language, no religion, that has lived long and changed much,
can be understood at any moment of its development,
unless we know what it became afterwards, and what it was
before. The language and religion of the Avesta record
but a moment in the long life of the Iranian language and
thought, so that we are unable to understand them, unless
we know what they became and whence they came. What
they became we learn directly from tradition, since the tradition arose from the very ideas which the Avesta expresses;
whence they came we learn indirectly from the Vedas, because the Vedas come from the same source as the Avesta.
Therefore it cannot happen that the tradition and the Veda
will really contradict one another, if we take care to ask
from each only what it knows, from one the present, and
the past from the other. Each method is equally right
and equally efficacious, at its proper time and in its right

place. The first place belongs to tradition, as it comes straight from the Avesta. The second inquiry, to be successful, requires infinite prudence and care: the Veda is not the past of the Avesta, as the Avesta is the past of tradition; the Avesta and Veda are not derived from one another, but from one and the same original, diversely altered in each, and, therefore, there are two stages of variation between them, whereas from the Avesta to tradition there is only one. The Veda, if first interrogated, gives no valuable evidence, as the words and gods, common to the two systems, may not have retained in both the same meaning they had in the Indo-Iranian period: they may have preserved it in one and lost it in the other, or they may have both altered it, but each in a different way. The Veda, generally speaking, cannot help in discovering matters of fact in the Avesta, but only in explaining them when discovered by tradition. If we review the discoveries made by the masters of the comparative school, it will be seen that they have in reality started, without noticing it, from facts formerly established by tradition. In fact tradition gives the materials, and comparison puts them in order. It is not possible, either to know the Avesta without the former, or to understand it without the latter.

The traditional school, and especially its indefatigable and well-deserving leader, Spiegel, made us acquainted with the nature of the old Iranian religion by gathering together all its materials; the comparative school tried to explain its growth. The traditional school published the text and the traditional translations, and produced the first Parsi grammar, the first Pahlavi grammar, and the first translation of the Avesta which had been made since Anquetil. The danger with it is that it shows itself too apt to stop at tradition, instead of going from it to comparison. When it undertakes to expound the history of the religion, it cannot but be misled by tradition. Any living people, although its existing state of mind is but the result of various and changing states through many successive ages, yet, at any particular moment of its life, keeps the remains of its former stages of thought in order, under the control of the principle that is then predominant. Thus it happens that their ideas are connected together in a way which seldom agrees with their historical sequence : chronological order is lost to sight and replaced by logical order, and the past is read into the present. Comparison alone can enable us to put things in their proper place, to trace their birth, their growth, their changes, their former relations, and lead us from the logical order, which is a shadow, to the historical order, which is the substance.

The comparative school developed Indo-Iranian mytho-logy. Roth showed after Burnouf how the epical history of Iran was derived from the same source as the myths of Vedic India, and pointed out the primitive identity of Ahura Mazda, the supreme god of Iran, with Varuna, the supreme god of the Vedic age. In the same direction Windischmann, in his 'Zoroastrian Essays' and in his studies on Mithra and Anâhita, displayed singular sagacity. But the dangers of the method came to light in the works of Haug, who, giving a definite form to a system still fluctuating, converted Mazdeism into a religious revolu-tion against Vedic polytheism, found historical allusions to that schism both in the Avesta and in the Veda, pointed out curses against Zoroaster in the Vedas, and, in short, transformed, as it were, the two books into historical pamphlets [1].

In the contest about the authenticity of the Avesta, one party must necessarily have been right and the other wrong ; but in the present struggle the issue is not so clear, as both parties are partly right and partly wrong. Both of them, by following their principles, have rendered such services to science as seem to give each a right to cling to its own method more firmly than ever. Yet it is to be hoped that they will see at last that they must be allies, not enemies, and that their common work must be begun by the one and completed by the other.

[1] It would be unjust, when speaking of Haug, not to recall the invaluable services he rendered in the second part of his career, as a Pahlavi scholar. He was the first who thought of illustrating the Pahlavi in the books by the Pahlavi in the inscriptions, and thus determined the reading of the principal elements in the manuscript Pahlavi.

CHAPTER III.

THE FORMATION OF THE ZEND-AVESTA.

§ 1. The collection of Zend fragments, known as the Zend-Avesta [1], is divided, in its usual form, into two parts.

The first part, or the Avesta properly so called, contains the Vendîdâd, the Vispêrad, and the Yasna. The Vendîdâd is a compilation of religious laws and of mythical tales; the Vispêrad is a collection of litanies for the sacrifice; and the Yasna is composed of litanies of the same kind and of five hymns or Gâthas written in a special dialect, older than the general language of the Avesta.

These three books are found in manuscripts in two different forms: either each by itself, in which case they are generally accompanied by a Pahlavi translation; or the three mingled together according to the requirements of the liturgy, as they are not each recited separately in their entirety, but the chapters of the different books are intermingled; and in this case the collection is called the Vendîdâd Sâdah or 'Vendîdâd pure,' as it exhibits the original text alone, without a translation.

The second part, generally known as the Khorda Avesta or 'Small Avesta,' is composed of short prayers which are recited not only by the priests, but by all the faithful, at certain moments of the day, month, or year, and in presence of the different elements; these prayers are the five Gâh, the thirty formulas of the Sîrôzah, the three Âfrigân, and the six Nyâyis. But it is also usual to include in the Khorda Avesta, although forming no real part of it, the Yasts or hymns of praise and glorification to the several

---

[1] A very improper designation, as Zend means 'a commentary or explanation,' and was applied only to explanatory texts, to the translations of the Avesta. Avesta (from the old Persian âbastâ, 'the law;' see Oppert, Journal Asiatique, 1872, Mars) is the proper name of the original texts. What it is customary to call 'the Zend language' ought to be named 'the Avesta language;' the Zend being no language at all; and, if the word be used as the designation of one, it can be rightly applied only to the Pahlavi. The expression 'Avesta and Zend' is often used in the Pahlavi commentary to designate 'the law with its traditional and revealed explanation.'

Izads, and a number of fragments, the most important of which is the Hadhôkht Nosk.

§ 2. That the extent of the sacred literature of Mazdeism was formerly much greater than it is now, appears not only from internal evidence, that is, from the fragmentary character of the book, but is also proved by historical evidence. In the first place, the Arab conquest proved fatal to the religious literature of the Sassanian ages, a great part of which was either destroyed by the fanaticism of the conquerors and the new converts, or lost during the long exodus of the Parsis. Thus the Pahlavi translation of the Vendîdâd, which was not finished before the latter end of the Sassanian dynasty, contains not a few Zend quotations from books which are no longer in existence; other quotations, as remarkable in their importance as in their contents, are to be found in Pahlavi and Parsi tracts, like the Nîrangistân and the Aogemaidê. The Bundahis contains much matter which is not spoken of in the existing Avesta, but which is very likely to have been taken from Zend books which were still in the hands of its compiler. It is a tradition with the Parsis, that the Yasts were originally thirty in number, there having been one for each of the thirty Izads who preside over the thirty days of the month; yet there are only eighteen still extant.

The cause that preserved the Avesta is obvious; taken as a whole, it does not profess to be a religious encyclopedia, but only a liturgical collection, and it bears more likeness to a Prayer Book than to the Bible. It can be readily conceived that the Vendîdâd Sâdah, which had to be recited every day, would be more carefully preserved than the Yasts, which are generally recited once a month; and these again more carefully than other books, which, however sacred they might be, were not used in the performance of worship. Many texts, no doubt, were lost in consequence of the Arab conquest, but mostly such as would have more importance in the eyes of the theologian than in those of the priest. We have a fair specimen of what these lost texts may have been in the few non-liturgical fragments which we still possess, such as the Vistâsp Yast and

the blessing of Zoroaster upon King Vistâsp, which belong
to the old epic cycle of Iran, and the Hadhôkht Nosk,
which treats of the fate of the soul after death.

§ 3. But if we have lost much of the Sassanian sacred
literature, Sassanian Persia herself, if we may trust Parsi
tradition, had lost still more of the original books. The
primitive Avesta, as revealed by Ormazd to Zoroaster and
by Zoroaster to Vistâsp, king of Bactria, was supposed to
have been composed of twenty-one Nosks or Books, the
greater part of which was burnt by Iskander the Rûmi
(Alexander the Great). After his death the priests of the
Zoroastrian religion met together, and by collecting the
various fragments that had escaped the ravages of the war
and others that they knew by heart, they formed the present
collection, which is a very small part of the original book,
as out of the twenty-one Nosks there was only one that was
preserved in its entirety, the Vendîdâd [1].

This tradition is very old, and may be traced back from
the present period even to Sassanian times [2]. It involves
the assumption that the Avesta is the remnant of the sacred
literature of Persia under the last Achæmenian kings. To
ascertain whether this inference is correct, and to what
extent it may be so, we must first try to define, as accurately as we can, the exact time at which the collection,
now in existence, was formed.

§ 4. The Ravâet quoted above states that it was formed
'after the death of Iskander,' which expression is rather
vague, and may as well mean 'centuries after his death' as
'immediately after his death.' It is, in fact, hardly to be
doubted that the latter was really what the writer meant;
yet, as the date of that Ravâet is very recent, we had better
look for older and more precise traditions. We find such
a one in the Dînkart, a Pahlavi book which enjoys great
authority with the Parsis of our days, and which, although
it contains many things of late origin [3], also comprises many

---

[1] Ravâet ap. Anquetil, Mémoires de l'Acad. des Inscr. et Belles-Lettres
XXXVIII, 216; Spiegel, Zeitschrift der Deutschen Morgenländischen Gesellschaft IX, 174.

[2] J. Darmesteter, La légende d'Alexandre chez les Parses.

[3] We find in it a description of the four classes, which strikingly reminds

old and valuable traditions.   According to a proclamation, ascribed to Khosrav Anôsharvân (531–579), the collection of the Avesta fragments was begun in the reign of the last Arsacides, and was finished under Shapûr II (309–380). King Valkash (Vologeses), it is said, first ordered all the fragments of the Avesta which might have escaped the ravages of Iskander, or been preserved by oral tradition, to be searched for and collected together.   The first Sassanian king, Ardeshîr Bâbagân, made the Avesta the sacred book of Iran, and Mazdeism the state religion : at last, Âdarbâd Mahraspand, under Shapûr II, purified the Avesta and fixed the number of the Nasks, and Shapûr proclaimed to the heterodox[1]: ' Now that we have recognised the law of the world here below, they shall not allow the infidelity of any one whatever[2], as I shall strive that it may be so[3].'

§ 5. The authenticity of this record has been called in question, chiefly, I think, on account of the part that it ascribes to an Arsacide prince, which seems hardly to agree with the ideas generally entertained about the character of the Sassanian revolution[4].   Most Parsi and Muhammedan writers agree that it was the Sassanian dynasty which raised the Zoroastrian religion from the state of humiliation into which the Greek invasion had made it sink, and, while it gave the signal for a revival of the old national spirit, made Mazdeism one of the corner stones of the new establishment[5].   Therefore it seems strange to hear that the first step taken to make Mazdeism a state religion was taken by one of those very Philhellenic Parthian princes, who were so fully imbued with Greek ideas and manners. Yet this is the

one of the Brahmanical account of the origin of the castes (Chap. XLII; cf. the first pages of the Shikan Gumânî), and which was certainly borrowed from India; whether at the time of the last Sassanians, when Persia learnt so much from India, or since the settlement of the Parsis in India, we are unable to decide: yet the former seems more probable.

[1] Gvêt rastakân. We are indebted to Mr. West for the right translation of this word.

[2] Thus translated by West (Glossary of the Book of Ardâ Vîrâf, p. 27).

[3] Haug, Essay on Pahlavi, p. 145 seq., 149 seq.

[4] Spiegel, Eranische Alterthumskunde III, 782, n. 1.

[5] S. de Sacy, Mémoires sur quelques antiquités de la Perse. Cf. Masudi, II, 125.

very reason why we ought to feel some hesitation in rejecting
this document, and its being at variance with the general
Parsi view speaks rather for its authenticity ; for as it was
the general post-Sassanian tradition that the restoration of
Mazdeism was the work of the first Sassanian kings, no
Parsi would ever have thought of making them share what
was in his eyes their first and best title of honour with any
of the despised princes of the Parthian dynasty.

§ 6. It is difficult, of course, to prove directly the authenticity of this record, the more so as we do not even know
who was the king alluded to. There were, in fact, four
kings at least [1] who bore the name of Valkhash : the most
celebrated and best known of the four was Vologeses I, the
contemporary of Nero. Now that Zoroastrianism prevailed
with him, or at least with members of his family, we see
from the conduct of his brother Tiridates, who was a Magian (Magus) [2] ; and by this term we must not understand a
magician [3], but a priest, and one of the Zoroastrian religion.
That he was a priest appears from Tacitus' testimony [4]; that
he was a Zoroastrian is shown by his scruples about the
worship of the elements. When he came from Asia to Rome
to receive the crown of Armenia at the hands of Nero, he
wanted not to come by sea, but rode along the coasts [5],
because the Magi were forbidden to defile the sea [6]. This
is quite in the spirit of later Zoroastrianism, and savours
much of Mazdeism. That Vologeses himself shared the religious scruples of his brother appears from his answer to Nero,

---

[1] Perhaps five (see de Longpérier, Mémoire sur la Numismatique des Arsacides, p. 111).

[2] ' Magus ad eum Tiridates venerat' (Pliny, Nat. Hist. XXX, 6).

[3] Pliny very often confounds Magism and Magia, Magians and Magicians.
We know from Pliny, too, that Tiridates refused to initiate Nero into his
art: but the cause was not, as he assumes, that it was 'a detestable, frivolous,
and vain art,' but because Mazdean law forbids the holy knowledge to be
revealed to laymen, much more to foreigners (Yast IV, 10; cf. Philostrati
Vita Soph. I, 10).

[4] 'Nec recusaturum Tiridatem accipiendo diademati in urbem venire, nisi
sacerdotii religione attineretur' (Ann. XV, 24).

[5] He crossed only the Hellespont.

[6] 'Navigare noluerat, quoniam inspuere in maria, aliisque mortalium necessi-
tatibus violare naturam eam fas non putant' (Pliny, l.l. Cf. Introd. V, 8 seq.)

who insisted upon his coming to Rome also : 'Come your-self, it is easier for you to cross such immensity of sea[1].'

§ 7. Thus we hear on one hand from the Parsis that the first collection of the Avesta was made by an Arsacide named Vologeses ; and we hear, on the other hand, from a quite independent source, that an Arsacide named Volo-geses behaved himself as a follower of the Avesta might have done. In all this there is no evidence that it is Volo-geses I who is mentioned in the Dînkar*t*, much less that he was really the first editor of the Avesta ; but it shows at all events that the first attempt to recover the sacred literature of Iran might very well have been made by an Arsacide, and that we may trust, in this matter, to a docu-ment which has been written perhaps by a Sassanian king, but, at any rate, in a Sassanian spirit. In fact, in the struggle between Ardavan and Ardeshîr, there was no religious interest at stake, but only a political one ; and we are expressly told by Hamza that between Ardeshîr and his adversaries there was perfect accordance in religious matters[2]. It can, therefore, be fairly admitted that even in the time and at the court of the Philhellenic Parthians a Zoroastrian movement may have originated, and that there came a time when they perceived that a national religion is a part of national life. It was the merit of the Sassa-nides that they saw the drift of this idea which they had the good fortune to carry out ; and this would not be the only instance, in the history of the world, of an idea being sown by one party and its advantages reaped by their adversaries.

---

[1] Dio Cassius, LXIII, 4. The answer was mistaken for an insult by Nero, and, as it seems, by Dio himself. In fact Vologeses remained to the last faithful to the memory of Nero (Suet. Nero, 57). What we know moreover of his personal character qualifies him for taking the initiative in a religious work. He seems to have been a man of contemplative mind rather than a man of action, which often excited the anger or scorn of his people against him ; and he had the glory of breaking with the family policy of Parthian kings (Tacitus, Annales, XV, 1, 2). It was under his reign that the first interference of religion with politics, of which the history of Persia speaks, took place, as he was called by the people of Adiabene against their king Izates, who had become a Jew (Josephus, Antiq. XX, 4, 2).

[2] Hamzae Ispahensis Annales, ed. Gottwaldt, p. 31 (in the translation).

§ 8. Another presumptive evidence of the groundwork
of the Avesta being anterior to the age of the Sassanians
is given by the language in which it is written. That language not only was not, but had never been, the national
language of Persia. It is indeed closely connected with
the ancient Persian, as found in the cuneiform inscriptions
of the Achæmenian kings, from which modern Persian is
derived; but the relations between ancient Persian and
Zend are of such a kind that neither language can be conceived as being derived from the other; they are not one
and the same language in two different stages of its development, but two independent dialects in nearly the same
stage, which is a proof that they did not belong to the
same country, and, therefore, that Zend was not the language of Persia. Now the language used in Persia after
the death of Alexander, under the Arsacides and Sassanides, that is, during the period in which the Avesta must
have been edited, was Pahlavi, which is not derived from
Zend, but from ancient Persian, being the middle dialect
between ancient and modern Persian. Therefore, if the
Sassanian kings had conceived the project of having religious books of their own written and composed, it is not
likely that they would have had them written in an old
foreign dialect, but in the old national language, the more
so, because, owing both to their origin and their policy, they
were bound to be the representatives of the genuine old
Persian tradition. Therefore, if they adopted Zend as the
language of religion, it must have been because it was already
so when they appeared, that is to say, because the only
remnants of sacred literature then extant were written in
Zend, and the editors of the Avesta had Zend writings
before them.

This does not, of course, prove that all we find in the
Avesta is pre-Sassanian, and that the editors did not com-
pose new Zend texts. Although Zend was not only a
dead language, but also a foreign one, it was not an
unknown language: that it was well understood by the
learned class, the priests, appears from the Pahlavi translation, which was made by them, and which, the deeper

one enters into the meaning of the text, has the fuller justice done to its merits. The earliest date that can be ascribed to that translation, in its present form, is the last century of the Sassanian dynasty, as it contains an allusion to the death of the heresiarch Mazdak, the son of Bâmdâd [1], who was put to death in the beginning of the reign of Khosrav Anôsharvân (about 531). Now the ability to translate a dead language is a good test of the ability to write in it, and in the question of the age of the Zend texts the possibility of new ones having been composed by the editors cannot be excluded à priori. Nay, we shall see further on that there are passages in these texts which look very modern, and may have been written at the time when the book took its last and definitive form. But whatever may be the proportion of the new texts to the old ones (which I believe to be very small), it is quite certain that the bulk of the Avesta is pre-Sassanian.

§ 9. The date assigned by the Dînkart to the final edition of the Avesta and to its promulgation as the sacred law of the nation, agrees with what we know of the religious state of Iran in the times of Shapûr II. Mazdeism had just been threatened with destruction by a new religion sprung from itself, the religion of Mânî, which for a while numbered a king amongst its followers (Shapûr I, 240–270). Mazdeism was shaken for a long time, and when Mânî was put to death, his work did not perish with him. In the Kissah-i Sangâh, Zoroaster is introduced prophesying that the holy religion will be overthrown three times and restored three times; overthrown the first time by Iskander, it will be restored by Ardeshîr; overthrown again, it will be restored by Shapûr II and Âdarbâd Mahraspand; and, lastly, it will be overthrown by the Arabs and restored at the end of time by Soshyos. The Parsi traditions about Âdarbâd, although they are mixed with much fable, allow some historical truth to show itself. He was a holy man under Shapûr II, who, as there were many religions and heresies in Iran and the true religion

_____

[1] Vide infra, p. xli, note 3.

was falling into oblivion, restored it through a miracle, as
he gave a sign of its truth by allowing melted brass to be
poured on his breast, without his being injured. Setting
aside the miracle, which is most probably borrowed from
the legend of Zoroaster, this account receives its true interpretation from the passages in the Kissah-i Sangâh and
the Dînkart, which imply that Âdarbâd restored Mazdeism,
which had been shaken by the Manichean heresy, and that
in order to settle it upon a solid and lasting base, he gave
a definitive form to the religious book of Iran and closed
the Holy Writ. And even nowadays the Parsi, while
reciting the Patet, acknowledges Âdarbâd as the third
founder of the Avesta; the first being Zoroaster, who received it from Ormazd; the second Gâmâsp, who received it
from Zoroaster; and the third Âdarbâd, who taught it and
restored it to its purity.

Therefore, so far as we can trust to inferences that rest
upon such scanty and vague testimonies, it seems likely
that the Avesta took its definitive form from the hands of
Âdarbâd Mahraspand, under King Shapûr II, in consequence of the dangers with which Mânî's heresy had
threatened the national religion. As the death of Mânî
and the first persecution of his followers took place some
thirty years before Shapûr's accession to the throne, it may
be presumed that the last revision of the Avesta was made
in the first years of the new reign, when the agitation
aroused by Mânî's doctrines and imperfectly allayed by the
persecution of his disciples had not yet subsided, and the
old religion was still shaking on its base [1].

§ 10. It follows hence that Zend texts may have been
composed even as late as the fourth century A. D. This is,
of course, a mere theoretical possibility, for although the
liturgical parts of the Yasna, the Vispêrad, the Sîrôzah, and

[1] Shapûr II ascended the throne about 309 (before being born, as the tradition goes): and as he appears from the Dînkart to have taken a personal part
in the work of Âdarbâd, the promulgation of the Avesta can hardly have taken
place at an earlier date than 325–330. Âdarbâd and the Fathers at Nicaea
lived and worked in the same age, and the Zoroastrian threats of the king of
Iran and the Catholic anathemas of the Kaisar of Rûm may have been issued
on the same day.

the Khorda Avesta .must be ascribed to a later time than the Gâthas, the Vendîdâd, and the Yasts, and may belong to some period of revision, they certainly do not belong to the period of this last revision. Âdarbâd was only the last editor of the Avesta, and it is likely, nay, it is beyond all question, that the doctors of the law, before his time, had tried to put the fragments in order, to connect them, and to fill up the gaps as far as the practical purposes of liturgy required it. Therefore instead of saying that there are parts of the Avesta that may belong to so late a period as the fourth century, it is more correct to say that no part of it can belong to a later date.

There are two passages in the Vendîdâd which seem to contain internal evidence of their date, and in both cases it points to Sassanian times, nay, the second of them points to the age of Manicheism. The first is found in the eighteenth Fargard (§ 10): Ahura Mazda, while cursing those who teach a wrong law, exclaims :

' And he who would set that man at liberty, when bound in prison, does no better deed than if he should flay a man alive and cut off his head.'

This anathema indicates a time when Mazdeism was a state religion and had to fight against heresy; it must, therefore, belong to Sassanian times. These lines are fully illustrated by a Parsi book of the same period [1], the Mainyô-i-Khard :

' Good government is that which maintains and orders the true law and custom of the city people and poor un-troubled, and thrusts out improper law and custom ; . . . and keeps in progress the worship of God, and duties, and good works; . . . and will resign the body, and that also which [is] its own life, for the sake of the good religion of the Mazdayasnians. And if [there] be any one who shall stay [away] from the way of God, then it orders him to return thereto, and makes him a prisoner, and brings [him] back to the way of God ; and will bestow, from the wealth that is his, the share of God, and the worthy, and good works,

---

[1] See the book of the Mainyô-i-Khard, ed. West; Introduction, p. x seq.

and the poor; and will deliver up the body on account
of the soul. A good king who [is] of that sort, is called
like the Yazads and the Ameshâspeñds [1].'

What doctrines are alluded to by the Vendîdâd is not
explained: it appears from the context that it had in view
such sects as released the faithful from the yoke of religious
practices, as it anathematizes, at the same time, those who
have continued for three years without wearing the sacred
girdle. We know too little of the Manichean liturgy to guess
if the Manicheans are here alluded to: that Mânî should
have rejected many Zoroastrian practices is not unlikely,
as his aim was to found a universal religion. While he
pushed to extremes several of the Zoroastrian tenets, especially those which had taken, or might receive, a moral or
metaphysical meaning, he must have been very regardless
of practices which could not be ennobled into moral sym-
bolism. However it may be with regard to the foregoing
passage, it is difficult not to see a direct allusion to
Manicheism in lines like the following (IV, 47 seq.):

'Verily I say it unto thee, O Spitama Zarathustra! the
man who has a wife is far above him who begets no sons;
he who keeps a house is far above him who has none; he
who has children is far above the childless man; he who
has riches is far above him who has none.

'And of two men, he who fills himself with meat is filled
with the good spirit much more than he who does not so;
the latter is all but dead; the former is above him by the
worth of an Asperena, by the worth of a sheep, by the
worth of an ox, by the worth of a man.

'It is this man that can strive against the onsets of Astô-
vîdhôtu; that can strive against the self-moving arrow;
that can strive against the winter fiend, with thinnest garment on; that can strive against the wicked tyrant and
smite him on the head; it is this man that can strive
against the ungodly Ashemaogha [2] who does not eat [3].'

---

[1] Chap. XV, 16 seq. as translated by West.

[2] Ashemaogha, 'the confounder of Asha' (see IV, 37), is the name of the
fiends and of the heretics. The Parsis distinguish two sorts of Ashemaoghas, the deceiver and the deceived; the deceiver, while alive, is mar-

That this is a bit of religious polemics, and that it refers to definite doctrines and tenets which were held at the time when it was written, can hardly be doubted. It may remind one of the Christian doctrines; and, in fact, it was nearly in the same tone, and with the same expressions, that in the fifth century King Yazdgard branded the Christians in Armenia[4]. But however eager the Christian propaganda may have been for a time in Persia, they never endangered the state religion. The real enemy was the heresy sprung from Mazdeism itself; and Christianity, coming from abroad, was more of a political than a religious foe. And, in point of fact, the description in the above passage agrees better with the Manichean doctrines than with the Christian[5]. Like Mânî, Christian teachers held the single life holier than the state of matrimony, yet they had not forbidden marriage, which Mânî did; they put poor Lazarus above Dives, but they never forbade trade and husbandry, which Mânî did; and, lastly, they never prohibited the eating of flesh, which was one of the chief precepts of Mânî[6]. We find, therefore, in this passage, an illustration, from the Avesta itself, of the celebrated doctrine of the three seals with which Mânî had sealed the bosom, the hand, and the mouth of his disciples (signaculum sinus, manus, oris)[6].

---

garzân, 'worthy of death,' and after death is a darvand (a fiend, or one of the damned); the deceived one is only margarzân.

[3] The Pahlavi translation illustrates the words 'who does not eat' by the gloss, 'like Mazdak, son of Bâmdâd,' which proves that this part of the commentary is posterior to, or contemporary with the crushing of the Mazdakian sect (in the first years of Khosrav Anôsharvân, about 531). The words 'against the wicked tyrant' are explained by the gloss, 'like Zarvândâd;' may it not be Kobâd, the heretic king, or 'Yazdgard the sinner,' the scorner of the Magi?

[4] Elisaeus, pp. 29, 52, in the French translation by Garabed.

[5] At least with orthodox Christianity, which seems to have alone prevailed in Persia till the arrival of the Nestorians. The description would apply very well to certain gnostic sects, especially that of Cerdo and Marcio, which is no wonder, as it was through that channel that Christianity became known to Mânî. Masudi makes Mânî a disciple of Kardûn (ed. B. de Meynard, II, 167), and the care which his biographer (ap. Flügel, Mânî, pp. 51, 85) takes to determine the length of time which intervened between Marcio and Mânî seems to betray some dim recollection of an historical connection between the two doctrines.

[6] The patriarch of Alexandria, Timotheus, allowed the other patriarchs,

§ 11. We must now go a step farther back, and try to solve the question whence came the original texts out of which the editors of the Avesta formed their collection. Setting aside the Dînkar*t*, we have no oriental document to help us in tracing them through the age of the Arsacides, a complete historical desert, and we are driven for information to the classical writers who are, on this point, neither very clear nor always credible. The mention of books ascribed to Zoroaster occurs not seldom during that period, but very often it applies to Alexandrian and Gnostic apocrypha[1]. Yet there are a few passages which make it pretty certain that there was a Mazdean literature in existence in those times. Pausanias, travelling through Lydia in the second century of our era, saw and heard Magian priests singing hymns from a book[2]; whether these hymns were the same as the Gâthas, still extant, we cannot ascertain, but this shows that there were Gâthas. The existence of a Zoroastrian literature might be traced back as far as the third century before Christ, if Pliny could be credited when he says that Hermippus[3] had given an analysis of the books of Zoroaster, which are said to have amounted to 2,000,000 lines[4]. For want of external evidence for ascertaining whether the original texts were already in existence in the later years of the Achæmenian dynasty, we must seek for internal evidence. A comparison between the ideas expressed in our texts and what we know of the ideas of Achæmenian Persia may perhaps lead to safer inferences.

§ 12. That all the Avesta ideas were already fully developed in the time, or, at least, at the end of the

---

bishops, and monks to eat meat on Sundays, in order to recognise those who belonged to the Manichean sect (Flügel, Mânî, p. 279).

[1] 'Those who follow the heresy of Prodicus boast of possessing secret books of Zoroaster,' Clemens Alex. Stromata I. Cf. the ἀποκαλύψεις Ζωροάστρου forged by Adelphius or Aquilinus (ap. Porphyr. Vita Plotini, § 16).

[2] 'Επᾴδει δὲ ἐπιλεγόμενος ἐκ βιβλίου (V, 27, 3).

[3] See Windischmann, Zoroastrische Studien, 288.

[4] 'Hermippus, qui de tota arte ea (magia) diligentissime scripsit et viciens centiens milia versuum a Zoroastre condita indicibus quoque voluminum ejus positis explanavit.' . . . (Hist. Nat. XXX, 1, 2). He had written a book περὶ μάγων (Diog. Laert. Prooem. 8).

Achæmenian dynasty, appears from the perfect accordance of the account of Mazdeism in Theopompos[1] with the data of the Zend books. All the main features of Mazdean belief, namely, the existence of two principles, a good and an evil one, Ormazd and Ahriman, the antithetical creations of the two supreme powers, the division of all the beings in nature into two corresponding classes, the limited duration of the world, the end of the struggle between Ormazd and Ahriman by the defeat and destruction of the evil principle, the resurrection of the dead, and the everlasting life, all these tenets of the Avesta had already been established at the time of Philip and Aristotle. Therefore we must admit that the religious literature then in existence, if there were any, must have differed but little, so far as its contents were concerned, from the Avesta; its extent was greater of course, and we have a proof of this in this very account of Theopompos, which gives us details nowhere to be found in the present texts, and yet the authenticity of which is made quite certain by comparative mythology[2]. Therefore there is nothing that forbids us to believe, with the Parsis, that the fragments of which the Avesta is composed were already in existence before the Greek invasion[3].

§ 13. But it does not follow hence that the Achæmenian Avesta was the sacred book of the Achæmenians and of Persia, and it must not be forgotten that the account in Plutarch is not about the religion of Persia, but about the belief of the Magi and the lore of Zoroaster. Now if we consider that the two characteristic features of Avestean Magism are, so far as belief goes, the admission of two principles, and so far as practice is concerned, the prohibition of burying the dead, we find that there is no evidence

---

[1] In Plutarch, De Iside et Osiride, §§ 46-47.

[2] Men, when raised from the dead, shall have no shadow any longer (μήτε σκιὰν ποιοῦντας). In India, gods have no shadows (Nalus); in Persia, Râshidaddîn was recognised to be a god from his producing no shadow (Guyard, Un grand maître des Assassins, Journal Asiatique, 1877, I, 392); the plant of eternal life, Haoma, has no shadow (Henry Lord).

[3] Persian tradition cannot be much relied on, when it tries to go back beyond Alexander, and on that special point it seems to be more an inference of later ages, than a real tradition; but the inference happens to be right.

that Achæmenian Persia admitted the former, and there is
evidence that she did not admit the latter. But, at the
same time, it appears that both the belief and the practice
were already in existence, though peculiar to one class, the
sacerdotal class, the Magi.

The question whether the Achæmenian kings believed
in dualism and knew of Ahriman, is not yet settled. Much
stress has often been laid on the absence of the name of
Ahriman in the religious formulae engraved by Darius and
Xerxes on the rocks at Persepolis and Naqs-i Rustam[1].
But it is never safe to draw wide conclusions from negative
facts: Darius and Xerxes speak of Aurâmazda quite in the
style of the Avesta, and their not speaking of Ahriman is
no sufficient proof of their not knowing him ; they did not
intend to publish a complete creed, nor had they to inscribe
articles of faith.

The account of the Persian religion in Herodotus also
leaves, or seems to leave, Ahriman unnoticed. But it must
be borne in mind that he does not expound the religious
conceptions of the Persians, but only their religious customs ; he describes their worship more than their dogmas,
and not a single tenet is mentioned. He seems even not
to know anything of Ormazd, who was, however, most
certainly the supreme god of Persia in his days ; yet, in
fact, he clearly alludes to Ormazd, when he states that the
Persians worship Zeus on the summits of mountains, and
call by the name of Zeus the whole circle of the heavens,
which exactly agrees with the character of Ormazd[2]. In
the same way the existence of Ahriman is indirectly
pointed to by the duty enforced upon the faithful to perse-
cute and kill noxious animals, as it was only on account of

---

[1] Professor Oppert thinks he has found in Darius' inscriptions an express
mention of Ahriman (Le peuple et le langue des Mèdes, p. 199) ; yet the
philological interpretation of the passage seems to me still too obscure to
allow of any decisive opinion. Plutarch introduces Artaxerxes I speaking of
'Αρειμάνιος, but whether the king is made to speak the language of his own
time, or that of Plutarch's time, is left doubtful. As to the allusions in Isaiah
(xlv), they do not necessarily refer to dualism in particular, but to all religions
not monotheistic. (Cf. Ormazd et Ahriman, § 241.)

[2] Vide infra, IV, 5.

their being creatures of the evil principle and incarnations of it, that this custom was enjoined as a religious duty[1]. It appears, it is true, from the words of Herodotus, that it was only a custom peculiar to the Magi[2]; but it shows, at least, that the belief in Ahriman was already then in existence, and that dualism was constituted, at least, as a Magian article of faith.

If we pass now from dogma to practice, we find that the most important practice of the Avesta law was either disregarded by the Achæmenian kings, or unknown to them. According to the Avesta burying corpses in the earth is one of the most heinous sins that can be committed[3]; we know that under the Sassanians a prime minister, Seoses, paid with his life for an infraction of that law[4]. Corpses were to be laid down on the summits of mountains, there to be devoured by birds and dogs; the exposure of corpses was the most striking practice of Mazdean profession, and its adoption was the sign of conversion[5]. Now under the Achæmenian rule, not only the burial of the dead was not forbidden, but it was the general practice. Persians, says Herodotus, bury their dead in the earth, after having coated them with wax[6]. But Herodotus, immediately after stating that the Persians inter their dead, adds that the Magi do not follow the general practice, but lay the corpses down on the ground, to be devoured by birds. So what became a law for all people, whether laymen or priests, under the rule of the Sassanians, was only the custom of the Magi, under the Achæmenians.

The obvious conclusion is that the ideas and customs which are found in the Avesta were already in existence under the Achæmenian kings; but that taken as a whole, they were not the general ideas and customs of the whole of Persia, but only of the sacerdotal caste[7]. There were

---

[1] Vide infra, IV, 35; cf. Fargard XIII, 5 seq.; XIV, 5.

[2] Herod. I, 140.   [3] Vide infra, V, 9.

[4] Procopius, De Bello Persico, I, 11.

[5] Ibid. I, 12.   [6] Herod. I, 140.

[7] There are other features of the Avesta religion which appear to have been foreign to Persia, but are attributed to the Magi. The ḳvaêtvôdatha, the holiness of marriage between next of kin, even to incest, was unknown to

therefore, practically, two religions in Iran, the one for
laymen and the other for priests. The Avesta was originally the sacred book only of the Magi, and the progress
of the religious evolution was to extend to laymen what
was the custom of the priests.

§ 14. We are now able to understand how it was that the
sacred book of Persia was written in a non-Persian dialect:
it had been written in the language of its composers, the
Magi, who were not Persians. Between the priests and the
people there was not only a difference of calling, but also
a difference of race, as the sacerdotal caste came from a
non-Persian province. What that province was we know
both from Greek historians and from Parsi traditions.

All classical writers, from Herodotus down to Ammianus,
agree in pointing to Media as the seat and native place of
the Magi. 'In Media,' says Marcellinus (XXIII, 6), 'are the
fertile fields of the Magi . . . (having been taught in the
magic science by King Hystaspes) they handed it down to
their posterity, and thus from Hystaspes to the present age
an immense family was developed, hereditarily devoted to
the worship of the gods. . . . In former times their number
was very scanty . . . , but they grew up by and by into the
number and name of a nation, and inhabiting towns without
walls they were allowed to live according to their own laws,
protected by religious awe.' Putting aside the legendary account of their origin, one sees from this passage that in the
time of Marcellinus[1] (fourth cent. A.D.) there was in Media a
tribe, called Magi, which had the hereditary privilege of pro-
viding Iran with priests. Strabo, writing three centuries before
Marcellinus, considered the Magi as a sacerdotal tribe
spread over the land[2]. Lastly, we see in Herodotus (III, 65)
that the usurpation of the Magian Smerdis was interpreted

Persia under Cambyses (Herod. III, 31), but it is highly praised in the Avesta,
and was practised under the Sassanians (Agathias II, 31); in the times before
the Sassanians it is mentioned only as a law of the Magi (Diog. Laert. Prooem.
6; Catullus, Carm. XC).

[1] Or of the historians from whom he copies. Still he seems to speak from
contemporary evidence. Sozomenus (Hist. Eccles. II, 9) states that the care
of worship belonged hereditarily to the Magi 'as to a sacerdotal race,' ὥσπερ
τι φῦλον ἱερατικόν.

[2] Τὸ τῶν Μάγων φῦλον (XV, 14).

by Cambyses as an attempt of the Medes to recover the
hegemony they had lost, and when we learn from Herodotus
(I, 101) that the Medes were divided into several tribes,
Busae, Paraetakeni, Strouchates, Arizanti, Budii, and Magi,
without his making any remark on the last name, we can
hardly have any doubt that the priests known as Magi
belonged to the tribe of the Magi, that they were named
after their origin, and that the account of Marcellinus may
be correct even for so early a period as that of Herodotus.

§ 15. Parsi traditions agree with Greek testimonies.

That the priesthood was hereditary, we see from the statement in the Bundahis, that all the Maubeds are descend-
ants from King Minochihr[1], and even nowadays the priesthood cannot extend beyond the priestly families ; the son
of a Dastur is not obliged to be a Dastur, but no one that
is not the son of a Dastur can become one[2].

That they came from Media, we see from the traditions
about the native place of Zoroaster, their chief and the
founder of their religion.   Although epic legends place the
cradle of Mazdean power in Bactria, at the court of King
Vîstâsp, Bactria was only the first conquest of Zoroaster, it
was neither his native place, nor the cradle of his religion.
Although there are two different traditions on this point,
both agree in pointing to Media ; according to the one he
was born in Rai, that is in Media, properly so called ;
according to the other he was born in Shîz, that is in
Media Atropatene.

The former tradition seems to be the older ; it is expressed directly in the Pahlavi Commentary to Vendîdâd I,
16[3]; and there is in the Avesta itself (Yasna XIX, 18 (50)) a
passage that either alludes to it or shows how it originated.

'How many masters are there?'

---

[1] Bundahis 79, 13.

[2] Dosabhoy Framjee, The Parsees, &c. p. 277.

[3] 'Ragha of the three races,' that is to say, Atropatene (vide infra); some
say it is 'Rai.' It is 'of the three races' because the three classes, priests,
warriors, husbandmen, 'were well organized there.   Some say that Zartust
was born there . . . , those three classes were born from him.'   Cf. Bundahis
79, 15, and Farg. II, 43, n. 2.   Rai is the Greek 'Ραγαί.

'There are the master of the house, the lord of the borough, the lord of the town, the lord of the province, and the Zarathuṣtra (the high-priest) as the fifth. So is it in all lands, except in the Zarathuṣtrian realm ; for there are there only four masters, in Ragha, the Zarathuṣtrian city [1].'

'Who are they?'

'They are the master of the house, the lord of the borough, the lord of the town, and Zarathuṣtra is the fourth [2].'

This amounts to saying that the high-priest, the Mau-bedân Maubed, held in Rai the position of the da h vy u m a, or lord of the land, and was the chief magistrate. It may be suspected that this was the independent sacerdotal state which is spoken of in Marcellinus, and this suspicion is raised to a certain degree of probability by the following lines in Yaqût :

'Ustûnâwand, a celebrated fortress in the district of Dan-bawand, in the province of Rai. It is very old, and was strongly fortified. It is said to have been in existence for more than 3000 years, and to have been the stronghold of the Masmoghân of the land during the times of paganism. This word, which designates the high-priest of the Zoroas-trian religion, is composed of mas, "great," and moghân, which means "magian." Khaled besieged it, and destroyed the power of the last of them [3].'

According to another tradition Zarathuṣtra was born in Atropatene. The very same commentary which describes Ragha as being identical with Rai, and the native place of Zartuṣt, also informs us that Ragha was thought by others

---

[1] Or possibly, ' in the Zarathuṣtrian Ragha.'

[2] The Commentary has here: 'that is to say, he was the fourth master in his own land.'

Their spreading and wandering over Mazdean lands appears from Yasna XLII, 6 (XLI, 34): 'We bless the coming of the Athravans, who come from afar to bring holiness to countries;' cf. infra, p. lii, note 1, and Farg. XIII, 22.

[3] Dictionnaire géographique de la Perse, traduit par Barbier de Meynard, p. 33. Cf. Spiegel, Eranische Alterthumskunde III, 565. A dim recollection of this Magian dynasty seems to survive in the account ap. Diog. Laert. (Prooem. 2) that Zoroaster was followed by a long series of Magi, Osthanae Astrampsychi, and Pazatae, till the destruction of the Persian empire by Alexander.

to be Atropatene. Traditions, of which unfortunately we have only late records, make him a native of Shîz, the capital of Atropatene[1]: ' In Shîz is the fire temple of Azerekhsh, the most celebrated of the Pyraea of the Magi; in the days of the fire worship, the kings always came on foot, upon pilgrimage. The temple of Azerekhsh is ascribed to Zeratusht, the founder of the Magian religion, who went, it is said, from Shîz to the mountain of Sebîlân, and, after remaining there some time in retirement, returned with the Zend-Avesta, which, although written in the old Persian language, could not be understood without a commentary. After this he declared himself to be a prophet[2].'

Now we read in the Bundahis that Zartust founded his religion by offering a sacrifice in Irân Vêg (Airyanem Vaêgô)[3]. Although this detail referred originally to the mythical character of Zoroaster, and Irân Vêg was primitively no real country, yet as it was afterwards identified with the basin of the Aras (Vanguhi Dâitya)[4], this identification is a proof that the cradle of the new religion was looked for on the banks of the Aras. In the Avesta itself we read that Zoroaster was born and received the law from Ormazd on a mountain, by the river Darega[5], a name which strikingly reminds one of the modern Darah river, which falls from the Sebîlân mount into the Aras.

To decide which of the two places, Rai or Atropatene, had the better claim to be called the native place of Zoroaster is of course impossible. The conflict of the two traditions must be interpreted as an indication that both places were important seats of the Magian worship. That both traditions may rely on the Avesta is perhaps a sign that the Avesta contains two series of documents, the one emanating from the Magi of Ragha, and the other from the

---

[1] The Persian Gazn, the Byzantine Gaza. Ganzaka, the site of which was identified by Sir Henry Rawlinson with Takht i Suleiman (Memoir on the Site of the Atropatenian Ecbatana, in the Journal of the Royal Geographical Society, X, 65).

[2] Kazwini, apud Rawlinson l. c. p. 69.

[3] Bund. 79, 12.   [4] See Farg. I, p. 3.

[5] See Farg. XIX, 4, 11.

Magi of Atropatene[1]. Which of the two places had the older claim is also a question hardly to be settled in the present state of our knowledge[2].

Whether Magism came from Ragha to Atropatene, or from Atropatene to Ragha, in either case it had its origin in Media[3]. That Persia should have submitted in religious matters to a foreign tribe will surprise no one who thinks of the influence of the Etruscan augurs in Rome. The Magi might be hated as Medes, but they were respected and feared as priests. When political revolutions gave vent to national hate, the Persian might willingly indulge it, and revel in the blood of the foreign priest[4]; yet whenever he had to invoke the favour of the gods, he was obliged to acknowledge that he could not do without the detested tribe, and that they alone knew how to make themselves heard by heaven[5]. When and how the religious hegemony of Media arose we cannot say: it is but natural that Media[6],

[1] This would be a principle of classification which unfortunately applies only to a small part of the Avesta.

[2] Still, if we follow the direction of the Zoroastrian legend, Magism must have spread from west to east, from Atropatene to Ragha, from Ragha to Bactria; and Atropatene must thus have been the first cradle of Mazdeism. Its very name points to its sacred character; oriental writers, starting from the modern form of the name, Adarbîgân, interpret it as 'the seed of fire,' with an allusion to the numerous fire springs to be found there. Modern scholars have generally followed the historical etymology given by Strabo, who states that, after the death of Alexander, the satrap Atropates made himself an independent sovereign in his satrapy, which was named after him Atropatene. This looks like a Greek etymology (scarcely more to be trusted than the etymology of 'Ραγαί, from ῥήγνυμι), and it is hardly to be believed that the land should have lost its former name to take a new one from its king; it was not a new-fangled geographical division, like Lotharingia, and had lived a life of its own for a long time before. Its name Âtarpatakân seems to mean ' the land of the descent of fire,' as it was there that fire came down from heaven (cf. Ammianus l. c.)

[3] The Pahlavi names of the cardinal points show that Media was the centre of orientation in Magian geography (Garrez, Journal Asiatique, 1869, II).

[4] Magophonia (Herod. III, 79).

[5] 'Ὡς αὐτοὺς μόνους ἀκουομένους (Diog. Laert. Prooem.); cf. Herod. I, 132; Ammian. l. l.

[6] An echo of the old political history of Media seems to linger in Yast V, 29, which shows Azi Dahâka reigning in Babylon (Bawru); as Azi, in his legendary character, represents the foreign invader, this passage can hardly be anything but a far remote echo of the struggles between Media and the Mesopotamian empires. The legend of Azi is localised only in Medic

having risen sooner to a high degree of civilisation, should have given to religion and worship a more systematic and elaborate form, and in religion, as in politics, the best organised power must sooner or later get the upper hand. It is likely that it began with the conquest of Media by Cyrus: Media capta ferum victorem cepit. . . . Cyrus is said to have introduced the Magian priesthood into Persia (Xenophon, Cyrop. VIII, 1, 23), which agrees with the legend mentioned by Nikolaus that it was on the occasion of the miraculous escape of Crœsus that the Persians remembered the old λογία of Zoroaster forbidding the dead to be burnt.

The Medic origin of the Magi accounts for a fact which perplexes at first sight, namely, the absence of the name of the Magi from the book written by themselves[1]; which is natural enough if the word Magu was not the name of the priest as a priest, but as a member of the tribe of the Magi. The proper word for a priest in the Avesta is Âthravan, literally, ‘fire-man,’ and that this was his name with the Persians too appears from the statement in Strabo (XV, 733) that the Magi are also called Πύραιθοι. It is easy to conceive that the Persians, especially in ordinary parlance, would rather designate their priests after their origin than after their functions[2]; but the Magi themselves had no reason to follow the Persian custom, which was not always free from an implication of spite or scorn. The only passage into which the word found its way is just one that betrays the existence of this feeling: the enemy of the priests is

lands: he addresses his prayers to Ahriman by the banks of the Sipît rût (Bundahis 52, 11), his adversary Ferîdûn is born in Ghilân, he is bound to Mount Damâvand (near Rai).

[1] In their own language, the Zend; of which the modern representatives, if there be any left, should therefore be looked for in Atropatene or on the banks of the Caspian sea. The research is complicated by the growing intrusion of Persian words into the modern dialects, but as far as I can see from a very inadequate study of the matter, the dialect which exhibits most Zend features is the Talis dialect, on the southern bank of the Aras.

[2] The Pahlavi has ‘one who hates the Magu-men.’ In the passage LIII (LII), 7, magéus is not a Magian, and it is translated by magî, ‘holiness, godliness,’ related to the Vedic magha. Afterwards the two words were confounded, whence came the Greek statement that μάγος means at the same time ‘a priest’ and ‘a god’ (Apollon. Tyan. Ep. XVII).

not called, as would be expected, an Âthrava-*t*bi*s*, 'a hater of the Âthravans' (cf. the Indian Brahma-dvish), but a Moghu-*t*bi*s*, 'a hater of the Magi[1].' The name, it is true, became current in Pahlavi and modern Persian, but it was at a time when the old national quarrels between Media and Persia were quenched, and the word could no longer carry any offensive idea with it.

§ 16. The results of the foregoing research may be summed up as follows :—

The original texts of the Avesta were not written by Persians, as they are in a language which was not used in Persia, they prescribe certain customs which were unknown to Persia, and proscribe others which were current in Persia. They were written in Media, by the priests of Ragha and Atropatene, in the language of Media, and they exhibit the ideas of the sacerdotal class under the Achæmenian dynasty.

It does not necessarily follow from this, that the original fragments were already written at the time of Herodotus[2].

---

[1] A further echo of the anti-Magian feelings may be heard in Yasna IX, 24 (75): 'Haoma overthrew Keresâni, who rose up to seize royalty, and he said, "No longer shall henceforth the Âthravans go through the lands and teach at their will."' This is a curious instance of how easily legendary history may turn myths to its advantage. The struggle of Haoma against Keresâni is an old Indo-European myth, Keresâni being the same as the Vedic K*ri*sânu, who wants to keep away Soma from the hands of men. His name becomes in the Avesta the name of an anti-Magian king [it may be Darius, the usurper (?)], and ten centuries later it was turned into an appellation of the Christian Kaisars of Rûm (Kalasyâk = *ἐκκλησια[κός] ; Tarsâka).

[2] If the interpretation of the end of the Behistun inscription (preserved only in the Scythian version) as given by Professor Oppert be correct, Darius must have made a collection of religious texts known as Avesta, whence it would follow, with great probability, that the present Avesta proceeded from Darius. The translation of the celebrated scholar is as follows: 'J'ai fait une collection de textes (dippimas) ailleurs en langue arienne qui autrefois n'existait pas. Et j'ai fait un texte de la Loi (de l'Avesta ; Haduk ukku) et un commentaire de la Loi, et la Bénédiction (la prière, le Zend) et les Traductions.' (Le peuple et la langue des Mèdes, pp. 155, 186.) The authority of Oppert is so great, and at the same time the passage is so obscure, that I hardly know if there be more temerity in rejecting his interpretation or in adopting it. Yet I beg to observe that the word dippimas is the usual Scythian transliteration of the Persian dipi, 'an inscription,' and there is no apparent reason for departing from that meaning in this passage; if the word translated 'la Loi,' ukku, really represents here a Persian word Aba*s*ta, it need not denote the Avesta, the religious book,

But as the Magi of that time sang songs of their gods during sacrifice, it is very likely that there was already a sacred literature in existence. The very fact that no sacrifice could be performed without the assistance of the Magi makes it highly probable that they were in possession of rites, prayers, and hymns very well composed and arranged, and not unlike those of the Brahmans ; their authority can only be accounted for by the power of a strongly defined ritual and liturgy. There must, therefore, have been a collection of formulae and hymns, and it is quite possible that Herodotus may have heard the Magi sing, in the fifth century B. C., the very same Gâthas which are sung nowadays by the Mobeds in Bombay. A part of the Avesta, the liturgical part, would therefore have been, in fact, a sacred book for the Persians. It had not been written by them, but it was sung for their benefit. That Zend hymns should have been sung before a Persian-speaking people is not stranger than Latin words being sung by Frenchmen, Germans, and Italians ; the only difference being that, owing to the close affinity of Zend to Persian, the Persians may have been able to understand the prayers of their priests.

§ 17. It may, therefore, be fairly admitted that, on the whole, the present texts are derived from texts already existing under the Achæmenian kings. Some parts of the collection are undoubtedly older than others ; thus, the Gâthas are certainly older than the rest of the Avesta, as they are often quoted and praised in the Yasna and the Vendîdâd ; but it is scarcely possibly to go farther than a logical chronology. One might feel inclined, at first sight, to assign to a very recent date, perhaps to the last revision of the Avesta, those long enumerations of gods so symmetrically elaborated in the Yasna, Vispêrad, and Vendîdâd. But the account of Mazdeism given by Plutarch shows that the

as in that case the word would most certainly not have been translated in the Scythian version, but only transliterated ; the ideogram for 'Bénédiction, prière,' may refer to religious inscriptions like Persepolis I ; the import of the whole passage would therefore be that Darius caused other inscriptions to be engraved, and wrote other edicts and religious formulae (the word 'traductions' is only a guess).

work of co-ordination was already terminated at the end of the Achæmenian period, and there is no part of the Avesta which, so far as the matter is concerned, may not have been written in those times. Nay, the Greek accounts of that period present us, in some measure, with a later stage of thought, and are pervaded with a stronger sense of symmetry, than the Avesta itself. Such passages as the latter end of the Zamyâd Yast and Vendîdâd X, 9 seq. prove that, when they were composed, the seven Arch-Dêvs were not yet pointedly contrasted with the seven Amshaspands, and therefore those passages might have been written long before the time of Philip. The theory of time and space as first principles of the world, of which only the germs are found in the Avesta, was fully developed in the time of Eudemos, a disciple of Aristotle.

§ 18. To what extent the Magian dogmatical conceptions were admitted by the whole of the Iranian population, or how and by what process they spread among it, we cannot ascertain for want of documentary evidence. As regards their observances we are better instructed, and can form an idea of how far and in what particulars they differed from the other Iranians. The new principle they introduced, or, rather, developed into new consequences, was that of the purity of the elements. Fire, earth, and water had always been considered sacred things, and had received worship[1]: the Magi drew from that principle the conclusion that burying the dead or burning the dead was defiling a god: as early as Herodotus they had already succeeded in preserving fire from that pollution, and cremation was a capital crime. The earth still continued to be defiled, notwithstanding the example they set; and it was only under the Sassanians, when Mazdeism became the religion of the state, that they won this point also.

The religious difference between the Persians and their Medic priests was therefore chiefly in observances. Out of the principles upon which the popular religion rested, the sacerdotal class drew by dint of logic, in a puritan spirit,

---

[1] Cf. V, 8.

the necessity of strict observances, the yoke of which was not willingly endured by the mass of the people. Many acts, insignificant in the eyes of the people, became repugnant to their consciences and their more refined logic. The people resisted, and for a time Magian observances were observed only by the Magi. The slow triumph of Magism can be dimly traced through the Achæmenian period. Introduced by Cyrus, it reigned supreme for a time with the Pseudo-Smerdis, and was checked by Darius[1]. It seems to have resumed its progress under Xerxes ; at least, it was reported that it was to carry out Magian principles that he destroyed the Greek temples, and that the first who wrote on the Zoroastrian lore was a Magian, named Osthanes, who had accompanied him to Greece[2]. New progress marked the reign of Artaxerxes Longimanus. The epic history of Iran, as preserved in the Shah Nâmah, passes suddenly from the field of mythology to that of history with the reign of that king, which makes it likely that it was in his time that the legends of Media became national in Persia, and that his reign was an epoch in the political history of Magism[3]. But the real victory was not won till six centuries later, when national interest required a national religion. Then, as happens in every revolution, the ultra party, that had pushed to the extreme the principles common to all, took the lead ; the Magi ascended the throne with Ardeshîr, one of their pupils[4], and the Magian

---

[1] Darius rebuilt the temples which the Magus Gaumata had destroyed (Behistun I, 63). The Magi, it is said, wanted the gods not to be imprisoned within four walls (Cic. de Legibus II, 10) : Xerxes behaved himself as their disciple, at least in Greece. Still the Magi seem to have at last given way on that point to the Perso-Assyrian customs, and there were temples even under the Sassanians.

[2] Pliny, Hist. Nat. XXX, 1, 8.

[3] Cf. Westergaard, Preface to the Zend-Avesta, p. 17. This agrees with what we know of the fondness of Artaxerxes for religious novelties. It was he who blended the worship of the Assyrian Anat-Mylitta with that of the Iranian Anâhita (the ascription of that innovation to Artaxerxes Mnemon by Clemens Alexandrinus (Stromata I) must rest on a clerical error, as in the time of Herodotus, who wrote under Longimanus, the worship of Mylitta had already been introduced into Persia (I, 131)).

[4] Agathias II, 26.

observances became the law of all Iran.   But their triumph
was not to be a long one; their principles required an effort
too continuous and too severe to be ever made by any but
priests, who might concentrate all their faculties in watching
whether they had not dropped a hair upon the ground.   A
working people could not be imprisoned in such a religion,
though it might be pure and high in its ethics.   The
triumph of Islam was a deliverance for the consciences of
many [1], and Magism, by enforcing its observances upon the
nation, brought about the ruin of its dogmas, which were
swept away at the same time: its triumph was the cause
and signal of its fall [2].

CHAPTER IV.

THE ORIGIN OF THE AVESTA RELIGION.

§ 1. What was the religion of the Magi which we find
reflected in the Avesta ? and whence did it arise ?

Magism, in its general form, may be summed up as
follows :—

The world, such as it is now, is twofold, being the work of
two hostile beings, Ahura Mazda, the good principle, and
Angra Mainyu, the evil principle ; all that is good in the
world comes from the former, all that is bad in it comes
from the latter.   The history of the world is the history of
their conflict, how Angra Mainyu invaded the world of
Ahura Mazda and marred it, and how he shall be expelled
from it at last.   Man is active in the conflict, his duty in it
being laid before him in the law revealed by Ahura Mazda
to Zarathustra.   When the appointed time is come, a son of
the lawgiver, still unborn, named Saoshyant, will appear,
Angra Mainyu and hell will be destroyed, men will rise
from the dead, and everlasting happiness will reign over the
world.

---

[1] De Gobineau, Histoire des Perses, II, 632 seq.

[2] We ought to discuss here the Scythian theory of Magism; but thus far we
have been unable to find anywhere a clear and consistent account of its thesis
and of its arguments.   Nothing is known of any Scythian religion, and what is
ascribed to a so-called Scythian influence, the worship of the elements, is one
of the oldest and most essential features of the Aryan religions.

We have tried in another book [1] to show that the religion of the Magi is derived from the same source as that of the Indian *R*íshis, that is, from the religion followed by the common forefathers of the Iranians and Indians, the Indo-Iranian religion. The Mazdean belief is, therefore, composed of two different strata ; the one comprises all the gods, myths, and ideas which were already in existence during the Indo-Iranian period, whatever changes they may have undergone during the actual Iranian period ; the other comprises the gods, myths, and ideas which were only developed after the separation of the two religions.

§ 2. There were two general ideas at the bottom of the Indo-Iranian religion ; first, that there is a law in nature, and, secondly, that there is a war in nature.

There is a law in nature, because everything goes on in a serene and mighty order. Days after days, seasons after seasons, years after years come and come again; there is a marvellous friendship between the sun and the moon, the dawn has never missed its appointed time and place, and the stars that shine in the night know where to go when the day is breaking. There is a God who fixed that never-failing law, and on whom it rests for ever [2].

There is a war in nature, because it contains powers that work for good and powers that work for evil : there are such beings as benefit man, and such beings as injure him : there are gods and fiends. They struggle on, never and nowhere more apparent than in the storm, in which, under our very eyes, the fiend that carries off the light and streams of heaven fights with the god that gives them back to man and the thirsty earth.

There were, therefore, in the Indo-Iranian religion a latent monotheism and an unconscious dualism [3]; both of which, in the further development of Indian thought, slowly disappeared ; but Mazdeism lost neither of these two notions

---

[1] Ormazd et Ahriman, Paris, 1877. We beg, for the sake of brevity, to refer to that book for further demonstration.

[2] Cf. Max Müller, Lectures on the Origin and Growth of Religion, p. 249.

[3] J. Darmesteter, The Supreme God in the Indo-European Mythology, in the Contemporary Review, October, 1879, p. 283.

nor did it add a new one, and its original action was to cling
strongly and equally to both ideas and push them to an
extreme.

§ 3. The God that has established the laws in nature is
the Heaven God. He is the greatest of gods, since there is
nothing above him nor outside of him; he has made everything, since everything is produced or takes place in him; he
is the wisest of all gods, since with his eyes, the sun, moon,
and stars, he sees everything[1].

This god was named either after his bodily nature Varana,
'the all-embracing sky[2],' or after his spiritual attributes
Asura, 'the Lord,' Asura visvavedas, 'the all-knowing
Lord,' Asura Mazdhâ, 'the Lord of high knowledge[3].'

§ 4. The supreme Asura of the Indo-Iranian religion, the
Heaven god, is called in the Avesta Ahura Mazda, 'the
all-knowing Lord[4];' his concrete name Varana, which
became his usual name in India (Varuna), was lost in Iran,
and remained only as the name of the material heaven, and
then of a mythical region, the Varena, which was the seat
of the mythical fight between a storm god and a storm
fiend[5].

§ 5. The spiritual attributes of the Heaven god were daily
more and more strongly defined, and his material attributes
were thrown farther into the background. Yet many features,
though ever dimmer and dimmer, betray his former bodily
or, rather, his sky nature. He is white, bright, seen afar,
and his body is the greatest and fairest of all bodies; he
has the sun for his eye, the rivers above for his spouses, the
fire of lightning for his son; he wears the heaven as a
star-spangled garment, he puts on the hard stone of heaven,
he is the hardest of all gods[6]. He dwells in the infinite
luminous space, and the infinite luminous space is his place,

[1] Ibid.

[2] Οὐρανός; or Dyaus, 'the shining sky' [Ζεύς, Jup-piter], or Svar.

[3] Or perhaps 'the Lord who bestows intelligence' (Benfey, 'Asura Medhâ
and Ahura Mazdâo ').

[4] This is, at least, the meaning that attached to the name in the consciences
of the composers of the Avesta.

[5] Vide infra, § 12.

[6] Orm. Ahr. §§ 27-36.

his body[1]. In the time of Herodotus, Persians, while in-
voking Aurâmazda, the creator of earth and heaven, still
knew who he was, and called the whole vault of the sky
Zeus, that is to say, called it the supreme god[2].

§ 6. In the Indo-Iranian religion, the supreme Asura,
although he was the supreme god, was not the only god.
There were near him and within him many mighty beings,
the sun, wind, lightning, thunder, rain, prayer, sacrifice, which
as soon as they struck the eye or the fancy of man, were at
once turned into gods. If the Heaven Asura, greater in
time and space, eternal and universal, everlasting and ever
present, was without effort raised to the supreme rank by
his twofold infinitude, there were other gods, of shorter but
mightier life, who maintained against him their right to
independence. The progress of religious thought might as
well have gone on to transfer power from him to any of
these gods, as to make his authority unrivalled. The former
was the case in India : in the middle of the Vedic period,
Indra, the dazzling god of storm, rose to supremacy in the
Indian Pantheon, and outshines Varuna with the roar and
splendour of his feats ; but soon to give way to a new and
mystic king, Prayer or Brahman[3].

Not so did Mazdeism, which struggled on towards unity.
The Lord slowly brought everything under his unquestioned
supremacy, and the other gods became not only his subjects,
but his creatures. This movement was completed as early
as the fourth century B.C. Nowhere can it be more clearly
traced than in the Amesha Spentas and Mithra.

§ 7. The Indo-Iranian Asura was often conceived as
sevenfold : by the play of certain mythical formulae and
the strength of certain mythical numbers, the ancestors of
the Indo-Iranians had been led to speak of seven worlds,
and the supreme god was often made sevenfold, as well as
the worlds over which he ruled[4]. The names and the several

---

[1] Bundahis 1, 7; Yasna LVIII, 8 (LVII, 22).

[2] Herod. I, 131.

[3] Cf. 'The Supreme God,' l. l. p. 287.

[4] The seven worlds became in Persia the seven Karshvare of the earth : the
earth is divided into seven Karshvare, only one of which is known and

attributes of the seven gods had not been as yet defined,
nor could they be then; after the separation of the two
religions, these gods, named Âditya, 'the infinite ones,'
in India, were by and by identified there with the sun, and
their number was afterwards raised to twelve, to correspond
to the twelve successive aspects of the sun. In Persia, the
seven gods are known as Amesha Spentas, 'the undying
and well-doing ones;' they by and by, according to the
new spirit that breathed in the religion, received the names
of the deified abstractions[1], Vohu-manô (good thought),
Asha Vahista (excellent holiness), Khshathra vairya (perfect sovereignty), Spenta Ârmaiti (divine piety), Haurvatât
and Ameretât (health and immortality). The first of them
all was and remained Ahura Mazda; but whereas formerly
he had been only the first of them, he was now their father.
' I invoke the glory of the Amesha Spentas, who all seven
have one and the same thinking, one and the same speaking,
one and the same doing, one and the same father and lord,
Ahura Mazda[2].'

§ 8. In the Indo-Iranian religion, the Asura of Heaven
was often invoked in company with Mitra[3], the god of the
heavenly light, and he let him share with himself the
universal sovereignty. In the Veda, they are invoked as a
pair (Mitrâ-Varunâ), which enjoys the same power and rights
as Varuna alone, as there is nothing more in Mitrâ-Varunâ
than in Varuna alone, Mitra being the light of Heaven,
that is, the light of Varuna. But Ahura Mazda could no
longer bear an equal, and Mithra became one of his

accessible to man, the one on which we live, namely, Hvaniratha; which
amounts to saying that there are seven earths. Parsi mythology knows also
of seven heavens. Hvaniratha itself was divided into seven climes (Orm. Ahr.
§ 72). An enumeration of the seven Karshvare is to be found in Farg. XIX, 39.

[1] Most of which were already either divine or holy in the Indo-Iranian period:
health and immortality are invoked in the Vedas as in the Avesta (see
J. Darmesteter, Haurvatât et Ameretât, §§ 49 seq.); Asha Vahista is revered
in the Vedas as Rita (vide infra, § 30); Spenta Ârmaiti is the Vedic goddess Aramati (§ 30); Khshathra vairya is the same as the Brahmanical
Kshatra; Vohu-manô is a personification of the Vedic sumati (Orm. Ahr.
§§ 196-201).

[2] Yast XIX, 16.

[3] Mitra means literally ' a friend;' it is the light as friendly to man (Orm.
Ahr. §§ 59-61).

creatures : 'This Mithra, the lord of wide pastures, I have created as worthy of sacrifice, as worthy of glorification, as I, Ahura Mazda, am myself[1].' But old formulae, no longer understood, in which Mithra and Ahura, or, rather, Mithra-Ahura, are invoked in an indivisible unity, dimly remind one that the Creator was formerly a brother to his creature.

§ 9. Thus came a time when Ahura was not only the maker of the world, the creator of the earth, water, trees, mountains, roads, wind, sleep, and light, was not only he who gives to man life, shape, and food, but was also the father of Tistrya, the rain-bestowing god, of Verethraghna, the fiend-smiting god, and of Haoma, the tree of eternal life, the father of the six Amesha Spentas, the father of all gods[2].

Yet, with all his might, he still needs the help of some god, of such as free the oppressed heavens from the grasp of the fiend. When storm rages in the atmosphere he offers up a sacrifice to Vayu, the bright storm god, who moves in the wind, he entreats him : 'Grant me the favour, thou Vayu whose action is most high[3], that I may smite the world of Angra Mainyu, and that he may not smite mine! Vayu, whose action is most high, granted the asked-for favour to the creator Ahura Mazda[4].' And when Zoroaster is born, Ahura entreats Ardvî Sûra Anâhita that the new-born hero may stand by him in the fight[5] (see § 40).

---

[1] He preserved, however, a high situation, both in the concrete and in the abstract mythology. As the god of the heavenly light, the lord of vast luminous space, of the wide pastures above (cf. § 16), he became later the god of the sun (Deo invicto Soli Mithrae; in Persian Mihr is the Sun). As light and truth are one and the same thing, viewed with the eyes of the body and of the mind, he became the god of truth and faith. He punishes the Mithra-drug, 'him who lies to Mithra' (or 'who lies to the contract,' since Mithra as a neuter noun means 'friendship, agreement, contract'); he is a judge in hell, in company with Rashnu, 'the true one,' the god of truth, a mere offshoot of Mithra in his moral character (Farg. IV, 54).

[2] Cf. Plut. de Iside, XLVII.

[3] Or, who workest in the heights above.

[4] Yt. XV, 3.

[5] In the same way his Greek counterpart, Zeus, the god of heaven, the lord and father both of gods and men, when besieged by the Titans, calls Thetis, Prometheus, and the Hecatonchirs to help him.

§ 10. Whereas in India the fiends were daily driven farther and farther into the background, and by the prevalence of the metaphysical spirit gods and fiends came to be nothing more than changing and fleeting creatures of the everlasting, indifferent Being, Persia took her demons in real earnest; she feared them, she hated them, and the vague and unconscious dualism that lay at the bottom of the Indo-Iranian religion has its unsteady outlines sharply defined, and became the very form and frame of Mazdeism. The conflict was no more seen and heard in the passing storm only, but it raged through all the avenues of space and time. The Evil became a power of itself, engaged in an open and never-ceasing warfare with the Good. The Good was centred in the supreme god, in Ahura Mazda, the bright god of Heaven, the all-knowing Lord, the Maker, who, as the author of every good thing, was 'the good Spirit,' Spenta Mainyu. In front of him and opposed to him slowly rose the evil Spirit, Angra Mainyu.

We will briefly explain what became, in Mazdeism, of the several elements of the Indo-Iranian dualism, and then we will show how the whole system took a regular form.

§ 11. The war in nature was waged in the storm. The Vedas describe it as a battle fought by a god, Indra, armed with the lightning and thunder, against a serpent, Ahi, who has carried off the dawns or the rivers, described as goddesses or as milch cows, and who keeps them captive in the folds of the cloud.

This myth appears in a still simpler form in the Avesta: it is a fight for the possession of the light of *hvarenô* between Âtar and Azi Dahâka[1].

Âtar means 'fire;' he is both a thing and a person. He is sometimes described as the weapon of Ahura[2], but usually as his son[3], as the fire that springs from heaven can be conceived either as flung by it, or as born of it[4].

Azi Dahâka, 'the fiendish snake,' is a three-headed

---

[1] Yt. XIX, 47-52.
[2] Yasna LI (L), 9.
[3] Farg. III, 15; V, 10; XV, 26, &c.
[4] Cf. Clermont-Ganneau, in the Revue Critique, 1877, No. 52.

dragon, who strives to seize and put out the *hvarenô*: he takes hold of it, but Âtar frightens him away and recovers the light.

The scene of the fight is the sea Vouru-kasha, a sea from which all the waters on the earth fall down with the winds and the clouds; in other words, they fight in the sea above[1], in the atmospheric field of battle[2].

§ 12. The same myth in the Vedas was described as a feat of Traitana or Trita Âptya, 'Trita, the son of waters,' who killed the three-headed, six-eyed fiend, and let loose the cows[3]. 'The son of waters[4]' is both in the Vedas and in the Avesta a name of the fire-god, as born from the cloud, in the lightning. The same tale is told in the same terms in the Avesta: Thraêtaona Âthwya killed Azi Dahâka (the fiendish snake), the three-mouthed, three-headed, six-eyed, ... the most dreadful Drug created by Angra Mainyu[5]. The scene of the battle is 'the four-cornered Varena[6],' which afterwards became a country on the earth, when Thraêtaona himself and Azi became earthly kings, but which was formerly nothing less than 'the four-pointed Varuna[7],' that is, 'the four-sided Οὐρανός,' the Heavens.

§ 13. The fight for the waters was described in a myth of later growth, a sort of refacimento, the myth of Tistrya and Apaosha. Apaosha[8] keeps away the rain: Tistrya[9], worsted at first, then strengthened by a sacrifice which has been offered to him by Mazda, knocks down Apaosha[10] with his club, the fire Vâzista[11], and the waters stream freely

---

[1] The *hvarenô*, Persian khurrah and farr, is properly the light of sovereignty, the glory from above which makes the king an earthly god. He who possesses it reigns, he who loses it falls down; when Yima lost it he perished and Azi Dahâka reigned; as when light disappears, the fiend rules supreme. Vide infra, § 39; and cf. Yt. XIX, 32 seq.

[2] See Farg. V, 15 seq.   [3] Rv. I, 158, 5; X, 99, 6.

[4] Generally, apâm napât.   [5] Yasna IX, 8 (25).

[6] Cathru-gaosho Varenô; v. Vendîdâd I, 18.

[7] Catur-asris Varuno, Rv. I, 152, 2. Cf Orm. Ahr. § 65.

[8] 'The extinguisher' (?).   [9] Cf. § 36.

[10] Called also Spengaghra (Farg. XIX, 40).

[11] It is the groaning of the fiend under the stroke of that club that is heard in thunder (Bundahis 17, 11; cf. Farg. XIX, 40).

down the seven Karshvare, led by the winds, by the son of
the waters, and by the light that dwells in the waters[1].

§ 14. The god that conquers light is chiefly praised in
the Vedas under the name of Indra V*ri*trahan, 'Indra the
fiend-smiter.' His Iranian brother is named Verethraghna,
which became by and by the genius of Victory (Bahrâm).
Yet although he assumed a more abstract character than
Indra, he retained the mythical features of the storm god[2],
and his original nature was so little forgotten that he was
worshipped on earth as a fire, the Bahrâm fire, which was
believed to be an emanation from the fire above[3], and the
most powerful protector of the land against foes and fiends.

§ 15. In the Indo-Iranian mythology, Vâyu was the word
for both the atmosphere and the bright god who fights and
conquers in it.

As a god, Vâyu became in Mazdeism Vayu, 'a god conqueror of light, a smiter of the fiends, all made of light,
who moves in a golden car, with sonorous rings[4].' Ahura
Mazda invokes him for help against Angra Mainyu[5].

§ 16. Another name of Vayu is Râma *hv*âstra: this
word meant originally 'the god of the resting-place with
good pastures,' the clouds in the atmosphere being often
viewed as a herd of cows[6], and the Indian Vâyu as a
good shepherd[7]. Hence came the connection of Râma
*hv*âstra with Mithra, 'the lord of the wide pastures[8].' In
later times, chiefly owing to a mistake in language (*hv*âstra
being thought to be related to the root *hv*arez, 'to taste'),
Râma *hv*âstra became the god who gives a good flavour to
aliments[9].

§ 17. Considered as a thing, as the atmosphere, Vayu is
the place where the god and the fiend meet: there is therefore a part of it which belongs to the good and another
part which belongs to the evil[10]. Hence came the later
notion that between Ormazd and Ahriman there is a void
space, Vâi, in which their meeting takes place[11].

---

[1] Yt. VIII.   [2] Yt. XIV.   [3] Cf. V, 8.
[4] Yt. XV.   [5] Cf. above, p. lxi.   [6] See above, § 11.
[7] Cf. Atharva-veda II, 26, 1; Rv. I, 134, 4.
[8] Farg. III, 2; Yasna I, 3 (9).   [9] Neriosengh ad Yasna, l. l.
[10] Yt. XV, 5.   [11] Bundahis I, 15.

Hence came also the distinction of two Vai[1], the good one and the bad one, which, probably by the natural connection of Vayu, the atmosphere, with the heavens[2] whose movement is Destiny[3], became at last the good Fate and the bad Fate, or Destiny bringing good and evil, life and death[4].

§ 18. Aźi is not always vanquished; he may also conquer; and it is just because the serpent has seized upon the sky and darkened the light, that the battle breaks out. Aźi has carried off the sovereign light, the *hvarenô*, from Yima Khshaêta, 'the shining Yima[5].

In the course of time Thraêtaona, Yima, and Aźi Dahâka became historical: it was told how King Jemshîd (Yima Khshâeta) had been overthrown and killed by the usurper Zohâk (Dahâka), a man with two snakes' heads upon his shoulders, and how Zohâk himself had been overthrown by a prince of the royal blood, Ferîdûn (Thraêtaona). Yet Zohâk, though vanquished, could not be killed; he was bound to Mount Damâvand, there to lie in bonds till the end of the world, when he shall be let loose, and then killed by Keresâspa[6]. The fiend is as long-lifed as the world, since as often as he is vanquished he appears again, as dark and fearful as ever[7].

§ 19. While the serpent passed thus from mythology into legend, he still continued under another name, or, more correctly, under another form of his name, âzi, a word which the Parsis converted into a pallid and lifeless abstraction by identifying it with a similar word from the same root, meaning 'want.' But that he was the very same being as Aźi, the snake, appears from his adversaries: like Aźi, he fights against Âtar, the fire, and strives to extinguish it[8], and together with the Pairikas, he wants to carry off the rain-floods, like the Indian Ahi[9].

§ 20. Mazdeism, as might be expected from its main

---

[1] Mainyô i-Khard II, 115; cf. Farg. V, 8, n. 3.
[2] Cf. Farg. XIX, 16.   [3] Orm. Ahr. § 257.
[4] Farg. V, 8-9, text and notes.
[5] See above, p. lxiii, n. 1, and Yast XIX.   [6] Cf. § 39.
[7] Cf. Roth, Zeitschrift der Deutschen Morgenl. Gesellschaft II, 216.
[8] Farg. XVIII, 19 seq.
[9] Yasna LXVIII, 7 (LXVII, 18).

principle, is very rich in demons. There are whole classes of them which belong to the Indo-Iranian mythology.

The Vedic Yâtus are found unaltered in the Avesta. The Yâtu in the Vedas is the demon taking any form he pleases, the fiend as a wizard : so he is in the Avesta also, where the name is likewise extended to the Yâtu-man, the sorcerer.

§ 21. With the Yâtus are often associated the Pairikas (the Paris)[1].

The Pairika corresponds in her origin (and perhaps as to her name) to the Indian Apsaras[2].

The light for which the storm god struggled was often compared, as is well known, to a fair maid or bride carried off by the fiend. There was a class of myths, in which, instead of being carried off, she was supposed to have given herself up, of her own free will, to the demon, and to have betrayed the god, her lover. In another form of myth, still more distant from the naturalistic origin, the Pairikas were ' nymphs of a fair, but erring line,' who seduced the heroes to lead them to their ruin. Afterwards the Pari became at length the seduction of idolatry[3].

In their oldest Avesta form they are still demoniac nymphs, who rob the gods and men of the heavenly waters: they hover between heaven and earth, in the midst of the sea Vouru-kasha, to keep off the rain-floods, and they work together with Âzi and Apaosha[4].

Then we see the Pairika, under the name of Knâthaiti, cleave to Keresâspa[5]. Keresâspa, like Thraêtaona, is a great smiter of demons, who killed the snake Srvara, a twin-brother of Azi Dahâka[6]. It was related in later tales that he was born immortal, but that having despised the holy religion he was killed, during his sleep, by a Turk, Niyâz[7], which, being translated into old myth, would mean that he

---

[1] Farg. VIII, 80. [2] Orm. Ahr. § 142.
[3] Ibid. p. 176, n. 6. Then pairikãm, the accusative of pairika, was interpreted as a Pahlavi compound, pari-kâm, ' love of the Paris' (Comm. ad Farg. XIX. 5).
[4] Yast VIII, 8, 39, 49–56; Yasna XVI, 8 (XVII, 46).
[5] Farg. I, 10. [6] Yasna IX, 11 (34); Yast XIX, 40.
[7] Bundahis 69, 13. On Niyâz, see Orm. Ahr. p. 216, n. 9.

gave himself up to the Pairika Khnâthaiti, who delivered
him asleep to the fiend.   Yet he must rise from his sleep, at
the end of time, to kill Aʑi, and Khnâthaiti will be killed
at the same time by Saoshyant[1], the son of Zarathuʂtra,
which shows her to be a genuine sister of Aʑi.

§ 22. Then come the host of storm fiends, the Drvanʦ,
the Dvaranʦ, the Dregvanʦ, all names meaning ' the running ones,' and referring to the headlong course of the
fiends in storm, ' the onsets of the wounding crew.'

One of the foremost amongst the Drvanʦ, their leader
in their onsets, is Aêshma, 'the raving,' 'a fiend with the
wounding spear.'   Originally a mere epithet of the storm
fiend, Aêshma was afterwards converted into an abstract,
the demon of rage and anger, and became an expression
for all moral wickedness, a mere name of Ahriman.

§ 23. A class of demons particularly interesting are the
Varenya daêvas[2]. The phrase, an old one belonging to the
Indo-European mythology, meant originally ' the gods in
heaven,' οὐράνιοι θεοί ; when the daêvas were converted
into demons (see § 41), they became ' the fiends in the
heavens,' the fiends who assail the sky ; and later on, as
the meaning of the word Varena was lost, 'the fiends of
the Varena land ;' and finally, nowadays, as their relation
to Varena is lost to sight, they are turned by popular etymology, now into demons of lust, and now into demons of
doubt[3].

§ 24. To the Pairika is closely related Bûshyãsta the
yellow, the long-handed[4].   She lulls back to sleep the
world as soon as awaked, and makes the faithful forget in
slumber the hour of prayer[5].   But as at the same time she
is said to have fallen upon Keresâspa[6], one sees that she
belonged before to a more concrete sort of mythology, and
was a sister to Khnâthaiti and to the Pairikas.

§ 25. A member of the same family is Gahi, who was

---

[1] Farg. XIX, 5.
[2] Farg. X, 14. The Mâzainya daêva (see Farg. X, 16 n.) are often invoked
with them (Yaʂt V, 22 ; XIII, 37 ; XX, 8).
[3] Aspendiârji.   [4] Farg. XI, 9.
[5] Farg. XVIII, 16 seq.   [6] Bundahiʂ 69, 15.

originally the god's bride giving herself up to the demon, and became then, by the progress of abstraction, the demon of unlawful love and unchastity[1]. The courtezan is her incarnation, as the sorcerer is that of the Yâtu.

§ 26. Death gave rise to several personations.

Sauru, which in our texts is only the proper name of a demon[2], was probably identical in meaning, as he is in name, with the Vedic Śaru, 'the arrow,' a personification of the arrow of death as a godlike being[3].

The same idea seems to be conveyed by Ishus hvâ-thakhtô, 'the self-moving arrow[4],' a designation to be accounted for by the fact that Śaru, in India, before becoming the arrow of death, was the arrow of lightning with which the god killed his foe.

A more abstract personification is Ithyêgô marshaonem[5], 'the unseen death,' death which creeps unawares.

Astô vîdôtus, 'the bone-divider[6],' who, like the Yama of the Sanskrit epic, holds a noose around the neck of all living creatures[7].

§ 27. In the conflict between gods and fiends man is active: he takes a part in it through the sacrifice.

The sacrifice is more than an act of worship, it is an act of assistance to the gods. Gods, like men, need drink and food to be strong; like men, they need praise and encouragement to be of good cheer[8]. When not strengthened by the sacrifice, they fly helpless before their foes. Tistrya, worsted by Apaosha, cries to Ahura: 'O Ahura Mazda! men do not worship me with sacrifice and praise: should they worship me with sacrifice and praise, they would bring me the strength of ten horses, ten bulls, ten mountains, ten rivers.' Ahura offers him a sacrifice, he brings him thereby the

---

[1] Orm. Ahr. § 145. Cf. Farg. XXI, 1.

[2] Vide infra, § 41; Farg. X, 9; Bundahis 5, 19.

[3] Orm. Ahr. § 212.   [4] Farg. IV, 49.   [5] Farg. XIX, 1.

[6] Farg. IV, 49. His mythical description might probably be completed by the Rabbinical and Arabian tales about the Breaking of the Sepulchre and the angels Monkir and Nakir (Sale, the Coran, Introd. p. 60, and Bargès, Journal Asiatique, 1843).

[7] See Farg. XIX, 29, n. 2. Closely related to Astô-vîdôtu is Vîzaresha (ibid.); on Bûiti, see Farg. XIX, 1, n. 3.

[8] See Orm. Ahr. §§ 87–88.

strength of ten horses, ten bulls, ten mountains, ten rivers, Tistrya runs back to the battle-field and Apaosha flies before him [1].

§ 28. The sacrifice is composed of two elements, offerings and spells.

The offerings are libations of holy water (zaothra) [2], holy meat (myazda) [3], and Haoma. The last offering is the most sacred and powerful of all.

Haoma, the Indian Soma, is an intoxicating plant, the juice of which is drunk by the faithful for their own benefit and for the benefit of their gods. It comprises in it the powers of life of all the vegetable kingdom.

There are two Haomas : one is the yellow or golden Haoma, which is the earthly Haoma, and which, when prepared for the sacrifice, is the king of healing plants [4] ; the other is the white Haoma or Gaokerena, which grows up in the middle of the sea Vouru-kasha, surrounded by the ten thousand healing plants [5]. It is by the drinking of Gaokerena that men, on the day of the resurrection, will become immortal [6].

§ 29. Spell or prayer is not less powerful than the offerings. In the beginning of the world, it was by reciting the Honover (Ahuna Vairya) that Ormazd confounded Ahriman [7]. Man, too, sends his prayer between the earth and the heavens, there to smite the fiends, the Kahvaredhas and the Kahvaredhis, the Kayadhas and the Kayadhis, the Zandas and the Yâtus [8].

§ 30. A number of divinities sprang from the hearth of the altar, most of which were already in existence during the Indo-Iranian period.

Piety, which every day brings offerings and prayers to the fire of the altar, was worshipped in the Vedas as Aramati, the goddess who every day, morning and evening,

---

[1] Yt. VIII, 23 seq.
[2] Prepared with certain rites and prayers; it is the Vedic hotrâ.
[3] A piece of meat placed on the draona (Farg. V, 25, n. 3).
[4] Bundahis 58, 10.   [5] Farg. XX, 4.
[6] Bundahis 42, 12 ; 59, 4.
[7] Bundahis. Cf. Farg. XIX, 9, 43 ; Yasna XIX.
[8] Yasna LXI (LX).

streaming with the sacred butter, goes and gives up herself to Agni [1]. She was praised in the Avesta in a more
sober manner as the abstract genius of piety; yet a few
practices preserved evident traces of old myths on her
union with Âtar, the fire-god [2].

Agni, as a messenger between gods and men, was known
to the Vedas as Narâ-sansa; hence came the Avesta messenger of Ahura, Nairyô-sangha [3].

The riches that go up from earth to heaven in the offerings
of man and come down from heaven to earth in the gifts of the
gods were deified as Râta [4], the gift, Ashi, the felicity [5], and
more vividly in Pârendi [6], the keeper of treasures, who comes
on a sounding chariot, a sister to the Vedic Puramdhi.

The order of the world, the Vedic Rita, the Zend Asha,
was deified as Asha Vahista, 'the excellent Asha [7].'

§ 31. Sraosha is the priest god [8]: he first tied the
Baresma into bundles, and offered up sacrifice to Ahura;
he first sang the holy hymns: his weapons are the Ahuna-
Vairya and the Yasna, and thrice in each day, in each night,
he descends upon this Karshvare to smite Angra Mainyu
and his crew of demons. It is he who, with his club
uplifted, protects the living world from the terrors of the
night, when the fiends rush upon the earth; it is he who
protects the dead from the terrors of death, from the
assaults of Angra Mainyu and Vîdôtus [9]. It is through a
sacrifice performed by Ormazd, as a Zôti, and Sraosha, as
a Raspî [10], that at the end of time Ahriman will be for ever
vanquished and brought to nought [11].

§ 32. Thus far, the single elements of Mazdeism do
not essentially differ from those of the Vedic and Indo-
European mythologies generally. Yet Mazdeism, as a
whole, took an aspect of its own by grouping these elements in a new order, since by referring everything either

---

[1] Orm. Ahr. § 205.
[2] Farg. XVIII, 51 seq.
[3] Farg. XXII, 7.
[4] Farg. XIX, 19.
[5] Neriosengh.
[6] Orm. Ahr. § 200.
[7] Parsi Ardibehest.
[8] Yasna LVI.
[9] Farg. VII, 52, n. 4; XIX, 46, n. 8.
[10] Cf. Farg. V, 57, n.
[11] Bundahis 76, 11.

to Ahura Mazda or Angra Mainyu as its source, it came to divide the world into two symmetrical halves, in both of which a strong unity prevailed. The change was summed up in the rising of Angra Mainyu, a being of mixed nature, who was produced by abstract speculation from the old Indo-European storm fiend, and who borrowed his form from the supreme god himself. On the one hand, as the world battle is only an enlarged form of the mythical storm fight, Angra Mainyu, the fiend of fiends and the leader of the evil powers, is partly an abstract embodiment of their energies and feats ; on the other hand, as the antagonist of Ahura, he is modelled after him, and is partly, as it were, a negative projection of Ahura[1].

Ahura is all light, truth, goodness, and knowledge; Angra Mainyu is all darkness, falsehood, wickedness, and ignorance[2].

Ahura dwells in the infinite light ; Angra Mainyu dwells in the infinite night.

Whatever the good Spirit makes, the evil Spirit mars. When the world was created, Angra Mainyu broke into it[3], opposed every creation of Ahura's with a plague of his own[4], killed the first-born bull that had been the first offspring and source of life on earth[5], he mixed poison with plants, smoke with fire, sin with man, and death with life.

§ 33. Under Ahura were ranged the six Amesha Spentas. They were at first mere personifications of virtues and moral or liturgical powers[6]; but as their lord and father ruled over the whole of the world, they took by and by each a part of the world under their care. The choice was not altogether artificial, but partly natural and spontaneous. The empire of waters and trees was vested in Haurvatât and Ameretât, health and immortality, through the influence of old Indo-Iranian formulae, in which waters and trees were invoked as the springs of health and life. More complex trains of ideas and partly the influence of analogy fixed the

---

[1] Orm. Ahr. § 85.
[2] Yast XIII, 77.
[3] Bundahis I ; cf. Yasna XXX.
[4] Cf. Farg. I.
[5] Cf. Farg. XXI, 1.
[6] See above, p. lx.

field of action of the others. Khshathra Vairya, the perfect sovereignty, had molten brass for its emblem, as the god in the storm established his empire by means of that 'molten brass,' the fire of lightning; he thus became the king of metals in general. Asha Vahista, the holy order of the world, as maintained chiefly by the sacrificial fire, became the genius of fire. Ârmaiti seems to have become a goddess of the earth as early as the Indo-Iranian period, and Vohu-manô had the living creation left to his superintendence [1].

§ 34. The Amesha Spentas projected, as it were, out of themselves, as many Daêvas or demons, who, either in their being or functions, were, most of them, hardly more than dim inverted images of the very gods they were to oppose, and whom they followed through all their successive evolutions. Haurvatât and Ameretât, health and life, were opposed by Tauru and Zairi, sickness and decay, who changed into rulers of thirst and hunger when Haurvatât and Ameretât had become the Amshaspands of waters and trees.

Vohu-manô, or good thought, was reflected in Akô-manô, evil thought. Sauru, the arrow of death [2], Indra, a name or epithet of fire as destructive [3], Nâunhaithya, an old Indo-Iranian divinity whose meaning was forgotten in Iran and misinterpreted by popular etymology [4], were opposed, respectively, to Khshathra Vairya, Asha Vahista, and Spenta Ârmaiti, and became the demons of tyranny, corruption, and impiety.

Then came the symmetrical armies of the numberless gods and fiends, Yazatas and Drvants.

§ 35. Everything in the world was engaged in the conflict. Whatever works, or is fancied to work, for the good of man or for his harm, for the wider spread of life or against it, comes from, and strives for, either Ahura or Angra Mainyu.

Animals are enlisted under the standards of either the one spirit or the other [5]. In the eyes of the Parsis, they

---

[1] Orm. Ahr. §§ 202-206.

[2] See above, p. lxviii.   [3] See § 41.   [4] Ibid.

[5] A strict discipline prevails among them. Every class of animals has a chief or ratu above it (Bund. XXIV). The same organisation extends to all the beings

belong either to Ormazd or Ahriman according as they are useful or hurtful to man; but, in fact, they belonged originally to either the one or the other, according as they had been incarnations of the god or of the fiend, that is, as they chanced to have lent their forms to either in the storm tales [1]. In a few cases, of course, the habits of the animal had not been without influence upon its mythic destiny: but the determinative cause was different. The fiend was not described as a serpent because the serpent is a subtle and crafty reptile, but because the storm fiend envelops the goddess of light, or the milch cows of the raining heavens, with the coils of the cloud as with a snake's folds. It was not animal psychology thàt disguised gods and fiends as dogs, otters, hedge-hogs, and cocks, or as snakes, tortoises, frogs, and ants, but the accidents of physical qualities and the caprice of popular fancy, as both the god and the fiend might be compared with, and transformed into, any object, the idea of which was suggested by the uproar of the storm, the blazing of the lightning, the streaming of the water, or the hue and shape of the clouds.

Killing the Ahrimanian creatures, the Khrafstras [2], is killing Ahriman himself, and sin may be atoned for by this means [3]. Killing an Ormazdean animal is an abomination, it is killing God himself. Persia was on the brink of zoolatry, and escaped it only by misunderstanding the principle she followed [4].

---

in nature: stars, men, gods have their respective ratus, Ti:trya, Zoroaster, Ahura.

[1] Orm. Ahr. §§ 227–231.

[2] Farg. III, 10; XIV, 5 seq., 8, n. 8; XVIII, 70, &c.

[3] There is scarcely any religious custom that can be followed through so continuous a series of historical evidence: fifth century B.C., Herodotus I, 140; first century A. D., Plutarch, De Isid. XLVI; Quaest Conviv. IV, 5, 2; sixth century, Agathias II, 24; seventeenth century, G. du Chinon.

[4] Thus arose a classification which was often at variance with its supposed principle. As the god who rushes in the lightning was said to move on a raven's wings, with a hawk's flight, birds of prey belonged to the realm of Ormazd. The Parsi theologians were puzzled at this fact but their ingenuity proved equal to the emergency: Ormazd, while creating the hunting hawk, said to him: ' O thou hunting hawk! I have created thee; but I ought rather to be sorry than glad of it: for thou doest the will of Ahriman much more than mine: like a wicked man who never has money enough, thou art never satisfied with killing birds.

§ 36. The fulgurating conqueror of Apaosha, Tistrya, was described in mythic tales sometimes as a boar with golden horns, sometimes as a horse with yellow ears, sometimes as a beautiful youth. But as he had been compared to a shining star on account of the gleaming of lightning, the stars joined in the fray, where they stood with Tistrya on Ahura's side; and partly for the sake of symmetry, partly owing to Chaldaean influences, the planets passed into the army of Ahriman.

§ 37. Man, according to his deeds, belongs to Ormazd or to Ahriman. He belongs to Ormazd, he is a man of Asha, a holy one, if he offers sacrifice to Ormazd and the gods, if he helps them by good thoughts, words, and deeds, if he enlarges the world of Ormazd by spreading life over the world, and if he makes the realm of Ahriman narrower by destroying his creatures. A man of Asha is the Athravan (priest) who drives away fiends and diseases by spells, the Rathaêsta (warrior) who with his club crushes the head of the impious, the Vâstryô (husbandman) who makes good and plentiful harvests grow up out of the earth. He who does the contrary is a Drvant, ' demon,' an Anashavan, ' foe of Asha,' an Ashemaogha, ' confounder of Asha.'

The man of Asha who has lived for Ahura Mazda will have a seat near him in heaven, in the same way as in India the man of Rita, the faithful one, goes to the palace of Varuna, there to live with the forefathers, the Pitris, a life of everlasting happiness [1]. Thence he will go out, at the end of time, when the dead shall rise, and live a new and all-happy life on the earth freed from evil and death.

But hadst thou not been made by me, Ahriman, bloody Ahriman, would have made thee with the size of a man, and there would no more be any small creature left alive' (Bundahis XIV). Inversely Ahriman created a lovely bird, the peacock, to show that he did not do evil from any incapacity of doing well, but through wilful wickedness (Eznik); Satan is still nowadays invoked by the Yezidis as Melek Taus (' angel peacock ').

[1] From the worship of the Pitris was developed in Iran the worship of the Fravashis, who being at first identical with the Pitris, with the souls of the departed, became by and by a distinct principle. The Fravashi was independent of the circumstances of life or death, an immortal part of the individual which existed before man and outlived him. Not only man was endowed with a Fravashi, but gods too, and the sky, fire, waters, and plants (Orm. Ahr. §§ 112-113).

§ 38. This brings us to speak of a series of myths which have done much towards obscuring the close connection between the Avesta and the Vedic mythologies: I mean the myths about the heavenly life of Yima.

In the Veda Yama, the son of Vivasvat, is the first man and, therefore, the first of the dead, the king of the dead. As such he is the centre of gathering for the departed, and he presides over them in heaven, in the Yamasâdanam, as king of men, near Varuna the king of gods.

His Avesta twin-brother, Yima, the son of Vîvanghat, is no longer the first man, as this character had been transferred to another hero, of later growth, Gayô Maratan; yet he has kept nearly all the attributes which were derived from his former character: on the one hand he is the first king, and the founder of civilisation; on the other hand, 'the best mortals' gather around him in a marvellous palace, in Airyanem Vaêgô, which appears to be identical with the Yamasâdanam from Yama meeting there with Ahura and the gods, and making his people live there a blessed life[1]. But, by and by, as it was forgotten that Yima was the first man and the first of the dead, it was also forgotten that his people were nothing else than the dead going to their common ancestor above and to the king of heaven: the people in the Vara were no longer recognised as the human race, but became a race of a supernatural character, different from those who continued going, day by day, from earth to heaven to join Ahura Mazda[2].

§ 39. But the life of the world is limited, the struggle is not to last for ever, and Ahriman will be defeated at last. The world was imagined as lasting a long year of twelve millenniums. There had been an old myth, connected with that notion, which made the world end in a frightful winter[3], to be succeeded by an eternal spring, when the blessed would come down from the Vara of Yima to repeople the earth. But as storm was the ordinary and more dramatic form of the strife, there was another version, according to

---

[1] See Farg. II.
[3] Cf. Farg. II, Introd. and § 21 seq.

[2] Farg. XIX, 28 seq.

which the world ended in a storm, and this version became
the definitive one.

The serpent, Azi Dahâka, let loose, takes hold of the
world again. As the temporary disappearance of the light
was often mythically described either as the sleeping of the
god, or as his absence, or death, its reappearance was indicative of the awakening of the hero, or his return, or the
arrival of a son born to him. Hence came the tales about
Keresâspa awakening from his sleep to kill the snake
finally[1]; the tales about Peshôtanu, Aghraêratha, Khumbya,
and others living in remote countries till the day of the last
fight is come[2]; and, lastly, the tales about Saoshyant, the
son who is to be born to Zarathustra at the end of time,
and to bring eternal light and life to mankind, as his father
brought them the law and the truth. This brings us to the
question whether any historical reality underlies the legend
of Zarathustra or Zoroaster.

§ 40. Mazdeism has often been called Zoroaster's religion
in the same sense as Islam is called Muhammed's religion,
that is, as being the work of a man named Zoroaster, a view
which was favoured, not only by the Parsi and Greek
accounts, but by the strong unity and symmetry of the
whole system. Moreover, as the moral and abstract spirit
which pervades Mazdeism is different from the Vedic spirit,
and as the word deva, which means a god in Sanskrit,
means a demon in the Avesta, it was thought that Zoroaster's work had been a work of reaction against Indian
polytheism, in fact, a religious schism. When he lived no
one knows, and every one agrees that all that the Parsis
and the Greeks tell of him is mere legend, through which
no solid historical facts can be arrived at. The question is
whether Zoroaster was a man converted into a god, or a god
converted into a man. No one who reads, with a mind free
from the yoke of classical recollections, I do not say the
Book of Zoroaster (which may be charged with being a
modern romance of recent invention), but the Avesta itself,
will have any doubt that Zoroaster is no less an essential

---

[1] See above, p. lxv.   [2] Bundahis XXX.

part of the Mazdean mythology than the son expected to
be born to him, at the end of time, to destroy Ahriman[1].
   Zoroaster is not described as one who brings new truth
and drives away error, but as one who overthrows the
demons: he is a smiter of fiends, like Verethraghna, Apâm
Napât, Tistrya, Vayu, or Keresâspa, and he is stronger and
more valiant than Keresâspa himself[2]; the difference between
him and them is that, whereas they smite the fiend with
material weapons, he smites them chiefly with a spiritual
one, the word or prayer. We say 'chiefly' because the holy
word is not his only weapon; he repels the assaults of
Ahriman with stones as big as a house which Ahura has
given to him[3], and which were furnished, no doubt, from the
same quarry as the stones which are cast at their enemies
by Indra, by Agni, by the Maruts, or by Thor, and which
are 'the flame, wherewith, as with a stone[4],' the storm god
aims at the fiend. Therefore his birth[5], like the birth of
every storm god, is longed for and hailed with joy as the
signal of its deliverance by the whole living creation, because
it is the end of the dark and arid reign of the demon: 'In
his birth, in his growth did the floods and trees rejoice; in
his birth, in his growth the floods and trees did grow up; in
his birth, in his growth the floods and trees exclaimed with
joy[6].' Ahura himself longs for him and fears lest the hero
about to be born may not stand by him: 'He offered up a
sacrifice to Ardvî Sûra Anâhita, he, the Maker, Ahura
Mazda; he offered up the Haoma, the Myazda, the Baresma, the holy words, he besought her, saying: Vouchsafe
me that boon, O high, mighty, undefiled goddess, that I
may bring about the son of Pourushaspa, the holy Zara-

---

[1] The same view as to the mythological character of Zoroaster was maintained, although with different arguments, by Professor Kern in an essay 'Over
het woord Zarathustra,' as I see from a short abstract of it which Professor
Max Müller kindly wrote for me.

[2] Yast XIX, 38.   [3] Farg. XIX, 4.   [4] Rig-veda II, 30, 4.

[5] A singular trait of his birth, according to Pliny, who is on this point in
perfect accordance with later Parsi tradition, is that, alone of mortals, he
laughed while being born; this shows that his native place is in the very same
regions where the Vedic Maruts are born, those storm genii 'born of the
laughter of the lightning' ('I laugh as I pass in thunder' says the Cloud in
Shelley; cf. the Persian Khandah i barq, 'the laughter of the lightning').

[6] Yast XIII, 93.

thustra, to think according to the law, to speak according to the law, to work according to the law!' Ardvî Surâ Anâhita granted that boon to him who was offering up libations, sacrificing and beseeching[1].

Zarathustra stands by Ahura. The fiends come rushing along from hell to kill him, and fly away terrified by his *hvarenô*: Angra Mainyu himself is driven away by the stones he hurls at him[2]. But the great weapon of Zarathustra is neither the thunder-stones he hurls, nor the glory with which he is surrounded, it is the Word[2].

In the voice of the thunder the Greeks recognised the warning of a god which the wise understand, and they worshipped it as ῎Οσσα Διὸς ἄγγελος, 'the Word, messenger of Zeus;' the Romans worshipped it as a goddess, Fama; India adores it as 'the Voice in the cloud,' Vâ*k* Âmbh*rinî*, which issues from the waters, from the forehead of the father, and hurls the deadly arrow against the foe of Brahman. So the word from above is either a weapon that kills, or a revelation that teaches: in the mouth of Zarathustra it is both: now 'he smites down Angra Mainyu with the Ahuna vairya (Honover) as he would do with stones as big as a house, and he burns him up with the Ashem vohu as with melted brass[3];' now he converses with Ahura, on the mountain of the holy questions, in the forest of the holy questions[4]. Any storm god, whose voice descends from above to the earth, may become a godlike messenger, a lawgiver, a Zarathustra. Nor is Zarathustra the only lawgiver, the only prophet, of whom the Avesta knows: Gayô Maratan, Yima, the bird Karsiptan[5], each of whom, under different names, forms, and functions, are one and the same being with Zarathustra, that is to say, the godlike champion in the struggle for light, knew the law as well as Zarathustra. But as mythology, like language and life, likes to reduce every organ to one function, Zarathustra became the titulary lawgiver[6].

---

[1] Yast V, 18.   [2] Orm. Ahr. § 162 seq.   [3] Yast XVII, 18.
[4] Farg. XXII, 19.   [5] Farg. II, 3, 42; Yast XIII, 87.
[6] The law is generally known as Dâtem vîdaêvô-dâtem (cf. V, 1); as emanating from Ahura it is Mathra Spenta, 'the holy word,' which is the soul of Ahura (Farg. XIX, 14).

As he overwhelmed Angra Mainyu during his lifetime by his spell, he is to overwhelm him at the end of time by the hands of a son yet unborn. 'Three times he came near unto his wife Hrôgvi, and three times the seed fell upon the ground. The Ized Neriosengh took what was bright and strong in it and intrusted it to the Ized Anâhita. At the appointed time, it will be united again with a maternal womb: 99,999 Fravashis of the faithful watch over it, lest the fiends destroy it[1].' A maid bathing in the lake Kâsava will conceive by it and bring forth the victorious Saoshyant (Sôshyôs), who will come from the region of the dawn to free the world from death and decay, from corruption and rottenness, ever living and ever thriving, when the dead shall rise and immortality commence[2].

All the features in Zarathustra point to a god: that the god may have grown up from a man, that pre-existent mythic elements may have gathered around the name of a man, born on earth, and by and by surrounded the human face with the aureole of a god, may of course be maintained, but only on condition that one may distinctly express what was the real work of Zoroaster. That he raised a new religion against the Vedic religion, and cast down into hell the gods of older days can no longer be maintained, since the gods, the ideas, and the worship of Mazdeism are shown to emanate directly from the old religion, and have nothing more of a reaction against it than Zend has against Sanskrit.

§ 41. The only evidence in favour of the old hypothesis of a religious schism is reduced to the evidence of a few words which might à priori be challenged, as the life of words is not the same as the life of the things they express, the nature of things does not change with the meaning of the syllables which were attached to them for a while, and the history of the world is not a chapter of grammar. And, in fact, the evidence appealed to, when more closely considered, proves to speak against the very theory it is meant

---

[1] Bund. XXXIII; Eznik. The whole of the myth belongs to the Avesta period, as appears from Yast XIII, 61; Vendîdâd XIX, 5.
[2] Yast XIX, 89 seq.

to support. The word Asura, which in the Avesta means 'the Lord,' and is the name of the supreme God, means 'a demon' in the Brahmanical literature; but in the older religion of the Vedas it is quite as august as in the Avesta, and is applied to the highest deities, and particularly to Varu*n*a, the Indian brother of Ahura. This shows that when the Iranians and Indians sallied forth from their common native land, the Asura continued for a long time to be the Lord in India as well as in Persia; and the change took place, not in Iran, but in India. The descent of the word daêva from 'a god' to 'a demon' is a mere accident of language. There were in the Indo-Iranian language three words expressive of divinity: Asura, 'the Lord,' Ya*g*ata, 'the one who is worthy of sacrifice,' Daêva, 'the shining one.' Asura became the name of the supreme God, Ya*g*ata was the general name of all gods. Now as there were old Indo-Iranian formulae which deprecated the wrath of both men and devas (gods), or invoked the aid of some god against the hate and oppression of both men and devas[1], that word daêva, which had become obsolete (because Asura and Ya*g*ata met all the wants of religious language), took by and by from formulae of this kind a dark and fiendish meaning. What favoured the change was the want of a technical word for expressing the general notion of a fiend, a want the more felt as the dualistic idea acquired greater strength and distinctness. Etymology was unable to preserve the Daêvas from this degradation, as the root div, 'to shine,' was lost in Zend, and thus the primitive meaning being forgotten, the word was ready to take any new meaning which chance or necessity should give to it. But only the word descended into hell, not the beings it denoted; neither Varu*n*a, nor Mitra, nor the Âdityas, nor Agni, nor Soma, in fact none of the old Aryan deities fell or tottered. Though the word Indra is the name of a fiend in the Avesta, the Vedic god it denotes was as bright and as mighty in Iran as in India under the name of Verethraghna: and as we do not know the etymological mean-

---

[1] Rig-veda VI, 62, 8; VII, 52, 1; VIII, 19, 6; Ya*s*t X, 34; Yasna IX (60).

ing of the name, it may have been such epithet as could be applied to a fiend as well as to a god. The same can be said of Naunghaithya. Moreover, both Indra and Naunghaithya are in the Avesta mere names: neither the Avesta nor old tradition knows anything about them, which would look very strange, had they been vanquished in a religious struggle, as they should have played the foremost part at the head of the fiends. As to the third comparison established between the Iranian demon Sauru and the Indian god Sarva, it fails utterly, as Sauru is the Vedic Saru, a symbol of death, and both are therefore beings of the same nature.

§ 42. Therefore, so far as the Vedic religion and the Avesta religion are concerned, there is not the abyss of a schism between them. They are quite different, and must be so, since each of them lived its own life, and living is changing; but nowhere is the link broken that binds both to their common source. Nowhere in the Avesta is the effort of any man felt who, standing against the belief of his people, enforces upon them a new creed, by the ascendancy of his genius, and turns the stream of their thoughts from the bed wherein it had flowed for centuries. There was no religious revolution: there was only a long and slow movement which led, by insensible degrees, the vague and unconscious dualism of the Indo-Iranian religion onwards to the sharply defined dualism of the Magi.

It does not follow hence, of course, that there was nothing left to individual genius in the formation of Mazdeism; the contrary is evident à priori from the fact that Mazdeism expresses the ideas of a sacerdotal caste. It sprang from the long elaboration of successive generations of priests, and that elaboration is so far from having been the work of one day and of one man that the exact symmetry which is the chief characteristic of Mazdeism is still imperfect in the Avesta on certain most important points. For instance, the opposition of six arch-fiends to the six arch-gods which we find in Plutarch and in the Bundahis was still unknown when the Xth Fargard of the Vendîdâd and the XIXth Yast were composed, and the stars were not yet members

[4]   f

of the Ormazdean army when the bulk of the VIIIth Yast
was written.

The reflective spirit that had given rise to Mazdeism
never rested, but continued to produce new systems; and
there is hardly any religion in which slow growth and con-
tinual change is more apparent. When the Magi had
accounted for the existence of evil by the existence of two
principles, there arose the question how there could be two
principles, and a longing for unity was felt, which found its
satisfaction in the assumption that both are derived from
one and the same principle. This principle was, according
to divers sects, either Space, or Infinite Light, or Boundless
Time, or Fate[1]. Of most of these systems no direct trace is
found in the Avesta[2], yet they existed already in the time
of Aristotle[3].

They came at last to pure monotheism. Some forty
years ago when the Rev. Dr. Wilson was engaged in his
controversy with the Parsis, some of his opponents repelled
the charge of dualism by denying to Ahriman any real
existence, and making him a symbolical personification of
bad instincts in man. It was not difficult for the Doctor to
show that they were at variance with their sacred books,
and critics in Europe occasionally wondered at the progress
made by the Parsis in rationalism of the school of Voltaire.
and Gibbon. Yet there was no European influence at the
bottom; and long before the Parsis had heard of Europe
and Christianity, commentators, explaining the myth of
Tahmurath, who rode for thirty years on Ahriman as a
horse, interpreted the feat of the old legendary king as the

---

[1] All these four principles are only abstract forms of Ormazd himself, at
least in his first naturalistic character of the Heaven God. Heaven is Infinite
Space, it is Infinite Light, and by its movement it gives rise to Time and to
Fate (Orm. Ahr. §§ 244–259). Time is twofold: there is the limited time that
measures the duration of the world (see above, § 39) and lasts 12,000 years,
which is Zrvan dareghô-Avadâta, 'the Sovereign Time of the long period;'
and there is 'the Boundless Time,' Zrvan akarana (Farg. XIX, 9).

[2] When Vendîdâd XIX, 9 was written, the Zervanitic system seems to have
been, if not fully developed, at least already existent.

[3] Eudemos (ap. Damascius, ed. Kopp, 384) knows of χρόνος and τόπος as the
first principles of the Magi; Boundless Time is already transformed into a
legendary hero in Berosus (third century B. C.)

curbing of evil passion and restraining the Ahriman in the heart of man [1]. That idealistic interpretation was current as early as the fifteenth century, and is prevalent now with most of the Dasturs [2]. To what extent that alteration may have been influenced by Islamism, can hardly be decided; there are even some faint signs that it began at a time when the old religion was still flourishing; at any rate, no one can think of ascribing to one man, or to one time, that slow change from dualism to monotheism, which is, however, really deeper and wider than the movement which, in prehistoric times, brought the Magi from an imperfect form of dualism to one more perfect.

CHAPTER V.

THE VENDÎDÂD.

§ 1. According to Parsi tradition the Vendîdâd [3] is the only Nosk, out of the twenty-one, that was preserved in its entirety [4]. This is a statement to which it is difficult to trust; for, if there is anything that shows how right the Parsis are in admitting that the Avesta is only a collection of fragments, it is just the fragmentary character of the Vendîdâd.

The Vendîdâd has often been described as the book of the laws of the Parsis; it may be more exactly called the code of purification, a description, however, which is itself only so far correct that the laws of purification are the object of the largest part of the book.

---

[1] Aogemaidê, ed. Geiger, p. 36, § 92; Mirkhond, History of the Early Kings of Persia, tr. Shea, p. 98. Cf. Revue Critique, 1879, II, 163.

[2] 'The Parsis are now strict monotheists, and whatever may have been the views of former philosophical writings, their one supreme deity is Ahura Mazda. Their views of Angra Mainyu seem to differ in no respect from what is supposed to be the orthodox Christian view of the devil.' Haug's Essays, 2nd ed. p. 53. Mandelslo, in the seventeenth century, speaks of Parsiism as a monotheistic religion.

[3] The word Vendîdâd is a corruption of Vîdaêvô-dâtem (dâtem), 'the antidemoniac law.' It is sometimes applied to the whole of the law (Vendîdâd Sâdah).

[4] See above, p. xxxii.

The first two chapters deal with mythical matter, without any direct connection with the general object of the Vendîdâd, and are remnants of an old epic and cosmogonic literature. The first deals with the creations and counter-creations of Ahura Mazda and Angra Mainyu; the second speaks of Yima, the founder of civilisation. Although there was no particular reason for placing them in the Vendîdâd, as soon as they were admitted into it they were put at the beginning, because they referred to the first ages of the world. Three chapters of a mythical character, about the origin of medicine, were put at the end of the book, for want of any better place, but might as well have been kept apart[1], as was the so-called Had-hokht Nosk fragment. There is also another mythical Fargard, the nineteenth, which, as it treats of the revelation of the law by Ahura to Zarathustra, would have been more suitably placed at the beginning of the Vendîdâd proper, that is, as the third Fargard.

The other seventeen chapters deal chiefly with religious observances, although mythical fragments, or moral digressions, are met with here and there, which are more or less artificially connected with the text, and which were most probably not written along with the passages which they follow[2].

§ 2. A rough attempt at regular order appears in these seventeen chapters : nearly all the matter contained in the eight chapters from V to XII deals chiefly with impurity from the dead and the way of dispelling it; but the subject is again treated, here and there, in other Fargards[3], and matter irrelevant to the subject has also found its way into these same eight Fargards[4]. Fargards XIII and XIV are devoted to the dog, but must be completed with a part of the XVth. Fargards XVI, XVII, and most part of XVIII deal with several sorts of uncleanness, and their proper

[1] As an introduction to a code of laws on physicians; see Farg. VII, 36-44.
[2] For instance, Farg. V, 15-20; III, 24-29; 30-32; 33; IV, 47-49.
[3] III, 14-22; 36 seq.; XIX, 11-25.
[4] The passages on medicine (VII, 36-44), and on the sea Vouru-kasha (V, 15-20).

place should rather have been after the XIIth Fargard. Fargard III is devoted to the earth[1]; Fargard IV stands by itself, as it deals with a matter which is treated only there, namely, civil and penal laws[2].

No better order prevails within these several parts: prescriptions on one and the same subject are scattered about through several Fargards, without any subject being treated at once in a full and exhaustive way; and this occasions needless repetitions[3].

The main cause of this disorder was, of course, that the advantage of order is rarely felt by Orientals; but it was further promoted by the very form of exposition adopted by the first composers of the Vendîdâd. The law is revealed by Ahura in a series of answers to questions put to him by Zarathuſtra[4]; and as these questions are not of a general character, but refer to details, the matter is much broken into fragments, each of which, consisting of a question with its answer, stands by itself, as an independent passage.

We shall treat in the following pages, first of the laws of purification, then of the civil laws, and, lastly, of the penalties both religious and civil.

A.

§ 3. The first object of man is purity, yaoždau : 'purity is for man, next to life, the greatest good[5].'

Purity and impurity have not in the Vendîdâd the exclusively spiritual meaning which they have in our languages: they do not refer to an inward state of the

---

[1] It contains two digressions, the one on funeral laws, the other on husbandry. See Farg. III, Introd.

[2] It contains one digression on physical weal, which must have belonged originally to Farg. III. See Farg. IV, Introd.

[3] V, 27-30 = VII, 6-9; V, 45-54 = VII, 60-69; V, 57-62 = VII, 17-22.

[4] The outward form of the Vendîdâd has been often compared with that of the Books of Moses. But in reality, in the Bible, there is no conversation between God and the lawgiver: the law comes down unasked, and God gives commands, but gives no answers. In the Vendîdâd, on the contrary, it is the wish of man, not the will of God, that is the first cause of the revelation. Man must ask of Ahura, who knows everything, and is pleased to answer (XVIII, 13 seq.); the law is 'the question to Ahura,' âhuri frasnô.

[5] Farg. V, 21, from Yasna XLVIII (XLVII), 5.

person, but chiefly to a physical state of the body. Impurity or uncleanness may be described as the state of a person or thing that is possessed of the demon; and the object of purification is to expel the demon.

The principal means by which uncleanness enters man is death, as death is the triumph of the demon.

When a man dies, as soon as the soul has parted from the body, the Drug Nasu or Corpse-Drug falls upon the dead from the regions of hell, and whoever thenceforth touches the corpse becomes unclean, and makes unclean whomsoever he touches [1].

The Drug is expelled from the dead by means of the Sag-dîd, 'the look of the dog:' 'a four-eyed dog' or 'a white one with yellow ears' is brought near the body and is made to look at the dead ; as soon as he has done so, the Drug flees back to hell [2].

The Drug is expelled from the living, whom she has seized through their contact with the dead, by a process of washings with ox's urine (gômêz or nîrang) and with water, combined with the Sag-dîd [3].

The real import of these ceremonies is shown by the spells which accompany their performance : 'Perish, O fiendish Drug! Perish, O brood of the fiend! Perish, O world of the fiend! Perish away, O Drug! Rush away, O Drug! Perish away, O Drug! Perish away to the regions of the north, never more to give unto death the living world of the holy spirit!'

Thus, in the death of a man, there is more involved than the death of one man : the power of death, called forth from hell, threatens from the corpse, as from a stronghold, the whole world of the living, ready to seize whatever may fall within his reach, and 'from the dead defiles the living, from the living rushes upon the living.' When a man dies in a house, there is danger for three days lest somebody else should die in that house [4].

---

[1] Farg. VII, 1 seq.

[2] In the shape of a fly. 'The fly that came to the smell of the dead body was thought to be the corpse-spirit that came to take possession of the dead in the name of Ahriman' (Justi, Persien, p. 88).

[3] Farg. VIII, 35-72; IX, 12-36.   [4] Saddar 78.

The notion or feeling, out of which these ceremonies grew, was far from unknown to the other Indo-European peoples: what was peculiar to Mazdeism was that it carried it to an extreme, and preserved a clearer sense of it, while elsewhere it grew dimmer and dimmer, and faded away. In fact, when the Greek, going out of a house where a dead man lay, sprinkled himself with water from the ἀρδανίον at the door, it was death that he drove away from himself. The Vedic Indian, too, although his rites were intended chiefly for the benefit of the dead, considered himself in danger and, while burning the corpse, cried aloud: 'Away, go away, O Death! injure not our sons and our men!' (Rig-veda X, 18, 1.)

§ 4. As to the rites by means of which the Drug is expelled, they are the performance of myths. There is nothing in worship but what existed before in mythology. What we call a practice is only an imitation of gods, an ὁμοίωσις θεῷ, as man fancies he can bring about the things he wants, by performing the acts which are supposed to have brought about things of the same kind when practised by the gods.

The Parsis, being at a loss to find four-eyed dogs, interpret the name as meaning a dog with two spots above the eyes[1]: but it is clear that the two-spotted dog's services are only accepted for want of a four-eyed one, or of a white one with yellow ears, which amounts to saying that there were myths, according to which the death-fiend was driven away by dogs of that description. This reminds one at once of the three-headed Kerberos, watching at the doors of hell, and, still more, of the two brown, four-eyed dogs of Yama, who guard the ways to the realm of death[2].

The identity of the four-eyed dog of the Parsi with Kerberos and Yama's dogs appears, moreover, from the Parsi tradition that the yellow-eared dog watches at the

---

[1] In practice they are still less particular: 'the Sag-dîd may be performed by a shepherd's dog, by a house dog, by a Vohunazga dog (see Farg. XIII, 19, n.), or by a young dog (a dog four months old), Comm. ad Farg. VII, 2. As birds of prey are as fiend-smiting as the dog (see above, p. lxxiii, n. 4), they are Nasu-smiters like him, and one may appeal to their services, when there is no dog at hand (see Farg. VII, 3, n. 5).

[2] Rig-veda X, 14, 10 seq.

head of the *K*inva*t* bridge, which leads from this to the next world, and with his barking drives away the fiend from the souls of the holy ones, lest he should drag them to hell [1].

Wherever the corpse passes by, death walks with it; all along the way it has gone, from the house to its last resting-place, a spirit of death is breathing and threatening the living. Therefore, no man, no flock, no being whatever that belongs to the world of Ahura, is allowed to pass by that way until the deadly breath, that blows through it, has been blown away to hell [2]. The four-eyed dog is made to go through the way three times, or six times, or nine times, while the priest helps the look of the dog with his spells, dreaded by the Dru*g*.

§ 5. The use of gômêz in cleansing the unclean is also derived from old mythic conceptions [3]. The storm floods that cleanse the sky of the dark fiends in it were described in a class of myths as the urine of a gigantic animal in the heavens. As the floods from the bull above drive away the fiend from the god, so they do from man here below, they make him 'free from the death-demon' (frânasu), and the death-fiend flees away hellwards, pursued by the fiend-smiting spell: 'Perish thou, O Dru*g* . . . , never more to give over to Death the living world of the good spirit !'

§ 6. As uncleanness is nothing else than the contagion of death, it is at its greatest intensity when life is just departing. The Nasu at that moment defiles ten persons around the

---

[1] Gr. Rav. p. 592. Allusions to this myth are found in Farg. XIII, 9, and XIX, 30. The Commentary ad Farg. XIII, 17 has: 'There are dogs who watch over the earthly regions; there are others who watch over the fourteen heavenly regions.' The birth of the yellow-eared dog is described in the Ravâet (l. c.) as follows: 'Ormazd, wishing to keep the body of the first man, Gayômart, from the assaults of Ahriman, who tried to kill him, cried out: "O thou yellow-eared dog, arise !" and directly the dog barked and shook his two ears; and the unclean Satan and the fiends, when they saw the dreadful looks of the yellow-eared dog, and heard his barking, were sore afraid and fled down to hell.'

[2] Farg. VIII, 14–22.

[3] Orm. Ahr. § 124. The use of gômêz has been lately found to be known in Basse-Bretagne (Luzel, Le Nirang des Parsis en Basse-Bretagne, Mélusine, 493).

corpse [1] : when a year is over, the corpse defiles no longer [2]. Thus the notion of uncleanness is quite the reverse of what is thought elsewhere : the corpse, when rotten, is less unclean than the body still all but warm with life ; death defiles least when it looks most hideous, and defiles most when it might look majestic. The cause is that in the latter case the death-demon has just arrived in the fulness of his strength, whereas in the former case time has exhausted his power.

§ 7. As the focus of the contagion is in the corpse, it must be disposed of so that death may not spread abroad. On this point the old Indo-European customs have been completely changed by Mazdeism. The Indo-Europeans either burnt the corpse or buried it : both customs are held to be sacrilegious in the Avesta.

§ 8. This view originated from the notion of the holiness of the elements being pushed to an extreme. The elements, fire, earth, and water are holy, and during the Indo-Iranian period they were already considered so, and in the Vedas they are worshipped as godlike beings. Yet this did not prevent the Indian from burning his dead ; death did not appear to him so decidedly a work of the demon, and the dead man was a traveller to the other world, whom the fire kindly carried to his heavenly abode 'on his undecaying, flying pinions, wherewith he killed the demons.' The fire was in that, as in the sacrifice, the god that goes from earth to heaven, from man to god, the mediator, the god most friendly to man. In Persia it remains more distant from him ; being an earthly form of the eternal, infinite, godly light [3], no death, no uncleanness can be allowed to enter it, as it is here below the purest offspring of the good spirit, the purest part of his pure creation. Its only function is to repel the fiends with its bright blazing. In every place where Parsis are settled, an everlasting fire is kept, the Bahrâm fire, which, ' preserved by a more than Vestal

---

[1] Farg. V, 27; cf. n. 5.
[2] Farg. VIII, 33-34.
[3] Ignem coelitus delapsum (Ammian. Marcel. XXVII, 6); Cedrenus; Elisaeus; Recogn. Clement. IV, 29 ; Clem. Homil. IX, 6; Henry Lord.

care [1],' and ever fed with perfumes and dry well-blazing wood, whichever side its flames are brought by the wind, it goes and kills thousands and thousands of fiends, as Bahrâm does in heaven [2]. If the necessities of life oblige us to employ fire for profane uses, it must be only for a time an exile on our hearth, or in the oven of the potter, and it must go thence to the Right-Place of the fire (Dâityô Gâtu), the altar of the Bahrâm fire, there to be restored to the dignity and rights of its nature [3].

At least, let no gratuitous and wanton degradation be inflicted upon it: even blowing it with the breath of the mouth is a crime [4]; burning the dead is the most heinous of sins: in the times of Strabo it was a capital crime [5], and the Avesta expresses the same, when putting it in the number of those sins for which there is no atonement [6].

Water was looked upon in the same light. Bringing dead matter to it is as bad as bringing it to the fire [7]. The Magi are said to have overthrown a king for having built bath-houses, as they cared more for the cleanness of water than for their own [8].

§ 9. Not less holy was the earth, or, at least, it became so. There was a goddess who lived in her, Speñta Âr-maiti [9]; no corpse ought to defile her sacred breast: burying the dead is, like burning the dead, a deed for which there is no atonement [10]. It was not always so in Persia: the burning of the dead had been forbidden for

---

[1] J. Fryer, A New Account of East India and Persia, 1698, p. 265.

[2] Farg. VIII, 81-96; 79-80. Cf. above, p. lxiv.

[3] Extinguishing it is a mortal sin (Ravâets; Elisaeus; cf. Strabo XV, 14).

[4] A custom still existing with the Tâzîk, an Iranian tribe in Eastern Persia (de Khanikoff, Ethnographie de la Perse). Strabo XV, 14. Manu has the same prescription (IV, 53). Cf. Farg. XIV, 8, n. 7.

[5] Strabo XV, 14; cf. Herod. III, 16.

[6] Farg. I, 17; cf. Farg. VIII, 74.

[7] Farg. VII, 25-27; Strabo XV, 14; Herod. I, 138.

[8] King Balash (Josué le Stylite, traduction Martin, § xx). It seems as if there were a confusion between Balash and Kavât; at any rate, it shows that bathing smacked of heresy. Jews were forbidden to perform the legal ablutions (Fürst, Culturgeschichte der Juden, 9).

[9] See above, p. lxxii.

[10] Farg. I, 13.

years[1], while the burying was still general[2]. Cambyses
had roused the indignation of the Persians by burning the
corpse of Amasis: yet, years later, Persians still buried
their dead. But the priests already felt scruples, and feared
to defile a god. Later on, with the ascendancy of the
Magian religion, the sacerdotal observances became the
general law[3].

§ 10. Therefore the corpse is laid on the summit of a
mountain, far from man, from water, from tree, from fire,
and from the earth itself, as it is separated from it by a
layer of stones or bricks[4]. Special buildings, the Dakhmas,
were erected for this purpose[5]. There far from the world
the dead were left to lie, beholding the sun[6].

§ 11. Not every corpse defiles man, but only those of
such beings as belong to the world of Ahura. They are
the only ones in whose death the demon triumphs. The
corpse of an Ahrimanian creature does not defile; as its
life was incarnate death, the spring of death that was in it
is dried up with its last breath: it killed while alive, it can

---

[1] From the reign of Cyrus (cf. above, p. li).   [2] Cf. above, p. xlv.

[3] Still the worship of the earth seems not to have so deeply penetrated the
general religion as the worship of fire. The laws about the disposal of the
dead were interpreted by many, it would seem, as intended only to secure the
purity of water and fire, and they thought that they might be at peace with
religion if they had taken care to bury the corpse, so that no part of it might
be taken by animals to fire or water (Farg. III, 41, n. 7).

[4] Farg. VI, 44 seq.; VIII, 10 seq. Cf. IX, 11, n. 4. Moreover, the Dakhma
is ideally separated from the ground by means of a golden thread, which is
supposed to keep it suspended in the air (Ravâet, ap. Spiegel, Uebersetzung des
Avesta II, XXXVI).

[5] 'The Dakhma is a round building, and is designated by some writers,
"The Tower of Silence." A round pit, about six feet deep, is surrounded by an
annular stone pavement, about seven feet wide, on which the dead bodies are
placed. This place is enclosed all round by a stone wall some twenty feet
high, with a small door on one side for taking the body in. The whole is
built up of and paved with stone. The pit has communication with three
or more closed pits, at some distance into which the rain washes out the liquids
and the remains of the dead bodies' (Dadabhai Naoroji, The Manners and
Customs of the Parsees, Bombay, 1864, p. 16). Cf. Farg. VI, 50. A Dakhma
is the first building the Parsis erect when settling on a new place (Dosabhoy
Framjee).

[6] The Avesta and the Commentator attach great importance to that point:
it is as if the dead man's life were thus prolonged, since he can still behold the
sun. 'Grant us that we may long behold the sun,' said the Indian Rishi.

do so no more when dead; it becomes clean by dying[1].
None of the faithful are defiled by the corpse of an Ashe-
maògha or of a Khrafstra. Nay, killing them is a pious
work, as it is killing Ahriman himself[2].

§ 12. Not only real death makes one unclean, but partial
death too. Everything that goes out of the body of man
is dead, and becomes the property of the demon. The
going breath is unclean, it is forbidden to blow the fire with
it[3], and even to approach the fire without screening it from
the contagion with a Penôm[4]. Parings of nails and cut-
tings or shavings of hair are unclean, and become weapons
in the hands of the demons unless they have been protected
by certain rites and spells[5]. Any phenomenon by which
the bodily nature is altered, whether accompanied with
danger to health or not, was viewed as a work of the demon,
and made the person unclean in whom it took place. One
of these phenomena, which is a special object of attention
in the Vendîdâd, is the uncleanness of women during their
menses. The menses are sent by Ahriman[6], especially
when they last beyond the usual time: therefore a woman,
as long as they last, is unclean and possessed of the demon:
she must be kept confined, apart from the faithful whom
her touch would defile, and from the fire which her very
look would injure; she is not allowed to eat as much as she
wishes, as the strength she might acquire would accrue to
the fiends. Her food is not given to her from hand to hand,
but is passed to her from a distance[7], in a long leaden
spoon. The origin of all these notions is in certain physical
instincts, in physiological psychology, which is the reason
why they are found among peoples very far removed from
one another by race or religion[8]. But they took in Persia
a new meaning as they were made a logical part of the
whole religious system.

§ 13. A woman that has been just delivered of a child

[1] Farg. V, 35 seq.   [2] See above, p. lxxiii.
[3] See above, p. xc.   [4] See Farg. XIV, 8, n. 7.
[5] Farg. XVII.   [6] Farg. I, 18–19; XVI, 11. Cf. Bund. III.
[7] Farg XVI, 15.   [8] Cf. Leviticus. See Pliny VII, 13.

is also unclean [1], although it would seem that she ought to be considered pure amongst the pure, since life has been increased by her in the world, and she has enlarged the realm of Ormazd. But the strength of old instincts overcame the drift of new principles. Only the case when the woman has been delivered of a still-born child is examined in the Vendîdâd. She is unclean as having been in contact with a dead creature; and she must first drink gômêz to wash over the grave in her womb. So utterly unclean is she, that she is not even allowed to drink water, unless she is in danger of death; and even then, as the sacred element has been defiled, she is liable to the penalty of a Peshô-tanu [2]. It appears from modern customs that the treatment is the same when the child is born alive: the reason of which is that, in any case, during the first three days after delivery she is in danger of death [3]. A great fire is lighted to keep away the fiends, who use then their utmost efforts to kill her and her child [4]. She is unclean only because the death-fiend is in her.

§ 14. Logic required that the sick man should be treated as an unclean one, that is, as one possessed. Sickness, being sent by Ahriman, ought to be cured like all his other works, by washings and spells. In fact, the medicine of spells was considered the most powerful of all [5], and although it did not oust the medicine of the lancet and that of drugs, yet it was more highly esteemed and less mistrusted. The commentator on the Vendîdâd very sensibly observes that if it does not relieve, it will surely do no harm [6], which seems not to have been a matter of course with those who heal by the knife and physic. It

---

[1] Farg. V, 45 seq.   [2] Farg. VII, 70 seq.

[3] 'When there is a pregnant woman in a house, one must take care that there be fire continually in it; when the child is brought forth, one must burn a candle, or, better still, a fire, for three days and three nights, to render the Dêvs and Drugs unable to harm the child; for there is great danger during those three days and nights after the birth of the child' (Saddar 16).

[4] 'When the child is being born, one brandishes a sword on the four sides, lest fairy Aal kill it' (Polack, Persien I, 223). In Rome, three gods, Intercidona, Pilumnus, and Deverra, keep her threshold, lest Sylvanus come in and harm her (Augustinus, De Civ. D. VI, 9).

[5] I arg. VII, 44.   [6] Ibid. p. 86, n. 1.

appears from the last Fargard that all or, at least, many diseases might be cured by spells and Barashnûm washing. It appears from Herodotus and Agathias that contagious diseases required the same treatment as uncleanness: the sick man was excluded from the community of the faithful [1], until cured and cleansed according to the rites [2].

§ 15. The unclean are confined in a particular place, apart from all clean persons and objects, the Armêst-gâh [3], which may be described, therefore, as the Dakhma for the living. All the unclean, all those struck with temporary death, the man who has touched dead matter, the woman in her menses, or just delivered of child, the leper [4], or the man who has made himself unclean for ever by carrying a corpse alone [5], stay there all the time of their uncleanness.

§ 16. Thus far for general principles. From the diversity of circumstances arises a system of casuistry, the development of which may be followed first through the glosses to the Vendîdâd, in which the labours of several generations of theologians are embodied, and, later on, through the Ravâets. We will give a few instances of it, as found in the Vendîdâd itself.

The process of the cleansing varies according to the degree of uncleanness; and, again, the degree of uncleanness depends on the state of the thing that defiles and the nature of the thing that is defiled.

The uncleanness from the dead is the worst of all, and it is at its utmost when contracted before the Nasu has been expelled from the corpse by the Sag-dîd [6]: it can be cured only by means of the most complicated system of cleansing, the nine nights' Barashnûm [7].

---

[1] Herod. I, 138.   [2] Agathias II, 23.
[3] The Armest-gâh for women in their menses is called Dashtânistân.
[4] Herod. l. l.; Farg. II, 29.
[5] Farg. III, 21, n. 2.
[6] Farg. VIII, 35-36; 98-99; cf. VII, 29-30, and n. 1 to 30.
[7] Farg. IX. The Barashnûm, originally meant to remove the uncleanness from the dead, became a general instrument of holiness. Children when putting on the Kôstî (Farg. XVIII, 9, n. 4) perform it to be cleansed from the natural uncleanness they have contracted in the womb of their mothers. It is good for every one to perform it once a year.

If the Nasu has already been expelled from the corpse, as the defiling power was less, a simple washing once made, the Ghosel, is enough [1].

The defiling power of the Nasu reaches farther, if the death has just taken place, and if the dying creature occupied a higher rank in the scale of beings [2]; for the more recent the victory of the demon, or the higher the being he has overcome, the stronger he must have been himself.

Menstruous women are cleansed by the Ghosel [3].

As for things they are more or less deeply defiled according to their degree of penetrability: metal vessels can be cleansed, earthen vessels cannot [4]; leather is more easily cleansed than woven cloth [5]; dry wood than soft wood [6]. Wet matter is a better conductor of uncleanness than dry matter, and corpses cease to defile after a year [7].

B.

§ 17. In the cases heretofore reviewed, only religious purposes are concerned. There is another order of laws, in which, although religion interferes, yet it is not at the root; namely, the laws about contracts and assaults, to which the fourth Fargard is devoted, and which are the only remains extant of the civil and penal legislation of Zoroastrianism.

The contracts were divided into two classes, according to their mode of being entered into, and according to the value of their object [8]. As to their mode they are word-contracts or hand-contracts: as to their object, they are sheep-contracts, ox-contracts, man-contracts, or field-contracts, which being estimated in money value are contracts to the amount of 3, 12, 500 istîrs, and upwards [9].

No contract can be made void by the will of one party

---

[1] Farg. VIII, 36.
[2] Farg. V, 27 seq.; VII, 1 seq.
[3] Farg. XVI, 12.
[4] Farg. VII, 73 seq.
[5] Farg. VII, 14 seq.
[6] Farg. VII, 28 seq.
[7] Farg. VIII, 33-34.
[8] See p. 34, n. 3.
[9] An istîr ($\sigma\tau\alpha\tau\acute{\eta}\rho$) is as much as four dirhems ($\delta\rho\alpha\chi\mu\acute{\eta}$). The dirhem is estimated by modern tradition a little more than a rupee.

alone; he who breaks a contract is obliged to pay the value of the contract next higher in value:

The family and the next of kin are, it would seem, answerable for the fulfilment of a contract, a principle of the old Indo-European civil law[1].

§ 18. Assaults are of seven degrees: âgerepta, avaoirista[2], stroke, sore wound, bloody wound, broken bone, and manslaughter. The gravity of the guilt does not depend on the gravity of the deed only, but also on its frequency. Each of these seven crimes amounts, by its being repeated without having been atoned for, to the crime that immediately follows in the scale, so that an âgerepta seven times repeated amounts to manslaughter.

C.

§ 19. Every crime makes the guilty man liable to two penalties, one here below, and another in the next world.

The penalty here below consists of a certain number of stripes with the Aspahê-astra or the Sraoshô-karana[3].

The unit for heavy penalties is two hundred stripes; the crime and the criminal thus punished are called Peshô-tanu or Tanu-peretha (Parsi: Tanâfûhr). The two words literally mean, 'one who pays with his own body,' and 'payment with one's body,' and seem to have originally amounted to

---

[1] Farg. IV, 5 seq.   [2] Two different sorts of menaces; see IV, 54.

[3] The general formula is literally, 'Let (the priest; probably, the Sraoshâ-varez) strike so many strokes with the Aspahê-astra, so many strokes with the Sraoshô-karana.' Astra means in Sanskrit 'a goad,' so that Aspahê-astra may mean 'a horse-goad;' but Aspendiârji translates it by durra, 'a thong,' which suits the sense better, and agrees with etymology too ('an instrument to drive a horse, a whip;' astra, from the root az, 'to drive;' it is the Aspahê-astra which is referred to by Sozomenos II, 13: ἱμάσιν ὠμοῖς χαλεπῶς αὐτὸν ἐβασά-νισαν οἱ μάγοι (the Sraoshâ-varez), βιαζόμενοι προσκυνῆσαι τὸν ἥλιον). Sraoshô-karana is translated by kâbuk, 'a whip,' which agrees with the Sanskrit translation of the sî-srôsh-karanâm sin, 'yat tribhir gokarmasâmghâtâis prâyas-kityam bhavati tâvanmâtram, a sin to be punished with three strokes with a whip.' It seems to follow that Aspahê-astra and Sraoshô-karana are one and the same instrument, designated with two names, first in reference to its shape, and then to its use (Sraoshô-karana meaning 'the instrument for penalty,' or 'the instrument of the Sraoshâ-varez?'). The Aspahê-astra is once called astra mairya, 'the astra for the account to be given,' that is, 'for the payment of the penalty' (Farg. XVIII, 4).

'worthy of death, worthiness of death;' and in effect the
word Peshô-tanu is often interpreted in the Pahlavi Commentary by margarzân, 'worthy of death.' But, on the
whole, it was attached to the technical meaning of 'one who
has to receive two hundred strokes with the horse-whip[1].'
The lowest penalty in the Vendîdâd is five stripes, and the
degrees from five stripes to Peshôtanu are ten, fifteen,
thirty, fifty, seventy, ninety, two hundred. For instance,
âgerepta is punished with five stripes, avaoirista with ten,
stroke with fifteen, sore wound with thirty, bloody wound
with fifty, broken bone with seventy, manslaughter with
ninety; a second manslaughter, committed without the
former being atoned for, is punished with the Peshôtanu
penalty. In the same way the six other crimes, repeated
eight, or seven, or six, or five, or four, or three times make
the committer go through the whole series of penalties up
to the Peshôtanu penalty.

§ 20. If one reviews the different crimes described in the
Vendîdâd, and the respective penalties prescribed for them,
one cannot but wonder at first sight at the strange inequality
between crime and penalty. Beccaria would have felt un-
comfortable while reading the Vendîdâd. It is safer to kill
a man than to serve bad food to a shepherd's dog, for the
manslayer gets off with ninety stripes, whereas the bad
master is at once a Peshôtanu[2], and will receive two hundred stripes. Two hundred stripes are awarded if one tills
land in which a corpse has been buried within the year[3],
if a woman just delivered of child drinks water[4], if one
suppresses the menses of a woman[5], if one performs a
sacrifice in a house where a man has just died[6], if one
neglects fastening the corpse of a dead man so that birds or
dogs may not take dead matter to trees and rivers[7]. Two
hundred stripes if one throws on the ground a bone of a
man's corpse, of a dog's carcase as big as two ribs, four

---

[1] Farg. IV, 20, 21, 24, 25, 28, 29, 32, 33, 35, 36, 38, 39, 41, 42; V, 44; VI,
5, 9, 19, 48, &c.
[2] Farg. IV, 40, and XIII, 24.   [3] Farg. VI, 5.
[4] Farg. VII, 70 seq.   [5] Farg. XVI, 13 seq.
[6] Farg. V, 39.   [7] Farg. VI, 47 seq.

hundred if one throws a bone as big as a breast bone, six
hundred if one throws a skull, one thousand if the whole
corpse[1]. Four hundred stripes if one, being in a state of
uncleanness, touches water or trees[2], four hundred if one
covers with cloth a dead man's feet, six hundred if one
covers his legs, eight hundred if the whole body[3]. Five
hundred stripes for killing a whelp, six hundred for killing
a stray dog, seven hundred for a house dog, eight hundred
for a shepherd's dog[4], one thousand stripes for killing a
Vanhâpara dog, ten thousand stripes for killing a water
dog[5].

Capital punishment is expressly pronounced only against
the false cleanser[6] and the 'carrier alone[7].'

Yet any one who bethinks himself of the spirit of the old
Aryan legislation will easily conceive that there may be in
its eyes many crimes more heinous, and to be punished
more severely, than manslaughter: offences against man
injure only one man; offences against gods endanger all
mankind. No one should wonder at the unqualified cleanser
being put to death who reads Demosthenes' Neaera; the
Persians who defiled the ground by burying a corpse were
not more severely punished than the Greeks were for defiling with corpses the holy ground of Delos[8], or than the
conquerors at Arginousae; nor would the Athenians, who
put to death Atarbes[9], have much stared at the awful
revenge taken for the murder of the sacred dog. There is
hardly any prescription in the Vendîdâd, however odd and
absurd it may seem, but has its counterpart or its explanation in other Aryan legislations: if we had a Latin or a
Greek Vendîdâd, I doubt whether it would look more
rational.

§ 21. Yet, if theoretically the very absurdity of its principles is nothing peculiar to the Mazdean law, nay, is a
proof of its authenticity, it may be doubted whether it could

---

[1] Farg. VI, 10 seq.   [2] Farg. VIII, 104 seq.
[3] Farg. VIII, 23 seq.   [4] Farg. XIII, 8 seq.
[5] Farg. XIV, 1 seq.   [6] Farg. IX, 47 seq.
[7] Farg. III, 14 seq. Yet there were other capital crimes. See below, § 23.
[8] Diodor. XII, 58.   [9] Aelianus, Hist. Var. V, 17.

ever have been actually applied in the form stated in the texts. It may be doubted whether the murder of a shepherd's dog could have been actually punished with eight hundred stripes, much more whether the murder of a water dog could have been really punished with ten thousand stripes, unless we suppose that human endurance was different in ancient Persia from what it is elsewhere, or even in modern Persia herself[1]. Now as we see that in modern tradition bodily punishment is estimated in money value, that is to say, converted into fines, a conversion which is alluded to in the Pahlavi translation[2], it may readily be admitted that as early as the time of the last edition of the Vendîdâd, that conversion had already been made. In the Ravâets, two hundred stripes, or a Tanâfûhr, are estimated as equal to three hundred istîrs or twelve hundred dirhems, or thirteen hundred and fifty rupees; a stripe is therefore about equal to six rupees[3]. How far that system prevailed in practice, whether the guilty might take advantage of this commutation of his own accord, or only with the assent of the judge, we cannot decide. It is very likely that the riches of the fire-temples came for the most part from that source, and that the sound of the dirhems often made the Sraoshô-karana fall from the hands of the Mobeds. That the system of financial penalties did not, however, suppress the system of bodily penalties, appears from the customs of the Parsis who apply both, and from the Pahlavi Commentary which expressly distinguishes three sorts of atonement: the atonement by money (khvâstak), the atonement by the Sraoshô-karana, and the atonement by cleansing.

§ 22. This third element of atonement is strictly religious. It consists in repentance, which is manifested by avowal of the guilt and by the recital of a formula of repentance,

---

[1] In the time of Chardin, the number of stripes inflicted on the guilty never exceeded three hundred; in the old German law, two hundred; in the Hebrew law, forty.

[2] Ad Farg. XIV, 2.

[3] In later Parsîism every sin (and every good deed) has its value in money fixed, and may thus be weighed in the scales of Rashnu. If the number of sin dirhems outweigh the number of the good deed dirhems, the soul is saved. Herodotus noticed the same principle of compensation in the Persian law of his time (I, 137; cf. VII, 194).

the Patet. The performance of the Patet has only a
religious effect: it saves the sinner from penalties in the
other world, but not from those here below: it delivers him
before God, but not before man. When the sacrilegious
cleanser has repented his sin, he is not the less flayed and
beheaded, but his soul is saved [1]. Yet, although it has no
efficacy in causing the sin to be remitted, the absence of it
has power to cause it to be aggravated [2].

§ 23. Thus far for sins that can be atoned for. There
are some that are anâperetha, 'inexpiable,' which means,
as it seems, that they are punished with death here below,
and with torments in the other world.

Amongst the anâperetha sins are named the burning of
the dead, the burying of the dead [3], the eating dead matter [4],
unnatural sin [5], and self-pollution [6]. Although it is not
expressly declared that these sins were punished with
death, yet we know it of several of them, either from
Greek accounts or from Parsi tradition. There are also
whole classes of sinners whose life, it would seem, can be
taken by any one who detects them in the act, such as the
courtezan, the highwayman, the Sodomite, and the corpse-
burner [7].

§ 24. Such are the most important principles of the Mazdean law that can be gathered from the Vendîdâd. These
details, incomplete as they are, may give us an idea, if not
of the Sassanian practice, at least of the Sassanian ideal.
That it was an ideal which intended to pass into practice,
we know from the religious wars against Armenia, and
from the fact that very often the superintendence of justice and the highest offices of the state were committed to
Mobeds.

We must now add a few words on the plan of the following translation. As to our method we beg to refer to
the second chapter above. It rests on the Parsi tradition,
corrected or confirmed by the comparative method. The

---

[1] Farg. IX, 49, n.; cf. III, 20 seq.
[2] Farg. IV, 20, 24, 28, 32, 35, &c.
[3] Farg. I, 13, 17; Strabo XV, 14.
[4] Farg. VII, 23 seq.
[5] Farg. I, 12; cf. VIII, 32.
[6] Farg. VIII, 27.
[7] See p. 111, n. 1; Farg. XVIII, 64.

Parsi tradition is found in the Pahlavi Commentary [1], the understanding of which was facilitated to us first by the Gujarathi translation and paraphrase of Aspendiârji [2], and by a Persian transliteration and translation belonging to the Haug collection in Munich [3], for the use of which we were indebted to the obliging kindness of the Director of the State Library in Munich, Professor von Halm. The Ravâets and the Saddar [4] frequently gave us valuable information as to the traditional meaning of doubtful passages. As for the works of European scholars, we are much indebted to the Commentary on the Avesta by Professor Spiegel, and to the translations in the second edition of Martin Haug's Essays.

We have followed the text of the Avesta as given by Westergaard; the division into paragraphs is according to Westergaard; but we have given in brackets the corresponding divisions of Professor Spiegel's edition.

Many passages in the Vendîdâd Sâdah are mere quotations from the Pahlavi Commentary which have crept into the Sâdah text: we have not admitted them into the text. They are generally known to be spurious from their not being translated in the Commentary [5]: yet the absence of a Pahlavi translation is not always an unmistakable sign of such spuriousness. Sometimes the translation has been lost in our manuscripts, or omitted as having already been given in identical or nearly identical terms. When we thought

---

[1] Our quotations refer to the text given in Spiegel's edition, but corrected after the London manuscript.

[2] Bombay, 1842, 2 vols. in 8°.

[3] Unfortunately the copy is incomplete: there are two lacunae, one from I, 11 to the end of the chapter; the other, more extensive, from VI, 26 to IX. The perfect accordance of this Persian translation with the Gujarathi of Aspendiârji shows that both are derived from one and the same source. Their accordance is striking even in mistakes; for instance, the Pahlavi avâstâr ڙﻮﺳﻌﺴﻤﻤ, a transliteration of the Zend a-vâstra, 'without pastures' (VII, 28), is misread by the Persian translator âvâstâr, خواستار 'he who wishes,' owing to the ambiguity of the Pahlavi letter ﻤ (av or âv), and it is translated by Aspendiârji Kâhânâr, 'the wisher.'

[4] The prose Saddar (as found in the Great Ravâet), which differs considerably from the Saddar in verse, as translated by Hyde.

[5] Without speaking of their not being connected with the context. See Farg. I, 4, 15, 20; II, 6, 20; V, 1; VII, 53-54.

that this was the case, we have admitted the untranslated passages into the text, but in brackets [1].

We have divided the principal Fargards into several sections according to the matter they contain: this division, which is meant as an attempt to resolve the Vendîdâd into its primitive fragments, has, of course, no traditional authority, the divisions into paragraphs being the only ones that rest upon the authority of the manuscripts.

The translation will be found, in many passages, to differ greatly from the translations published heretofore [2]. The nature of this series of translations did not allow us to give full justificatory notes, but we have endeavoured in most cases to make the explanatory notes account to scholars for the new meanings we have adopted, and, in some cases, we hope that the original text, read anew, will by itself justify our translation [3].

We must not conclude this introduction without tendering our warmest thanks to Mr. E. W. West, who kindly revised the MS. of the translation before it went to press, and who has, we hope, succeeded in making our often imperfect English more acceptable to English readers.

JAMES DARMESTETER.

Paris,
November, 1879.

---

[1] Farg. VII, 3; VIII, 95. Formulae and enumerations are often left untranslated, although they must be considered part of the text (VIII, 72; XI, 9, 12; XX, 6, &c.)

[2] Complete translations of the Vendîdâd have been published by Anquetil Duperron in France (Paris, 1771), by Professor Spiegel in Germany (Leipzig, 1852), by Canon de Harlez in Belgium (Louvain, 1877). The translation of Professor Spiegel was translated into English by Professor Bleeck, who added useful information from inedited Gujarathi translations (Hertford, 1864).

[3] The following is a list of the principal abbreviations used in this volume :—
Asp. = Aspendiârji's translation.
Bund. = Bundahis; Arabic numbers refer to the chapter (according to Justi's edition); Roman numbers refer to the page and line.
Comm. = The Pahlavi Commentary.
Gr. Rav. = Le Grand Ravâet (in the Bibliothèque Nationale in Paris, Supplément Persan, No. 47).
Orm. Ahr. = Ormazd et Ahriman, Paris, Vieweg, 1877.

VENDÎDÂD.

VENDÎDÂD.

FARGARD I.

THIS chapter is an enumeration of sixteen lands created by
Ahura Mazda, and of as many plagues created in opposition by
Angra Mainyu.

Many attempts have been made, not only to identify these sixteen lands, but also to draw historical conclusions from their order
of succession, as representing the actual order of the migrations
and settlements of the old Iranian tribes[1]. But there is nothing in
the text that would authorise us to look to it even for legendary
records, much less for real history. We have here nothing more
than a geographical description of Iran, such as might be expected
in a religious work like the Vendîdâd, that is to say, one that
contains mythical lands as well as real countries. It is not easy to
decide with perfect certainty, in every case, whether we have to do
with a land of the former or of the latter kind, owing partly to our
deficient knowledge of the geography of ancient Iran, partly to the
fact that names, originally belonging to mythical lands, are often
in later times attached to real ones.

Of these sixteen lands there are certainly nine which have really
existed, and of which we know the geographical position, as we
are able to follow their names from the records of the Achæmenian
kings or the works of classical writers down to the map of modern
Iran. They are the following :—

---

[1] Rhode, Die heilige Sage des Zendvolks, p. 61; Heeren, Ideen
zur Geschichte, I, p. 498; Lassen, Indische Alterthumskunde I,
p. 526; Haug in Bunsen's work, Aegypten's Stellung, V, 2nd part,
p. 104; Kiepert, Monatsberichte der Berliner Akademie, 1856,
p. 621.—New light was thrown on this record by M. Bréal in his
paper 'De la géographie de l'Avesta' (in the Mélanges de mythologie et de linguistique, p. 187 seq.)

ZEND NAME.	OLD PERSIAN.	GREEK.	MODERN NAME.
Sughdha (2)	Suguda	Σογδιανή	(Samarkand)
Môuru (3)	Margu	Μαργιανή	Merv
Bâkhdhi (4)	Bâkhtri	Βάκτρα	Balkh
Harôyu (6)	Haraiva	Ἄρεια	Hari-rûd
Vehrkâna (9)	Varkâna	Ὑρκανία	Gorgân
Harahvaiti (10)	Harauvati	Ἀράχωτος	Harût
Haêtumant (11)		Ἐτύμανδρος	Helmend
Ragha (12)	Raga	Ῥαγαί	Raï
Hapta hindu (15)	Hindavas	Ἰνδοί	(Pañgâb)

The real existence of Nisâya (5) is certain, although its position cannot be exactly determined (see the note to § 8).

For the other lands we are confined for information to the Pahlavi Commentary. Kakhra (13) is only transliterated, whether the name was then too much known to require any further explanation or too little to allow of any. Urva (8) is described as being Masân ('the land of Masân' or 'the land of the Great'), a name which applied, in the Sassanian ages, to the land around Ispahân (Firdausi, ed. Mohl, V, 270).

For 'Varena, the four-cornered' (14), the Commentary hesitates between the Padashkhvârgar mountains (the Elborz) and Kirmân, a hesitation easily accounted for by the fact that Varena is the seat of the struggle between Azis Dahâka and Thraêtaona, between the storm serpent and the storm god, and was formerly 'the four-sided Heaven' (see Introd. IV, 12, 23). Modern tradition decides in favour of Padashkhvârgar, probably because the serpent was at last bound to Demavand, the highest peak in that chain. The claims of Kirmân were probably founded on the popular etymology of its name, 'the land of snakes.'

'Vaêkereta, of the evil shadows' (8), is identified with Kapul (Cabul); whether rightly or wrongly, we are unable to decide; yet, as it is spoken of only as the seat of the adventures of Keresâspa (see Introd. IV, 21), it may be suspected that this assimilation rests merely on the fact that, in later tradition, the legend of Keresâspa was localised in the table-land of Peshyansâi, in Kabulistan (Bund. XXX).

In the enumeration there is no apparent order whatever, and Ormazd, in his creations, seems to travel all over the map, forward and backward, without the slightest regard to the cardinal points. Yet, the starting point and the final point have not been arbitrarily chosen: the first land created was 'the Airyana Vaêgô by the Vanguhi Dâitya,' and the last was the land by the Rangha. Now, the Vanguhi and the Rangha were originally the celestial rivers that came down from heaven (as two heavenly Gangâs) to surround the earth, the one in the east, the other in the west (Bund. XX); this is why the creation begins with a land by the Vanguhi and ends with a land by the Rangha.

In the Sassanian ages, when the Tigris was definitively the border of Iran in the west, the Rangha was identified with it, and the sixteenth land is accordingly described in the Commentary as being Arvastân-i-Rûm, or Roman Mesopotamia. But all the Avesta passages in which the Rangha is cited refer to its mythical nature, as the river in the far-off horizon, as the surrounding Okeanos, and, now and then, still resembling its Vedic homonym, the Rasâ, as the river that divides the gods from the fiends.

The first land, the Airyana Vaêgô by the Vanguhi Dâitya, remained to the last a mythical region. It was originally the abode of Yima and of the righteous, that is to say, a particular form of paradise (see Introd. IV, 38, and Farg. II). Later on, it was looked for in the countries north of Adarbaijan, probably in order that it should be as near as possible to the seat of the Zoroastrian religion, yet without losing its supernatural character by the counter-evidence of facts. This brought about the division of the Vanguhi Dâitya into two rivers: as the Airyana Vaêgô was localised in the country north of Adarbaijan, the river in it must become identified with the Araxes (Aras); but, at the same time, it continued to surround the world eastward under the name of Veh (Vanguhi), which was the Sassanian name of the Oxus—Indus [1]. It seems that in the time of Herodotus, the Araxes and the Oxus were considered one and the same river [2], as the Oxus and the Indus were later on; this would account for his strange statement that the Araxes, which is confessedly with him the Oxus or Yaxartes, springs from the land of the Matianians, like the Gyndes, and flows eastwards (I, 202; IV, 40; cf. III, 36; IV, 11); and, at the same time, this would account both for how the Airyana Vaêgô could be localised in the basin of the Araxes and how the Oxus could flow eastwards to fall into the Arabian sea [3].

---

[1] The Oxus and the Indus were believed to be one and the same river (Bund. l. c.; see Garrez, Journal Asiatique, 1869, II, 195 seq.)

[2] Running under the Caspian sea, as Arethusa runs under the Sicilian sea and the Rangha itself under the Persian gulf (Bund. XX; cf. Garrez l. c.)

[3] Whether in the time when this Fargard was written, the Airyana

It follows hence that no historical conclusions can be drawn from this description : it was necessary that it should begin with the Vanguhi and end with the Rangha. To look to it for an account of geographical migrations, is converting cosmology into history.

Of the counter-creations of Angra Mainyu there is little to be said : they are different vices and plagues, which are generally unconnected with the country to the creation of which they answer. Some of them are expressed by ἅπαξ λεγόμενα, the meaning of which is doubtful or unknown.

If we assume that only lands belonging to the Iranian world were admitted into the list, the mention of the Seven Rivers would indicate that the first Fargard was not composed earlier than the time when the basin of the Indus became a part of Iran, that is, not earlier than the reign of Darius the First.

1. Ahura Mazda[1] spake unto Spitama[2] Zarathustra[3], saying :

2. I have made every land dear to its dwellers, even though it had no charms whatever in it[4] : had I not made every land dear to its dwellers, even though it had no charms whatever in it, then the whole living world would have invaded the Airyana Vaêgô[5].

3 (5). The first of the good lands and countries

Vaêgô was still believed to be in the far-off lands of the rising sun, or already on the banks of the Aras, we leave undecided.

[1] See Introd. IV, 4.

[2] Literally 'the most beneficent,' an epithet of Zarathustra, which was later mistaken for a family name, 'the Spitamide.'

[3] See Introd. IV, 40.

[4] 'Every one fancies that the land where he is born and has been brought up is the best and fairest land that I have created.' (Comm.)

[5] See following clause. Clause 2 belongs to the Commentary; it is composed of quotations that illustrate the alternative process of the creation : 'First, Ahura Mazda would create a land of such kind that its dwellers might like it, and there could be nothing more delightful. Then he who is all death would bring against it a counter-creation.'

which I, Ahura Mazda, created, was the Airyana Vaêgô [1], by the good river Dâitya [2].

Thereupon came Angra Mainyu, who is all death, and he counter-created by his witchcraft the serpent in the river [3] and winter, a work of the Daêvas [4].

4 (9). There are ten winter months there, two summer months [5]; and those are cold for the waters [6], cold for the earth, cold for the trees [7]. Winter falls there, with the worst of its plagues.

5 (13). The second of the good lands and countries which I, Ahura Mazda, created, was the plains [8] in Sughdha [9].

---

[1] See the Introd. to the Fargard.

[2] 'The good Dâitya.' 'The Dâitîk (Dâitya) comes from Irân Vêg (Airyana Vaêgô), it flows through the mountains of Gorgistân (Georgia,' Bund. p. 51, 19). It was therefore, in the time of the Sassanides, a name of the Araxes.

[3] 'There are many Khrafstras in the Dâitîk, as it is said, The Dâitîk full of Khrafstras' (Bund. p. 51, 20). The serpent in the river was originally the mythical Serpent, Azis, who overthrew and killed the king of Irân Vêg, Yima (see Introd. IV, 18); then it was identified, as appears from the Bundahis, with the snakes that abound on the banks of the Araxes (Morier, A Second Journey, p. 250).

[4] As Irân Vêg is a place of refuge for mankind and all life from the winter that is to destroy the world (see Farg. II, 21 seq.), winter was thought, by a mythical misunderstanding, to be the counter-creation of Irân Vêg: hence the glacial description of that strange paradise (see the following clause).

[5] Vendîdâd Sâdah: 'It is known that [in the ordinary course of nature] there are seven months of summer and five of winter' (see Bund. XXV).

[6] Some say: 'Even those two months of summer are cold for the waters . . .' (Comm.; cf. Mainyô-i-khard XLIV, 20, and above, n. 4).

[7] Vend. Sâdah: 'There reigns the core and heart of winter.'

[8] Doubtful: possibly the name of a river (the Zarafshand).

[9] Suguda; Sogdiana.

Thereupon came Angra Mainyu, who is all death, and he counter-created by his witchcraft the fly Skaitya[1], which brings death to the cattle.

6 (17). The third of the good lands and countries which I, Ahura Mazda, created, was the strong, holy Môuru[2].

Thereupon came Angra Mainyu, who is all death, and he counter-created by his witchcraft sinful lusts[3].

7 (21). The fourth of the good lands and countries which I, Ahura Mazda, created, was the beautiful Bâkhdhi[4] with high-lifted banners.

Thereupon came Angra Mainyu, who is all death, and he counter-created by his witchcraft the Bravara[5].

8 (25). The fifth of the good lands and countries which I, Ahura Mazda, created, was Nisâya[6], that lies between Môuru and Bâkhdhi.

Thereupon came Angra Mainyu, who is all death, and he counter-created by his witchcraft the sin of unbelief[7].

9 (29). The sixth of the good lands and countries

---

[1] A word unknown: possibly 'the cattle fly.' It is a fly that hides itself among the corn and the fodder, and thence stings with a venomous sting the ox that eats of it (Comm. and Asp.)

[2] Margu; Margiana; Merv.

[3] Translated according to the Comm. and Asp.

[4] Bâkhtri; Bactra; Balkh.

[5] 'The corn-carrying ants' (Asp.; cf. Farg. XIV, 5).

[6] There were several towns of this name, but none between Môuru and Bâkhdhi. But the sentence may be translated also: 'Nisâya between which and Bâkhdhi Môuru lies,' which would point to Νίσαια, the capital of Parthia (Παρθαύνισα ap. Isid. of Charax 12); cf. Pliny 6, 25 (29).

[7] 'One must believe in the law, and have no doubt whatever about it in the heart, and firmly believe that the good and right law that Ormazd sent to the world is the same law that was brought to us by Zardust' (Saddar 1).

which I, Ahura Mazda, created, was Harôyu[1] with
its lake[2].

Thereupon came Angra Mainyu, who is all death,
and he counter-created by his witchcraft the stained
mosquito[3].

10 (33). The seventh of the good lands and
countries which I, Ahura Mazda, created, was
Vaêkereta[4], of the evil shadows.

Thereupon came Angra Mainyu, who is all death,
and he counter-created by his witchcraft the Pairika
Knâthaiti, who clave unto Keresâspa[5].

11 (37). The eighth of the good lands and
countries which I, Ahura Mazda, created, was Urva
of the rich pastures[6].

Thereupon came Angra Mainyu, who is all death,
and he counter-created by his witchcraft the sin
of pride[7].

12 (41). The ninth of the good lands and
countries which I, Ahura Mazda, created, was
Khnenta in Vehrkâna[8].

Thereupon came Angra Mainyu, who is all death,
and he counter-created by his witchcraft a sin for
which there is no atonement, the unnatural sin[9].

13 (45). The tenth of the good lands and
countries which I, Ahura Mazda, created, was the
beautiful Harahvaiti[10].

---

[1] Haraiva; Areia; the basin of the Hari river, or Herat.
[2] Doubtful.   [3] Doubtful.
[4] 'Kapul' (Comm.; see the Introd. to the Fargard).
[5] See Introd. IV, 21.
[6] According to Asp. Tus (in Khorasan); more probably the
land around Ispahan. See the Introd. to the Fargard.
[7] Or better, tyranny: 'the great are proud there' (Comm.)
[8] Varkâna; Hyrcania. 'Khnenta is a river in Vehrkâna'
(Comm.); consequently the river Gorgân.
[9] See Farg. VIII, 31.   [10] Harauvati; 'Αράχωτος; Harût.

Thereupon came Angra Mainyu, who is all death, and he counter-created by his witchcraft a sin for which there is no atonement, the burying of the dead [1].

14 (49). The eleventh of the good lands and countries which I, Ahura Mazda, created, was the bright, glorious Haêtuma*n*t [2].

Thereupon came Angra Mainyu, who is all death, and he counter-created by his witchcraft the evil witchcraft of the Yâtus [3].

15 (53). And this is how the Yâtu's nature shows itself: it shows itself by the look [4]; and then, whenever the wizard goes and howls forth his spells [5], most deadly works of witchcraft go forth [6].

16 (59). The twelfth of the good lands and countries which I, Ahura Mazda, created, was Ragha of the three races [7].

Thereupon came Angra Mainyu, who is all death, and he counter-created by his witchcraft the sin of utter unbelief [8].

17 (63). The thirteenth of the good lands and

---

[1] See Farg. III, 36 seq.

[2] The basin of the 'Ἐτύμανδρος or Erymanthus; now Helmend. Cf. Farg. XIX, 39.

[3] The wizards; see Introd. IV, 20.   [4] The evil eye.

[5] As a Γόης. Witchcraft is exercised either by the eye or by the voice (Asp.)

[6] Vendîdâd Sâdah: 'Then they come forth to kill and to strike to the heart.' A gloss cites, as productions of the wizard, 'snow and hail' (cf. Hippocrates, De Morbo Sacro 1, and Pausanias 2, 34, 4). To that gloss seems to belong the corrupt Zend sentence that follows, and that may mean 'they increase the plague of locusts' (cf. Farg. VII, 26).

[7] Raï. See Introd. III, 15.

[8] 'They doubt themselves and cause other people to doubt' (Comm.)

countries which I, Ahura Mazda, created, was the strong, holy *K*akhra[1].

Thereupon came Angra Mainyu, who is all death, and he counter-created by his witchcraft a sin for which there is no atonement, the burning of corpses[2].

18 (67). The fourteenth of the good lands and countries which I, Ahura Mazda, created, was the four-cornered Varena[3], for which was born Thraê-taona, who smote A*z*is Dahâka.

Thereupon came Angra Mainyu, who is all death, and he counter-created by his witchcraft abnormal issues in women[4] and the oppression of foreign rulers[5].

19 (72). The fifteenth of the good lands and countries which I, Ahura Mazda, created, was the Seven Rivers[6].

Thereupon came Angra Mainyu, who is all death, and he counter-created by his witchcraft abnormal issues in women and excessive heat.

20 (76). The sixteenth of the good lands and countries which I, Ahura Mazda, created, was the land by the floods of the Rangha[7], where people live without a head[8].

---

[1] A land unknown. Asp.: China, which is certainly wrong. There was a town of that name in Khorasan (*K*arkh).

[2] See Farg. VIII, 73.

[3] See the Introd. to the Farg.   [4] Farg. XVI, 11 seq.

[5] Possibly an allusion to A*z*is Dahâka (Zohâk), who, as a king, represents the foreign conqueror (in later tradition the Tâzî or Arab; possibly in older tradition the Assyrian).

[6] The basin of the affluents of the Indus, the modern Pañgâb (=the Five Rivers).

[7] 'Arvastân-i-Rûm (Roman Mesopotamia),' (Comm.; see the Introd. to the Farg.)

[8] It is interpreted in a figurative sense as meaning 'people who

Thereupon came Angra Mainyu, who is all death, and he counter-created by his witchcraft winter, a work of the Daêvas [1].

21 (81). There are still other lands and countries, beautiful and deep, desirable and bright, and thriving.

FARGARD II.

Yima (Gamshêd).

This Fargard may be divided into two parts.

First part (1–20). Ahura Mazda proposes to Yima, the son of Vivanghat, to receive the law from him and to bring it to men. On his refusal, he bids him keep his creatures and make them prosper. Yima accordingly makes them thrive and increase, keeps death and disease away from them, and three times enlarges the earth, which had become too narrow for its inhabitants.

Second part (21 to the end). On the approach of a dire winter, which is to destroy every living creature, Yima, being advised by Ahura, builds a Vara to keep there the seeds of every kind of animals and plants, and the blessed live there a most happy life under his rule.

The tale in the first part refers to Yima as the first man, the first king, and the founder of civilisation (see Introd. IV, 38); the tale in

---

do not hold the chief for a chief' (Comm.), which is the translation for asraosha (Comm. ad XVI, 18), 'rebel against the law,' and would well apply in the Sassanian ages to the non-Mazdean people of Arvastân-i-Rûm. I think we must adopt the literal meaning, and recognise in this passage the source, or at least the oldest form, of those tales about people without a head, with eyes on their shoulders, which Pliny received from the half-Persian Ctesias (Hist. N. VII, 2; V, 8; cf. Aul. Gell. IX, 4; Sanct. August. De Civit. Dei, XVI, 8). Persian geographers mention such people, they place them in the Oriental islands near China, whence they sent ambassadors to the Khan of the Tatars (Ouseley, Catalogue). The mythical origin of those tales may be traced in Indian and Greek mythology (Orm. Ahr. § 222; cf. Pausanias IX, 20).

[1] Vendîdâd Sâdah: 'And the oppression of the land that comes from taoza (?).'

the second part is a combination of the myths of Yima, as the first dead and the king of the dead over whom he rules in a region of bliss, and of old myths about the end of the world. The world, lasting a long year of twelve millenniums, was to end by a dire winter, like the Eddic Fimbul winter, to be followed by an everlasting spring, when men, sent back to earth from the heavens, should enjoy, in an eternal earthly life, the same happiness that they had enjoyed after their death in the realm of Yima. But as in the definitive form which was taken by Mazdean cosmology the world was made to end by fire, its destruction by winter was no longer the last incident of its life, and therefore, the Var of Yima, instead of remaining, as it was originally, the paradise that gives back to earth its inhabitants, came to be nothing more than a sort of Noah's ark (see Introd. IV, 39, and Orm. Ahr. §§ 94, 131, 184, 185).

I.

1. Zarathustra asked Ahura Mazda :

O Ahura Mazda, most beneficent Spirit, Maker of the material world, thou Holy One!

Who was the first mortal, before myself, Zarathustra, with whom thou, Ahura Mazda, didst converse[1], whom thou didst teach the law of Ahura, the law of Zarathustra?

2 (4). Ahura Mazda answered:

The fair Yima, the great shepherd, O holy Zarathustra! he was the first mortal, before thee, Zarathustra, with whom I, Ahura Mazda, did converse, whom I taught the law of Ahura, the law of Zarathustra.

3 (7). Unto him, O Zarathustra, I, Ahura Mazda, spake, saying: 'Well, fair Yima, son of Vivanghat, be thou the preacher and the bearer of my law!'

And the fair Yima, O Zarathustra, replied unto me, saying :

---

[1] 'On the law' (Comm.)

'I was not born, I was not taught to be the preacher and the bearer of thy law [1].'

4 (11). Then I, Ahura Mazda, said thus unto him, O Zarathustra:

'Since thou wantest not to be the preacher and the bearer of my law, then make thou my worlds thrive, make my worlds increase: undertake thou to nourish, to rule, and to watch over my world.'

5 (14). And the fair Yima replied unto me, O Zarathustra, saying:

'Yes! I will make thy worlds thrive, I will make thy worlds increase. Yes! I will nourish, and rule, and watch over thy world. There shall be, while I am king, neither cold wind nor hot wind, neither disease nor death.'

7 (17)[2]. Then I, Ahura Mazda, brought two implements unto him: a golden ring and a poniard inlaid with gold [3]. Behold, here Yima bears the royal sway!

8 (20). Thus, under the sway of Yima, three hundred winters passed away, and the earth was replenished with flocks and herds, with men and

---

[1] In the Vedas, Yama, as the first man, is the first priest too; he brought worship here below as well as life, and 'first he stretched out the thread of sacrifice.' Yima had once the same right as his Indian brother to the title of a founder of religion: he lost it as, in the course of the development of Mazdeism, Zarathustra became the titular law-giver (cf. Introd. IV, 40; Orm. Ahr. § 156).

[2] The § 6 is composed of unconnected Zend quotations, that are no part of the text and are introduced by the commentator for the purpose of showing that 'although Yima did not teach the law and train pupils, he was nevertheless a faithful and a holy man, and rendered men holy too (?).'

[3] As the symbol and the instrument of sovereignty. 'He reigned supreme by the strength of the ring and of the poniard' (Asp.)

dogs and birds and with red blazing fires, and there was no more room for flocks, herds, and men.

9. Then I warned the fair Yima, saying: 'O fair Yima, son of Vîvanghat, the earth has become full of flocks and herds, of men and dogs and birds and of red blazing fires, and there is no more room for flocks, herds, and men.'

10. Then Yima stepped forward, towards the luminous space, southwards, to meet the sun[1], and (afterwards) he pressed the earth with the golden ring, and bored it with the poniard, speaking thus:

'O Spenta Ârmaiti[2], kindly open asunder and stretch thyself afar, to bear flocks and herds and men.'

11. And Yima made the earth grow larger by one-third than it was before, and there came flocks and herds and men, at his will and wish, as many as he wished[3].

---

[1] Thence is derived the following tradition recorded by G. du Chinon: 'Ils en nomment un qui s'allait tous les jours promener dans le Ciel du Soleil d'où il aportait la sciance des Astres, aprez les avoir visités de si prez. Ils nomment ce grand personnage Gemachid' (Relations nouvelles du Levant, Lyon, 1671, p. 478). There is no direct connexion, as it seems, between the two acts of Yima, namely, between his going to the heaven of the sun and his enlarging the surface of the earth. The meaning of the first is given, perhaps, by the tale about the dream of Cyrus: 'He saw in a dream the sun at his feet: thrice he tried vainly to seize it with his hands, as the sun was rolling and sliding away. The Magi said to him that the threefold effort to seize the sun presaged to him a reign of thirty years' (Dino ap. Cicero, De Divin. I, 23). Yima goes three times to the sun, to take thence royal power for three times three hundred years. In Aryan mythology, the sun is, as is well known, the symbol and source of royalty: Persian kings in particular are 'the brothers of the sun.'

[2] The genius of the earth (see Introd. IV, 33).

[3] The happiness which Yima made reign on the earth is also

12 (23). Thus, under the sway of Yima, six hundred winters passed away, and the earth was replenished with flocks and herds, with men and dogs and birds and with red blazing fires, and there was no more room for flocks, herds, and men.

13. And I warned the fair Yima, saying: 'O fair Yima, son of Vîvanghat, the earth has become full of flocks and herds, of men and dogs and birds and of red blazing fires, and there is no more room for flocks, herds, and men.'

14. Then Yima stepped forward, towards the luminous space, southwards, to meet the sun, and (afterwards) he pressed the earth with the golden ring, and bored it with the poniard, speaking thus:

'O Spenta Ârmaiti, kindly open asunder and stretch thyself afar, to bear flocks and herds and men.'

15. And Yima made the earth grow larger by two-thirds than it was before, and there came flocks and herds and men, at his will and wish, as many as he wished.

16 (26). Thus, under the sway of Yima, nine hundred winters passed away, and the earth was replenished with flocks and herds, with men and dogs and birds and with red blazing fires, and there was no more room for flocks, herds, and men.

17 (28). And I warned the fair Yima, saying: 'O fair Yima, son of Vîvanghat, the earth has become full of flocks and herds, of men and dogs and birds and of red blazing fires, and there is no more room for flocks, herds, and men.'

---

described Ys. IX, 4; Yt. IX, 8 seq.; Yt. XV, 15. In the Shâh Nâmah he is the founder of civilisation, of social order, of arts and sciences, and the first builder (cf. § 25 seq.)

18 (31). Then Yima stepped forward, towards the luminous space, southwards, to meet the sun, and (afterwards) he pressed the earth with the golden ring, and bored it with the poniard, speaking thus:

'O Spenta Ârmaiti, kindly open asunder and stretch thyself afar, to bear flocks and herds and men.'

19 (37). And Yima made the earth grow larger by three-thirds than it was before, and there came flocks and herds and men, at his will and wish, as many as he wished.

II.

21 (42)[1]. The Maker, Ahura Mazda, of high renown[2] in the Airyana Vaêgô, by the good river Dâitya[3], called together a meeting of the celestial gods.

The fair Yima, the good shepherd, of high renown[2] in the Airyana Vaêgô, by the good river Dâitya, called together a meeting of the excellent mortals[4].

To that meeting came Ahura Mazda, of high renown in the Airyana Vaêgô, by the good river Dâitya; he came together with the celestial gods.

To that meeting came the fair Yima, the good shepherd, of high renown in the Airyana Vaêgô, by the good river Dâitya; he came together with the excellent mortals.

22 (46). And Ahura Mazda spake unto Yima, saying:

'O fair Yima, son of Vîvanghat! Upon the material

---

[1] § 20 belongs to the Commentary.

[2] Or perhaps, 'whose voice was loud,' &c. (while proclaiming the law).

[3] See Farg. I, Introd., and notes to § 2.

[4] Primitively the souls of the righteous (see Introd. IV, 38).

world the fatal winters are going to fall, that shall
bring the fierce, foul frost; upon the material world
the fatal winters [1] are going to fall, that shall make
snow-flakes fall thick, even an aredvî deep on the
highest tops of mountains [2].

23 (52). And all the three sorts of beasts shall
perish, those that live in the wilderness, and those
that live on the tops of the mountains, and those
that live in the bosom of the dale, under the shelter
of stables.

24 (57). Before that winter, those fields would
bear plenty of grass for cattle: now with floods
that stream, with snows that melt, it will seem a
happy land in the world, the land wherein footprints
even of sheep may still be seen [3].

25 (61). Therefore make thee a Vara [4], long as a

---

[1] The Commentary has here: Malkôsân, which is the plural of
the Hebrew Malkôs, 'rain;' this seems to be an attempt to
identify the Iranian legend with the biblical tradition of the deluge.
The attempt was both a success and a failure; Malkôs entered
the Iranian mythology and became naturalised there, but it was
mistaken for a proper noun, and became the name of a demon,
who by witchcraft will let loose a furious winter on the earth to
destroy it (Saddar 9). What may be called the diluvial version
of the myth is thus summed up in the Mainyô-i-khard: 'By him
(Gamshîd) the enclosure of Jam-kard was made; when there is
that rain of Malakosân, as it is declared in the religion, that
mankind and the remaining creatures and creations of Hôrmezd,
the lord, will mostly perish; then they will open the gate of that
enclosure of Jam-karđ, and men and cattle and the remaining
creatures and creation of the creator Hôrmezd will come from
that enclosure and arrange the world again' (XXVII, 27 seq.;
edited and translated by E. West).

[2] 'Even where it (the snow) is least, it will be one Vîtasti two
fingers deep' (Comm.); that is, fourteen fingers deep.

[3] Doubtful.

[4] Literally, 'an enclosure.' This Vara is known in later mythology as the Var-Gam-kard, 'the Var made by Yima.'

riding-ground on every side of the square[1], and thither bring the seeds of sheep and oxen, of men, of dogs, of birds, and of red blazing fires.

Therefore make thee a Vara, long as a riding-ground on every side of the square, to be an abode for men; a Vara, long as a riding-ground on every side of the square, to be a fold for flocks.

26 (65). There thou shalt make waters flow in a bed a hâthra long; there thou shalt settle birds, by the ever-green banks that bear never-failing food. There thou shalt establish dwelling places, consisting of a house with a balcony, a courtyard, and a gallery[2].

27 (70). Thither thou shalt bring the seeds[3] of men and women, of the greatest, best, and finest kinds on this earth; thither thou shalt bring the seeds of every kind of cattle, of the greatest, best, and finest kinds on this earth.

28 (74). Thither thou shalt bring the seeds of every kind of tree, of the greatest, best, and finest kinds on this earth; thither thou shalt bring the seeds of every kind of fruit, the fullest of food and sweetest of odour. All those seeds shalt thou bring, two of every kind, to be kept inexhaustible there, so long as those men shall stay in the Vara.

29 (80). There shall be no humpbacked, none bulged forward there; no impotent, no lunatic; no poverty, no lying; no meanness, no jealousy; no

---

[1] 'Two hâthras long on every side' (Comm.) A hâthra is about an English mile.

[2] The last three words are ἅπαξ λεγόμενα of doubtful meaning.

[3] To be sown in the ground, and to grow up into life in due time (? see § 41, text and note).

[4]   C

decayed tooth, no leprous to be confined[1], nor any of the brands wherewith Angra Mainyu stamps the bodies of mortals.

30 (87). In the largest part of the place thou shalt make nine streets, six in the middle part, three in the smallest. To the streets of the largest part thou shalt bring a thousand seeds of men and women; to the streets of the middle part, six hundred; to the streets of the smallest part, three hundred. That Vara thou shalt seal up with the golden ring[2], and thou shalt make a door, and a window self-shining within.

31 (93). Then Yima said within himself: 'How shall I manage to make that Vara which Ahura Mazda has commanded me to make?'

And Ahura Mazda said unto Yima: 'O fair Yima, son of Vîvanghat! Crush the earth with a stamp of thy heel, and then knead it with thy hands, as the potter does when kneading the potter's clay[3].'

[32. And Yima did as Ahura Mazda wished; he crushed the earth with a stamp of his heel, he kneaded it with his hands, as the potter does when kneading the potter's clay[4].]

33 (97). And Yima made a Vara, long as a riding-ground on every side of the square. There he brought the seeds of sheep and oxen, of men, of

---

[1] See Introd. V, 14.   [2] Doubtful.

[3] In the Shâh Nâmah Gamshîd teaches the Dîvs to make and knead clay; and they build palaces at his bidding. It was his renown, both as a wise king and a great builder, that caused the Musulmans to identify him with Solomon.

[4] From the Vendîdâd Sâdah.

dogs, of birds, and of red blazing fires. He made a Vara, long as a riding-ground on every side of the square, to be an abode for men; a Vara, long as a riding-ground on every side of the square, to be a fold for flocks.

34 (101). There he made waters flow in a bed a hâthra long; there he settled birds, by the ever-green banks that bear never-failing food.   There he established dwelling places, consisting of a house with a balcony, a courtyard, and a gallery.

35 (106). There he brought the seeds of men and women, of the greatest, best, and finest kinds on this earth ; there he brought the seeds of every kind of cattle, of the greatest, best, and finest kinds on this earth.

36 (110). There he brought the seeds of every kind of tree, of the greatest, best, and finest kinds on this earth ; there he brought the seeds of every kind of fruit, the fullest of food and sweetest of odour.   All those seeds he brought, two of every kind, to be kept inexhaustible there, so long as those men shall stay in the Vara.

37 (116). And there were no humpbacked, none bulged forward there; no impotent, no lunatic; no poverty, no lying; no meanness, no jealousy; no decayed tooth, no leprous to be confined, nor any of the brands wherewith Angra Mainyu stamps the bodies of mortals.

38 (123). In the largest part of the place he made nine streets, six in the middle part, three in the smallest.   To the streets of the largest part he brought a thousand seeds of men and women; to the streets of the middle part, six hundred; to the streets of the smallest part, three hundred.   That

Vara he sealed up with the golden ring, and he made a door, and a window self-shining within.

39 (129). O Maker of the material world, thou Holy One! What [lights are there to give light[1]] in the Vara which Yima made ?

40 (131). Ahura Mazda answered : 'There are uncreated lights and created lights[2]. There the stars, the moon, and the sun are only once (a year) seen to rise and set[3], and a year seems only as a day.

41 (133). 'Every fortieth year, to every couple two are born, a male and a female[4]. And thus it is for every sort of cattle. And the men in the Vara which Yima made live the happiest life[5].'

---

[1] From the Vendîdâd Sâdah.

[2] Heavenly lights and material lights. The Commentary has here the following Zend quotation : 'All uncreated light shines from above ; all the created lights shine from below.'

We give here the description of Irân-vêg according to a later source, the Mainyô-i-khard (as translated by West) : 'Hôrmezd created Erã-vêz better than the remaining places and districts ; and its goodness was this, that men's life is three hundred years ; and cattle and sheep, one hundred and fifty years ; and their pain and sickness are little, and they do not circulate falsehood, and they make no lamentation and weeping ; and the sovereignty of the demon of Avarice, in their body, is little, and in ten men, if they eat one loaf, they are satisfied ; and in every forty years, from one woman and one man, one child is born ; and their law is goodness, and religion the primeval religion, and when they die, they are righteous (=blessed) ; and their chief is Gôpatshâh, and the ruler and king is Srôsh' (XLIV, 24).

[3] Doubtful.

[4] From the seeds deposited in the Vara (see §§ 27 seq., 35 seq.) ; in the same way as the first human couple grew up, after forty years, in the shape of a Reivas shrub, from the seed of Gayômard received by Spenta Ârmaiti (the Earth. See Bund. XV).

[5] 'They live there for 150 years ; some say, they never die.' (Comm.) The latter are right, that is to say, are nearer the mythical

42 (137). O Maker of the material world, thou
Holy One! Who is he who brought the law of
Mazda into the Vara which Yima made?

Ahura Mazda answered: 'It was the bird Karshipta[1], O holy Zarathustra!'

43 (140). O Maker of the material world, thou
Holy One! Who is the lord and ruler there?

Ahura Mazda answered: 'Urvatad-nara[2], O Zarathustra! and thyself, Zarathustra.'

FARGARD III.

The Earth.

I (1–6). The five places where the Earth feels most joy.
II (7–11). The five places where the Earth feels most sorrow.
III (12–35). The five things which most rejoice the Earth.
IV (36–42). Corpses ought not to be buried in the Earth.

There is a resemblance as to words between the first and

---

truth, as the inhabitants of the Vara were primitively the departed
and therefore immortal.

[1] 'The bird Karshipta dwells in the heavens: were he living on
the earth, he would be the king of birds. He brought the law
into the Var of Yima, and recites the Avesta in the language of
birds' (Bund. XIX and XXIV). As the bird, because of the
swiftness of his flight, was often considered an incarnation of
lightning, and as thunder was supposed to be the voice of a god
speaking from above, the song of the bird was often thought to be
the utterance of a god and a revelation (see Orm. Ahr. § 157).

[2] Zarathustra had three sons during his lifetime (cf. Introd. IV,
40), Isad-vâstra, Hvare-kithra, and Urvatad-nara, who were respectively the fathers and chiefs of the three classes, priests, warriors,
and husbandmen. They play no great part in Mazdean mythology, and are little more than three subdivisions of Zarathustra
himself, who was 'the first priest, the first warrior, the first husbandman' (Yt. XIII, 88). Zarathustra, as a heavenly priest, was,
by right, the ratu in Airyana Vaêgô, where he founded the religion
by a sacrifice (Bund. XXXIII and Introd. III, 15).

second parts, but there is none as to matter; no clause in the former has its counterpart in the latter. There is more resemblance between the second part and the third; as the first three clauses of the third part (§§ 12, 13, 22) relate to the same things as the second, third, and fourth clauses of the second part (§§ 8, 9, 10).

Parts I and II are nothing more than dry enumerations. Part III is more interesting, as it contains two long digressions, the one (§§ 14–21) on funeral laws, the other (§§ 24–33) on the holiness of husbandry. The fourth part of the chapter may be considered as a digression relating to the first clause of the third part (§ 12).

The things which rejoice or grieve the Earth are those that produce fertility and life or sterility and death, either in it or on it.

The subject of this chapter has become a commonplace topic with the Parsis, who have treated it more or less antithetically in the Mainyô-i-khard (chaps. V and VI) and in the Ravaets (Gr. Rav. pp. 434–437).

The second digression (§§ 24–33) is translated in Haug's Essays, p. 235 seq.

I.

1. O Maker of the material world, thou Holy One! Which is the first place where the Earth feels most happy?

Ahura Mazda answered: 'It is the place whereon one of the faithful steps forward, O Spitama Zarathustra! with the holy wood in his hand [1], the baresma [2] in his hand, the holy meat in his hand,

---

[1] The wood for the fire altar.

[2] The baresma (now called barsom) is a bundle of sacred twigs which the priest holds in his hand while reciting the prayers. They were formerly twigs of the pomegranate, date, or tamarind tree, or of any tree that had no thorns, and were plucked with particular ceremonies, which alone made them fit to be used for liturgic purposes (cf. Farg. XIX, 18 seq.) The Parsis in India found it convenient to replace them by brass wires, which, when once consecrated, can be used for an indefinite period. It is the baresma which is alluded to by Strabo, when speaking of the bundle of thin twigs of heath, which the Magi hold in their hand

the holy mortar [1] in his hand, fulfilling the law with love, and beseeching aloud Mithra, the lord of wide pastures, and Râma *Hv*âstra [2].'

2, 3 (6–10). O Maker of the material world, thou Holy One! Which is the second place where the Earth feels most happy?

Ahura Mazda answered: 'It is the place whereon one of the faithful erects a house with a priest within, with cattle, with a wife, with children, and good herds within; and wherein afterwards the cattle go on thriving, holiness is thriving [3], fodder is thriving, the dog is thriving, the wife is thriving, the child is thriving, the fire is thriving, and every blessing of life is thriving.'

4 (11). O Maker of the material world, thou Holy One! Which is the third place where the Earth feels most happy?

Ahura Mazda answered: 'It is the place where one of the faithful cultivates most corn, grass, and fruit, O Spitama Zarathustra! where he waters ground that is dry, or dries ground that is too wet.'

5 (15). O Maker of the material world, thou Holy One! Which is the fourth place where the Earth feels most happy?

Ahura Mazda answered: 'It is the place where there is most increase of flocks and herds.'

---

while reciting their hymns (τὰς δὴ ἐπῳδὰς ποιοῦνται πολὺν χρόνον ῥάβδων μυρικίνων λεπτῶν δέσμην κατέχοντες, XV, 3, 14).

[1] The Hâvana or mortar used in crushing the Haoma or Hom (see Introd. IV, 28).

[2] The god that gives good folds and good pastures to cattle (see Introd. IV, 16).

[3] By the performance of worship.

6 (18). O Maker of the material world, thou Holy One! Which is the fifth place where the Earth feels most happy?

Ahura Mazda answered: 'It is the place where flocks and herds yield most dung.'

II.

7 (21). O Maker of the material world, thou Holy One! Which is the first place where the Earth feels sorest grief?

Ahura Mazda answered: 'It is the neck of Arezûra[1], whereon the hosts of fiends rush forth from the burrow of the Drug[2].'

8 (25). O Maker of the material world, thou Holy One! Which is the second place where the Earth feels sorest grief?

Ahura Mazda answered: 'It is the place wherein most corpses of dogs and of men lie buried[3].

9 (28). O Maker of the material world, thou Holy One! Which is the third place where the Earth feels sorest grief?

Ahura Mazda answered: 'It is the place whereon stand most of those Dakhmas on which corpses of men are deposited[4].'

10 (31). O Maker of the material world, thou

---

[1] The neck of Arezûra (Arezûrahê grîva) is 'a mount at the gate of hell, whence the demons rush forth' (Bund. 22, 16); it is also called 'the head of Arezûra' (Farg. XIX, 45), or 'the back of Arezûra' (Bund. 21, 17). Arezûra was first the name of a fiend who was killed by Gayômard (Mainyô-i-khard XXVII, 15); and mount Arezûra was most likely the mountain to which he was bound, as Azi Dahâka was to Demâvend (see Introd. IV, 18).

[2] Hell.   [3] See Introd. V, 9.

[4] With regard to Dakhmas, see Introd. V, 10. 'Nor is the Earth happy at that place whereon stands a Dakhma with corpses upon it; for that patch of ground will never be clean again till the day of

Holy One! Which is the fourth place where the Earth feels sorest grief?

Ahura Mazda answered : ' It is the place wherein are most burrows of the creatures of Angra Mainyu [1].'

11 (34). O Maker of the material world, thou Holy One! Which is the fifth place where the Earth feels sorest grief?

Ahura Mazda answered: 'It is the place whereon the wife and children of one of the faithful [2], O Spitama Zarathustra! are driven along the way of captivity, the dry, the dusty way, and lift up a voice of wailing.'

III.

12 (38). O Maker of the material world, thou Holy One! Who is the first that rejoices the Earth with greatest joy?

Ahura Mazda answered : ' It is he who digs out of it most corpses of dogs and men [3].'

13 (41). O Maker of the material world, thou

---

resurrection' (Gr. Rav. 435, 437). Although the erection of Dakhmas is enjoined by the law, yet the Dakhma in itself is as unclean as any spot on the earth can be, since it is always in contact with the dead (cf. Farg. VII, 55). The impurity which would otherwise be scattered over the whole world, is thus brought together to one and the same spot. Yet even that spot, in spite of the Ravaet, is not to lie defiled for ever, as every fifty years the Dakhmas ought to be pulled down, so that their sites may be restored to their natural purity (V. i. Farg. VII, 49 seq. and this Farg. § 13).

[1] 'Where there are most Khrafstras' (Comm.); cf. Introd. V, 11.

[2] Killed by an enemy.

[3] There is no counterpart given to the first grief (§ 7), because, as the Commentary naively expresses it, 'it is not possible so to dig out hell, which will be done at the end of the world' (Bund. XXXI, sub fin.)

Holy One! Who is the second that rejoices the Earth with greatest joy?

Ahura Mazda answered: 'It is he who pulls down most of those Dakhmas on which corpses of men are deposited.'

14 (44). Let no man alone by himself carry a corpse[1]. If a man alone by himself carry a corpse, the Nasu[2] rushes upon him, to defile him, from the nose of the dead, from the eye, from the tongue, from the jaws, from the sexual organ, from the hinder parts. This Drug, this Nasu, falls upon him, stains him even to the end of the nails, and he is unclean, thenceforth, for ever and ever.

15 (49). O Maker of the material world, thou Holy One! What shall be the place of that man who has carried a corpse alone[3]?

Ahura Mazda answered: 'It shall be the place on this earth wherein is least water and fewest plants, whereof the ground is the cleanest and the driest and the least passed through by flocks and herds, by Fire, the son of Ahura Mazda, by the consecrated bundles of baresma, and by the faithful.'

---

[1] No ceremony in general can be performed by one man alone. Two Mobeds are wanted to perform the Vendîdâd service, two priests for the Barashnûm, two persons for the Sag-dîd (Anquetil, II, 584 n.) It is never good that the faithful should be alone, as the fiend is always lurking about, ready to take advantage of any moment of inattention. If the faithful be alone, there is no one to make up for any negligence and to prevent mischief arising from it. Never is the danger greater than in the present case, when the fiend is close at hand, and in direct contact with the faithful.

[2] See Introd. V, 3.

[3] As the Nasu has taken hold of him, he has become a Nasu incarnate, and must no longer be allowed to come into contact with men, whom he would defile.

16 (55). O Maker of the material world, thou Holy One! How far from the fire? How far from the water? How far from the consecrated bundles of baresma? How far from the faithful?

17 (57). Ahura Mazda answered: 'Thirty paces from the fire, thirty paces from the water, thirty paces from the consecrated bundles of baresma, three paces from the faithful.

18, 19 (58–63). 'There, on that place, shall the worshippers of Mazda erect an enclosure[1], and therein shall they establish him with food, therein shall they establish him with clothes, with the coarsest food and with the most worn-out clothes. That food he shall live on, those clothes he shall wear, and thus shall they let him live, until he has grown to the age of a Hana, or of a Zaurura, or of a Pairista-khshudra[2].

20, 21 (64–71). 'And when he has grown to the age of a Hana, or of a Zaurura, or of a Pairista-khshudra, then the worshippers of Mazda shall order a man strong, vigorous, and skilful[3], to flay the skin off his body and cut the head off his neck[4], on the top of the mountain: and they shall deliver his corpse unto the greediest of the corpse-eating creatures made by Ahura Mazda, to the greedy ravens, with these words: "The man here has repented of all his evil thoughts, words, and deeds.

---

[1] The Armest-gâh, the place for the unclean; see Introd. V, 15.

[2] Hana means, literally, 'an old man;' Zaurura, 'a man broken down by age;' Pairista-khshudra, 'one whose seed is dried up.' These words seem to have acquired the technical meanings of 'fifty, sixty, and seventy years old.'

[3] 'Trained to operations of that sort' (Comm.); a headsman.

[4] Cf. Farg. IX, 49, text and note.

If he has committed any other evil deed, it is remitted by his repentance[1]: if he has committed no
other evil deed, he is absolved by his repentance,
for ever and ever[2]."'

22 (72). O Maker of the material world, thou
Holy One! Who is the third that rejoices the
Earth with greatest joy?

Ahura Mazda answered: 'It is he who fills up
most burrows of the creatures of Angra Mainyu.'

23 (75). O Maker of the material world, thou
Holy One! Who is the fourth that rejoices the
Earth with greatest joy?

Ahura Mazda answered : ' It is he who cultivates
most corn, grass, and fruit, O Spitama Zarathustra!
who waters ground that is dry, or dries ground that
is too wet[3].

24 (79). 'Unhappy is the land that has long lain
unsown with the seed of the sower and wants a
good husbandman, like a well-shapen maiden who
has long gone childless and wants a good husband.

25 (84). 'He who would till the earth, O Spitama
Zarathustra! with the left arm and the right, with
the right arm and the left, unto him will she bring

[1] The performance of the Patet. See Introd. V, 22.

[2] It seems as if the law had formerly directed that he should be
immediately put to death; but that afterwards, when the rigour of
the law had abated, the object which had previously been fulfilled
by his death, was then attained by his confinement. He was
allowed to live in confinement till he was old and all but dead, and
he was put to death by the law, just before he would have died in
the usual course of nature (see §§ 19, 20). Certain Ravaets put
the 'carrier alone' among the number of the margarzân (East
India Office Library, Zend MSS. VIII, 144); he is not only to be
punished in this world, but in the other too; he is condemned to
feed in hell on corpses of men (Ardâ Vîrâf XXXVIII).

[3] Cf. § 4.

forth plenty, like a loving bride on her bed, unto her beloved ; the bride will bring forth children, the earth will bring forth plenty of fruit.

26, 27 (87–90). ' He who would till the earth, O Spitama Zarathustra! with the left arm and the right, with the right arm and the left, unto him thus says the Earth: " O thou man! who dost till me with . the left arm and the right, with the right arm and the left [hither shall people ever come and beg (for bread¹)], here shall I ever go on bearing, bringing forth all manner of food, bringing forth profusion of corn²."

28, 29 (91–95). ' He who does not till the earth, O Spitama Zarathustra! with the left arm and the right, with the right arm and the left, unto him thus says the Earth: " O thou man! who dost not till me with the left arm and the right, with the right arm and the left, ever shalt thou stand at the door of the stranger, among those who beg for bread ; ever shalt thou wait there for the refuse that is brought unto thee³, brought by those who have profusion of wealth."'

30 (96). O Maker of the material world, thou Holy One! What is the food that fills the law of Mazda⁴ ?

Ahura Mazda answered : ' It is sowing corn again and again, O Spitama Zarathustra!

31 (99). ' He who sows corn, sows holiness: he

---

¹ From the Vendîdâd Sâdah.

² Or 'bearing corn first for thee.' ' When something good grows up, it will grow up for thee first' (Comm.)

³ ' They take for themselves what is good and send to thee what is bad' (Comm.)

⁴ Literally, ' What is the stomach of the law ?'

makes the law of Mazda grow higher and higher:
he makes the law of Mazda as fat as he can with a
hundred acts of adoration, a thousand oblations, ten
thousand sacrifices [1].

32 (105). 'When barley is coming forth, the
Daêvas start up [2]; when the corn is growing rank [3],
then faint the Daêvas' hearts; when the corn is
being ground [4], the Daêvas groan; when wheat is
coming forth, the Daêvas are destroyed. In that
house they can no longer stay, from that house they
are beaten away, wherein wheat is thus coming
forth [5]. It is as though red hot iron were turned
about in their throats, when there is plenty of corn.

33 (111). 'Then let (the priest) teach people this
holy saying: "No one who does not eat, has
strength to do works of holiness, strength to do
works of husbandry, strength to beget children. By
eating every material creature lives, by not eating
it dies away [6]."'

34 (116). O Maker of the material world, thou
Holy One! Who is the fifth that rejoices the
Earth with greatest joy?

---

[1] The translation 'acts of adoration' and 'oblations' is doubtful: the words in the text are ἅπαξ λεγόμενα, which are traditionally
translated 'feet' and 'breasts.' The Commentary has as follows:
'He makes the law of Mazda as fat as a child could be made by
means of a hundred feet, that is to say, of fifty servants walking to
rock him; of a thousand breasts, that is, of five hundred nurses;
of ten thousand sacrifices performed for his weal.'

[2]   John Barleycorn got up again,
              And sore surpris'd them all.

[3] Doubtful; possibly, 'When sudhus (a sort of grain) is coming
forth.'

[4] Doubtful; possibly, 'When pistra (a sort of grain) is coming
forth.'

[5] Doubtful.   [6] See Farg. IV, 47.

Ahura Mazda answered: '[It is he who tilling the earth, O Spitama Zarathuſtra! kindly and piously gives[1] to one of the faithful.]

35 (118). 'He who tilling the earth, O Spitama Zarathuſtra! would not kindly and piously give to one of the faithful, he shall fall down into the darkness of Speɴta Ârmaiti[2], down into the world of woe, the dismal realm, down into the house of hell.'

IV.

36 (122). O Maker of the material world, thou Holy One! If a man shall bury in the earth either the corpse of a dog or the corpse of a man, and if he shall not disinter it within half a year, what is the penalty that he shall pay?

Ahura Mazda answered: 'Five hundred stripes with the Aspahê-aſtra[3], five hundred stripes with the Sraoshô-ꝁarana.'

37 (126). O Maker of the material world, thou Holy One! If a man shall bury in the earth either the corpse of a dog or the corpse of a man, and if he shall not disinter it within a year, what is the penalty that he shall pay?

Ahura Mazda answered: 'A thousand stripes with the Aspahê-aſtra, a thousand stripes with the Sraoshô-ꝁarana.'

38 (130). O Maker of the material world, thou Holy One! If a man shall bury in the earth either the corpse of a dog or the corpse of a man, and if he shall not disinter it within the second year, what

---

[1] The Ashô-dâd or alms. The bracketed clause is from the Vendîdâd Sâdah.

[2] The earth.   [3] See Introd. V, 19.

is the penalty for it? What is the atonement for
it? What is the cleansing from it?

39 (135). Ahura Mazda answered: 'For that
deed there is nothing that can pay, nothing that can
atone, nothing that can cleanse from it; it is a
trespass for which there is no atonement, for ever
and ever.'

40 (137). When is it so?

'It is so, if the sinner be a professor of the law
of Mazda, or one who has been taught in it[1]. But
if he be not a professor of the law of Mazda, nor
one who has been taught in it[2], then this law of
Mazda takes his sin from him, if he confesses it[3]
and resolves never to commit again such forbidden
deeds.

41 (142). 'The law of Mazda indeed, O Spitama
Zarathustra! takes away from him who confesses it
the bonds of his sin[4]; it takes away (the sin of)
breach of trust[5]; it takes away (the sin of) murdering one of the faithful[6]; it takes away (the sin
of) burying a corpse[7]; it takes away (the sin of)

---

[1] As he must have known that he was committing sin.

[2] If he did not know that he was committing sin.

[3] If he makes Patet (see Introd. V, 22), and says to himself, 'I
will never henceforth sin again' (Comm.)

[4] If not knowingly committed; see § 40 and the following notes.

[5] Draosha: refusing to give back a deposit (Comm. ad IV, 1):
'He knows that it is forbidden to steal, but he fancies that robbing
the rich to give to the poor is a pious deed' (Comm.)

[6] Or better, 'a Mazdean,' but one who has committed a capital
crime; 'he knows that it is allowed to kill the margarzân, but he
does not know that it is not allowed to do so without an order
from the judge.' Cf. VIII, 74 note.

[7] 'He knows that it is forbidden to bury a corpse; but he fancies
that if one manages so that dogs or foxes may not take it to the fire
and to the water, he behaves piously' (Comm.) See Introd. V, 9.

deeds for which there is no atonement; it takes away the heaviest penalties of sin[1]; it takes away any sin that may be sinned.

42 (149). 'In the same way the law of Mazda, O Spitama Zarathustra! cleanses the faithful from every evil thought, word, and deed, as a swift-rushing mighty wind cleanses the plain[2].

'So let all the deeds thou doest be henceforth good, O Zarathustra! a full atonement for thy sin is effected by means of the law of Mazda.'

FARGARD IV.
Contracts and Outrages.

1–16. Contracts (see Introd. V, 17):—
2. Classification of contracts;
3–4. Damages for breach of contract;
5–10. Kinsmen responsible;
11–16. Penalties for breach of contract.
17–55. Outrages (see Introd. V, 18):—
18–21. Menaces;
22–25. Assaults;
26–29. Blows;
30–33. Wounds;
34–36. Wounds causing blood to flow;
37–39. Broken bones;
40–43. Manslaughter;
46, 49 (bis)–55. False oaths.

Clauses 44–45 refer to contracts, and ought to be placed after § 16. Clauses 47–49, which are in praise of physical weal, have been probably misplaced here from the preceding Fargard (see Farg. III, 33). The right order of this chapter would, therefore, seem to be as follows: 1–16; 44–45; 17–43; 46; 49 (bis)–55.

---

[1] Or, possibly, 'the sin of usury.' 'He knows that it is lawful to take high interest, but he does not know that it is not lawful to do so from the faithful' (Comm.)

[2] 'From chaff' (Comm.)

[4]   D

I.

1. He that does not restore (a thing lent), when it is asked for back again, steals the thing; he robs the man[1]. So he does every day, every night, as long as he keeps in his house his neighbour's property, as though it were his own[2].

II a.

2 (4). O Maker of the material world, thou Holy One! How many in number are thy contracts, O Ahura Mazda?

Ahura Mazda answered: 'They are six in number[3]. The first is the word-contract[4]; the second

---

[1] 'He is a thief when he takes with a view not to restore; he is a robber when, being asked to restore, he answers, I will not' (Comm.)

[2] Every moment that he holds it unlawfully, he steals it anew. 'The basest thing with Persians is to lie; the next to it is to be in debt, for this reason among many others, that he who is so, must needs sink to lying at last' (Herod. I, 183). The debtor in question is of course the debtor of bad faith, 'he who says to a man, Give me this, I will restore it to thee at the proper time, and he says to himself, I will not restore it' (Comm.)

[3] The following classification is in fact twofold, the contracts being defined in the first two clauses by their mode of being entered into, and in the last four by their amount. Yet it appears from the following clauses that even the word-contract and the hand-contract became at last, or were misunderstood as, indicative of a certain amount. The commentators, however, were unable to determine that amount, or, at least, they do not state how much it was, which they do with regard to the last four.

[4] The contract entered into by simple word of mouth. 'The immortal Zartuſt Isfitamân asked of the good, beneficent Hormazd, "Which is the worst of the sins that men commit?" The good, beneficent Hormazd answered, "There is no sin worse than when a man, having given his word to another, there being no witness but myself, Hormazd, one of them breaks his word and says, I don't know anything about it ... there is no sin worse than this "' (Gr. Rav. 94).

is the hand-contract[1]; the third is the contract to
the amount of a sheep[2]; the fourth is the contract
to the amount of an ox[3]; the fifth is the contract to
the amount of a man[4]; the sixth is the contract
to the amount of a field[5], a field in good land, a
fruitful one, in good bearing[6].'

II b.

3 (13). If a man make the word-contract a mere
word[7], it shall be redeemed by the hand-contract;
he shall give in pledge[8] the amount of the hand-
contract.

4 (16). The hand-contract[9] shall be redeemed by
the sheep-contract; he shall give in pledge the
amount of the sheep-contract. The sheep-contract
shall be redeemed by the ox-contract; he shall give
in pledge the amount of the ox-contract. The ox-
contract shall be redeemed by the man-contract; he

---

[1] 'When they strike hand in hand and make then agreement
by word' (Gr. Rav. l. l.)   It would be of interest to know whether
word and hand are to be taken in the strict meaning or if they
allude to certain formulas and gestures like those in the Roman
stipulatio.

[2] 'Viz. to the amount of 3 istîrs [in weight],' (Comm.)   An
istîr (στατήρ) is as much as 4 dirhems (δραχμή).   On the value
of the dirhem, see Introd. V, 22.

[3] 'To the amount of 12 istîrs (=48 dirhems),' (Comm.)

[4] 'To the amount of 500 istîrs (=2000 dirhems).'   The exact
translation would be rather, 'The contract to the amount of a
human being,' as the term is applied to promises of marriage and
to the contract between teacher and pupil.

[5] 'Upwards of 500 istîrs.'

[6] A sort of gloss added to define more accurately the value of
the object and to indicate that it is greater than that of the preceding one.

[7] If he fail to fulfil it.   [8] Or, 'as damages (?).'

[9] The breach of the hand-contract.

shall give in pledge the amount of the man-contract. The man-contract shall be redeemed by the field-contract; he shall give in pledge the amount of the field-contract.

II c.

5 (24). O Maker of the material world, thou Holy One! If a man break the word-contract, how many are involved in his sin[1]?

Ahura Mazda answered: 'His sin makes his Nabânazdistas[2] answerable for the[3] three hundred-fold atonement.'

6 (26). O Maker of the material world, thou Holy One! If a man break the hand-contract, how many are involved in his sin?

Ahura Mazda answered: 'His sin makes his Nabânazdistas answerable for the six hundred-fold atonement[4].'

---

[1] Literally, how much is involved? The joint responsibility of the family was a principle in the Persian law, as it was in the old German law, which agrees with the statement in Am. Marcellinus: 'Leges apud eos impendio formidatae, et abominandae aliae, per quas ob noxam unius omnis propinquitas perit' (XXIII, 6).

[2] The next of kin to the ninth degree.

[3] See § 11. This passage seems to have puzzled tradition. The Commentary says, 'How long, how many years, has one to fear for the breach of a word-contract?—the Nabânazdistas have to fear for three hundred years;' but it does not explain farther the nature of that fear; it only tries to reduce the circle of that liability to narrower limits: 'only the son born after the breach is liable for it; the righteous are not liable for it; when the father dies, the son, if righteous, has nothing to fear from it.' And finally, the Ravaets leave the kinsmen wholly aside; the penalty falling entirely upon the real offender, and the number denoting only the duration of his punishment in hell: 'He who breaks a word-contract, his soul shall abide for three hundred years in hell' (Gr. Rav. 94).

[4] See § 12. 'His soul shall abide for six hundred years in hell' (Gr. Rav. l. l.)

7 (28). O Maker of the material world, thou
Holy One! If a man break the sheep-contract,
how many are involved in his sin?

Ahura Mazda answered: 'His sin makes his
Nabânazdistas answerable for the seven hundred-
fold atonement[1].'

8 (30). O Maker of the material world, thou
Holy One! If a man break the ox-contract, how
many are involved in his sin?

Ahura Mazda answered: 'His sin makes his
Nabânazdistas answerable for the eight hundred-
fold atonement[2].'

9 (32). O Maker of the material world, thou
Holy One! If a man break the man-contract, how
many are involved in his sin?

Ahura Mazda answered: 'His sin makes his
Nabânazdistas answerable for the nine hundred-fold
atonement[3].'

10 (34). O Maker of the material world, thou
Holy One! If a man break the field-contract, how
many are involved in his sin?

Ahura Mazda answered: 'His sin makes his
Nabânazdistas answerable for the thousand-fold
atonement[4].'

II d.

11 (36). O Maker of the material world, thou
Holy One! If a man break the word-contract,
what is the penalty that he shall pay?

Ahura Mazda answered: 'Three hundred stripes

---

[1] See § 13. 'His soul shall abide for seven hundred years in
hell' (Gr. Rav. l. l.)

[2] See § 14. 'His soul shall abide for eight hundred years in hell.'

[3] See § 15. 'His soul shall abide for nine hundred years in hell.'

[4] See § 16. 'His soul shall abide for a thousand years in hell.'

with the Aspahê-astra, three hundred stripes with
the Sraoshô-karana [1].'

12 (39). O Maker of the material world, thou
Holy One! If a man break the hand-contract,
what is the penalty that he shall pay?

Ahura Mazda answered: 'Six hundred stripes
with the Aspahê-astra, six hundred stripes with
the Sraoshô-karana [2].'

13 (42). O Maker of the material world, thou
Holy One! If a man break the sheep-contract,
what is the penalty that he shall pay?

Ahura Mazda answered: 'Seven hundred stripes
with the Aspahê-astra, seven hundred stripes with
the Sraoshô-karana [3].'

14 (45). O Maker of the material world, thou
Holy One! If a man break the ox-contract, what
is the penalty that he shall pay?

Ahura Mazda answered: 'Eight hundred stripes
with the Aspahê-astra, eight hundred stripes with
the Sraoshô-karana [4].'

15 (48). O Maker of the material world, thou
Holy One! If a man break the man-contract, what
is the penalty that he shall pay?

Ahura Mazda answered: 'Nine hundred stripes
with the Aspahê-astra, nine hundred stripes with
the Sraoshô-karana [5].'

16 (51). O Maker of the material world, thou
Holy One! If a man break the field-contract, what
is the penalty that he shall pay?

---

[1] One tanâfûhr and a half, that is 1800 dirhems.
[2] Three tanâfûhrs, or 3600 dirhems.
[3] Three tanâfûhrs and a half, or 4200 dirhems.
[4] Four tanâfûhrs, or 4800 dirhems.
[5] Four tanâfûhrs and a half, or 5400 dirhems.

Ahura Mazda answered: 'A thousand stripes with the Aspahê-a*s*tra, a thousand stripes with the Sraoshô-*k*arana[1].'

III a.

1̣7̣ (54). If a man rise up to smite a man, it is an Âgerepta[2]. If a man come upon a man to smite him, it is an Avaoiri*s*ta. If a man actually smite a man with evil aforethought, it is an Aredu*s*. Upon the fifth Aredu*s*[3] he becomes a Peshôtanu[4].

18 (58). O Maker of the material world, thou Holy One! He that committeth an Âgerepta, what penalty shall he pay?

Ahura Mazda answered: 'Five stripes with the Aspahê-a*s*tra, five stripes with the Sraoshô-*k*arana; on the second Âgerepta, ten stripes with the Aspahê-a*s*tra, ten stripes with the Sraoshô-*k*arana; on the third, fifteen stripes with the Aspahê-a*s*tra, fifteen stripes with the Sraoshô-*k*arana.

19 (63). 'On the fourth, thirty stripes with the

---

[1] Five tanâfûhrs, or 6000 dirhems.

[2] In this paragraph are defined the first three of the eight outrages with which the rest of the Fargard deals. Only these three are defined, because they are designated by technical terms. We subjoin the definitions of them found in a Sanskrit translation of a Patet (Paris, Bibl. Nat. f. B. 5, 154), in which their etymological meanings are better preserved than in the Zend definition itself:—

Âgerepta, 'seizing,' is when a man seizes a weapon with a view to smite another.

Avaoiri*s*ta, 'brandishing,' is when a man brandishes a weapon with a view to smite another.

Aredu*s* is when a man actually smites another with a weapon, but without wounding him, or inflicts a wound which is healed within three days.

[3] Viz. on the sixth commission of it, as appears from § 28.

[4] He shall receive two hundred stripes, or shall pay 1200 dirhems (see Introd. V, 19).

Aspahê-a*s*tra, thirty stripes with the Sraoshô-*k*arana;
on the fifth, fifty stripes with the Aspahê-a*s*tra, fifty
stripes with the Sraoshô-*k*arana; on the sixth, sixty
stripes with the Aspahê-a*s*tra, sixty stripes with the
Sraoshô-*k*arana; on the seventh, ninety stripes with
the Aspahê-a*s*tra, ninety stripes with the Sraoshô-
*k*arana.'

20 (67). If a man commit an Âgerepta for the
eighth time, without having atoned for the preceding, what penalty shall he pay?

Ahura Mazda answered: 'He is a Peshôtanu:
two hundred stripes with the Aspahê-a*s*tra, two
hundred stripes with the Sraoshô-*k*arana.'

21 (70). If a man commit an Âgerepta[1] and refuse
to atone for it[2], what penalty shall he pay?

Ahura Mazda answered: 'He is a Peshôtanu:
two hundred stripes with the Aspahê-a*s*tra, two
hundred stripes with the Sraoshô-*k*arana.'

22 (73). O Maker of the material world, thou
Holy One! If a man commit an Avaoiri*s*ta, what
penalty shall he pay?

Ahura Mazda answered: 'Ten stripes with the
Aspahê-a*s*tra, ten stripes with the Sraoshô-*k*arana;
on the second Avaoiri*s*ta, fifteen stripes with the
Aspahê-a*s*tra, fifteen stripes with the Sraoshô-*k*arana.

23 (75). 'On the third, thirty stripes with the
Aspahê-a*s*tra, thirty stripes with the Sraoshô-*k*arana;
on the fourth, fifty stripes with the Aspahê-a*s*tra,
fifty stripes with the Sraoshô-*k*arana; on the fifth,
seventy stripes with the Aspahê-a*s*tra, seventy

---

[1] Even though the Âgerepta has been committed for the first
time.

[2] If he does not offer himself to bear the penalty, and does not
perform the Patet (see Introd. V, 22).

stripes with the Sraoshô-*k*arana; on the sixth, ninety stripes with the Aspahê-a*s*tra, ninety stripes with the Sraoshô-*k*arana.'

24 (76). O Maker of the material world, thou Holy One! If a man commit an Avaoiri*s*ta for the seventh time, without having atoned for the preceding, what penalty shall he pay?

Ahura Mazda answered: 'He is a Peshôtanu: two hundred stripes with the Aspahê-a*s*tra, two hundred stripes with the Sraoshô-*k*arana.'

25 (77). O Maker of the material world, thou Holy One! If a man commit an Avaoiri*s*ta, and refuse to atone for it, what penalty shall he pay?

Ahura Mazda answered: 'He is a Peshôtanu: two hundred stripes with the Aspahê-a*s*tra, two hundred stripes with the Sraoshô-*k*arana.'

26 (79). O Maker of the material world, thou Holy One! If a man commit an Aredu*s*, what penalty shall he pay?

Ahura Mazda answered: 'Fifteen stripes with the Aspahê-a*s*tra, fifteen stripes with the Sraoshô-*k*arana.

27 (81). 'On the second Aredu*s*, thirty stripes with the Aspahê-a*s*tra, thirty stripes with the Sraoshô-*k*arana; on the third, fifty stripes with the Aspahê-a*s*tra, fifty stripes with the Sraoshô-*k*arana; on the fourth, seventy stripes with the Aspahê-a*s*tra, seventy stripes with the Sraoshô-*k*arana; on the fifth, ninety stripes with the Aspahê-a*s*tra, ninety stripes with the Sraoshô-*k*arana.'

28. O Maker of the material world, thou Holy One! If a man commit an Aredu*s* for the sixth time, without having atoned for the preceding, what penalty shall he pay?

Ahura Mazda answered: 'He is a Peshôtanu: two hundred stripes with the Aspahê-astra, two hundred stripes with the Sraoshô-karana.'

29 (82). O Maker of the material world, thou Holy One! If a man commit an Aredus, and refuse to atone for it, what penalty shall he pay?

Ahura Mazda answered: 'He is a Peshôtanu: two hundred stripes with the Aspahê-astra, two hundred stripes with the Sraoshô-karana.'

30 (85). O Maker of the material world, thou Holy One! If a man smite another and hurt him sorely, what is the penalty that he shall pay?

31 (87). Ahura Mazda answered: 'Thirty stripes with the Aspahê-astra, thirty stripes with the Sraoshô-karana; the second time, fifty stripes with the Aspahê-astra, fifty stripes with the Sraoshô-karana; the third time, seventy stripes with the Aspahê-astra, seventy stripes with the Sraoshô-karana; the fourth time, ninety stripes with the Aspahê-astra, ninety stripes with the Sraoshô-karana.'

32 (89). If a man commit that deed for the fifth time, without having atoned for the preceding, what is the penalty that he shall pay?

Ahura Mazda answered: 'He is a Peshôtanu: two hundred stripes with the Aspahê-astra, two hundred stripes with the Sraoshô-karana.'

33 (90). If a man commit that deed and refuse to atone for it, what is the penalty that he shall pay?

Ahura Mazda answered: 'He is a Peshôtanu: two hundred stripes with the Aspahê-astra, two hundred stripes with the Sraoshô-karana.'

34 (93). O Maker of the material world, thou Holy One! If a man smite another so that the

blood comes, what is the penalty that he shall pay?

Ahura Mazda answered : ' Fifty stripes with the Aspahê-astra, fifty stripes with the Sraoshô-karana ; the second time, seventy stripes with the Aspahê-astra, seventy stripes with the Sraoshô-karana ; the third time, ninety stripes with the Aspahê-astra, ninety stripes with the Sraoshô-karana.'

35 (95). If he commit that deed for the fourth time, without having atoned for the preceding, what is the penalty that he shall pay?

Ahura Mazda answered : ' He is a Peshôtanu : two hundred stripes with the Aspahê-astra, two hundred stripes with the Sraoshô-karana.'

36 (96). O Maker of the material world, thou Holy One! If a man smite another so that the blood comes, and if he refuse to atone for it, what is the penalty that he shall pay?

Ahura Mazda answered : ' He is a Peshôtanu : two hundred stripes with the Aspahê-astra, two hundred stripes with the Sraoshô-karana.'

37 (99). O Maker of the material world, thou Holy One! If a man smite another so that he breaks a bone, what is the penalty that he shall pay?

Ahura Mazda answered : ' Seventy stripes with the Aspahê-astra, seventy stripes with the Sraoshô-karana ; the second time, ninety stripes with the Aspahê-astra, ninety stripes with the Sraoshô-karana.'

38 (102). If he commit that deed for the third time, without having atoned for the preceding, what is the penalty that he shall pay?

Ahura Mazda answered : ' He is a Peshôtanu :

two hundred stripes with the Aspahê-astra, two hundred stripes with the Sraoshô-karana.'

39 (104). O Maker of the material world, thou Holy One! If a man smite another so that he breaks a bone, and if he refuse to atone for it, what is the penalty that he shall pay?

Ahura Mazda answered: 'He is a Peshôtanu: two hundred stripes with the Aspahê-astra, two hundred stripes with the Sraoshô-karana.'

40 (106). O Maker of the material world, thou Holy One! If a man smite another so that he gives up the ghost, what is the penalty that he shall pay?

Ahura Mazda answered: 'Ninety stripes with the Aspahê-astra, ninety stripes with the Sraoshô-karana.'

41 (109). If he commit that deed again, without having atoned for the preceding, what is the penalty that he shall pay?

Ahura Mazda answered: 'He is a Peshôtanu: two hundred stripes with the Aspahê-astra, two hundred stripes with the Sraoshô-karana.'

42 (112). O Maker of the material world, thou Holy One! If a man smite another so that he gives up the ghost, and if he refuse to atone for it, what is the penalty that he shall pay?

Ahura Mazda answered: 'He is a Peshôtanu: two hundred stripes with the Aspahê-astra, two hundred stripes with the Sraoshô-karana.'

43 (115). And they shall thenceforth in their doings walk after the way of holiness, after the word of holiness, after the ordinance of holiness.

II e [1].

44 (118). If men of the same faith, either friends or brothers, come to an agreement together, that one may obtain from the other, either goods [2], or a wife [3], or knowledge [4], let him who wants to have goods have them delivered to him; let him who wants to have a wife receive and wed her; let him who wants to have knowledge be taught the holy word.

45 (123). He shall learn on, during the first part of the day and the last, during the first part of the night and the last, that his mind may be increased in knowledge and wax strong in holiness : so shall he sit up, giving thanks and praying to the gods, that he may be increased in knowledge : he shall rest during the middle part of the day, during the middle part of the night, and thus shall he continue until he can say all the words which former Aêthra-paitis [5] have said.

III b.

46 (128). Before the water and the blazing fire [6],

---

[1] We return here to contracts; the proper place of §§ 44–45 is after § 16.

[2] The goods-contract is a general expression for the sheep, ox, and field-contracts (see above, § 2).

[3] Woman is an object of contract, like cattle or fields ; she is disposed of by contracts of the fifth sort, being more valuable than cattle and less so than fields. She is sold by her father or her guardian, often from the cradle. ' Instances are not wanting of the betrothal of a boy of three years of age to a girl of two' (see Dosabhoy Framjee's work on The Parsees, p. 77; cf. 'A Bill to Define and Amend the Law relating to Succession, Inheritance, Marriage, &c.,' Bombay, 1864).

[4] The contract between pupil and teacher falls into the same class (the man-contract, see p. 35, n. 4).

[5] A teaching priest (Parsi Hêrbad).

[6] Doubtful. This clause is intended, as it seems, against false

O Spitama Zarathuʃtra! let no one make bold to
deny having received from his neighbour the ox or
the garment (he has received from him).

47 (130). . . . Verily I say it unto thee, O Spitama
Zarathuʃtra! the man who has a wife is far above
him who begets no sons[1]; he who keeps a house is
far above him who has none; he who has children
is far above the childless man; he who has riches is
far above him who has none.

48 (134). And of two men, he who fills himself
with meat is filled with the good spirit[2] much more
than he who does not do so[3]; the latter is all but
dead; the former is above him by the worth of an
Asperena[4], by the worth of a sheep, by the worth
of an ox, by the worth of a man.

49 (137). It is this man that can strive against
the onsets of Astô-vîdhôtu[5]; that can strive against

---

oaths. The water and the blazing fire are the water and the fire
before which the oath is taken (see § 54 n.); putting aside §§ 47–49,
which are misplaced from Farg. III, 34, one comes to § 50, in
which the penalty for a false oath is described.

[1] 'In Persia there are prizes given by the king to those who
have most children' (Herod. I, 136). 'He who has no child, the
bridge (of paradise) shall be barred to him. The first question the
angels there will ask him is, whether he has left in this world a sub-
stitute for himself; if he answers, No, they will pass by and he will
stay at the head of the bridge, full of grief and sorrow' (Saddar 18;
Hyde 19). The primitive meaning of this belief is explained by
Brahmanical doctrine; the man without a son falls into hell, because
there is nobody to pay him the family worship.

[2] Or, 'with Vôhu Manô,' who is at the same time the god of
good thoughts and the god of cattle (see Introd. IV, 33).

[3] 'There are people who strive to pass a day without eating,
and who abstain from any meat; we strive too and abstain, namely,
from any sin in deed, thought, or word: . . . in other religions, they
fast from bread; in ours, we fast from sin' (Saddar 83; Hyde 25).

[4] A dirhem.   [5] See Introd. IV, 26.

the self-moving arrow [1]; that can strive against the winter fiend, with thinnest garment on; that can strive against the wicked tyrant and smite him on the head; it is this man that can strive against the ungodly Ashemaogha who does not eat [2].

---

49 (bis).... The very first time when that deed [3] has been done, without waiting until it is done again [4].

50 (143). Down there [5] the pain for that deed shall be as hard as any in this world: should one cut off the limbs from his perishable body with knives of brass, yet still worse shall it be.

51 (146). Down there the pain for that deed shall be as hard as any in this world: should one nail [6] his perishable body with nails of brass, yet still worse shall it be.

52 (149). Down there the pain for that deed shall be as hard as any in this world: should one by force throw his perishable body headlong down a precipice a hundred times the height of a man, yet still worse shall it be.

53 (152). Down there the pain for that deed shall be as hard as any in this world: should one by force impale [7] his perishable body, yet still worse shall it be.

54 (154). Down there the pain for that deed shall be as hard as any in this world: to wit, that deed which is done, when a man, knowingly lying, confronts the brimstoned, golden [8], truth-knowing [9]

---

[1] See Introd. IV, 26. [2] See Introd. III, 10.
[3] The taking of a false oath. [4] See Introd. V, 18.
[5] In hell. [6] Doubtful. [7] Doubtful.
[8] The water before which the oath is taken contains some incense, brimstone, and one danak of molten gold (Gr. Rav. 101).
[9] Doubtful. Possibly 'bright.'

water with an appeal unto Rashnu[1] and a lie unto
Mithra[2].

55 (156). O Maker of the material world, thou
Holy One! He who, knowingly lying, confronts the
brimstoned, golden, truth-knowing water with an
appeal unto Rashnu and a lie unto Mithra, what is
the penalty that he shall pay[3]?

Ahura Mazda answered: 'Seven hundred stripes
with the Aspahê-astra, seven hundred stripes with
the Sraoshô-karana.'

FARGARD V.

This chapter and the following ones, to the end of the twelfth,
deal chiefly with uncleanness arising from the dead, and with the
means of removing it from men and things.

The subjects treated in this Fargard are as follows :—

I (1–7). If a man defile the fire or the earth involuntarily, or
unconsciously, it is no sin.

II (8–9). Water and fire do not kill.

III (10–14). Disposal of the dead during winter.

IV (15–20). How the Dakhmas are cleansed by water from the
heavens.

V (21–26). On the excellence of purity and of the law that
shows how to recover it, when lost.

VI (27–38). On the defiling power of the Nasu being greater or
less, according to the greater or less dignity of the being that dies.

VII (39–44). On the management of sacrificial implements
defiled by the dead.

---

[1] The god of truth. The formula is as follows: 'Before the
Amshaspand Bahman, before the Amshaspand Ardibehesht, here
lighted up . . . &c., I swear that I have nothing of what is thine,
N. son of N., neither gold, nor silver, nor brass, nor clothes, nor
any of the things created by Ormazd' (l. l. 96).

[2] See Introd. IV, 8. He is a Mithra-drug, 'one who lies to
Mithra.'

[3] In this world.

VIII (45–62). On the treatment of a woman who has been delivered of a still-born child; and what is to be done with her clothes.

I a.

1. There dies a man in the depths of the vale: a bird takes flight from the top of the mountain down into the depths of the vale, and it eats up the corpse of the dead man there: then, up it flies from the depths of the vale to the top of the mountain: it flies to some one of the trees there, of the hard-wooded or the soft-wooded, and upon that tree it vomits, it deposits dung, it drops pieces from the corpse.

2 (7). Now, lo! here is a man coming up from the depths of the vale to the top of the mountain; he comes to the tree whereon the bird is sitting; from that tree he wants to take wood for the fire. He fells the tree, he hews the tree, he splits it into logs, and then he lights it in the fire, the son of Ahura Mazda. What is the penalty that he shall pay[1]?

3 (11). Ahura Mazda answered: 'There is no sin upon a man for any dead matter that has been brought by dogs, by birds, by wolves, by winds, or by flies.

4 (12). 'For were there sin upon a man for any dead matter that might have been brought by dogs, by birds, by wolves, by winds, or by flies, how soon this material world of mine would have in it only Peshôtanus[2], shut out from the way of holiness,

---

[1] For defiling the fire by bringing dead matter into it, see Farg. VII, 25 seq. The Vendîdâd Sâdah has here, 'Put ye only proper and well-examined fuel (in the fire).' For the purification of unclean wood, see Farg. VII, 28 seq.

[2] 'People guilty of death' (Comm.; cf. Introd. V, 19).

whose souls will cry and wail[1]! so numberless are
the beings that die upon the face of the earth.'

I b.

5 (15). O Maker of the material world, thou
Holy One! Here is a man watering a corn field.
The water streams down the field; it streams again;
it streams a third time; and the fourth time, a dog,
a fox, or a wolf carries a corpse into the bed of the
stream: what is the penalty that the man shall
pay[2]?

6 (19). Ahura Mazda answered: 'There is no
sin upon a man for any dead matter that has been
brought by dogs, by birds, by wolves, by winds, or
by flies.

7 (20). 'For were there sin upon a man for any
dead matter that might have been brought by dogs,
by birds, by wolves, by winds, or by flies, how soon
this material world of mine would have in it only
Peshôtanus, shut out from the way of holiness,
whose souls will cry and wail! so numberless are
the beings that die upon the face of the earth.'

II a.

8 (23). O Maker of the material world, thou
Holy One! Does water kill[3]?

---

[1] After their death, 'When the soul, crying and beaten off, is
driven far away from paradise' (Comm.) Possibly, 'Whose soul
shall fly (from paradise) amid howls' (cf. Farg. XIII, 8).

[2] For defiling the earth and the water: 'If a man wants to irri-
gate a field, he must first look after the water-channel, whether
there is dead matter in it or not. . . . . If the water, unknown to
him, comes to a corpse, there is no sin upon him. If he has not
looked after the rivulet and the stream, he is unclean' (Saddar 75;
Hyde 85).

[3] Water and fire belong to the holy part of the world, and come

Ahura Mazda answered: 'Water kills no man: Astô-vîdhôtu[1] ties the noose around his neck, and, thus tied, Vaya[2] carries him off: then the flood takes him up[3], the flood takes him down[4], the flood throws him ashore; then birds feed upon him, and chance brings him here, or brings him there[5].'

II b.

9 (29). O Maker of the material world, thou Holy One! Does fire kill?

Ahura Mazda answered: 'Fire kills no man: Astô-vîdhôtu ties the noose around his neck, and, thus tied, Vaya carries him off. The fire burns up life and limb, and then chance brings him here, or brings him there[6].'

III.

10 (34). O Maker of the material world, thou Holy One! If the summer is past and the winter has come, what shall the worshippers of Mazda do[7]?

---

from God: how then is it that they kill? 'Let a Gueber light a sacred fire for a hundred years, if he once fall into it, he shall be burnt.' Even the Mobeds, if we may trust Elisaeus, complained that the fire would burn them without regard for their piety, when to adore it they came too near (Vartan's War, p. 211 of the French translation by l'Abbé Garabed). The answer was that it is not the fire nor the water that kills, but the demon of Death and Fate. 'Nothing whatever that I created in the world, said Ormazd, does harm to man; it is the bad Nâi (lege Vâi) that kills the man' (Gr. Rav. 124).

[1] Literally, 'binds him;' see Introd. IV, 26; cf. Farg. XIX, 29.
[2] 'The bad Vâi' (Comm.); see Introd. IV, 17.
[3] To the surface.   [4] To the bottom.
[5] Or perhaps, 'When he departs, it is by the will of Destiny that he departs' (Comm.)
[6] See preceding note.
[7] In case a man dies during the snowy season, while it is diffi-

E 2

Ahura Mazda answered: 'In every house, in every borough[1], they shall raise three small houses for the dead[2].'

11 (37). O Maker of the material world, thou Holy One! How large shall be those houses for the dead?

Ahura Mazda answered: 'Large enough not to strike the skull, or the feet, or the hands of the man, if he[3] should stand erect, and hold out his feet, and stretch out his hands: such shall be, according to the law, the houses for the dead.

12 (41). 'And they shall let the lifeless body lie there, for two nights, or for three nights, or a month long, until the birds begin to fly[4], the plants to grow, the floods to flow, and the wind to dry up the waters from off the earth[5].

13 (44). 'And as soon as the birds begin to fly, the plants to grow, the floods to flow, and the wind to dry up the waters from off the earth, then the worshippers of Mazda shall lay down the dead (on the Dakhma) his eyes towards the sun.

14 (46). 'If the worshippers of Mazda have not, within a year, laid down the dead (on the Dakhma),

cult or impossible to take the corpse to the Dakhma, which usually stands far from inhabited places. The same case is treated more clearly and fully in Farg. VIII, 4 seq.

[1] In every isolated house, in every group of houses.

[2] Thence is derived the modern usage of the Zâd-marg, a small mud house where the corpse is laid, to lie there till it can be taken to the Dakhma (Anquetil, Zend-Avesta II, 583). The object of that provision is to remove the uncleanness of the dead from the place of the living. An older form of the same provision is found in Farg. VIII, 8.

[3] 'Being in life' (Comm.)   [4] To come back.

[5] 'Until the winter is past' (Comm.)

his eyes towards the sun, thou shalt prescribe for
that trespass the same penalty as for the murder of
one of the faithful.   [And there shall it lie] until
the corpse has been rained on, until the Dakhma
has been rained on, until the unclean remains have
been rained on, until the birds have eaten up the
corpse.'

IV.

15 (49). O Maker of the material world, thou
Holy One! Is it true that thou, Ahura Mazda,
sendest the waters from the sea Vouru-kasha [1]
down with the wind and with the clouds?

16 (51). That thou, Ahura Mazda, makest them
flow down to the corpses[2]? that thou, Ahura Mazda,
makest them flow down to the Dakhmas? that thou,
Ahura Mazda, makest them flow down to the unclean remains? that thou, Ahura Mazda, makest
them flow down to the bones? and that then thou,
Ahura Mazda, makest them flow back unseen? that
thou, Ahura Mazda, makest them flow back to the
sea Pûitika [3]?

17 (53). Ahura Mazda answered: 'It is even so

---

[1] The sea above, the clouds.   See Introd. IV, 11.

[2] Zoroaster seems to wonder that Ormazd fears so little to in-
fringe his own laws by defiling waters with the dead. In a Ravaet,
he asks him bluntly why he forbids men to take corpses to the
water, while he himself sends rain to the Dakhmas (Gr. Rav. 125).

[3] The sea where waters are purified before going back to their
heavenly seat, the sea Vouru-kasha (see § 19). Pûitika, 'the
clean,' is very likely to have been originally a name or epithet of
the sea Vouru-kasha.   When the mythic geography of Mazdeism
was reduced into a system, the epithet took a separate existence, as
it gave a ready answer to that question, which, it may be, was
raised first by the name itself: 'Where are the waters cleansed
which have been defiled here below, and which we see falling again
to us pure and clean?'

as thou hast said, O righteous Zarathustra! I,
Ahura Mazda, send the waters from the sea Vouru-
kasha down with the wind and with the clouds.

18 (55). ' I, Ahura Mazda, make them stream
down to the corpses; I, Ahura Mazda, make them
stream down to the Dakhmas; I, Ahura Mazda,
make them stream down to the unclean remains; I,
Ahura Mazda, make them stream down to the
bones; then I, Ahura Mazda, make them flow back
unseen; I, Ahura Mazda, make them flow back to
the sea Pûitika [1].

19 (56). ' The waters stand there boiling, boiling
up in the heart of the sea Pûitika, and, when
cleansed there, they run back again from the sea
Pûitika to the sea Vouru-kasha, towards the well-
watered tree [2], whereon grow the seeds of my
plants of every kind [by hundreds, by thousands, by
hundreds of thousands].

20 (60). ' Those plants, I, Ahura Mazda, rain
down upon the earth [2], to bring food to the faithful,
and fodder to the beneficent cow; to bring food to
my people that they may live on it, and fodder to
the beneficent cow.'

---

[1] In later mythology, the sea Vouru-kasha and the sea Pûitika
were assimilated to the Arabian sea and to the gulf of Oman: the
moving to and fro of the waters from heaven to earth and from
the earth to heaven was interpreted as the coming and going of
the tide (Bund. XIII).

[2] The tree of all seeds (Harvisptokhm), which grows in the
middle of the sea Vouru-kasha; the seeds of all plants are on it.
There is a godlike bird, the Sinamru, sitting on that tree; whenever he flies off the tree, there grow out of it a thousand boughs;
whenever he alights on it, there break a thousand boughs, the seeds
of which are scattered about, and rained down on the earth by
Tistar (Tistrya), the rain-god (Yt. XII, 17; Minokhired LXII, 37
seq.; Bundahis XXVII; cf. Farg. XX, 4 seq.)

V.

21 (63). 'This[1] is the best of all things, this is the fairest of all things, even as thou hast said, O righteous Zarathustra!'

With these words the holy Ahura Mazda rejoiced the holy Zarathustra[2]: 'Purity is for man, next to life, the greatest good[3], that purity that is procured by the law of Mazda to him who cleanses his own self with good thoughts, words, and deeds[4].'

22 (68). O Maker of the material world, thou Holy One! This law, this fiend-destroying law of Zarathustra, by what greatness, goodness, and fairness is it great, good, and fair above all other utterances?

23 (69). Ahura Mazda answered: 'As much above all other floods as is the sea Vouru-kasha, so much above all other utterances in greatness, goodness, and fairness is this law, this fiend-destroying law of Zarathustra.

24 (71). 'As much as a great stream flows swifter than a slender rivulet, so much above all other utterances in greatness, goodness, and fairness is this law, this fiend-destroying law of Zarathustra.

'As high as the great tree[5] stands above the small plants it overshadows, so high above all other

---

[1] The cleansing, the purification.

[2] 'When Zoroaster saw that man is able to escape sin by performing good works, he was filled with joy' (Comm.)

[3] As uncleanness is nothing less than a form of death (see Introd. V, 3).

[4] That is to say, 'Who performs the rites of cleansing according to the prescriptions of the law.'

[5] 'The royal cypress above small herbs' (Comm.)

utterances in greatness, goodness, and fairness is this
law, this fiend-destroying law of Zarathuꭍtra.

25, 26 (73–81). 'As high as heaven is above the
earth that it compasses around, so high above all
other utterances is this law, this fiend-destroying law
of Mazda.

'[Therefore], when the Ratu has been applied to [1],
when the Sraoshâ-varez has been applied to [2];
whether for a draona-service [3] that has been undertaken [4], or for one that has not been undertaken [5];
whether for a draona that has been offered up, or
for one that has not been offered up; whether for a
draona that has been shared, or for one that has
not been shared [6]; the Ratu has power to remit. him

---

[1] 'To take the rule' (Comm.), which probably means, 'to know
what sort of penance he must undergo;' as, when a man has
sinned with the tongue or with the hand, the Dastur (or Ratu) must
prescribe for him the expiation that the sin requires. The Ratu is
the chief priest, the spiritual head of the community.

[2] 'To weep for his crime' (Comm.), which may mean, 'to recite
to him the Patet, or, to receive at his hand the proper number of
stripes.' It is difficult to say exactly what were the functions of the
Sraoshâ-varez, which seem to have been twofold. The cock is
compared to him, as being 'the one who sets the world in motion,'
and wakes men for prayer (Farg. XVIII, 14, text and note),
which would make him a sort of Zoroastrian Muezzin; at the same
time he is the priest of penance. His name may refer to either of
his functions, according as it is translated, 'the one who causes
hearing,' or 'the executor of punishment;' in the first case he
would be the priest who pronounces the favete linguis, the
ꭍrâushaꬵ; in the other case he would be the priest who wields
the Sraoshô-ꬵarana (see Introd. V, 19).

[3] A service in honour of any of the angels, or of deceased persons, in which small cakes, called draona, are consecrated in their
names, and then given to those present to eat.

[4] When it ought not to be.

[5] When it ought to be.

[6] The meaning of the sentence is not certain; it alludes to

one-third of the penalty he had to pay[1]: if he has committed any other evil deed, it is remitted by his repentance; if he has committed no other evil deed, he is absolved by his repentance for ever and ever[2].'

VI.

27 (82). O Maker of the material world, thou Holy One! If there be a number of men resting in the same place, on adjoining carpets, on adjoining pillows, be there two men near one another, or five, or fifty, or a hundred, close by one another; and of those people one happens to die; how many of them does the Drug Nasu envelope with infection, pollution, and uncleanness[3]?

28 (86). Ahura Mazda answered: 'If the dead one be a priest, the Drug Nasu rushes forth[4], O Spitama Zarathustra! she falls on the eleventh and defiles the ten[5].

---

religious customs which are not well known. The Commentary interprets it as amounting to, ' Whether he has thought what he ought not to have thought, or has not thought what he ought to have thought; whether he has said what he ought not to have said, or has not said what he ought to have said; whether he has done what he ought not to have done, or has not done what he ought to have done.'

[1] When the Ratu remits one-third of the sin, God remits the whole of it (Saddar 29).

[2] Cf. Farg. III, 21.   [3] See Introd. V, 3.

[4] In opposition to the case when the dead one is an Ashe-maogha (§ 35), as no Nasu issues then.

[5] Literally, ' If she falls on the eleventh, she defiles the tenth.' The word if refers to the supposition that there are eleven persons at least, and the words ' she defiles the tenth' must be understood to mean ' she defiles to the tenth.' In the Ravaets, the Avesta distinctions are lost, and the defiling power of the Nasu is the same, whatever may have been the rank of the dead: ' If there be a

'If the dead one be a warrior, the Dru*g* Nasu
rushes forth, O Spitama Zarathu*s*tra! she falls on
the tenth and defiles the nine.

'If the dead one be a husbandman, the Dru*g*
Nasu rushes forth, O Spitama Zarathu*s*tra! she
falls on the ninth and defiles the eight.

29 (92). 'If it be a shepherd's dog, the Dru*g*
Nasu rushes forth, O Spitama Zarathu*s*tra! 'she
falls on the eighth and defiles the seven.

'If it be a house dog, the Dru*g* Nasu rushes
forth, O Spitama Zarathu*s*tra! she falls on the
seventh and defiles the six.

30 (96). 'If it be a Vohunazga dog[1], the Dru*g*
Nasu rushes forth, O Spitama Zarathu*s*tra! she
falls on the sixth and defiles the five.

'If it be a young dog[2], the Dru*g* Nasu rushes
forth, O Spitama Zarathu*s*tra! she falls on the fifth
and defiles the four.

31 (100). 'If it be a Sukuruna dog[3], the Dru*g*
Nasu rushes forth, O Spitama Zarathu*s*tra! she
falls on the fourth and defiles the three.

'If it be a *Ga*zu dog[4], the Dru*g* Nasu rushes
forth, O Spitama Zarathu*s*tra! she falls on the
third and defiles the two.

32 (104). 'If it be an Aiwizu dog, the Dru*g*

---

number of people sleeping in the same place, and if one of them
happen to die, all those around him, in any direction, as far as the
eleventh, become unclean if they have been in contact with one
another' (Gr. Rav. 470).

[1] A dog without a master (see Farg. XIII, 19).

[2] A dog not more than four months old.

[3] According to Aspendiârji, a siyâ-gosh, or 'black-eared'
lynx, the messenger of the lion.

[4] This name and the two following, Aiwizu and Vîzu, are left
untranslated, not being clear, in the Pahlavi translation.

Nasu rushes forth, O Spitama Zarathustra! she falls on the second and defiles the next.

'If it be a Vîzu dog, the Drug Nasu rushes forth, O Spitama Zarathustra! she falls on the next, she defiles the next.'

33 (108). O Maker of the material world, thou Holy One! If it be an Urupi dog[1], how many of the creatures of the good spirit does it directly defile, how many does it indirectly defile in dying?

34 (110). Ahura Mazda answered: 'An Urupi dog does neither directly nor indirectly defile any of the creatures of the good spirit, but him who smites and kills it; to him the uncleanness clings for ever and ever[2].'

35 (113). O Maker of the material world, thou Holy One! If the dead one be a wicked, two-footed ruffian, an ungodly Ashemaogha[3], how many of the creatures of the good spirit does he directly defile, how many does he indirectly defile in dying?

36 (115). Ahura Mazda answered: 'No more than a frog does whose venom is dried up, and that has been dead more than a year[4]. Whilst alive, indeed, O Spitama Zarathustra! that wicked, two-

---

[1] A weasel. The weasel is one of the creatures of Ahura, for 'it has been created to fight against the serpent garza and the other khrafstras that live in holes' (Bund. 47, 8).

[2] Not that the unclean one cannot be cleansed, but that his uncleanness does not pass from him to another.

[3] See Introd. IV, 10; V, 11.

[4] The frog is a creature of Ahriman's, and one of the most hateful; for, in the sea Vouru-kasha, it goes swimming around the white Hom, the tree of everlasting life, and would gnaw it down, but for the godlike fish Kar-mâhî, that keeps watch and guards the tree wherever the frog would slip in (Bund. XVIII; cf. Orm. Ahr. § 146).

legged ruffian, that ungodly Ashemaogha, directly defiles the creatures of the good spirit, and indirectly defiles them.

37 (119). 'Whilst alive he smites the water[1]; whilst alive he blows out the fire[2]; whilst alive he carries off the cow[3]; whilst alive he smites the faithful man with a deadly blow, that parts the soul from the body[4]; not so will he do when dead.

38 (120). 'Whilst alive, indeed, O Spitama Zarathustra! that wicked, two-legged ruffian, that ungodly Ashemaogha, never ceases depriving the faithful man of his food, of his clothing, of his house, of his bed, of his vessels[5]; not so will he do when dead.'

VII.

39 (122). O Maker of the material world, thou Holy One! When into our houses here below we have brought the fire, the baresma, the cups, the Haoma, and the mortar[6], O holy Ahura Mazda! if it come to pass that either a dog or a man dies there, what shall the worshippers of Mazda do?

40 (125). Ahura Mazda answered: 'Out of the house, O Spitama Zarathustra! shall they take the fire, the baresma, the cups, the Haoma, and the mortar; they shall take the dead one out to the proper place[7] whereto, according to the law, corpses must be brought, to be devoured there.'

41 (128). O Maker of the material world, thou

---

[1] By defiling it (a capital crime; see Introd. V, 8, and Farg. VII, 25).

[2] He extinguishes the Bahrâm fire (a capital crime; Introd. V, 8).

[3] As a cattle-lifter.   [4] As an assassin.

[5] By defiling or by stealing them.

[6] In order to perform a sacrifice.   [7] The Dakhma.

Holy One! When shall they bring back the fire into the house wherein the man has died?

42 (129). Ahura Mazda answered: 'They shall wait for nine nights in winter, for a month in summer, and then they shall bring back the fire to the house wherein the man has died.'

43 (131). O Maker of the material world, thou Holy One! And if they shall bring back the fire to the house wherein the man has died, within the nine nights, or within the month, what penalty shall they pay?

44 (134). Ahura Mazda answered: 'They shall be Peshôtanus: two hundred stripes with the Aspahê-astra, two hundred stripes with the Sraoshô-karana.'

VIII.

45 (135)[1]. O Maker of the material world, thou Holy One! If in the house of a worshipper of Mazda there be a woman with child, and if being a month gone, or two, or three, or four, or five, or six, or seven, or eight, or nine, or ten months gone, she bring forth a still-born child, what shall the worshippers of Mazda do?

46 (139). Ahura Mazda answered: 'The place in that Mazdean house whereof the ground is the cleanest and the driest, and the least passed through by flocks and herds, by Fire, the son of Ahura Mazda, by the consecrated bundles of baresma, and by the faithful;'—

47 (143). O Maker of the material world, thou Holy One! How far from the fire? How far from the water? How far from the consecrated bundles of baresma? How far from the faithful?

---

[1] §§ 45–54 = Farg. VII, 60–69.

48 (144). Ahura Mazda answered : 'Thirty paces from the fire; thirty paces from the water; thirty paces from the consecrated bundles of baresma; three paces from the faithful;—

49 (145). 'On that place shall the worshippers of Mazda erect an enclosure[1], and therein shall they establish her with food, therein shall they establish her with clothes.'

50 (147). O Maker of the material world, thou Holy One! What is the food that the woman shall first take ?

51 (148). Ahura Mazda answered : 'She shall drink gômêz[2] mixed with ashes, three cups of it, or six, or nine, to wash over the grave within her womb.

52 (151). 'Afterwards she may drink boiling[3] milk of mares, cows, sheep, or goats, with pap or without pap[4]; she may take cooked meat without water, bread without water, and wine without water[5].'

53 (154). O Maker of the material world, thou Holy One! How long shall she remain so ? How long shall she live only on that sort of meat, bread, and wine ?

54 (155). Ahura Mazda answered: 'Three nights

---

[1] The Armêst-gâh (cf. Farg. III, 15 seq., and Introd. V, 15).

[2] Urine of the ox : it destroys the Nasu in her womb (Introd. V, 5). The ashes work to the same end, as they are taken from the Bahrâm fire (Comm.), the earthly representative of the fire of lightning, and the most powerful destroyer of fiends (see Introd. V, 8, and Farg. VIII, 80 seq.) 'Three cups, or six, or nine, according to her strength' (Asp.)

[3] Doubtful.   [4] Doubtful.

[5] See Introd. V, 13. 'The water would be defiled;' cf. Farg. VII, 70 seq.

long shall she remain so; three nights long shall she
live on that sort of meat, bread, and wine. Then,
when three nights have passed, she shall wash her
body, she shall wash her clothes, with gômêz and
water, by the nine holes[1], and thus shall she be
clean.'

55 (157). O Maker of the material world, thou
Holy One! How long shall she remain so? How
long, after the three nights have gone, shall she sit
confined, and live separated from the rest of the
worshippers of Mazda, as to her seat, her food, and
her clothing?

56 (158). Ahura Mazda answered: 'Nine nights
long shall she remain so: nine nights long, after the
three nights have gone, shall she sit confined, and
live separated from the rest of the worshippers of
Mazda, as to her seat, her food, and her clothing.
Then, when the nine nights have gone, she shall
wash her body, and cleanse her clothes with gômêz
and water[2].'

57 (160)[3]. O Maker of the material world, thou
Holy One! Can those clothes, when once washed
and cleansed, ever be used either by a Zaotar, or by
a Hâvanan, or by an Âtare-vakhsha, or by a Frabaretar, or by an Âbered, or by an Âsnâtar, or by a

---

[1] She shall perform the nine nights' Barashnûm, for the
details of which see Farg. IX.

[2] The modern custom is somewhat different: 'If a woman
brings forth a still-born child, after a pregnancy of one month to
ten months, the first food she shall take is nîrang (=gômêz) . . .
fire and ashes; and she is not allowed until the fourth day to take
water or salt, or any food that is cooked with water or salt: on the
fourth day they give her nîrang, that she may cleanse herself and
wash her clothes with it, and she is not allowed to wash herself and
her clothes with water until the forty-first day' (Gr. Rav. 568).

[3] §§ 57-62=Farg. VII, 17-22.

Rathwiskar, or by a Sraoshâ-varez[1], or by any priest, warrior, or husbandman[2]?

58 (162). Ahura Mazda answered: 'Never can those clothes, even when washed and cleansed, be used either by a Zaotar, or by a Hâvanan, or by an Âtare-vakhsha, or by a Frabaretar, or by an Âbered, or by an Âsnâtar, or by a Rathwiskar, or by a Sraoshâ-varez, or by any priest, warrior, or husbandman.

59 (164). 'But if there be in a Mazdean house a woman who is in her sickness, or a man who has become unfit for work[3], and who must sit in the place of infirmity[4], those clothes shall serve for their coverings and for their sheets[5], until they can withdraw and move their hands[6].

---

[1] These are the names of the different priests who were engaged in the sacrifices. The Hâvanan strains the Haoma; the Âtare-vakhsha kindles the fire; the Frabaretar brings all that is necessary for the sacrifice (Anquetil); the Âbered brings the water (Anquetil and Zand-Pahlavi Glossary, 21); the Âsnâtar cleanses the vessels. Those are the priests who are entrusted with the preparatory or accessory proceedings; the essential duties are performed by the Zaotar and the Rathwiskar, the former chanting the hymns and saying the prayers, the latter performing the various operations during the sacrifice. Nowadays there are only two priests, the Zaotar (Zûtî) and the Rathwiskar (Raspî), the latter performing all the accessory services formerly performed by several priests. As to the Sraoshâ-varez, see above, § 25, note 2.

[2] In short, by any of the faithful, when in state of purity.

[3] An Armêst; literally, 'an infirm person,' that is to say, one who is unclean, during the time of his uncleanness (Farg. IX, 33 seq.), when all work is forbidden to him (cf. Introd. V, 15).

[4] The Armêst-gâh (cf. Introd. V, 15).

[5] The clothing defiled by the dead can only serve for Dashtân women, even after it has been washed and exposed for six months to the light of the sun and of the moon (Saddar 91; cf. Farg. VII, 10 seq.)

[6] Until they are clean. The unclean must have their hands

60 (168). 'Ahura Mazda, indeed, does not allow us to waste anything of value that we may have, not even so much as an Asperena's[1] weight of thread, not even so much as a maid lets fall in spinning.

61 (171). 'Whosoever throws any clothing on a dead body[2], even so much as a maid lets fall in spinning, is not a pious man whilst alive, nor shall he, when dead, have a place in the happy realm[3].

62 (174). 'He shall go away into the world of the fiends, into that dark world[4], made of darkness, the offspring of darkness[5]. To that world, to the

---

wrapped in an old piece of linen, lest they should touch and defile anything clean.

[1] See Farg. IV, 48, note 4.

[2] Cf. Farg. VIII, 23 seq. It appears from those passages that the dead must lie on the mountain naked, or 'clothed only with the light of heaven' (Farg. VI, 51). The modern custom is to clothe them with old clothing (Dadabhai Naoroji, Manners and Customs of the Parsis, p. 15). 'When a man dies and receives the order (to depart), the older the shroud they make for him, the better. It must be old, worn out, but well washed: they must not lay anything new on the dead. For it is said in the Zend Vendîdâd, If they put on the dead even so much as a thread from the distaff more than is necessary, every thread shall become in the other world a black snake clinging to the heart of him who made that shroud, and even the dead shall rise against him and seize him by the skirt, and say, That shroud which thou madest for me has become food for worms and vermin' (Saddar 12). The Greeks entertained quite different ideas, and dressed the dead in their gayest attire, as if for a feast. Yet the difference is only in appearance; for, after the fourth day, when the soul is in heaven, then rich garments are offered up to it, which it will wear in its celestial life (Saddar 87, Hyde 64).

[3] The Behesht or paradise.

[4] 'Where darkness can be seized with the hand' (Comm.; cf. Aogemaidê 28); something more than the 'visible darkness.'

[5] The Commentary has, 'the place of those who impregnate

dismal realm, you are delivered by your own doings, by your own souls, O sinners!'

FARGARD VI.

I (1–9). How long the earth remains unclean, when defiled by the dead.

II (10–25). Penalties for defiling the ground with dead matter.

III (26–41). Purification of the different sorts of water, when defiled by the dead.

IV (42–43). Purification of the Haoma.

V (44–51). The place for corpses; the Dakhmas.

I.

1. How long shall the ground lie fallow whereon dogs or men have died?

Ahura Mazda answered: 'A year long shall the ground lie fallow whereon dogs or men have died, O holy Zarathustra!

2 (3). 'A year long shall no worshipper of Mazda sow or water that part of the ground whereon dogs or men have died; he may sow as he likes the rest of the ground; he may water it as he likes [1].

3 (5). 'If within the year they shall sow or water the ground whereon dogs or men have died, the sin is the same as if they had brought dead matter to the water, to the earth, and to the plants [2].'

4 (7). O Maker of the material world, thou Holy One! If worshippers of Mazda shall sow or water,

---

darkness, for the Drug who conceives seed from the sinner comes from that place' (cf. Farg. XVIII, 30 seq.)

[1] Cf. Farg. VII, 45 seq.

[2] 'To the water which they pour out, to the earth which they plough, to the plants which they sow' (Comm.)

within the year, the ground whereon dogs or men have died, what is the penalty that they shall pay?

5 (9). Ahura Mazda answered : 'They are Peshô-tanus: two hundred stripes with the Aspahê-astra, two hundred stripes with the Sraoshô-karana¹.'

6 (10). O Maker of the material world, thou Holy One! If worshippers of Mazda want to make the ground fit to be tilled again², that they may water it, sow it, and plough it, what shall they do?

7 (12). Ahura Mazda answered: 'They shall look on the ground for any bones, hair, flesh, dung, or blood that may be there.'

8 (13). O Maker of the material world, thou Holy One! If they shall not look on the ground for any bones, hair, flesh, dung, or blood that may be there, what is the penalty that they shall pay?

9 (15). Ahura Mazda answered: 'They are Peshô-tanus: two hundred stripes with the Aspahê-astra, two hundred stripes with the Sraoshô-karana.'

II.

10 (16). O Maker of the material world, thou Holy One! If a man shall throw on the ground a bone of a dead dog, or of a dead man, as large as the top joint of the little finger, and if grease or marrow flow from it on to the ground, what penalty shall he pay?

11 (18). Ahura Mazda answered: 'Thirty stripes with the Aspahê-astra, thirty stripes with the Sraoshô-karana.'

---

¹ 'If they plough and sow it, one tanâfûhr (see Introd. V, 19); if they pour water on it, one tanâfûhr; if they plough, sow, and water it, two tanâfûhrs' (Comm.)

² Even when a year's space is past, the ground is not free ipso facto.

12 (20). O Maker of the material world, thou Holy One! If a man shall throw on the ground a bone of a dead dog, or of a dead man, as large as the top joint of the fore-finger, and if grease or marrow flow from it on to the ground, what penalty shall he pay?

13 (24). Ahura Mazda answered: 'Fifty stripes with the Aspahê-astra, fifty stripes with the Sraoshô-karana.'

14 (25). O Maker of the material world, thou Holy One! If a man shall throw on the ground a bone of a dead dog, or of a dead man, as large as the top joint of the middle finger, and if grease or marrow flow from it on to the ground, what penalty shall he pay?

15 (29). Ahura Mazda answered: 'Seventy stripes with the Aspahê-astra, seventy stripes with the Sraoshô-karana.'

16 (30). O Maker of the material world, thou Holy One! If a man shall throw on the ground a bone of a dead dog, or of a dead man, as large as a finger or as a rib, and if grease or marrow flow from it on to the ground, what penalty shall he pay?

17 (34). Ahura Mazda answered: 'Ninety stripes with the Aspahê-astra, ninety stripes with the Sraoshô-karana.'

18 (35). O Maker of the material world, thou Holy One! If a man shall throw on the ground a bone of a dead dog, or of a dead man, as large as two fingers or as two ribs, and if grease or marrow flow from it on to the ground, what penalty shall he pay?

19 (39). Ahura Mazda answered: 'He is a Peshô-tanu: two hundred stripes with the Aspahê-astra, two hundred stripes with the Sraoshô-karana.'

20 (40). O Maker of the material world, thou
Holy One! If a man shall throw on the ground
a bone of a dead dog, or of a dead man, as large as
an arm-bone or as a thigh-bone, and if grease or
marrow flow from it on to the ground, what penalty
shall he pay?

21 (44). Ahura Mazda answered: 'Four hundred
stripes with the Aspahê-astra, four hundred stripes
with the Sraoshô-karana.'

22 (45). O Maker of the material world, thou
Holy One! If a man shall throw on the ground
a bone of a dead dog, or of a dead man, as large as
a man's skull, and if grease or marrow flow from it
on to the ground, what penalty shall he pay?

23 (49). Ahura Mazda answered: 'Six hundred
stripes with the Aspahê-astra, six hundred stripes
with the Sraoshô-karana.'

24 (50). O Maker of the material world, thou
Holy One! If a man shall throw on the ground
the whole body of a dead dog, or of a dead man,
and if grease or marrow flow from it on to the
ground, what penalty shall he pay?

25 (53). Ahura Mazda answered: 'A thousand
stripes with the Aspahê-astra, a thousand stripes with
the Sraoshô-karana.'

III.

26 (54). O Maker of the material world, thou
Holy One! If a worshipper of Mazda, walking, or
running, or riding, or driving, come upon a corpse in
a stream of running water, what shall he do?

27 (56). Ahura Mazda answered: 'Taking off
his shoes, putting off his clothes, boldly, O Zarathustra! he shall enter the river, and take the dead
out of the water; he shall go down into the water

ankle-deep, knee-deep, waist-deep, or a man's full depth, till he can reach the dead body[1].'

28 (61). O Maker of the material world, thou Holy One! If, however, the body be already falling to pieces and rotting, what shall the worshipper of Mazda do?

29 (63). Ahura Mazda answered: 'He shall draw out of the water as much of the corpse as he can grasp with both hands, and he shall lay it down on the dry ground; no sin attaches to him for any bone, hair, grease, flesh, dung, or blood that may drop back into the water.'

30 (65). O Maker of the material world, thou Holy One! What part of the water in a pond does the Drug Nasu defile with infection, pollution, and uncleanness?

31 (66). Ahura Mazda answered: 'Six steps on each of the four sides. As long as the corpse has not been taken out of the water, so long shall that water be unclean and unfit to drink. They shall, therefore, take the corpse out of the pond, and lay it down on the dry ground.

32 (69). 'And of the water they shall draw off the half, or the third, or the fourth, or the fifth part, according as they are able; and after the corpse has been taken out and the water has been drawn off, the rest of. the water is clean, and both cattle and men may drink of it at their pleasure, as before.'

33 (72). O Maker of the material world, thou

---

[1] 'If he is able to draw out the corpse and does so, it is a pious deed worth a tanâfûhr (that is, one by which a tanâfûhr sin can be cancelled); if he is able to draw it out and does not do so, it is a tanâfûhr sin. Gûgôsasp says, It is a margarzân sin (a capital crime),' (Comm.)

Holy One! What part of the water in a well does the Dru*g* Nasu defile with infection, pollution, and uncleanness?

34 (73). Ahura Mazda answered: 'As long as the corpse has not been taken out of the water [1], so long shall that water be unclean and unfit to drink. They shall, therefore, take the corpse out of the well, and lay it down on the dry ground.

35 (73). 'And of the water in the well they shall draw off the half, or the third, or the fourth, or the fifth part, according as they are able; and after the corpse has been taken out and the water has been drawn off, the rest of the water is clean, and both cattle and men may drink of it at their pleasure, as before.'

36 (74). O Maker of the material world, thou Holy One! What part of a sheet of snow or hail does the Dru*g* Nasu defile with infection, pollution, and uncleanness?

37 (75). Ahura Mazda answered: ' Three steps on each of the four sides. As long as the corpse has not been taken out of the water, so long shall that water be unclean and unfit to drink. They shall, therefore, take the corpse out of the water, and lay it down on the dry ground.

38 (78). 'After the corpse has been taken out, and the snow or the hail has melted, the water is clean, and both cattle and men may drink of it at their pleasure, as before.'

39 (79). O Maker of the material world, thou Holy One! What part of the water of a running

---

[1] All the water in the well is unclean, ' as the well has the length and breadth of a man's stature' (Brouillons d'Anquetil, Vendidâd, p. 206).

stream does the Dru*g* Nasu defile with infection,
pollution, and uncleanness?

40 (80). Ahura Mazda answered: 'Three steps
down the stream, nine steps up the stream, six steps
across. As long as the corpse has not been taken
out of the water, so long shall the water be unclean
and unfit to drink. They shall, therefore, take the
corpse out of the water, and lay it down on the dry
ground.

41 (83). 'After the corpse has been taken out and
the stream has flowed three times[1], the water is clean,
and both cattle and men may drink of it at their
pleasure, as before.'

IV.

42 (84). O Maker of the material world, thou
Holy One! Can the Haoma that has been touched
by the corpse of a dead dog, or the corpse of a dead
man, be made clean again?

43 (85). Ahura Mazda answered: 'It can, O
holy Zarathu*s* ra! If it has been strained for the
sacrifice, no corpse that has been brought unto it,
makes corruption or death enter it[2]. If it has not
been strained for the sacrifice, the stem is defiled
the length of four fingers. That length of stem shall
be buried in the ground, in the middle of the house,
for a year long. When the year is passed, the faithful
may drink of its juice at their pleasure, as before.'

V.

44 (92). O Maker of the material world, thou

---

[1] When three waves have passed.

[2] Because the Haoma is the plant of life; when strained for the
sacrifice, it is the king of healing plants (Bund. XXIV); the dead
shall become immortal by tasting of the white Haoma (ib. XXXI).

Holy One! Whither shall we bring, where shall we lay the bodies of the dead, O Ahura Mazda?

45 (93). Ahura Mazda answered: 'On the highest summits[1], where they know there are always corpse-eating dogs and corpse-eating birds, O holy Zarathustra!

46 (95). 'There shall the worshippers of Mazda fasten the corpse, by the feet and by the hair, with brass, stones, or lead, lest the corpse-eating dogs and the corpse-eating birds shall go and carry the bones to the water and to the trees.

47 (98). 'If they shall not fasten the corpse, so that the corpse-eating dogs and the corpse-eating birds may go and carry the bones to the water and to the trees, what is the penalty that they shall pay?'

48 (100). Ahura Mazda answered: 'They shall be Peshôtanus: two hundred stripes with the Aspahê-astra, two hundred stripes with the Sraoshô-karana.'

49 (101). O Maker of the material world, thou Holy One[2]! Whither shall we bring, where shall we lay the bones of the dead, O Ahura Mazda?

50 (102). Ahura Mazda answered: 'The worshippers of Mazda shall erect a building[3] out of the reach of the dog, of the fox, and of the wolf, and wherein rain-water cannot stay[4].

---

[1] 'On the top of a mountain' (Comm.) See Introd. V, 10; cf. VIII, 10.

[2] The foregoing clauses (§§ 44–47) refer to the place where the corpse must be laid; the following (49–51) refer to the building, which must be erected on that place, if possible, to receive the corpse.

[3] The Dakhma.

[4] The rain-water that washes away the remains of corpses (V, 16 seq.) must not remain on the Dakhmas (cf. Comm. ad VIII, 7),

51 (105). 'Such a building shall they erect, if they can afford it, with stones, mortar, and earth[1]; if they cannot afford it, they shall lay down the dead man on the ground, on his carpet and his pillow, clothed with the light of heaven, and beholding the sun.'

FARGARD VII.

This chapter would offer tolerable unity, but for a digression on medicine, which would be better placed as an introduction to the last three chapters. Sections II and IX, parts of which have already been found in Fargard V, are more suitably placed here. This chapter, as a whole, deals with the action of the Drug Nasu, from the moment she takes hold of the corpse, and shows how and when the several objects she has defiled become clean, namely, clothes, wood, corn, earth, women, vessels, and cows.

I.

1. Zarathustra asked Ahura Mazda: 'O Ahura Mazda, most beneficent Spirit, Maker of the material

---

but is brought out through trenches dug for that purpose (cf. Introd. V, 10).

[1] This word is doubtful.

world, thou Holy One! When a man dies, 'at what moment does the Dru*g* Nasu rush upon him[1]?'

2 (3). Ahura Mazda answered: 'Directly after death, as soon as the soul has left the body, O Spitama Zarathustra! the Dru*g* Nasu comes and rushes upon him, from the regions of the north[2], in the shape of a raging fly, with knees and tail sticking out, all stained with stains, and like unto the foulest Khrafstras[3].

[3. 'On him she stays until the dog has seen the corpse[4] or eaten it up, or until the flesh-eating birds have taken flight towards it[5]. When the dog has seen it or eaten it up, or when the flesh-eating birds have taken flight towards it, then the Dru*g* Nasu rushes away to the regions of the north in the shape of a raging fly, with knees and tail sticking out, all stained with stains, and like unto the foulest Khrafstras.']

4 (5). O Maker of the material world, thou Holy One! If the man has been killed by a dog, or by a wolf, or by witchcraft, or by the artifices of hatred[6], or by falling down a precipice, or by the law[7], or by a murderer, or by the noose[8], how long after death does the Dru*g* Nasu come and rush upon the dead?

---

[1] See Introd. V, 3.

[2] Hell lies in the north; cf. XIX, 1; Yt. XXII, 25; Bundahi*s* 36, 12.

[3] See Introd. V, 3.

[4] Until the Sag-dîd has been performed (see Introd. V, 4).

[5] The Sag-dîd may be performed by birds of prey as well as by dogs (see Introd. V, 4). The dog smites the Nasu when it brings its muzzle near to the dead, the bird (mountain hawk, sparrow (?), or eagle) when its shadow passes over the body (Comm. ad § 2; cf. § 29). § 3 is from the Vendîdâd Sâdah.

[6] 'By poison' (Comm.)

[7] Literally, 'by men;' that is to say, put to death by the community according to law (Comm.)

[8] If he has strangled himself. Or possibly, 'by want.'

5 (6). Ahura Mazda answered: ' At the next watch after death [1], the Drug Nasu comes and rushes upon the dead, from the regions of the north, in the shape of a raging fly, with knees and tail sticking out, all stained with stains, and like unto the foulest Khrafstras.'

II [2].

6 (7). O Maker of the material world, thou Holy One! If there be a number of men resting in the same place, on adjoining carpets, on adjoining pillows, be there two men near one another, or five, or fifty, or a hundred, close by one another; and of those people one happens to die; how many of them does the Drug Nasu envelope with infection, pollution, and uncleanness?

7 (11). Ahura Mazda answered: ' If the dead one be a priest, the Drug Nasu rushes forth, O Spitama Zarathustra! she falls on the eleventh and defiles the ten.

' If the dead one be a warrior, the Drug Nasu rushes forth, O Spitama Zarathustra! she falls on the tenth and defiles the nine.

' If the dead one be a husbandman, the Drug Nasu rushes forth, O Spitama Zarathustra! she falls on the ninth and defiles the eight.

8 (17). 'If it be a shepherd's dog, the Drug Nasu rushes forth, O Spitama Zarathustra! she falls on the eighth and defiles the seven.

---

[1] The day is divided into five watches or ratu. If the man dies a natural death, the Drug comes directly; if the death be violent and unlooked for, the Drug is taken unawares, and it requires time for her to be warned of it and to come.

[2] §§ 6–9 = Farg. V, 27–30.

'If it be a house dog, the Dru*g* Nasu rushes
forth, O Spitama Zarathu*s*tra! she falls on the
seventh and defiles the six.

9 (21). 'If it be a Vohunazga dog, the Dru*g*
Nasu rushes forth, O Spitama Zarathu*s*tra! she
falls on the sixth and defiles the five.

'If it be a young dog, the Dru*g* Nasu rushes
forth, O Spitama Zarathu*s*tra! she falls on the fifth
and defiles the four [1].'

. . . 'those clothes shall serve for their coverings
and for their sheets [2].' . . .

III.

10 (26). O Maker of the material world, thou
Holy One! What part of his bedding [3] and pillow
does the Dru*g* Nasu defile with infection, uncleanness, and pollution?

11 (27). Ahura Mazda answered: 'The Dru*g*
Nasu defiles with infection, uncleanness, and pollution the upper sheet and the inner garment [4].'

12 (28). O Maker of the material world, thou
Holy One! Can that garment be made clean, O
holy Ahura Mazda! that has been touched by the
carcase of a dog or the corpse of a man?

13 (29). Ahura Mazda answered: 'It can, O holy
Zarathu*s*tra!'

How so?

---

[1] This enumeration is less complete than that in the fifth Fargard,
as it comprises only the first four sorts of dogs, viz. only those that
can perform the Sag-dîd (Comm. ad § 2).

[2] This phrase, which forms part of § 19, is wrongly inserted
here.

[3] The bedding on which he has died.

[4] That is to say, only those clothes which have been in direct
contact with the dead.

'If, indeed, the garment has been defiled with seed, or sweat, or dirt, or vomit, the worshippers of Mazda shall rend it to pieces, and bury it under the ground[1].

14 (33). 'But if it has not been defiled with seed, or sweat, or dirt, or vomit, then the worshippers of Mazda shall wash it with gômêz.

15 (35). 'If it be leather, they shall wash it with gômêz three times, they shall rub it with earth three times, they shall wash it with water three times, and afterwards they shall expose it to the air for three months at the window of the house.

'If it be woven cloth, they shall wash it with gômêz six times[2], they shall rub it with earth six times, they shall wash it with water six times, and afterwards they shall expose it to the air for six months at the window of the house.

16 (37). 'The spring named Ardvî Sûra, O Spitama Zarathustra! that spring of mine, purifies the seed in man, the fruit in a woman's womb, the milk in a woman's breast[3].'

17[4] (41). O Maker of the material world, thou Holy One! Can those clothes, when once washed and cleansed, ever be used either by a Zaotar, or by a Hâvanan, or by an Âtare-vakhsha, or by a Frabaretar, or by an Âbered, or by an Âsnâtar, or by a Rathwiskar, or by a Sraoshâ-varez, or by any priest, warrior, or husbandman?

---

[1] According to the Commentary only that part which has been defiled is rent off; the rest may still be used.

[2] See Introd. V, 16.

[3] This clause is a quotation from Yasna LXV, 5, intended to illustrate the cleansing power of water. Ardvî Sûra is the goddess of the waters.

[4] §§ 17–22 = Farg. V, 57–62.

18 (43). Ahura Mazda answered: 'Never can those clothes, even when washed and cleansed, be used either by a Zaotar, or by a Hâvanan, or by an Âtare-vakhsha, or by a Frabaretar, or by an Âbered, or by an Âsnâtar, or by a Rathwiskar, or by a Sraoshâ-varez, or by any priest, warrior, or husbandman.

19 (45). 'But if there be in a Mazdean house a woman who is in her sickness, or a man who has become unfit for work, and who must sit in the place of infirmity, those clothes shall serve for their coverings and for their sheets, until they can withdraw and move their hands.

20 (49). 'Ahura Mazda, indeed, does not allow us to waste anything of value that we may have, not even so much as an Asperena's weight of thread, not even so much as a maid lets fall in spinning.

21 (52). 'Whosoever throws any clothing on a dead body, even so much as a maid lets fall in spinning, is not a pious man whilst alive, nor shall he, when dead, have a place in the happy realm.

22 (55). 'He shall go away into the world of the fiends, into that dark world, made of darkness, the offspring of darkness. To that world, to the dismal realm, you are delivered by your own doings, by your own souls, O sinners!'

IV.

23 (59). O Maker of the material world, thou Holy One! Can he be clean again who has eaten of the carcase of a dog or of the carcase of a man[1]?

---

[1] The carcase-eater lodges the Nasu in himself; he becomes a Nasu, and therefore must be destroyed; cf. infra § 76 seq.

24 (60). Ahura Mazda answered: 'He cannot, O holy Zarathustra! His burrow[1] shall be dug out, his life shall be torn out, his bright eyes shall be put out; the Drug Nasu falls upon him, takes hold of him even to the end of the nails, and he is unclean, thenceforth, for ever and ever[2].'

V.

25 (65). O Maker of the material world, thou Holy One! Can he be clean again, O holy Ahura Mazda! who has brought a corpse with filth into the waters, or unto the fire, and made either unclean?

26 (66). Ahura Mazda answered: 'He cannot, O holy Zarathustra! Those wicked ones it is, those men turned to Nasus[3], that most increase gnats and locusts[4]; those wicked ones it is, those men turned to Nasus, that most increase the grass-destroying drought.

27 (69). 'Those wicked ones it is, those men turned to Nasus, that increase most the power of the winter, produced by the fiends, the cattle-killing, thick-snowing, overflowing, the piercing,

---

[1] His house, as he is assimilated to a devouring Khrafstra.

[2] Till the resurrection. 'It is prescribed in the Vendîdâd that if a man shall eat of a carcase, his house and family shall be destroyed, his heart shall be torn out of his body, his eyes shall be put out, and his soul shall abide in hell till the resurrection' (Saddar 71, Hyde 79). 'He who eats of a carcase with sinful intent is both unclean and margarzân; Barashnûm and Nireng are of no avail for him, he must die. If there has been no sinful intent, he may wash himself; one may give him the ashes and the gômêz (Comm.); he is unclean, he is not margarzân' (Old Rav. 115 b).

[3] Doubtful; possibly, 'those Nasu-makers.'

[4] 'It is said in the Avesta that when there are many gnats and locusts it is owing to corpses having been brought to water and to fire' (Saddar 72, Hyde 80).

fierce, mischievous winter[1]. Upon them comes
and rushes the Dru*g* Nasu, she takes hold of them
even to the end of the nails, and they are unclean,
thenceforth, for ever and ever [2].'

VI.

28 (72). O Maker of the material world, thou
Holy One! Can the wood be made clean, O holy
Ahura Mazda! whereunto dead matter has been
brought from a dead dog, or from a dead man?

29 (73). Ahura Mazda answered: 'It can, O holy
Zarathu*s*tra!'

How so?

'If the Nasu has not yet been smitten[3] by the
corpse-eating dogs, or by the corpse-eating birds[4],
they shall lay down, apart on the ground, the wood
on the length of a Vîtasti[5] all around the dead
matter, if the wood be dry; on the length of a
Frârâthni[6] all around, if it be wet; then they shall
sprinkle it once over with water, and it shall be
clean[7].

---

[1] 'In the same way (by the bringing of corpses to water and to
fire), winter grows colder, and summer grows warmer' (Saddar 72,
Hyde 80).

[2] Whoever shall do that deed, shall pay for it in this world and
in the next; they shall flay his body in the presence of the as-
sembly, they shall tear him limb from limb, and his corpse shall be
thrown away to dogs and ravens, . . . and when his soul comes
to the other world, he shall suffer tortures from the dêvs (Gr. Rav.
p. 123).

[3] That is to say, if the Sag-dîd has not yet been performed.

[4] See above, p. 75, n. 5.

[5] Twelve fingers.

[6] The Frârâthni is, as it seems, as much as one foot (fourteen
fingers, Vd. II, 22, Comm.)

[7] 'After a year,' according to the Commentary.

[4]   G

30 (78). 'But if the Nasu has already been
smitten[1] by the corpse-eating dogs, or by the corpse-
eating birds, they shall lay down, apart on the
ground, the wood on the length of a Frârâthni all
around the dead matter, if the wood be dry; on the
length of a Frâbâzu[2] all around, if it be wet; then
they shall sprinkle it once over with water, and it
shall be clean.

31 (81). 'This is the quantity of wood around
the dead matter, that they shall lay down, apart on
the ground, according as the wood is dry or wet;
according as it is hard or soft; they shall sprinkle it
once over with water, and it shall be clean.'

32 (83). O Maker of the material world, thou
Holy One! Can the corn or the fodder be made
clean, O holy Ahura Mazda! whereunto dead matter has been brought from a dead dog, or from a
dead man?

33 (84). Ahura Mazda answered: 'It can, O holy
Zarathustra!'

How so?

'If the Nasu has not yet been smitten by the
corpse-eating dogs, or by the corpse-eating birds, they
shall lay down, apart on the ground, the corn on the
length of a Frârâthni all around the dead matter, if
the corn be dry; on the length of a Frâbâzu all

---

[1] It appears from the similar passages (VIII, 35, 36, and 98, 99)
and from the general principles of uncleanness (see Introd. V, 16)
that the words 'If the Nasu has not yet been smitten,' in § 29,
have been misplaced there from § 30, and that the corresponding
words in § 30 belong to § 29; because uncleanness spreads less far,
when the Sag-dîd has taken place.

[2] A measure of unknown extent; 'an arm's length,' it would
seem.

around, if it be wet; then they shall sprinkle it once over with water, and it shall be clean.

34 (89). 'But if the Nasu has already been smitten[1] by the corpse-eating dogs, or by the corpse-eating birds, they shall lay down, apart on the ground, the corn on the length of a Frâbâzu all around the dead matter, if the corn be dry; on the length of a Vîbâzu[2] all around, if it be wet; then they shall sprinkle it once over with water, and it shall be clean.

35 (92). 'This is the quantity of corn around the dead matter, that they shall lay down, apart on the ground, according as the corn is dry or wet; according as it is sown or not sown; according as it is reaped or not reaped; according as it is ground or not ground[3]; according as it is (kneaded)[4] or not kneaded; they shall sprinkle it once over with water, and it shall be clean.'

VII a.

36 (94). 'O Maker of the material world, thou Holy One! If a worshipper of Mazda want to practice the art of healing, on whom shall he first prove his skill? on worshippers of Mazda or on worshippers of the Daêvas?

37 (96). Ahura Mazda answered: 'On worshippers of the Daêvas shall he first prove himself,

---

[1] The same observation applies to the first words of §§ 33, 34, as was observed of §§ 29, 30.

[2] A measure of unknown extent; 'an ell,' it would seem.

[3] This clause is preceded and followed, in the Vendîdâd Sâdah, by clauses which seem to refer to the process of grinding being more or less advanced.

[4] This word is supplied, as it appears, from the context, and from the Pahlavi translation, to be wanting.

rather than on worshippers of Mazda. If he treat
with the knife a worshipper of the Daêvas and he
die; if he treat with the knife a second worshipper of
the Daêvas and he die; if he treat with the knife for
the third time a worshipper of the Daêvas and he
die, he is unfit to practise the art of healing for ever
and ever.

38 (99). 'Let him therefore never attend any
worshipper of Mazda; let him never treat with the
knife any worshipper of Mazda, nor wound him with
the knife. If he shall ever attend any worshipper
of Mazda, if he shall ever treat with the knife any
worshipper of Mazda, and wound him with the knife,
he shall pay for it the same penalty as is paid for
wilful murder [1].

39 (102). 'If he treat with the knife a worshipper
of the Daêvas and he recover; if he treat with the
knife a second worshipper of the Daêvas and he
recover; if for the third time he treat with the knife
a worshipper of the Daêvas and he recover; then
he is fit to practise the art of healing for ever and
ever [2].

40 (104). 'He may henceforth at his will attend
worshippers of Mazda; he may at his will treat with
the knife worshippers of Mazda, and heal them with
the knife.

VII b.

41 (105). 'A healer shall heal a priest for a holy

---

[1] For baodhô-varsta, which word is wrongly understood by the
Parsis as the designation of a penalty, consisting in the amputation
of six fingers (Asp.)

[2] 'Some say, One who has been qualified may become disqualified; one who has been disqualified shall never become
qualified' (Comm. ad § 43).

blessing [1]; he shall heal the master of a house for the value of an ox of low value; he shall heal the lord of a borough [2] for the value of an ox of average value; he shall heal the lord of a town for the value of an ox of high value; he shall heal the lord of a province for the value of a chariot and four [3].

42 (110). 'He shall heal the wife of the master of a house for the value of a she-ass; he shall heal the wife of the lord of a borough for the value of a cow; he shall heal the wife of the lord of a town for the value of a mare; he shall heal the wife of the lord of a province for the value of a she-camel.

43 (114). 'He shall heal the son of the lord of a borough for the value of an ox of high value; he shall heal an ox of high value for the value of an ox of average value; he shall heal an ox of average value for that of an ox of low value; he shall heal an ox of low value for the value of a sheep; he shall heal a sheep for the value of a meal of meat [4].

44 (118). 'If several healers offer themselves together, O Spitama Zarathustra! namely, one who heals with the knife, one who heals with herbs, and one who heals with the holy word [5], it is this one

---

[1] 'Thus he will become holy (i.e. he will go to paradise); there is no equivalent in money. Some say, It is given when the priest has not 3000 stîrs' (Comm.)

[2] A group of several houses; Aspendiârji and Anquetil say, 'a street.'

[3] 'A value of seventy stîrs' (Comm.)

[4] Cf. the tariff of fees for the cleanser, Farg. IX, 37 seq.

[5] 'By spells' (Comm.; cf. Odyssea XIX, 457). This classification was not unknown to Asclepios: he relieved the sick 'now with caressing spells, now with soothing drink or balsam, now with the knife' (Pindaros, Pyth. III, 51).

who will best drive away sickness from the body of the faithful [1].'

VIII.

45 (122). O Maker of the material world, thou Holy One! How long after the corpse of a dead man has been laid down on the ground, clothed with the light of heaven and beholding the sun, is the ground itself again [2]?

46 (123). Ahura Mazda answered: 'When the corpse of a dead man has lain on the ground for a year, clothed with the light of heaven, and beholding the sun, then the ground is itself again, O holy Zarathustra [3]!'

47 (124). O Maker of the material world, thou Holy One! How long after the corpse of a dead man has been buried in the earth, is the earth itself again?

48 (125). Ahura Mazda answered: 'When the corpse of a dead man has lain buried in the earth for fifty years, O Spitama Zarathustra! then the earth is itself again [4].'

49 (126). O Maker of the material world, thou Holy One! How long after the corpse of a dead

---

[1] 'It may be that he may not relieve, but he will not harm' (Comm.) The Vendîdâd Sâdah, instead of 'it is this one,' &c., reads as follows: 'Let them address themselves to the one who heals with the holy word; for he is the best healer among all healers, who heals by the holy word; this one it is who will drive away sickness from the body of the faithful.' The treatment by the holy word seems not to consist only in the recitation of spells, but the spells must be accompanied by the ceremony of the Barashnûm (see Farg. XXII and Introd. V, 14).

[2] Restored to the purity of its nature, and fit to till; as it remains Nasu till that time.

[3] See Farg. VI, 1 seq.   [4] Cf. Farg. III, 36 seq.

man has been laid down on a Dakhma, is the ground, whereon the Dakhma stands, itself again?

50 (127). Ahura Mazda answered : ' Not until the dust of the corpse, O Spitama Zarathustra! has mingled with the dust of the earth [1]. Urge every one in the material world, O Spitama Zarathustra! to pull down Dakhmas [2].

51 (129). ' He who should pull down Dakhmas, even so much thereof as the size of his own body, his sins in thought, word, and deed are remitted as they would be by a Patet; his sins in thought, word, and deed are atoned for [3].

52 (132). ' Not for his soul shall the two spirits wage war with one another [4]; and when he enters the blissful world, the stars, the moon, and the sun shall rejoice in him; and I, Ahura Mazda, shall rejoice in him, saying: " Hail, O man! thou who hast just passed from the decaying world into the undecaying one!"'

55 [5] (137). O Maker of the material world, thou

---

[1] A space of time estimated at fifty years (Comm.) Cf. Farg. III, 13.

[2] Cf. Farg. III, 9, text and note, and § 13.

[3] ' A tanâfûhr sin is remitted thereby ' (Comm.)

[4] When a man dies, hell and paradise, fiends and gods struggle for the possession of his soul : Astôvîdhôtus, Vîzaresha, and the bad Vayu drag the souls of the wicked to hell ; Mithra, Sraosha, Rashnu, and the good Vayu take the souls of the good to paradise (see Farg. XIX, 29 seq.; Yt. XXII; Mainyô-i-khard II). The struggle lasts for three days and three nights (the sadis), during which time the relatives of the dead offer up prayers and sacrifices to Sraosha, Rashnu, and Vayu, to assure him their protection (cf. IX, 56).

[5] §§ 53, 54 belong to the Commentary; they are composed of disconnected quotations, part of which refers to the different deeds by which a tanâfûhr sin may be redeemed, while the other part refers to the rules of what may be called the book-keeping of good actions and sins.

Holy One! Where are the fiends? Where are
the worshippers of the fiends? What is the place
whereon the troops of fiends rush together? What
is the place whereon the troops of fiends come
rushing along? What is the place whereon they
rush together to kill their fifties and their hundreds,
their hundreds and their thousands, their thousands
and their tens of thousands, their tens of thousands
and their myriads of myriads?

56 (138). Ahura Mazda answered: 'Those Dakhmas that are built upon the face of the earth, O Spitama Zarathustra! and whereon are laid the corpses
of dead men, that is the place where the fiends are,
that is the place whereon the troops of fiends rush
together, that is the place whereon the troops of
fiends come rushing along, that is the place whereon
they rush together to kill their fifties and their
hundreds, their hundreds and their thousands, their
thousands and their tens of thousands, their tens of
thousands and their myriads of myriads.

57 (140). 'On those Dakhmas, O Spitama Zarathustra! those fiends take food and void filth, (eating
up corpses) in the same way as you, men, in the
material world, eat cooked meal and cooked meat.
It is, as it were, the smell of their feeding that you
smell there, O men!

58 (143). 'Thus the fiends revel on there, until
that stench is rooted in the Dakhmas. Thus from
the Dakhmas arise the infection of diseases, itch,
hot fever, humours[1], cold fever, rickets, and hair
untimely white. There death has most power on
man, from the hour when the sun is down.

---

[1] Doubtful (naêza).

59 (148). 'And if there be people of evil spirit who do not seek for better spirit, the Gainis[1] make those diseases grow stronger by a third[2], on their thighs, on their hands, on their plaited hair[3].'

IX.

60[4] (151). O Maker of the material world, thou Holy One! If in the house of a worshipper of Mazda there be a woman with child, and if being a month gone, or two, or three, or four, or five, or six, or seven, or eight, or nine, or ten months gone, she bring forth a still-born child, what shall the worshippers of Mazda do?

61 (155). Ahura Mazda answered: 'The place in that Mazdean house whereof the ground is the cleanest and the driest, and the least passed through by flocks and herds, by Fire, the son of Ahura Mazda, by the consecrated bundles of baresma, and by the faithful;'—

62 (158). O Maker of the material world, thou Holy One! How far from the fire? How far from the water? How far from the consecrated bundles of baresma? How far from the faithful?

63 (159). Ahura Mazda answered: 'Thirty paces from the fire; thirty paces from the water; thirty paces from the consecrated bundles of baresma; three paces from the faithful;—

---

[1] 'The Gahi' (Comm.) The Gaini seems to be the Gahi as bringing sickness (cf. Farg. XXI, 2).

[2] The general meaning of the sentence is that the Dakhmas are seats of infection, of which the action becomes worse and stronger when people live in impiety and vices.

[3] Doubtful.

[4] §§ 60–69=Farg. V, 45–54.

64 (160). 'On that place shall the worshippers of Mazda erect an enclosure, and therein shall they establish her with food, therein shall they establish her with clothes.'

65 (162). O Maker of the material world, thou Holy One! What is the food that the woman shall first take?

66 (163). Ahura Mazda answered: 'She shall drink gômêz mixed with ashes, three cups of it, or six, or nine, to wash over the grave in her womb.

67 (166). 'Afterwards she may drink boiling milk of mares, cows, sheep, or goats, with pap or without pap; she may take cooked meat without water, bread without water, and wine without water.'

68 (169). O Maker of the material world, thou Holy One! How long shall she remain so? How long shall she live only on that sort of meat, bread, and wine?

69 (170). Ahura Mazda answered: 'Three nights long shall she remain so; three nights long shall she live on that sort of meat, bread, and wine. Then, when three nights have passed, she shall wash her body, she shall wash her clothes, with gômêz and water, by the nine holes, and thus shall she be clean.'

70 (172). O Maker of the material world, thou Holy One! But if fever befall her unclean body, if that twofold plague, hunger and thirst, befall her, may she be allowed to drink water?

71 (175). Ahura Mazda answered: 'She may; the first thing for her is to have her life saved. Having been allowed by one of the holy men, by a holy faithful man, who knows the holy know-

ledge[1], she shall drink of the strength-giving water.
But you, worshippers of Mazda, fix ye the penalty
for it. The Ratu being applied to, the Sraoshâ-
varez being applied to[2], shall prescribe the penalty
to be paid[3].'

72 (181). What is the penalty to be paid?

Ahura Mazda answered: ' The deed is that of a
Peshôtanu : two hundred stripes with the Aspahê-
astra, two hundred stripes with the Sraoshô-karana[4].'

X.

73 (183). O Maker of the material world, thou
Holy One! Can the eating vessels be made clean
that have been touched by the carcase of a dog,
or by the corpse of a man?

74 (184). Ahura Mazda answered : ' They can,
O holy Zarathustra !'

How so?

' If they be of gold, you shall wash them once
with gômêz, you shall rub them once with earth,
you shall wash them once with water, and they
shall be clean.

' If they be of silver, you shall wash them twice
with gômêz, you shall rub them twice with earth,
you shall wash them twice with water, and they
shall be clean.

[75. ' If they be of brass, you shall wash them
thrice with gômêz, you shall rub them thrice with

---

[1] The Dastur.   [2] See Farg. V, 25.

[3] For the water having been defiled.

[4] A penalty to be undergone by the husband, at least in modern
practice : ' If through fear of death or of serious illness she has
drunk water before the appointed time, her husband shall make
Patet for her fault before the Dastur ' (Old Rav. 98 b).

earth, you shall wash them thrice with water, and they shall be clean.

'If they be of steel, you shall wash them four times with gômêz, you shall rub them four times with earth, you shall wash them four times with water, and they shall be clean.

'If they be of stone, you shall wash them six times with gômêz, you shall rub them six times with earth, you shall wash them six times with water, and they shall be clean [1].]

'If they be of earth, of wood, or of clay, they are unclean for ever and ever [2].'

XI.

76 (189). O Maker of the material world, thou Holy One! Can the cow be made clean that has eaten of the carcase of a dog, or of the corpse of a man?

77 (190). Ahura Mazda answered: 'She can, O holy Zarathustra! The priest shall not, within a year, take from her to the baresma neither the milk and cheese that accompany the libation, nor the meat that accompanies the libation [3]. When a year has passed, then the faithful may eat of her as before [4].'

XII.

78 (193). Who is he, O holy Ahura Mazda! who,

---

[1] From the Vendîdâd Sâdah.   [2] See Introd. V, 16.

[3] The offering of the libation waters (Zaothra) is accompanied with offerings of milk, cheese, and meat, which the priest eats holding the baresma in his hand.

[4] 'Whatever comes from her, if dropped, is clean; if taken, unclean. If she be big with young, the young is born clean, if conceived before her eating of the corpse; if conceived afterwards, it is born unclean' (Comm.)

with a godly intent, with a godly wish, goes astray from the ways of God? Who is he who, with a godly intent, falls into the ways of the Drug[1]?

79 (194). Ahura Mazda answered: 'The one who, with a godly intent, with a godly wish, goes astray from the ways of God; the one who with a godly intent falls into the ways of the Drug, is he who offers up for libation water defiled by the dead; or who offers up libations in the dead of the night[2].'

Fargard VIII.

I (1-3). Purification of the house where a man has died.
II (4-13). Funerals.
III (14-22). Purification of the ways along which the corpse has been carried.
IV (23-25). No clothes to be wasted on a corpse.
V (26-32). Unlawful lusts.
VI (33-34). A corpse when dried up does not contaminate.
VII (35-72). Purification of the man defiled by the dead.
VIII (73-80). Purification of the fire defiled by the dead.
IX (81-96). The Bahrâm fire.
X (97-107). Purification in the wilderness.

This chapter, putting aside section V, may be entitled: Funerals and Purification. Logical order may easily be introduced into it, by arranging the sections as follows: I, IV, II, III, VI, VII, X, VIII, IX.

I.

1. If a dog or a man die under the timber-work of a house or the wattlings of a hut, what shall the worshippers of Mazda do?

---

[1] Possibly, works for the Drug.

[2] 'From what hour may the good waters be offered up? From sunrise to sunset. He who offers up the good waters after sunset, before sunrise, does no better deed than if he should shed them downright into the jaws of the venomous snake' (Nîrangistân, in the Zand-Pahlavi Glossary, p. 76).

2 (4). Ahura Mazda answered : ' They shall look for a Dakhma, they shall look for a Dakhma all around. If they find it easier to remove the dead than to remove the house, they shall take out the dead, they shall let the house stand, and shall perfume it with Urvâsni, or Vohu-gaona, or Vohu-kereti, or Hadhâ-naêpata, or any other sweet-smelling plant [1].

3 (8). ' If they find it easier to remove the house than to remove the dead [2], they shall take away the house, they shall let the dead lie on the spot, and shall perfume the house with Urvâsni, or Vohu-gaona, or Vohu-kereti, or Hadhâ-naêpata, or any other sweet-smelling plant.'

II.

4 (11). O Maker of the material world, thou Holy One ! If in the house of a worshipper of Mazda a dog or a man happens to die, and it is raining [3], or snowing, or blowing [4], or the darkness is coming on, when flocks and men lose their way, what shall the worshippers of Mazda do [4] ?

---

[1] ' So, when a dog or a man dies, the first thing to do is to take the corpse out (from the house), and to purify the house, inside and outside, with perfumes burnt on the fire ' (Comm.) Cf. XI, 4. Urvâsni is the râsan plant, a sort of garlic; Vohu-gaona, Vohu-kereti, and Hadhâ-naêpata are respectively (according to Aspendiârji) benzoin, aloe, and pomegranate.

[2] If the house is simply a hut or a tent.

[3] ' No corpse must be taken to the Dakhma when rain is falling, or threatening. If one is overtaken by rain on the way, if there be a place to lay it down, they shall lay it down ; if there be none, they must go on and take it to the Dakhma, they must not retrace their steps. . . . . When arrived at the Dakhma, if they find it full of water, they may nevertheless lay down the corpse ' (Comm.)

[4] If it is the season of rain or snow. Cf. V, 10 seq.

5 (14). Ahura Mazda answered: 'The place in that house whereof the ground is the cleanest and the driest, and the least passed through by flocks and herds, by Fire, the son of Ahura Mazda, by the consecrated bundles of baresma, and by the faithful;'—

6 (16). O Maker of the material world, thou Holy One! How far from the fire? How far from the water? How far from the consecrated bundles of baresma? How far from the faithful?

7 (17). Ahura Mazda answered: 'Thirty paces from the fire; thirty paces from the water; thirty paces from the consecrated bundles of baresma; three paces from the faithful;—

8 (18). 'On that place they shall dig a grave, half a foot deep if the earth be hard, half the height of a man if it be soft; [they shall cover the surface of the grave with ashes or cowdung][1]; they shall cover the surface of it with dust of bricks, of stones, or of dry earth [2].

9 (21). 'And they shall let the lifeless body lie there, for two nights, or three nights, or a month long, until the birds begin to fly, the plants to grow, the floods to flow, and the wind to dry up the waters from off the earth.

10 (23). 'And when the birds begin to fly, the plants to grow, the floods to flow, and the wind to dry up the waters from off the earth, then the worshippers of Mazda shall make a breach in the wall

---

[1] Vendîdâd Sâdah.

[2] In the similar case in V, 10, it is prescribed to isolate the corpse in a permanent dead house (the Zâd-marg); the rule prescribed here seems to be older, as it is now obsolete; it was besides less convenient.

of the house[1], and they shall call for two men, strong and skilful[2], and those, having stripped their clothes off[3], shall take the body to the building of clay, stones, and mortar[4], raised on a place where they know there are always corpse-eating dogs and corpse-eating birds.

11 (29). 'Afterwards the corpse-bearers shall sit down, three paces from the dead; then the holy Ratu[5] shall proclaim to the worshippers of Mazda thus: "Let the worshippers of Mazda here bring the urine wherewith the corpse-bearers there shall wash their hair and their bodies!"'

12 (32). O Maker of the material world, thou Holy One! Which is the urine wherewith the corpse-bearers shall wash their hair and their bodies? Is it of sheep or of oxen? Is it of man or of woman?

13 (35). Ahura Mazda answered: 'It is of sheep or of oxen; not of man nor of woman, except these two: the nearest kinsman (of the dead) or his nearest kinswoman. The worshippers of Mazda

---

[1] 'The master and mistress of the house are carried away through a breach (made in the wall of the house); others through the door' (Comm.)   In some parts of Germany the dead must not be carried away through the usual house-door, as the dead and the living must not pass through the same door.

[2] The corpse-bearers or nasu-kasha. 'The corpse must be carried by two persons (see Farg. III, 13 seq.), no matter who they are; they may be a man and a woman, or two women' (Comm.)

[3] 'As they are exchanged for the special clothes in which they carry corpses' (Comm.), the so-called *gâmah-i dakhma*, 'the Dakhma clothes.'

[4] The Dakhma (see Farg. VI, 50 seq.)

[5] The priest who directs the funerals, 'the chief of the Nasu-kashas' (Comm.)

shall therefore procure the urine wherewith the corpse-bearers shall wash their hair and their bodies [1].'

III.

14 (38). O Maker of the material world, thou Holy One! Can the way, whereon the carcases of dogs or corpses of men have been carried, be passed through again by flocks and herds, by men and women, by Fire, the son of Ahura Mazda, by ·the consecrated bundles of baresma, and by the faithful?

15 (40). Ahura Mazda answered: 'It cannot be passed through again by flocks and herds, nor by men and women, nor by Fire, the son of Ahura Mazda, nor by the consecrated bundles of baresma, nor by the faithful.

16 (41). 'You shall therefore cause the yellow dog with four eyes, or the white dog with yellow ears [2], to go three times through that way [3]. When either the yellow dog with four eyes, or the white dog with yellow ears, is brought there, then the Drug Nasu flies away to the regions of the north, in the shape of a raging fly, with knees and tail sticking out, all stained with stains, and like unto the foulest Khrafstras [4].

17 (45). 'If the dog goes unwillingly, they shall cause the yellow dog with four eyes, or the white

---

[1] When back in the village they perform the regular Barash-nûm with consecrated gômêz (Comm.)

[2] See Introd. V, 4.

[3] 'Afrag says, the dog goes straight along the length of the way; Maidyô-mâh says, he goes across it from side to side' (Comm.)

[4] Cf. Farg. VII, 3.

[4]   H

dog with yellow ears, to go six times[1] through that
way. When either the yellow dog with four eyes,
or the white dog with yellow ears, is brought there,
then the Drug Nasu flies away to the regions of the
north, in the shape of a raging fly, with knees and
tail sticking out, all stained with stains, and like
unto the foulest Khrafstras.

18 (47). 'If the dog goes unwillingly, they shall
cause the yellow dog with four eyes, or the white
dog with yellow ears, to go nine times through that
way. When either the yellow dog with four eyes,
or the white dog with yellow ears, has been brought
there, then the Drug Nasu flies away to the regions
of the north, in the shape of a raging fly, with knees
and tail sticking out, all stained with stains, and like
unto the foulest Khrafstras.

19 (49). 'An Âthravan shall first go along the
way and shall say aloud these fiend-smiting words:
"Yathâ ahû vairyô[2]: — the will of the Lord is
the law of holiness; the riches of Vohu-manô[3] shall
be given to him who works in this world for Mazda,
and wields according to the will of Ahura the power
he gave to him to relieve the poor.

20 (52). '"Kem nâ mazdâ:—whom hast thou
placed to protect me, O Mazda! while the hate of

---

[1] 'Three times suffice if the dog goes of his own accord; if he
goes by force, it counts as nothing; if he goes but with reluctance,
that shall suffice' (Comm. ad § 18).

[2] A prayer in frequent use, and considered of great efficacy,
generally known as the Ahuna Vairya or Honover. It was by
reciting it that Ormazd in his first conflict with Ahriman drove
him back to hell (Bund. I).

[3] Of paradise, as Vohu-manô (Good Thought) is the door-
keeper of heaven (cf. Farg. XIX, 31).

the fiend is grasping me? Whom but thy Âtar
and Vohu-manô[1], by whose work the holy world
goes on? Reveal to me the rules of thy law!

'"K*e* verethrem *g*â:—who is he who will
smite the fiend in order to maintain thy ordinances?
Teach me clearly thy rules for this world and for
the next, that Sraosha[2] may come with Vohu-manô
and help whomsoever thou pleasest.

21 (60). '"Keep us from our hater, O Mazda
and Ârmaiti Spe*n*ta! Perish, O fiendish Dru*g*!
Perish, O brood of the fiend! Perish, O world of
the fiend! Perish away, O Dru*g*! Rush away, O
Dru*g*! Perish away, O Dru*g*! Perish away to the
regions of the north, never more to give unto death
the living world of the holy spirit!"

22 (63). 'Then the worshippers of Mazda may
at their will bring by those ways sheep and oxen,
men and women, and Fire, the son of Ahura
Mazda, the consecrated bundles of baresma, and
the faithful.

'The worshippers of Mazda may afterwards[3] pre-
pare meals with meat and wine in that house; it
shall be clean, and there will be no sin, as before.'

IV.

23 (65). O Maker of the material world, thou
Holy One! If a man shall throw clothes, either of

---

[1] When Ahriman broke into the world he was repelled by Âtar
and Vohu-manô (Yasht XIII, 77; cf. Orm. Ahr. § 107).

[2] Sraosha fights for the soul of the good after death (see p. 87,
note 4). K*e*m nâ mazdâ and k*e* verethrem *g*â are lines taken
from the Gâthas (Yasna XLVI, 7; XLIV, 16) and diverted from
their primitive meaning to suit the present case.

[3] On the fourth day. For three days and nights after the death
it is forbidden to cook meat in the house (Comm.)

skin or woven, upon a dead body, enough to cover the feet, what is the penalty that he shall pay[1]?

Ahura Mazda answered : 'Four hundred stripes with the Aspahê-astra, four hundred stripes with the Sraoshô-karana.'

24 (68). O Maker of the material world, thou Holy One! If a man shall throw clothes, either of skin or woven, upon a dead body, enough to cover both legs, what is the penalty that he shall pay?

Ahura Mazda answered : 'Six hundred stripes with the Aspahê-astra, six hundred stripes with the Sraoshô-karana.'

25 (71). O Maker of the material world, thou Holy One! If a man shall throw clothes, either of skin or woven, upon a dead body, enough to cover the whole body, what is the penalty that he shall pay ?

Ahura Mazda answered : 'A thousand stripes with the Aspahê-astra, a thousand stripes with the Sraoshô-karana.'

V.

26 (74). O Maker of the material world, thou Holy One! If a man involuntarily emits his seed, what is the penalty that he shall pay ?

Ahura Mazda answered : 'Eight hundred stripes with the Aspahê-astra, eight hundred stripes with the Sraoshô-karana.'

27 (77). O Maker of the material world, thou Holy One! If a man voluntarily emits his seed, what is the penalty for it ? What is the atonement for it ? What is the cleansing from it ?

---

[1] See Farg. V, 60 ; VII, 20.

Ahura Mazda answered : ' For that deed there is nothing that can pay, nothing that can atone, nothing that can cleanse from it; it is a trespass for which there is no atonement, for ever and ever.'

28 (83). When is it so ?

' It is so, if the sinner be a professor of the law of Mazda, or one who has been taught in it.   But if he be not a professor of the law of Mazda, nor one who has been taught in it, then this law of Mazda takes his sin from him, if he confesses it and resolves never to commit again such forbidden deeds.

29 (88). 'The law of Mazda indeed, O Spitama Zarathustra! takes away from him who confesses it the bonds of his sin; it takes away (the sin of) breach of trust; it takes away (the sin of) murdering one of the faithful; it takes away (the sin of) burying a corpse; it takes away (the sin of) deeds for which there is no atonement; it takes away the heaviest penalties of sin; it takes away any sin that may be sinned.

30 (95). 'In the same way the law of Mazda, O Spitama Zarathustra! cleanses the faithful from every evil 'thought, word, and deed, as a swift-rushing mighty wind cleanses the plain.

' So let all the deeds thou doest be henceforth good, O Zarathustra! a full atonement for thy sin is effected by means of the law of Mazda [1].'

31 (98). O Maker of the material world, thou Holy One! Who is the man that is a Daêva ? Who is he that is a worshipper of the Daêvas? that is a male paramour of the Daêvas ? that is a female paramour of the Daêvas ? that is a she-Daêva ?

---

[1] See Farg. III, 38–42, text and notes.

that is in his inmost self a Daêva? that is in his
whole being a Daêva¹? Who is he that is a
Daêva before he dies, and becomes one of the unseen Daêvas after death²?

32 (102). Ahura Mazda answered: 'The man
that lies with mankind as man lies with womankind,
or as woman lies with mankind, is the man that is
a Daêva; this one is the man that is a worshipper
of the Daêvas, that is a male paramour of the
Daêvas, that is a female paramour of the Daêvas,
that is a she-Daêva; this is the man that is in his
inmost self a Daêva, that is in his whole being a
Daêva; this is the man that is a Daêva before he
dies, and becomes one of the unseen Daêvas after
death: so is he, whether he has lain with mankind
as mankind, or as womankind³.'

---

¹ The text has a Vîspô-daêva, a curious expression which comes
from the time when daêva still meant 'a god' (see Introd. IV, 41).
In the time of the Indo-Iranian, nay, as early as the time of the
Indo-European religion, it was the custom, beside special invoca-
tions to the several gods, to address one to all the gods, for fear
of the resentment of those who might have been forgotten or
ignored; thus the Greeks never failed to invoke all gods and
goddesses (θεοῖς πᾶσι καὶ πάσαις); in the same way the Indian
invoked visvê devâs, 'all the gods,' which, in course of time, gave
rise to a special class of gods. Hence, in Mazdeism, arose a class
of fiends, the vîspê daêva; but tradition lost the meaning of the
word, and the vîspô daevô became 'one who is entirely a Daêva
by his wickedness' (Comm.)

² Demons are often the restless souls of the wicked, excluded
from heaven. The Persian sect of the Mahâbâdians believed that
the soul that had not spoken and done good became an Ahriman
or *g*in (Dabistân).

³ The guilty may be killed by any one, without an order from
the Dastur (see § 74 n.), and by this execution an ordinary capital
crime may be redeemed (Comm. ad VII, 52).

VI.

33 (107). O Maker of the material world, thou Holy One! Shall the man be clean who has touched a corpse that has been dried up and dead more than a year?

34 (108). Ahura Mazda answered: 'He shall. The dry mingles not with the dry[1]. Should the dry mingle with the dry, how soon this material world of mine would have in it only Peshôtanus, shut out from the way of holiness, and whose souls will cry and wail! so numberless are the beings that die upon the face of the earth[2].'

VII.

35 (111). O Maker of the material world, thou Holy One! Can the man be made clean that has touched the corpse of a dog or the corpse of a man?

36 (113). Ahura Mazda answered: 'He can, O holy Zarathustra!'

How so?

'If the Nasu has already been smitten by the corpse-eating dogs, or by the corpse-eating birds,

---

[1] See Introd. V. This principle still prevails even with Musulman Persians: 'Pour encourir leur immondicité dans l'attouchement des Chretiens et autres idolatres, il est nécessaire que s'ils les touchent, leurs vêtements soient mouillés. C'est à cause, disent-ils, qu'étans secs l'immondicité ne s'attache pas; . . . . ce qui est cause que dans les villes où leurs Mullas et Docteurs ont plus d'autorité, ils font par fois défendre par leurs Kans que lorsqu'il pleut, les Chrétiens ne sortent pas de leurs maisons, de crainte que par accident, venans à les heurter, ils ne soient rendus immondes' (G. du Chinon, p. 88 seq.; cf. Chardin).

[2] See Farg. V, 4.

he shall cleanse his body with gômêz and water, and he shall be clean [1].

37 (117). 'If the Nasu has not yet been smitten by the corpse-eating dogs, or by the corpse-eating birds [2], then the worshippers of Mazda shall dig three holes in the ground [3], and he shall thereupon wash his body with gômêz, not with water. They shall then lift and bring my dog [4], they shall bring him (thus shall it be done and not otherwise) in front of the man [5].

38 (121). 'The worshippers of Mazda shall dig three other holes [6] in the ground, and he shall thereupon wash his body with gômêz, not with water. They shall then lift and bring my dog, they shall bring him (thus shall it be done and not otherwise) in front of the man. Then they shall wait until he is dried [7] even to the last hair on the top of his head.

39 (125). 'They shall dig three more holes [8] in the ground, and he shall thereupon wash his body with water, not with gômêz.

40 (127). 'He shall first wash his hands; if his

---

[1] If the Sag-dîd has been performed, a simple ghosel is enough (see Introd. V, 16).

[2] If the Sag-dîd has not been performed, the Barashnûm is necessary (see Introd. V, 16).

[3] The first three holes, which contain gômêz. For the disposition of the holes, see the following Fargard.

[4] Three times; every time that the unclean one passes from one hole to another (Comm. ad IX, 32).

[5] To look at him, or, rather, at the Nasu in him, whilst the priest sings the 'fiend-smiting spells.'

[6] Containing gômêz too.

[7] He rubs himself dry with handfuls of dust (see IX, 29 seq.)

[8] Containing water.

hands be not first washed, he makes the whole of his body unclean. When he has washed his hands three times, after his hands have been washed, thou shalt sprinkle with water the forepart of his skull.'

41 (131). O Maker of the material world, thou Holy One! When the good waters reach the forepart of the skull, whereon does the Drug Nasu rush [1]?

Ahura Mazda answered: 'In front, between the brows, the Drug Nasu rushes.'

42 (134). O Maker of the material world, thou Holy One! When the good waters reach in front between the brows, whereon does the Drug Nasu rush?

Ahura Mazda answered: 'On the back part of the skull the Drug Nasu rushes.'

43 (137). O Maker of the material world, thou Holy One! When the good waters reach the back part of the skull, whereon does the Drug Nasu rush?

Ahura Mazda answered: 'In front, on the jaws, the Drug Nasu rushes.'

44 (140). O Maker of the material world, thou Holy One! When the good waters reach in front, on the jaws, whereon does the Drug Nasu rush?

Ahura Mazda answered: 'Upon the right ear the Drug Nasu rushes.'

45 (143). O Maker of the material world, thou Holy One! When the good waters reach the right ear, whereon does the Drug Nasu rush?

---

[1] The Nasu is expelled symmetrically, from limb to limb, from the right side of the body to the left, from the forepart to the back parts, and she flies, thus pursued, downwards from the top of the head to the tips of the toes.

Ahura Mazda answered : ' Upon the left ear the
Drug Nasu rushes.'

46 (146). O Maker of the material world, thou
Holy One! When the good waters reach the left
ear, whereon does the Drug Nasu rush ?

Ahura Mazda answered:. 'Upon the right shoulder
the Drug Nasu rushes.'

47 (149). O Maker of the material world, thou
Holy One! When the good waters reach the right
shoulder, whereon does the Drug Nasu rush ?

Ahura Mazda answered : ' Upon the left shoulder
the Drug Nasu rushes.'

48 (152). O Maker of the material world, thou
Holy One! When the good waters reach the left
shoulder, whereon does the Drug Nasu rush ?

Ahura Mazda answered : ' Upon the right arm-pit
the Drug Nasu rushes.'

49 (155). O Maker of the material world, thou
Holy One! When the good waters reach the right
arm-pit, whereon does the Drug Nasu rush ?

Ahura Mazda answered: ' Upon the left arm-pit
the Drug Nasu rushes.'

50 (158). O Maker of the material world, thou
Holy One! When the good waters reach the left
arm-pit, whereon does the Drug Nasu rush ?

Ahura Mazda answered : ' In front, upon the
chest, the Drug Nasu rushes.'

51 (161). O Maker of the material world, thou
Holy One! When the good waters reach the
chest in front, whereon does the Drug Nasu
rush ?

Ahura Mazda answered : ' Upon the back the
Drug Nasu rushes.'

52 (164). O Maker of the material world, thou

Holy One! When the good waters reach the back, whereon does the Drug Nasu rush?

Ahura Mazda answered: 'Upon the right nipple the Drug Nasu rushes.'

53 (167). O Maker of the material world, thou Holy One! When the good waters reach the right nipple, whereon does the Drug Nasu rush?

Ahura Mazda answered: 'Upon the left nipple the Drug Nasu rushes.'

54 (170). O Maker of the material world, thou Holy One! When the good waters reach the left nipple, whereon does the Drug Nasu rush?

Ahura Mazda answered: 'Upon the right rib the Drug Nasu rushes.'

55 (173). O Maker of the material world, thou Holy One! When the good waters reach the right rib, whereon does the Drug Nasu rush?

Ahura Mazda answered: 'Upon the left rib the Drug Nasu rushes.'

56 (176). O Maker of the material world, thou Holy One! When the good waters reach the left rib, whereon does the Drug Nasu rush?

Ahura Mazda answered: 'Upon the right hip the Drug Nasu rushes.'

57 (179). O Maker of the material world, thou Holy One! When the good waters reach the right hip, whereon does the Drug Nasu rush?

Ahura Mazda answered: 'Upon the left hip the Drug Nasu rushes.'

58 (182). O Maker of the material world, thou Holy One! When the good waters reach the left hip, whereon does the Drug Nasu rush?

Ahura Mazda answered: 'Upon the sexual parts the Drug Nasu rushes. If the unclean one be a

man, thou shalt sprinkle him first behind, then
before; if the unclean one be a woman, thou shalt
sprinkle her first before, then behind.

59 (187). O Maker of the material world, thou
Holy One! When the good waters reach the
sexual parts, whereon does the Drug Nasu rush?

Ahura Mazda answered: 'Upon the right thigh
the Drug Nasu rushes.'

60 (190). O Maker of the material world, thou
Holy One! When the good waters reach the
right thigh, whereon does the Drug Nasu rush?

Ahura Mazda answered: 'Upon the left thigh
the Drug Nasu rushes.'

61 (193). O Maker of the material world, thou
Holy One! When the good waters reach the left
thigh, whereon does the Drug Nasu rush?

Ahura Mazda answered: 'Upon the right knee
the Drug Nasu rushes.'

62 (196). O Maker of the material world, thou
Holy One! When the good waters reach the right
knee, whereon does the Drug Nasu rush?

Ahura Mazda answered: 'Upon the left knee the
Drug Nasu rushes.'

63 (199). O Maker of the material world, thou
Holy One! When the good waters reach the left
knee, whereon does the Drug Nasu rush?

Ahura Mazda answered: 'Upon the right leg the
Drug Nasu rushes.'

64 (202). O Maker of the material world, thou
Holy One! When the good waters reach the right
leg, whereon does the Drug Nasu rush?

Ahura Mazda answered: 'Upon the left leg the
Drug Nasu rushes.'

65 (205). O Maker of the material world, thou

Holy One! When the good waters reach the left leg, whereon does the Drug Nasu rush?

Ahura Mazda answered: 'Upon the right ankle the Drug Nasu rushes.'

66 (208). O Maker of the material world, thou Holy One! When the good waters reach the right ankle, whereon does the Drug Nasu rush?

Ahura Mazda answered: 'Upon the left ankle the Drug Nasu rushes.'

67 (211). O Maker of the material world, thou Holy One! When the good waters reach the left ankle, whereon does the Drug Nasu rush?

Ahura Mazda answered: 'Upon the right instep the Drug Nasu rushes.'

68 (214). O Maker of the material world, thou Holy One! When the good waters reach the right instep, whereon does the Drug Nasu rush?

Ahura Mazda answered: 'Upon the left instep the Drug Nasu rushes.'

69 (217). O Maker of the material world, thou Holy One! When the good waters reach the left instep, whereon does the Drug Nasu rush?

Ahura Mazda answered: 'She is driven to the sole of the foot, where what is seen of her is like the wing of a fly.

70 (220). 'He shall press his toes upon the ground, and shall raise up his heels; thou shalt sprinkle his right sole with water; then the Drug Nasu rushes upon the left sole. Thou shalt sprinkle the left sole with water; then the Drug Nasu is driven to the toes, where what is seen of her is like the wing of a fly.

71 (225). 'He shall press his heels upon the ground and shall raise up his toes; thou shalt

sprinkle his right toe with water; then the Drug
Nasu rushes upon the left toe. Thou shalt sprinkle
the left toe with water; then the Drug Nasu
flies away to the regions of the north, in the shape
of a raging fly, with knees and tail sticking out,
all stained with stains, and like unto the foulest
Khrafstras.

[72. 'And thou shalt say aloud these fiend-smiting
and most-healing words :

'"The will of the Lord is the law of holiness," &c.

'"Whom hast thou placed to protect me, O
Mazda! while the hate of the fiend is grasping
me?" &c.

'"Who is he who will smite the fiend in order to
maintain thy ordinances?" &c.[1]

'"Keep us from our hater, O Mazda and Ârmaiti
Spenta! Perish, O fiendish Drug! Perish, O
brood of the fiend! Perish, O world of the fiend!
Perish away, O Drug! Rush away, O Drug!
Perish away, O Drug! Perish away to the regions
of the north, never more to give unto death the
living world of the holy spirit[2]!"']

VIII.

73 (229). O Maker of the material world, thou
Holy One! If worshippers of Mazda, walking, or
running, or riding, or driving, come upon a corpse-
burning fire, whereon a corpse is being cooked or
roasted, what shall they do?

74 (233). Ahura Mazda answered : 'They shall
kill the man that burns the corpse; surely they shall

---

[1] As in §§ 19, 20.   [2] From the Vendîdâd Sâdah.

kill him[1]. They shall take off the cauldron, they shall take off the tripod.

75 (237). 'Then they shall kindle wood from that fire; either wood of those trees that have the seed of fire in them, or bundles of the very wood that was prepared for that fire; and they shall separate and disperse it, that it may die out the sooner.

76 (242). 'Thus they shall lay a first bundle on the ground[2], a Vîtasti[3] away from the corpse-burning fire, and they shall separate and disperse it, that it may die out the sooner.

77 (245). 'They shall lay down a second bundle on the ground, a Vîtasti away from the corpse-burning fire, and they shall separate and disperse it, that it may die out the sooner.

'They shall lay down a third bundle on the ground, a Vîtasti away from the corpse-burning fire, and they shall separate and disperse it, that it may die out the sooner.

'They shall lay down a fourth bundle on the ground, a Vîtasti away from the corpse-burning fire, and they shall separate and disperse it, that it may die out the sooner.

---

[1] 'He who burns Nasâ (dead matter) must be killed. Burning or roasting Nasâ from the dead is a capital crime. . . . Four men can be put to death by any one without an order from the Dastur: the Nasâ-burner, the highwayman, the Sodomite, and the criminal taken in the deed' (Comm.)

[2] In a hole dug for that purpose; such is at least the custom nowadays. The ceremony seems to be an imitation of the Barashnûm. The unclean fire, represented by the nine bundles, passes through the nine holes, as the unclean man does (see above, § 37 seq. and Farg. IX, 12 seq.), and leaves at each of them some of the uncleanness it has contracted.

[3] A span of twelve fingers.

'They shall lay down a fifth bundle on the ground, a Vîtasti away from the corpse-burning fire, and they shall separate and disperse it, that it may die out the sooner.

'They shall lay down a sixth bundle on the ground, a Vîtasti away from the corpse-burning fire, and they shall separate and disperse it, that it may die out the sooner.

'They shall lay down a seventh bundle on the ground, a Vîtasti away from the corpse-burning fire, and they shall separate and disperse it, that it may die out the sooner.

'They shall lay down an eighth bundle on the ground, a Vîtasti away from the corpse-burning fire, and they shall separate and disperse it, that it may die out the sooner.

78 (245). 'They shall lay down a ninth bundle on the ground, a Vîtasti away from the corpse-burning fire, and they shall separate and disperse it, that it may die out the sooner.

79, 80 (246). 'If a man shall then piously bring unto the fire, O Spitama Zarathustra! wood of Urvâsna, or Vohu-gaona, or Vohu-kereti, or Hadhâ-naêpata, or any other sweet-smelling wood, wheresoever the wind shall bring the perfume of the fire, thereunto Fire, the son of Ahura Mazda, shall go and kill thousands of unseen Daêvas, thousands of fiends, the brood of darkness, thousands of couples of Yâtus and Pairikas[1].'

IX.

81 (251). O Maker of the material world, thou Holy One! If a man bring a corpse-burning fire

[1] See Introd. IV, 20–21.

to the Dâityô-gâtu [1], what shall be his reward when his soul has parted with his body?

Ahura Mazda answered: 'His reward shall be the same as if he had, here below, brought ten thousand fire-brands to the Dâityô-gâtu.'

82 (254). O Maker of the material world, thou Holy One! If a man bring to the Dâityô-gâtu the fire wherein excrement has been burnt [2], what shall be his reward when his soul has parted with his body?

Ahura Mazda answered: 'His reward shall be the same as if he had, here below, brought a thousand fire-brands to the Dâityô-gâtu.'

83 (257). O Maker of the material world, thou Holy One! If a man bring to the Dâityô-gâtu the fire wherein cowdung has been burnt [3], what shall be his reward when his soul has parted with his body?

Ahura Mazda answered: 'His reward shall be the same as if he had, here below, brought five hundred fire-brands to the Dâityô-gâtu.'

84 (258). O Maker of the material world, thou Holy One! If a man bring to the Dâityô-gâtu the fire from the kiln of a brick-maker [4], what shall be

---

[1] 'The proper abode,' the Bahrâm fire (see Introd. V, 8). The Bahrâm fire is composed of a thousand and one fires belonging to sixteen different classes (ninety-one corpse-burning fires, eighty dyers' fires, &c.) As the earthly representative of the heavenly fire, it is the sacred centre to which every earthly fire longs to return, in order to be united again, as much as possible, with its native abode. The more it has been defiled by worldly uses, the greater is the merit acquired by freeing it from defilement.

[2] 'The fire of the lac-makers and of the dyers' (Asp. and Gr. Rav. 120).

[3] 'The fire of a bath,' according to Aspendiârji; but see Introd. V, 8.

[4] Or, 'from a lime-kiln' (Comm.)

his reward when his soul has parted with his body?

Ahura Mazda answered: 'His reward shall be the same as if he had, here below, brought four hundred fire-brands to the Dâityô-gâtu.'

85 (259). O Maker of the material world, thou Holy One! If a man bring to the Dâityô-gâtu the fire from a potter's kiln, what shall be his reward when his soul has parted with his body?

Ahura Mazda answered: 'His reward shall be the same as if he had, here below, brought to the Dâityô-gâtu as many fire-brands as there were pots baked in that fire [1].'

86 (260). O Maker of the material world, thou Holy One! If a man bring to the Dâityô-gâtu the fire of the reapers [1], what shall be his reward when his soul has parted with his body?

Ahura Mazda answered: 'His reward shall be the same as if he had, here below, brought to the Dâityô-gâtu as many fire-brands as there were plants in the crop [1].'

87 (261). O Maker of the material world, thou Holy One! If a man bring to the Dâityô-gâtu the fire of a goldsmith, what shall be his reward when his soul has parted with his body?

Ahura Mazda answered: 'His reward shall be the same as if he had, here below, brought a hundred fire-brands to the Dâityô-gâtu.'

88 (262). O Maker of the material world, thou Holy One! If a man bring to the Dâityô-gâtu the fire of a silversmith, what shall be his reward when his soul has parted with his body?

---

[1] Doubtful.

Ahura Mazda answered: 'His reward shall be the same as if he had, here below, brought ninety fire-brands to the Dâityô-gâtu.'

89 (263). O Maker of the material world, thou Holy One! If a man bring to the Dâityô-gâtu the fire of a worker in brass, what shall be his reward when his soul has parted with his body?

Ahura Mazda answered: 'His reward shall be the same as if he had, here below, brought eighty fire-brands to the Dâityô-gâtu.'

90 (264). O Maker of the material world, thou Holy One! If a man bring to the Dâityô-gâtu the fire of a blacksmith, what shall be his reward when his soul has parted with his body?

Ahura Mazda answered: 'His reward shall be the same as if he had, here below, brought seventy fire-brands to the Dâityô-gâtu.'

91 (265). O Maker of the material world, thou Holy One! If a man bring to the Dâityô-gâtu the fire of an oven [1], what shall be his reward when his soul has parted from his body?

Ahura Mazda answered: 'His reward shall be the same as if he had, here below, brought sixty fire-brands to the Dâityô-gâtu.'

92 (266). O Maker of the material world, thou Holy One! If a man bring to the Dâityô-gâtu the fire from under a cauldron [2], what shall be his reward when his soul has parted with his body?

Ahura Mazda answered: 'His reward shall be the same as if he had, here below, brought fifty fire-brands to the Dâityô-gâtu.'

93 (267). O Maker of the material world, thou

---

[1] A baker's fire.　　　　[2] The kitchen-fire.

Holy One! If a man bring to the Dâityô-gâtu the fire from an encampment [1], what shall be his reward when his soul has parted with his body?

Ahura Mazda answered: 'His reward shall be the same as if he had, here below, brought forty fire-brands to the Dâityô-gâtu.'

94 (268). O Maker of the material world, thou Holy One! If a man bring a herdsman's fire to the Dâityô-gâtu, what shall be his reward when his soul has parted with his body?

Ahura Mazda answered: 'His reward shall be the same as if he had, here below, brought thirty fire-brands to the Dâityô-gâtu.'

[95 (269) [2]. O Maker of the material world, thou Holy One! If a man bring to the Dâityô-gâtu the fire of the field [3], what shall be his reward when his soul has parted with his body?

Ahura Mazda answered: 'His reward shall be the same as if he had, here below, brought twenty fire-brands to the Dâityô-gâtu.']

96 (270). O Maker of the material world, thou Holy One! If a man bring to the Dâityô-gâtu the fire of his own hearth, what shall be his reward when his soul has parted with his body?

Ahura Mazda answered: 'His reward shall be the same as if he had, here below, brought ten fire-brands to the Dâityô-gâtu.'

X.

97 (271). O Maker of the material world, thou Holy One! Can a man be made clean, O holy

---

[1] Doubtful.

[2] From the Vendîdâd Sâdah.   [3] The hunter's fire.

Ahura Mazda! who has touched a corpse in a distant place in the fields [1]?

98 (272). Ahura Mazda answered: 'He can, O holy Zarathustra.'

How so?

'If the Nasu has already been smitten by the corpse-eating dogs or the corpse-eating birds, he shall wash his body with gômêz; he shall wash it thirty times, he shall rub it dry with the hand thirty times, beginning every time with the head [2].

99 (278). 'If the Nasu has not yet been smitten by the corpse-eating dogs or the corpse-eating birds, he shall wash his body with gômêz; he shall wash it fifteen times, he shall rub it dry with the hand fifteen times [3].

100 (280). 'Then he shall run a distance of a Hâthra [4]. He shall run until he meets some man on his way, then he shall cry out aloud: "Here am I, one who has touched the corpse of a man, without any wilful sin of mind, tongue, or hand, and who wishes to be made clean." Thus shall he run until he overtakes the man. If the man will not cleanse him, he takes upon his own head the third of his trespass.

101 (287). 'Then he shall run another Hâthra, he shall run off again until he overtakes a man; if

---

[1] Where the regular process of purification cannot be performed.

[2] If the Sag-dîd has been performed, the Sî-shû (thirtyfold washing) is enough. Cf. above, §§ 35, 36.

[3] If the Sag-dîd has not been performed, he cleanses himself in a summary way till he comes to a place where the Barashnûm can be performed.

[4] See p. 17, n. 1.

the man will not cleanse him, he takes upon his own head the half of his trespass.

102 (291). 'Then he shall run a third Hâthra, he shall run off a third time until he overtakes a man; if the man will not cleanse him, he takes upon his own head the whole of his trespass.

103 (294). 'Thus shall he run forwards until he comes near a house, a borough, a town, an inhabited district, and he shall cry out with a loud voice: "Here am I, one who has touched the corpse of a man, without any wilful sin of mind, tongue, or hand, and who wishes to be made clean." If they will not cleanse him, he shall cleanse his body with gômêz and water; thus shall he be clean[1].'

104 (300). O Maker of the material world, thou Holy One! If he found water on his way, the water requires an atonement[2]; what is the penalty that he shall pay?

105 (303). Ahura Mazda answered: 'Four hundred stripes with the Aspahê-astra, four hundred stripes with the Sraoshô-karana.'

106 (304). O Maker of the material world, thou Holy One! If he found trees[3] on his way, the fire requires an atonement; what is the penalty he shall pay?

Ahura Mazda answered: 'Four hundred stripes with the Aspahê-astra, four hundred stripes with the Sraoshô-karana.

[1] 'He may then attend to his business; he may work and till; some say he must abstain from sacrifice (till he has undergone the Barashnûm),' (Comm.)

[2] As he defiled it by crossing it.

[3] 'Trees fit for the fire' (Comm.) If he touches those trees, the fire to which they are brought becomes unclean by his fault.

107 (308). 'This is the penalty, this is the atonement, which saves him who submits to it; he who does not submit to it, shall surely be an inhabitant in the mansion of the Drug[1].'

FARGARD IX.

The nine nights' Barashnûm.

I a (1-11). Description of the place for cleansing the unclean (the Barashnûm-gâh).

I b (12-36). Description of the cleansing.

II (37-44). Fees of the cleanser.

III (47-57). The false cleanser; his punishment.

§§ 45, 46 belong better to the following Fargard.

The ceremony described in this Fargard is known among the Parsis as Barashnûm nû shaba, or 'nine nights' Barashnûm,' because it lasts for nine nights (see § 35)[2]. It is the great purification, the most efficacious of all; it not only makes the defiled man clean, but it opens to him the heavens (see Farg. XIX, 33; cf. Introd. V, 16). So, although it was formerly intended only for the man defiled by the dead, it became, during the Parsi period, a pious work which might be performed without any corpse having been touched; nay, its performance was prescribed, once at least, at the time of the Nû zûdî (at the age of fifteen, when the young Parsi becomes a member of the community), in order to wash away the natural uncleanness that has been contracted in the maternal womb (Saddar 36, Hyde 40)[3].

I a.

1. Zarathustra asked Ahura Mazda : 'O most

---

[1] Hell. Cf. Farg. XIV, 18.

[2] As to the word Barashnûm, it seems not to refer to the ceremony itself, and to be nothing more than the Zend word bareshnûm, 'the top of the head, the skull,' the part of the body that is first to be washed (§ 15).

[3] For the plan of the Barashnûm-gâh, see Anquetil II, p. 456.

beneficent Spirit, Maker of the material world, thou Holy One! How shall they manage here below, who want to cleanse the body of one defiled by the dead?'

2 (4). Ahura Mazda answered: 'A godly man, O Spitama Zarathustra! who speaks truth, who learns the Holy Word, and who knows best the rites of cleansing according to the law of Mazda[1], such a man shall fell the trees off the surface of the ground on a space of nine Vîbâzus[2] square.

3 (9). 'It should be the part of the ground where there is least water and where there are fewest trees, the part which is the cleanest and driest, and the least passed through by sheep and oxen, and by Fire, the son of Ahura Mazda, by the consecrated bundles of baresma, and by the faithful.'

4 (11). How far from the fire? How far from the water? How far from the consecrated bundles of baresma? How far from the faithful?

5 (12). Ahura Mazda answered: 'Thirty paces from the fire, thirty paces from the water, thirty paces from the consecrated bundles of baresma, three paces from the faithful.

6 (13). 'Then thou shalt dig a hole, two fingers deep if the summer has come, four fingers deep if the winter and ice have come[3].

7 (14). 'Thou shalt dig a second hole, two fingers deep if the summer has come, four fingers deep if the winter and ice have come.

'Thou shalt dig a third hole, two fingers deep if

---

[1] A priest.

[2] The Vîbâzu seems to have been as much as ten paces.

[3] See Introd. V, 16.

the summer has come, four fingers deep if the winter and ice have come.

'Thou shalt dig a fourth hole, two fingers deep if the summer has come, four fingers deep if the winter and ice have come.

'Thou shalt dig a fifth hole, two fingers deep if the summer has come, four fingers deep if the winter and ice have come.

'Thou shalt dig a sixth hole[1], two fingers deep if the summer has come, four fingers deep if the winter and ice have come.'

8 (14). How far from one another?
'One pace.'

How much is the pace?

'As much as three feet.

9 (16). 'Then thou shalt dig three holes more[2], two fingers deep if the summer has come, four fingers deep if the winter and ice have come.'

How far from the former six?

'Three paces.'

What sort of paces?

'Such as are taken in walking.'

How much are those (three) paces?

'As much as nine feet.

10 (22). 'Then thou shalt draw a furrow all around with a metal knife.'

How far from the holes?

'Three paces.'

What sort of paces?

'Such as are taken in walking.'

---

[1] These six holes contain gômêz. 'The holes must be dug from the north to the south' (Comm.)

[2] The three holes to contain water.

How much are those (three) paces?

'As much as nine feet.

11 (24). 'Thou shalt draw twelve furrows [1]; three of which thou shalt draw around (the first) three holes; three thou shalt draw around (the first) six holes; three thou shalt draw around the nine holes; three thou shalt draw around the three holes, outside the six holes [2]. At each of the three times nine feet [3], thou shalt place stones as steps to the holes; or potsherds, or stumps, or clods, or any hard matter [4].'

I b.

12 (31). 'Then the unclean one shall walk to the holes; thou, O Zarathustra! shalt stand outside by the furrow, and thou shalt recite, Nemaskâ yâ

---

[1] 'The furrows must be drawn during the day; they must be drawn with a knife; they must be drawn with recitation of spells. While drawing the furrows the cleanser recites three Ashem-vohus ("holiness is the best of all good," &c.), the Fravarânê ("I declare myself a worshipper of Mazda, a follower of Zarathustra, a foe of the fiend," &c.), the Khshnûman of Serosh, and the Bâg of Serosh; they must be drawn from the north' (Comm. ad § 32). The furrow, or kesh, plays a greater part in the Mazdean liturgy than in any other. By means of the furrow, drawn with proper spells, and according to the laws of spiritual war, man either besieges the fiend or intrenches himself against him (cf. Farg. XVII, 5). In the present case the Drug, being shut up inside the kesh and thus excluded from the world outside, and being driven back, step by step, by the strength of the holy water and spells, finds at last no place of refuge but hell, and the world is freed from her presence.

[2] 'The three holes for water, the six holes for gômêz' (Comm.)

[3] The nine feet between the holes containing gômêz and those containing water, the nine feet between the first holes and the furrows, and the nine feet between the last hole and the furrows.

[4] That the foot of the unclean one may not touch the earth (see Introd. V, 10).

ârmaiti*s* î*za*kâ [1]; and the unclean one shall repeat, Nemas*k*â yâ ârmaiti*s* î*za*kâ.

13 (35). 'The Dru*g* becomes weaker and weaker at every one of those words which are to smite the fiend Angra Mainyu, to smite Aêshma of the bloody spear [2], to smite the Mâzainya fiends [3], to smite all the fiends.

14 (40). 'Then thou shalt sprinkle him with gômêz from a spoon of brass or of lead; thou shalt take a stick with nine knots [4], O Spitama Zarathu*s*tra! and thou shalt fasten the leaden spoon to the upper part of the stick.

15 (43). 'They shall wash his hands first. If his hands be not washed first, he makes his whole body unclean. When he has washed his hands three times, after his hands have been washed, thou shalt sprinkle the forepart of his skull; then the Dru*g* Nasu rushes in front, between his brows [5].

16 (50). 'Thou shalt sprinkle him in front between the brows; then the Dru*g* Nasu rushes upon the back part of the skull.

'Thou shalt sprinkle the back part of the skull; then the Dru*g* Nasu rushes upon the jaws.

'Thou shalt sprinkle the jaws; then the Dru*g* Nasu rushes upon the right ear.

17 (56). 'Thou shalt sprinkle the right ear; then the Dru*g* Nasu rushes upon the left ear.

'Thou shalt sprinkle the left ear; then the Dru*g* Nasu rushes upon the right shoulder.

---

[1] Yasna XLIX, 10. [2] See Introd. IV, 22. [3] See Introd. IV, 23.

[4] So long that the cleanser may take gômêz or water from the holes and sprinkle the unclean one, without touching him and without going inside the furrows.

[5] Cf. Farg. VIII, 40–71.

'Thou shalt sprinkle the right shoulder; then the Drug Nasu rushes upon the left shoulder.

'Thou shalt sprinkle the left shoulder; then the Drug Nasu rushes upon the right arm-pit.

18 (64). 'Thou shalt sprinkle the right arm-pit; then the Drug Nasu rushes upon the left arm-pit.

'Thou shalt sprinkle the left arm-pit; then the Drug Nasu rushes upon the chest.

'Thou shalt sprinkle the chest; then the Drug Nasu rushes upon the back.

19 (70). 'Thou shalt sprinkle the back; then the Drug Nasu rushes upon the right nipple.

'Thou shalt sprinkle the right nipple; then the Drug Nasu rushes upon the left nipple.

'Thou shalt sprinkle the left nipple; then the Drug Nasu rushes upon the right rib.

20 (76). 'Thou shalt sprinkle the right rib; then the Drug Nasu rushes upon the left rib.

'Thou shalt sprinkle the left rib; then the Drug Nasu rushes upon the right hip.

'Thou shalt sprinkle the right hip; then the Drug Nasu rushes upon the left hip.

21 (82). 'Thou shalt sprinkle the left hip; then the Drug Nasu rushes upon the sexual parts.

'Thou shalt sprinkle the sexual parts. If the unclean one be a man, thou shalt sprinkle him first behind, then before; if the unclean one be a woman, thou shalt sprinkle her first before, then behind; then the Drug Nasu rushes upon the right thigh.

22 (88). 'Thou shalt sprinkle the right thigh; then the Drug Nasu rushes upon the left thigh.

'Thou shalt sprinkle the left thigh; then the Drug Nasu rushes upon the right knee.

'Thou shalt sprinkle the right knee; then the Drug Nasu rushes upon the left knee.

23 (94). 'Thou shalt sprinkle the left knee; then the Drug Nasu rushes upon the right leg.

'Thou shalt sprinkle the right leg; then the Drug Nasu rushes upon the left leg.

'Thou shalt sprinkle the left leg; then the Drug Nasu rushes upon the right ankle.

'Thou shalt sprinkle the right ankle; then the Drug Nasu rushes upon the left ankle.

24 (102). 'Thou shalt sprinkle the left ankle; then the Drug Nasu rushes upon the right instep.

'Thou shalt sprinkle the right instep; then the Drug Nasu rushes upon the left instep.

'Thou shalt sprinkle the left instep; then the Drug Nasu is driven to the sole of the foot, where what is seen of her is like the wing of a fly.

25 (108). 'He shall press his toes upon the ground and shall raise up his heels; thou shalt sprinkle his right sole; then the Drug Nasu rushes upon the left sole.

'Thou shalt sprinkle the left sole; then the Drug Nasu is driven to the toes, where what is seen of her is like the wing of a fly.

26 (113). 'He shall press his heels upon the ground and shall raise up his toes; thou shalt sprinkle his right toe; then the Drug Nasu rushes upon the left toe.

'Thou shalt sprinkle the left toe; then the Drug Nasu flies away to the regions of the north, in the shape of a raging fly, with knees and tail sticking out, all stained with stains, and like unto the foulest Khrafstras.

27 (118). 'And thou shalt say those fiend-smiting and most-healing words :—

'"Yathâ ahû vairyô:—The will of the Lord is the law of holiness; the riches of Vohu-manô shall be given to him who works in this world for Mazda, and wields according to the will of Ahura the power he gave to him to relieve the poor.

'"Kem nâ mazdâ:—Whom hast thou placed to protect me, O Mazda! while the hate of the fiend is grasping me? Whom, but thy Âtar and Vohu-manô, by whose work the holy world goes on? Reveal to me the rules of thy law!

'"Ke verethrem gâ:—Who is he who will smite the fiend in order to maintain thy ordinances? Teach me clearly thy rules for this world and for the next, that Sraosha may come with Vohu-manô and help whomsoever thou pleasest.

'"Keep us from our hater, O Mazda and Ârmaiti Spenta! Perish, O fiendish Drug! Perish, O brood of the fiend! Perish, O world of the fiend! Perish away, O Drug! Rush away, O Drug! Perish away, O Drug! Perish away to the regions of the north, never more to give unto death the living world of the holy spirit[1]!"

28 (119). 'At the first hole the man becomes freer from the Nasu; then thou shalt say those fiend-smiting and most-healing words :—"Yathâ ahû vairyô," &c.[2]

'At the second hole he becomes freer from the Nasu; then thou shalt say those fiend-smiting and most-healing words :—"Yathâ ahû vairyô," &c.

---

[1] Cf. Farg. VIII, 19–21.
[2] As in preceding clause.

'At the third hole he becomes freer from the Nasu; then thou shalt say those fiend-smiting and most-healing words:—"Yathâ ahû vairyô," &c.

'At the fourth hole he becomes freer from the Nasu; then thou shalt say those fiend-smiting and most-healing words:—"Yathâ ahû vairyô," &c.

'At the fifth hole he becomes freer from the Nasu; then thou shalt say those fiend-smiting and most-healing words :—"Yathâ ahû vairyô," &c.

'At the sixth hole he becomes freer from the Nasu; then thou shalt say those fiend-smiting and most-healing words :—"Yathâ ahû vairyô," &c.

29 (120). 'Afterwards the unclean one shall sit down, inside the furrows [1], outside the furrows of the six holes, four fingers from those furrows. There he shall cleanse his body with thick handfuls of dust.

30 (123). 'Fifteen times shall they take up dust from the ground for him to rub his body, and they shall wait there until he is dry even to the last hair on his head.

31 (125). 'When his body is dry, then he shall step over the holes (containing water). At the first hole he shall wash his body once with water; at the second hole he shall wash his body twice with water; at the third hole he shall wash his body thrice with water.

32 (130). 'Then he shall perfume (his body) [2] with perfumes from Urvâsna, or Vohu-gaona, or Vohu-kereti, or Hadhâ-naêpata, or from any sweet-

---

[1] Between the furrows of the six holes containing gômêz and the furrows of the holes containing water.

[2] Or, possibly, 'his clothes' (see Farg. XIX, 24).

smelling plant; then he shall put on his clothes, and shall go back to his house.

33 (133). 'He shall sit down there in the place of infirmity [1], inside the house, apart from the other worshippers of Mazda. He shall not go near the fire, nor near the water, nor near the earth, nor near the cow, nor near the trees, nor near the faithful, either man or woman. Thus shall he continue until three nights have passed. When three nights have passed, he shall wash his body, he shall wash his clothes with gômêz and water to make them clean.

34 (137). 'Then he shall sit down again in the place of infirmity, inside the house, apart from the other worshippers of Mazda. He shall not go near the fire, nor near the water, nor near the earth, nor near the cow, nor near the trees, nor near the faithful, either man or woman. Thus shall he continue until six nights have passed. When six nights have passed, he shall wash his body, he shall wash his clothes with gômêz and water to make them clean.

35 (141). 'Then he shall sit down again in the place of infirmity, inside the house, apart from the other worshippers of Mazda. He shall not go near the fire, nor near the water, nor near the earth, nor near the cow, nor near the trees, nor near the faithful, either man or woman. Thus shall he continue, until nine nights have passed. When nine nights have passed, he shall wash his body, he shall wash his clothes with gômêz and water to make them clean.

36 (145). 'He may thenceforth go near the fire, near the water, near the earth, near the cow, near

---

[1] The Armêst-gâh (see Introd. V, 15).

the trees, and near the faithful, either man or woman.

II.[1]

37 (146). 'Thou shalt cleanse a priest for a holy blessing[2]; thou shalt cleanse the lord of a province for the value of a camel of high value; thou shalt cleanse the lord of a town for the value of a stallion; thou shalt cleanse the lord of a borough for the value of a bull; thou shalt cleanse the master of a house for the value of a cow three years old.

38 (151). 'Thou shalt cleanse the wife of the master of a house for the value of a ploughing[3] cow; thou shalt cleanse a menial for the value of a draught cow[4]; thou shalt cleanse a young child for the value of a lamb.

39 (154). 'These are the different cattle that the worshippers of Mazda shall give to him who has cleansed them, if they can afford it; if they cannot afford it, they shall give him any other reward that may make him leave their houses well-pleased with them, and free from anger.

40 (157). 'For if the man who has cleansed them leave their houses displeased with them, and full of anger, then the Drug Nasu enters them by the nose, by the eyes, by the tongue, by the jaws, by the sexual organs, by the hinder parts.

41 (159). 'And the Drug Nasu rushes upon them even to the end of the nails, and they are unclean thenceforth for ever and ever.

'It grieves the sun indeed, O Spitama Zarathustra!

---

[1] Cf. the tariff for the fees of physicians, Farg. VII, 41–43.
[2] See Farg. VII, 41, note.
[3] Doubtful.　　　　　　　　　　　　[4] Doubtful.

[4]　　　　　　　　K

to shine upon a man defiled by the dead; it grieves
the moon, it grieves the stars.

42 (162). 'That man delights them, O Spitama
Zarathustra! who cleanses from the Nasu those
whom she has defiled; he delights the fire, he delights the water, he delights the earth, he delights
the cow, he delights the trees, he delights the
faithful, both men and women.'

43 (164). Zarathustra asked Ahura Mazda : ' O
Maker of the material world, thou Holy One! What
shall be his reward, after his soul has parted from
his body, who has cleansed from the Nasu any one
defiled by her?'

44 (166). Ahura Mazda answered : ' The welfare
of the blessed abode thou canst promise to that
man, for his reward in the other world.'

45 [1] (167). Zarathustra asked Ahura Mazda : ' O
Maker of the material world, thou Holy One! How
shall I fight against that Drug who from the dead
rushes upon the living ? How shall I fight against
that Nasu who from the dead defiles the living?'

46 (169). Ahura Mazda answered : ' Say aloud
those words in the Gâthas that are to be said twice;
say aloud those words in the Gâthas that are to be
said thrice ; say aloud those words in the Gâthas
that are to be said four times; and the Drug shall
fade away like the self-moving arrow [2], like the
carpet of the earth [3] when the year is over, like its
garment [3] which lasts a season.'

---

[1] This clause and the following one as far as 'and the Drug'
are further developed in the following Fargard.
[2] See Introd. IV, 26.　　　　[3] The grass.

III.

47 (172). O Maker of the material world, thou Holy One! If a man who does not know the rites of cleansing according to the law of Mazda, offers to cleanse the unclean, what shall the worshippers of Mazda do? How shall I then fight against that Drug who from the dead rushes upon the living? How shall I fight against that Drug who from the dead defiles the living?

48 (175). Ahura Mazda answered: 'Then, O Spitama Zarathustra! the Drug Nasu waxes stronger than she was before. Stronger then are sickness and death and the working of the fiend than they were before.'

49 (177). O Maker of the material world, thou Holy One! What is the penalty that he shall pay?

Ahura Mazda answered: 'The worshippers of Mazda shall bind him; they shall bind his hands first; then they shall strip him of his clothes, they shall flay him alive, they shall cut off his head, and they shall give over his corpse unto the greediest of the birds of the beneficent spirit, unto the corpse-eating birds, unto the ravens, with these words [1]:—

'"The man here has repented of all his evil thoughts, words, and deeds.

50 (183). '"If he has committed any other evil

---

[1] 'The cleanser who has not performed the cleansing according to the rites, shall be taken to a desert place; there they shall nail him with four nails, they shall take off the skin from his body, and cut off his head. If he has performed Patet for his sin, he shall be holy (that is, he shall go to paradise); if he has not performed Patet, he shall stay in hell till the day of resurrection' (Fraser Ravaet, p. 398). Cf. Farg. III, 20 seq.

K 2

deed, it is remitted by his repentance; if he has committed no other evil deed, he is absolved by his repentance for ever and ever [1]." '

51 (187). Who is he, O Ahura Mazda! who threatens to take away fulness and increase from the world, and to bring in sickness and death?

52 (188). Ahura Mazda answered : 'It is the ungodly Ashemaogha [2], O Spitama Zarathustra! who in this material world cleanses the unclean without knowing the rites of cleansing according to the law of Mazda.

53 (190). 'For until then, O Spitama Zarathustra! sweetness and fatness would flow out from that land and from those fields, with health and healing, with fulness and increase and growth, and a growing of corn and grass [3].'

54 (191). O Maker of the material world, thou Holy One! When are sweetness and fatness to come back again to that land and to those fields, with health and healing, with fulness and increase and growth, and a growing of corn and grass?

55, 56 (192, 193). Ahura Mazda answered: 'Sweetness and fatness will never come back again to that land and to those fields, with health and healing, with fulness and increase and growth, and a growing of corn and grass, until that ungodly Ashemaogha has been put to death, and the holy Sraosha has been in that place, offered up a sacrifice [4], for three

---

[1] See Farg. III, 20 seq., and Introd. V.
[2] See Introd. IV.   [3] Cf. XIII, 52 seq.
[4] The so-called zanda ravân, 'the sacrifice that makes the soul living,' that is to say, that makes it enter heaven. It is probably to be performed only in case the sinner has performed the Patet (see the note to § 49).

days and three nights, with fire blazing, with baresma tied up, and with Haoma uplifted.

57 (196). 'Then sweetness and fatness will come back again to that land and to those fields, with health and healing, with fulness and increase and growth, and a growing of corn and grass.'

FARGARD X.

During the process of cleansing, the voice works with the hand. The spells which must be recited while the unclean one is cleansing himself have already been mentioned in the preceding Fargard, but we find here a detailed list of spells which are to be spoken twice, or thrice, or four times. The exact time when they are to be uttered is not mentioned, and we do not know whether they are to accompany those prescribed in the last Fargard, and are, therefore, to be repeated as often as the unclean one is washed, or whether they are only intended to close the whole ceremony.

These spells, like the former ones, are taken from the hymns or Gâthas, the oldest and holiest part of the Avesta. They were not written for this particular purpose, but, as happens in all religions, advantage was taken of whatever there might be in the old sacred hymns which could be more or less easily applied to the special circumstances of the case. The recitation of these lines is followed by an exorcism, written in the ordinary language of the Avesta, which has been expressly composed for the occasion.

1. Zarathustra asked Ahura Mazda: 'O Ahura Mazda! most beneficent spirit, Maker of the material world, thou Holy One! How shall I fight against that Drug who from the dead rushes upon the living? How shall I fight against that Drug who from the dead defiles the living?'

2 (3). Ahura Mazda answered: 'Say aloud those words in the Gâthas that are to be said twice [1]; say

---

[1] The so-called bis-âmrûta.

aloud those words in the Gâthas that are to be said thrice [1]; say aloud those words in the Gâthas that are to be said four times [2].'

3 (7). O Maker of the material world, thou Holy One! Which are those words in the Gâthas that are to be said twice?

4 (10). Ahura Mazda answered: 'These are the words in the Gâthas that are to be said twice, and thou shalt twice say them aloud :—

ahyâ yâsâ . . . urvânem (Yasna XXVIII, 2),
humatenăm . . . mahî (Yas. XXXV, 2),
ashahyâ âad sairê . . . ahubyâ (Yas. XXXV, 8),
yathâ tû î . . . ahurâ (Yas. XXXIX, 4),
humâim thwâ . . . hudaustemâ (Yas. XLI, 3),
thwôi staotaraskâ . . . ahurâ (Yas. XLI, 5),
ustâ ahmâi . . . mananghô (Yas. XLIII, 1),
spentâ mainyû . . . ahurô (Yas. XLVII, 1),
vohu khshathrem . . . vareshânê (Yas. LI, 1),
vahistâ îstis . . . skyaothanâkâ (Yas. LIII, 1).

5 (10). 'And after thou hast twice said those words, thou shalt say aloud these fiend-smiting and most-healing words :—

'"I drive away Angra Mainyu from this house, from this borough, from this town, from this land; from the very body of the man defiled by the dead, from the very body of the woman defiled by the dead; from the master of the house, from the lord of the borough, from the lord of the town, from the lord of the land; from the whole of the holy world.

6 (12). '"I drive away the Nasu, I drive away direct defilement, I drive away indirect defilement, from this house, from this borough, from this town,

---

[1] The thris-âmrûta.   [2] The kathrus-âmrûta.

from this land; from the very body of the man defiled by the dead, from the very body of the woman
defiled by the dead; from the master of the house,
from the lord of the borough, from the lord of the
town, from the lord of the land; from the whole of
the holy world."'

7 (13). O Maker of the material world, thou
Holy One! Which are those words in the Gâthas
that are to be said thrice?

8 (16). Ahura Mazda answered: 'These are the
words in the Gâthas that are to be said thrice, and
thou shalt thrice say them aloud:—

ashem vohu . . . (Yas. XXVII, 14),

ye sevistô . . . paitî (Yas. XXXIII, 11),

hukhshathrôtemâi . . . vahistâi (Yas. XXXV, 5),

duzvarenâis . . . vahyô (Yas. LIII, 9).

9 (16). 'After thou hast thrice said those words,
thou shalt say aloud these fiend-smiting and most-
healing words:—

'" I drive away Indra[1], I drive away Sauru[1], I
drive away the daêva Naunghaithya[1], from this
house, from this borough, from this town, from this
land; from the very body of the man defiled by the
dead, from the very body of the woman defiled by
the dead; from the master of the house, from the
lord of the borough, from the lord of the town, from
the lord of the land; from the whole of the holy
world.

10 (18). '" I drive away Tauru[2], I drive away
Zairi[2], from this house, from this borough, from this
town, from this land; from the very body of the
man defiled by the dead, from the very body of the

---

[1] See Introd. IV, 41.   [2] See Introd. IV, 34.

woman defiled by the dead; from the master of the house, from the lord of the borough, from the lord of the town, from the lord of the land; from the whole of the holy world." '

11 (19). O Maker of the material world, thou Holy One! Which are those words in the Gâthas that are to be said four times?

12 (22). Ahura Mazda answered: ' These are the words in the Gâthas that are to be said four times, and thou shalt four times say them aloud :—

yathâ ahû vairyô . . .¹ (Yas. XXVII, 13),

mazdâ ad môi . . . dau ahûm² (Yas. XXXIV, 15),

â airyamâ ishyô . . . masatâ mazdau³ (Yas. LIV, 1).

13 (22). 'After thou hast said those words four times, thou shalt say aloud these fiend-smiting and most-healing words :—

' " I drive away Aêshma, the fiend of the wounding spear⁴, I drive away the daêva Akatasha⁵, from this house, from this borough, from this town, from this land; from the very body of the man defiled by the dead, from the very body of the woman defiled by the dead; from the master of the house, from the lord of the borough, from the lord of the town, from the lord of the land; from the whole of the holy world.

14 (24). ' " I drive away the Varenya daêvas⁶, I drive away the wind-daêva⁷, from this house, from

---

¹ Translated Farg. VIII, 19.   ² Translated Farg. XI, 14.

³ Translated Farg. XX, 11.

⁴ See Introd. IV, 22.

⁵ ' The worker of evil,' a personification of the evil powers, it may be a mere name of Ahriman.

⁶ See Introd. IV, 23.

⁷ The demon Vâteh, who raises storms (Brouillons d'Anquetil).

this borough, from this town, from this land; from
the very body of the man defiled by the dead, from
the very body of the woman defiled by the dead;
from the master of the house, from the lord of the
borough, from the lord of the town, from the lord of
the land; from the whole of the holy world."

15 (25). 'These are the words in the Gâthas that
are to be said twice; these are the words in the
Gâthas that are to be said thrice; these are the
words in the Gâthas that are to be said four times.

16 (26). 'These are the words that smite down
Angra Mainyu; these are the words that smite
down Aêshma, the fiend of the wounding spear;
these are the words that smite down the Mâzainya
daêvas[1]; these are the words that smite down all
the daêvas.

17 (30). 'These are the words that stand against
that Drug, against that Nasu, who from the dead
rushes upon the living, who from the dead defiles
the living.

18 (32). 'Therefore, O Zarathustra! thou shalt
dig nine holes[2] in the part of the ground where
there is least water and where there are fewest
trees; where there is nothing that may be food
either for man or beast; for purity is for man, next
to life, the greatest good; that purity that is pro-

---

[1] According to tradition, 'the Dîvs in Mazanderan;' Mazanderan is known, in fact, as a land of fiends and sorcerers; a reputa-
tion for which it is very likely indebted to the neighbouring mount
Damâvand, to which Azis Dahâka is said to be bound. Yet one
may doubt whether it gave its name to the Mâzainya daêvas, or if
it took its name from them. Mâzainya was, most probably, like
Varenya, an epithet of the Dîvs, which, in course of time, became
the name of a class of demons.

[2] The nine holes for the Barashnûm; see above, p. 120, § 6 seq.

cured by the law of Mazda for him who cleanses himself with good thoughts, words, and deeds.

19 (38). 'Make thyself pure, O righteous man! any one in the world here below can win purity for himself, namely, when he cleanses himself with good thoughts, words, and deeds.

20. 'The will of the Lord is the law of holiness,' &c. [1]

'Whom hast thou placed to protect me, O Mazda! while the hate of the fiend is grasping me?' &c.

'Who is he who will smite the fiend in order to maintain thy ordinances?' &c.

'Keep us from our hater, O Mazda and Ârmaiti Spenta! Perish, O fiendish Drug! ... Perish away to the regions of the north, never more to give unto death the living world of the holy spirit!'

FARGARD XI.

This chapter, like the preceding, is composed of spells intended to drive away the Nasu. But they are of a more special character, as they refer to the particular objects to be cleansed, such as the house, the fire, the water, &c. Each incantation consists of two parts, a line from the Gâthas which alludes, or rather is made to allude, to the particular object, and a general exorcism, in the usual dialect, which is the same for all the objects.

1. Zarathustra asked Ahura Mazda: 'O Ahura Mazda! most beneficent spirit, Maker of the material world, thou Holy One! How shall I cleanse the house? how the fire? how the water? how the earth? how the cow? how the tree? how the faithful man and the faithful woman? how the stars? how the moon? how the sun? how the boundless light?

---

[1] The rest as in Farg. VIII, 19, 20.

how all good things, made by Mazda, the offspring
of the holy principle ?'

2 (4). Ahura Mazda answered: 'Thou shalt chant
the cleansing words, and the house shall be clean;
clean shall be the fire, clean the water, clean the
earth, clean the cow, clean the tree, clean the faithful
man and the faithful woman, clean the stars, clean
the moon, clean the sun, clean the boundless light,
clean all good things, made by Mazda, the offspring
of the holy principle.

3 (7). 'So thou shalt say these fiend-smiting and
most-healing words; thou shalt chant the Ahuna-
Vairya five times : " The will of the Lord is the law
of holiness," &c.

' The Ahuna-Vairya preserves the person of man:
" The will of the Lord is the law of holiness," &c.

' " Whom hast thou placed to protect me, O
Mazda ! while the hate of the fiend is grasping
me ?" &c.

' " Who is he who will smite the fiend in order to
maintain thy ordinances?" &c.

' " Keep us from our hater, O Mazda and Ârmaiti
Spenta!" &c.[1]

4 (9). ' If thou wantest to cleanse the house, say
these words aloud : " He is my greatest support as
long as lasts this dreary world[2]."

' If thou wantest to cleanse the fire, say these
words aloud: " Thy fire, first of all, do we approach
with worship, O Ahura Mazda[3]!"

---

[1] As in Farg. VIII, 19, 20.

[2] Yasna XLIX, 1. The allusion is not quite clear, but there
seems to be a comparison between the small house of man and
that great house the world.

[3] Yasna XXXVI, 1.

5 (13). 'If thou wantest to cleanse the water, say these words aloud: "Waters we worship, the waters in the tree, the waters in the stream, the waters in the rain [1]."

'If thou wantest to cleanse the earth, say these words aloud: "This earth we worship, this earth with the women, this earth which bears us and those women who are thine, O Ahura [2]!"

6 (17). 'If thou wantest to cleanse the cow, say these words aloud: "For the cow we order thee to do these most excellent deeds, that she may have a resting place and fodder [3]."

'If thou wantest to cleanse the trees, say these words aloud: "Out of him [4], through his holiness Mazda made the plants grow up [5]."

7 (21). 'If thou wantest to cleanse the faithful man or the faithful woman, say these words aloud: "May the beloved Airyaman come hither, for the men and women of Zarathustra to rejoice, for the faithful to rejoice; with the desirable reward that is won by means of the law, and with that boon for holiness that is vouchsafed by Ahura [6]!"

---

[1] Yasna XXXVIII, 3.

[2] Yasna XXXVIII, 1. 'Who are thine,' that is, 'who are thy wives;' these women are, or rather were, the rivers in heaven, which were considered as the wives of the heaven-god; the rain waters are called 'Ahura's spouses,' Ahurânîs (Yasna LXVIII); cf. Orm. Ahr. § 32 and Introd. IV. Tradition wrongly recognises in these women the Faroers of godly men.

[3] Yasna XXXV, 4. 'Let those excellent deeds be done for the behoof of cattle, that is to say, let stables be made, and water and fodder be given' (Comm.)

[4] The first-born bull from whose body, after his death, grew up all kinds of plants (Bund. IV; cf. Orm. Ahr. § 129 seq.)

[5] Yasna XLVIII, 6. Cf. Farg. XVII, 5.

[6] Yasna LIV, 1. Cf. Farg. XX, 11. There is no special spell for the cleansing of the sun, the moon, the stars, and the boundless

8 (25). 'Then thou shalt say these fiend-smiting and most-healing words. Thou shalt chant the Ahuna-Vairya eight times :—

'"The will of the Lord is the law of holiness," &c.

'"Whom hast thou placed to protect me, O Mazda?" &c.

'"Who is he who will smite the fiend?" &c.

'"Keep us from our hater, O Mazda!" &c.[1]

9 (26). 'I drive away Aêshma[2], I drive away the Nasu, I drive away direct defilement, I drive away indirect defilement.

[I drive away Khrû, I drive away Khrûighni[3]; I drive away Bûidhi, I drive away Bûidhiza[4]; I drive away Kundi, I drive away Kundiza.[5]]

'I drive away the yellow Bûshyãsta, I drive away the long-handed Bûshyãsta[6]; [I drive away Mûidhi[7], I drive away Kapasti.[8]]

---

light (see §§ 1, 2), because they are not defiled by the unclean one, they are only pained by seeing him (Farg. IX, 41); as soon as he is clean, they are freed from the pain.

[1] As in Farg. VIII, 19, 20.   [2] See Introd. IV, 22.

[3] Khrû and Khrûighni are not met with elsewhere; their names mean, apparently, 'wound' and 'the wounding one;' whether they belonged to concrete mythology, or were mere abstractions, is difficult to decide. They may have been mere names or epithets of Aêshma khrûidru, 'Aêshma of the wounding spear.'

[4] Bûidhiza is 'the offspring of Bûidhi,' but the meaning of Bûidhi is unknown.

[5] Kundiza is 'the offspring of Kundi;' Kundi is contracted from Kavandi or Kavanda; the Indian homonym kavandha means literally 'a tub,' and by a mythical metaphor 'a raining cloud' (Rig-veda V, 85, 3; IX, 74, 7); he becomes then the demon in the cloud (Farg. XIX, 41). He is known in Greek mythology under the name of Κάανθος (Kuhn, Herabkunft des Feuers, p. 134).

[6] See Introd. IV, 24; cf. Farg. XVIII, 16.

[7] A demon unknown. Aspendiârji translates it by 'Destruction.'

[8] Unknown. Aspendiârji çalls it 'Revenge.'

'I drive away the Pairika [1] that comes upon the fire, upon the water, upon the earth, upon the cow, upon the tree. I drive away the demon of uncleanness that comes upon the fire, upon the water, upon the earth, upon the cow, upon the tree.

10 (32). 'I drive thee away, O mischievous Angra Mainyu! from the fire, from the water, from the earth, from the cow, from the tree, from the faithful man and from the faithful woman, from the stars, from the moon, from the sun, from the boundless light, from all good things, made by Mazda, the offspring of the holy principle.

11 (33). 'Then thou shalt say these fiend-smiting and most-healing words; thou shalt chant four Ahuna-Vairyas :—

'"The will of the Lord is the law of holiness," &c.

'"Whom hast thou placed to protect me?" &c.

'"Who is he who will smite the fiend?" &c.

'"Keep us from our hater, O Mazda!" &c. [2]

12 (34). 'Away is Aêshma driven; away is the Nasu driven; away is direct defilement; away is indirect defilement driven.

['Away is Khrû, away is Khrûighni driven; away is Bûidhi, away is Bûidhiza driven; away is Kundi, away is Kundiza driven.]

'Away is Bûshyãsta driven, the yellow; away is Bûshyãsta driven, the long-handed; [away is Mûidhi, away is Kapasti driven.]

'Away is the Pairika driven that comes upon the fire, upon the water, upon the earth, upon the cow, upon the tree. Away is the demon of uncleanness driven that comes upon the fire, upon the water, upon the earth, upon the cow, upon the tree.

---

[1] See Introd. IV, 21.   [2] As in Farg. VIII, 19, 20.

13 (40). 'Away art thou driven, O mischievous
Angra Mainyu! from the fire, from the water, from
the earth, from the cow, from the tree, from the
faithful man and from the faithful woman, from the
stars, from the moon, from the sun, from the boundless light, from all good things, made by Mazda, the
offspring of the holy principle.

14 (41). 'Then thou shalt say these fiend-smiting
and most-healing words; thou shalt chant " Mazdâ
a*d* môi" four times : "O Mazda! teach me excellent
words and excellent works, that through the good
thought and the holiness of him who offers thee due
praise, thou mayest, O Lord! make the world thrive
for ever and ever, at thy will, under thy sovereign
rule [1]."

15. 'I drive away Aêshma, I drive away the
Nasu,' &c.[2]

16. 'I drive thee away, O mischievous Angra
Mainyu! from the fire, from the water,' &c.[3]

17. 'Then thou shalt say these fiend-smiting and
most-healing words; thou shalt chant the Airyama-
ishyô four times : "May the beloved Airyaman
come hither!" &c.[4]

18. 'Away is Aêshma driven; away is the Nasu
driven,' &c.[5]

19. 'Away art thou driven, O mischievous Angra
Mainyu! from the fire, from the water,' &c.[6]

20. 'Then thou shalt say these fiend-smiting and
most-healing words; thou shalt chant five Ahuna-
Vairyas:—

'"The will of the Lord is the law of holiness," &c.

---

[1] Yasna XXXIV, 15.
[2] The rest as in § 9.
[3] The rest as in § 10.
[4] As in § 7.
[5] As in § 12.
[6] As in § 13.

' " Whom hast thou placed to protect me ?" &c.

' " Who is he who will smite the fiend ?" &c.[1]

' " Keep us from our hater, O Mazda and Ârmaiti Spe*n*ta! Perish, O fiendish Dru*g*! Perish, O brood of the fiend! Perish, O world of the fiend! Perish away, O Dru*g*! Rush away, O Dru*g*! Perish away, O Dru*g*! Perish away to the regions of the north, never more to give unto death the living world of the holy spirit!"'

FARGARD XII.

This chapter is found only in the Vendîdâd Sâdah; it is missing in the Zend-Pahlavi Vendîdâd. This is owing, as it seems, only to the accidental loss of some folios in the one manuscript from which all the copies as yet known have been derived; and, in fact, even in the most ancient manuscripts the following Fargard is numbered the thirteenth (Westergaard, Zend-Avesta, preface, p. 5).

The directions in the preceding chapter are general, and do not depend on the relationship of the faithful with the deceased person; but those in this Fargard are of a special character, and apply only to the near relatives of the dead. Their object is to determine how long the time of 'staying'(upaman) should last for different relatives. What is meant by this word is not explained; but, as the word upaman is usually employed to indicate the staying of the unclean in the Armêst-gâh, apart from the faithful and from every clean object, it seems to follow that the relatives of a dead person were considered unclean from the mere fact of being related to him, and were, on this account, shut out of the frequented parts of the house. So, besides the general uncleanness arising from actual contact with a corpse, there was another form of uncleanness arising from relationship with the dead. The natural link that connects the members of one and the same family is of such a kind that no one can die without death entering all of them. Whether this is the primitive form of mourning, or only a later form of it, we will not discuss here.

---

[1] See Farg. VIII, 19, 20.

On the other hand, the house is unclean too, at least with regard to the relatives; for the time of 'staying' is followed by a purification of the house, that is not to be confounded with that described in the eighth Fargard, which takes place directly after the death and, as it appears, opens the house again only to those who were not connected with the dead man. Even nowadays, in Persia, the house where a relative has died is unlucky, and is looked upon with even more repugnance than is shown in the Avesta. The son deserts the house where his father has died; he could not live and walk in it, 'the unlucky step,' the bad qadîm is in it; 'every man's house must die with him;' therefore, he lets it fall into ruin, and builds another house farther off[1]; a custom to which there seems to be some allusion in the Pahlavi Commentary (ad I, 9).

1. If one's father or mother dies, how long shall they stay[2], the son for his father, the daughter for her mother? How long for the righteous? How long for the sinners[3]?

Ahura Mazda answered: 'They shall stay thirty days for the righteous, sixty days for the sinners.'

2 (5). O Maker of the material world, thou Holy One! How shall I cleanse the house? How shall it be clean again?

Ahura Mazda answered: 'They shall wash their bodies three times, they shall wash their clothes three times, they shall chant the Gâthas three times; they shall offer up a sacrifice to my Fire, they shall offer up the bundles of baresma, they shall bring libations to the good waters; then the house shall be clean, and then the waters may enter, then the fire may enter, and then the Amesha-Spentas may enter[4], O Spitama Zarathustra!'

---

[1] Chardin, Voyages, III, p. 7, 33 (ed. d'Amsterdam, 1711). Cf. Polack, Persien (I, p. 52). [2] See the Introd. to the Farg.

[3] How long if the dead person died in a state of holiness? How long if in the state of a Peshôtanu?

[4] All the other objects over which the Amesha-Spentas preside (such as the cow, the metals, &c.)

3 (9). If one's son or daughter dies, how long shall they stay, the father for his son, the mother for her daughter? How long for the righteous? How long for the sinners?

Ahura Mazda answered: 'They shall stay thirty days for the righteous, sixty days for the sinners.'

4 (13). O Maker of the material world, thou Holy One! How shall I cleanse the house? How shall it be clean again?

Ahura Mazda answered: 'They shall wash their bodies three times, they shall wash their clothes three times, they shall chant the Gâthas three times; they shall offer up a sacrifice to my Fire, they shall offer up the bundles of baresma, they shall bring libations to the good waters; then the house shall be clean, and then the waters may enter, then the fire may enter, and then the Amesha-Spentas may enter, O Spitama Zarathustra!'

5 (17). If one's brother or sister dies, how long shall they stay, the brother for his brother, the sister for her sister? How long for the righteous? How long for the sinners?

Ahura Mazda answered: 'They shall stay thirty days for the righteous, sixty days for the sinners.'

6 (21). O Maker of the material world, thou Holy One! How shall I cleanse the house? How shall it be clean again?

Ahura Mazda answered: 'They shall wash their bodies three times, they shall wash their clothes three times, they shall chant the Gâthas three times; they shall offer up a sacrifice to my Fire, they shall offer up the bundles of baresma, they shall bring libations to the good waters; then the house shall be clean, and then the waters may enter, then the fire may enter, and then the Amesha-Spe*n*tas may enter, O Spitama Zarathu*s*tra!'

7 (25). If the master of the house[1] dies, or if the mistress of the house dies, how long shall they stay? How long for the righteous? How long for the sinners?

Ahura Mazda answered: 'They[2] shall stay six months for the righteous, a year for the sinners.'

8 (28). O Maker of the material world, thou Holy One! How shall I cleanse the house? How shall it be clean again?

Ahura Mazda answered: 'They shall wash their bodies three times, they shall wash their clothes three times, they shall chant the Gâthas three times; they shall offer up a sacrifice to my Fire, they shall offer up the bundles of baresma, they shall bring libations to the good waters; then the house shall be clean, and then the waters may enter, then the fire may enter, and then the Amesha-Spe*n*tas may enter, O Spitama Zarathu*s*tra!'

9 (31). If one's grandfather or grandmother dies, how long shall they stay, the grandson for his grandfather, the granddaughter for her grandmother? How long for the righteous? How long for the sinners?

Ahura Mazda answered: 'They shall stay twenty-five days for the righteous, fifty days for the sinners.'

10 (34). O Maker of the material world, thou Holy One! How shall I cleanse the house? How shall it be clean again?

Ahura Mazda answered: 'They shall wash their

---

[1] The chief of the family, the paterfamilias.
[2] All the familia, both relatives and servants.

bodies three times, they shall wash their clothes three times, they shall chant the Gâthas three times; they shall offer up a sacrifice to my Fire, they shall offer up the bundles of baresma, they shall bring libations to the good waters; then the house shall be clean, and then the waters may enter, then the fire may enter, and then the Amesha-Spentas may enter, O Spitama Zarathustra!'

11 (37). If one's grandson or granddaughter dies, how long shall they stay, the grandfather for his grandson, the grandmother for her granddaughter? How long for the righteous? How long for the sinners?

`Ahura Mazda answered: 'They shall stay twenty-five days for the righteous, fifty days for the sinners.'

12 (40). O Maker of the material world, thou Holy One! How shall I cleanse the house? How shall it be clean again?

Ahura Mazda answered: 'They shall wash their bodies three times, they shall wash their clothes three times, they shall chant the Gâthas three times; they shall offer up a sacrifice to my Fire, they shall offer up the bundles of baresma, they shall bring libations to the good waters; then the house shall be clean, and then the waters may enter, then the fire may enter, and then the Amesha-Spentas may enter, O Spitama Zarathustra!'

13 (43). If one's uncle or aunt dies, how long shall they stay, the nephew for his uncle, the niece for her aunt? How long for the righteous? How long for the sinners?

Ahura Mazda answered: 'They shall stay twenty days for the righteous, forty days for the sinners.'

14 (45). O Maker of the material world, thou

Holy One! How shall I cleanse the house? How shall it be clean again?

Ahura Mazda answered: 'They shall wash their bodies three times, they shall wash their clothes three times, they shall chant the Gâthas three times; they shall offer up a sacrifice to my Fire, they shall offer up the bundles of baresma, they shall bring libations to the good waters; then the house shall be clean, and then the waters may enter, then the fire may enter, and then the Amesha-Spentas may enter, O Spitama Zarathustra!'

15 (48). If one's male cousin or female cousin dies, how long shall they stay? How long for the righteous? How long for the sinners?

Ahura Mazda answered: 'They shall stay fifteen days for the righteous, thirty days for the sinners.'

16 (50). O Maker of the material world, thou Holy One! How shall I cleanse the house? How shall it be clean again?

Ahura Mazda answered: 'They shall wash their bodies three times, they shall wash their clothes three times, they shall chant the Gâthas three times; they shall offer up a sacrifice to my Fire, they shall offer up the bundles of baresma, they shall bring libations to the good waters; then the house shall be clean, and then the waters may enter, then the fire may enter, and then the Amesha-Spentas may enter, O Spitama Zarathustra!'

17 (53). If the son or the daughter of a cousin dies, how long shall they stay? How long for the righteous? How long for the sinners?

Ahura Mazda answered: 'They shall stay ten days for the righteous, twenty days for the sinners.'

18 (55). O Maker of the material world, thou

Holy One! How shall I cleanse the house? How shall it be clean again?

Ahura Mazda answered : 'They shall wash their bodies three times, they shall wash their clothes three times, they shall chant the Gâthas three times; they shall offer up a sacrifice to my Fire, they shall offer up the bundles of baresma, they shall bring libations to the good waters; then the house shall be clean, and then the waters may enter, then the fire may enter, and then the Amesha-Spentas may enter, O Spitama Zarathustra!'

19 (58). If the grandson of a cousin or the granddaughter of a cousin dies, how long shall they stay? How long for the righteous? How long for the sinners?

Ahura Mazda answered : 'They shall stay five days for the righteous, ten days for the sinners.'

20 (60). O Maker of the material world, thou Holy One! How shall I cleanse the house? How shall it be clean again?

Ahura Mazda answered : 'They shall wash their bodies three times, they shall wash their clothes three times, they shall chant the Gâthas three times; they shall offer up a sacrifice to my Fire, they shall offer up the bundles of baresma, they shall bring libations to the good waters; then the house shall be clean, and then the waters may enter, then the fire may enter, and then the Amesha-Spentas may enter, O Spitama Zarathustra!'

21 (63). If a stranger dies who does not profess the true faith, or the true law[1], what part of the

---

[1] The case of a stranger (no relative) who professes the true faith is not provided for here, because it has been sufficiently considered in the preceding chapters.

creation of the good spirit does he directly defile (in dying)?   What part does he indirectly defile?

22[1](65). Ahura Mazda answered: 'No more than a frog does whose venom is dried up, and that has been dead more than a year. Whilst alive, indeed, O Spitama Zarathustra! that wicked, two-legged ruffian, that ungodly Ashemaogha, directly defiles the creatures of the good spirit, and indirectly defiles them.

23 (70). 'Whilst alive he smites the water; whilst alive he blows out the fire; whilst alive he carries off the cow; whilst alive he smites the faithful man with a deadly blow, that parts the soul from the body; not so will he do when dead.

24 (71). 'Whilst alive, indeed, O Spitama Zarathustra! that wicked, two-legged ruffian, that ungodly Ashemaogha, never ceases depriving the faithful man of his food, of his clothing, of his house, of his bed, of his vessels; not so will he do when dead.'

FARGARD XIII.

The Dog.

I (1-7). The dog of Ormazd and the dog of Ahriman.
  (a. 1-4). The dog Vanghâpara ('the hedge-hog').
  (b. 4-7). The dog Zairimyangura ('the tortoise').
II (8-16). Offences against the dog.
III (17-19). On the several duties of the dog.
IV (20-28). On the food due to the dog.
V (29-38). On the mad dog; how he is to be kept, and cured.
VI (39-40). On the excellence of the dog.
VII (41-43). On the wolf-dog.

---

[1] §§ 22-24 are the same as Farg. V, 36-38.

VIII (44–48). On the virtues and vices of the dog.
IX (49–50). Praise of the dog.
X (50–54). The water dog.
See Introd. IV, 35.

I a.

1. Which is the good creature among the creatures of the good spirit that from midnight till the sun is up goes and kills thousands of the creatures of the evil spirit?

2 (3). Ahura Mazda answered: 'The dog with the prickly back, with the long and thin muzzle, the dog Vanghâpara[1], which evil-speaking people call the Duzaka[2]; this is the good creature among the creatures of the good spirit that from midnight till the sun is up goes and kills thousands of the creatures of the evil spirit.

3 (6). 'And whosoever, O Zarathustra! shall kill the dog with the prickly back, with the long and thin muzzle, the dog Vanghâpara, which evil-speaking people call the Duzaka, kills his own soul for nine generations, nor shall he find a way over the Kinvad bridge[3], unless he has, while alive, atoned for his sin by offering up a sacrifice to Sraosha[4].

---

[1] The hedge-hog. As it struggles from midnight till the dawn, this supposes the existence of a myth, in which the rays of the sun, beginning from midnight to pierce the veil of darkness, were compared to the prickles of a heavenly hedge-hog.

[2] Duzaka is the popular name of the hedge-hog (Pers. zuzah). The name Vanghâpara must have referred to its mythical qualities. It is not without importance which name is given to it: 'When called by its high name, it is powerful' (Comm.); cf. § 6, and Farg. XVIII, 15. The nature of every being lies partly in its name.

[3] The bridge leading to paradise; see Farg. XIX, 30.

[4] Cf. § 54. Aspendiârji translates: 'He cannot atone for it in his life even by performing a sacrifice to Sraosha.'

4 (10). O Maker of the material world, thou
Holy One! If a man kill the dog with the prickly
back, with the long and thin muzzle, the dog Vanghâpara, which evil-speaking people call the Du*z*aka,
what is the penalty that he shall pay?

Ahura Mazda answered: 'A thousand stripes
with the Aspahê-a*s*tra, a thousand stripes with the
Sraoshô-*k*arana.'

I b.

5 (13). Which is the evil creature among the
creatures of the evil spirit that from midnight till
the sun is up goes and kills thousands of the creatures of the good spirit?

6 (15). Ahura Mazda answered : 'The daêva Zairimyangura [1], which evil-speaking people call the
Zairimyâka [2], this is the evil creature among the
creatures of the evil spirit that from midnight till
the sun is up goes and kills thousands of the creatures of the good spirit.

7 (18). 'And whosoever, O Zarathu*s*tra! shall kill
the daêva Zairimyangura, which evil-speaking people
call the Zairimyâka, his sins in thought, word, and
deed are redeemed as they would be by a Patet; his
sins in thought, word, and deed are atoned for.

II.

8 (21). 'Whosoever shall smite either a shepherd's dog, or a house dog, or a Vohunazga dog [3], or

---

[1] The tortoise (Asp.)

[2] 'When not so called it is less strong' (Comm.) Zairimyâka
is a lucky name, as it is connected with a word (zairimya) which
denotes the freshness of water and verdure ; and it seems to designate the tortoise as ' the fresh-water creature' (Asp.); therefore the
name is corrected into ' the injurer (?) of fresh water.'

[3] See § 19 n.

a trained dog[1], his soul when passing to the other world, shall fly[2] amid louder howling and fiercer pursuing than the sheep does when the wolf rushes upon it in the lofty forest.

9 (24). 'No soul will come and meet his departing soul and help it through the howls and pursuit[3] in the other world; nor will the dogs that keep the Kinvad bridge[4] help his departing soul through the howls and pursuit in the other world.

10 (26). 'If a man shall smite a shepherd's dog so that it becomes unfit for work, if he shall cut off its ear or its paw, and thereupon a thief or a wolf break in and carry away sheep from the fold, without the dog giving any warning, the man shall pay for the lost sheep, and he shall pay for the wound of the dog as for wilful wounding[5].

11 (31). 'If a man shall smite a house dog so that it becomes unfit for work, if he shall cut off its ear or its paw, and thereupon a thief or a wolf break in and carry away goods from the house, without the dog giving any warning, the man shall pay for the lost goods, and he shall pay for the wound of the dog as for wilful wounding.'

12 (36). O Maker of the material world, thou Holy One! If a man shall smite a shepherd's dog, so that it gives up the ghost and the soul parts from the body, what is the penalty that he shall pay?

Ahura Mazda answered : 'Eight hundred stripes with the Aspahê-astra, eight hundred stripes with the Sraoshô-karana.'

---

[1] A hunting dog (?). [2] 'From paradise' (Comm.)
[3] Of the Dîvs. [4] See Introd. V, 4.
[5] Baodhô-varsta; see Farg. VII, 38 n.

13 (39). O Maker of the material world, thou Holy One! If a man shall smite a house dog so that it gives up the ghost and the soul parts from the body, what is the penalty that he shall pay?

Ahura Mazda answered: 'Seven hundred stripes with the Aspahê-astra, seven hundred stripes with the Sraoshô-karana.'

14 (42). O Maker of the material world, thou Holy One! If a man shall smite a Vohunazga dog so that it gives up the ghost and the soul parts from the body, what is the penalty that he shall pay?

Ahura Mazda answered: 'Six hundred stripes with the Aspahê-astra, six hundred stripes with the Sraoshô-karana.'

15 (45). O Maker of the material world, thou Holy One! If a man shall smite a young dog[1] so that it gives up the ghost and the soul parts from the body, what is the penalty that he shall pay?

Ahura Mazda answered: 'Five hundred stripes with the Aspahê-astra, five hundred stripes with the Sraoshô-karana.'

16 (48). 'This is the penalty for the murder of a Gazu dog, of a Vîzu dog[2], of a Sukuruna dog[3], of a sharp-toothed Urupi dog[4], of a swift-running Raopi[5] dog; this is the penalty for the murder of any kind of dog but the water dog[6].'

---

[1] A dog not older than four months.

[2] Unknown. Cf. V, 31, 32.   [3] A lynx. Cf. V, 31.

[4] A weazel. Cf. V, 33.

[5] A fox. The fox belongs to the good creation, as he fights against the demon Khava (Bund. XIX; cf. Orm. Ahr. § 228).

[6] The beaver. 'For the penalty in that case is most heavy' (Comm.) Cf. § 52 seq. and Farg. XIV.

III.

17 (49). O Maker of the material world, thou Holy One! Which is the dog that must be called a shepherd's dog?

Ahura Mazda answered: ' It is the dog who goes a Yuɡyêsti [1] round about the fold, watching for the thief and the wolf.'

18 (51). O Maker of the material world, thou Holy One! Which is the dog that must be called a house dog?

Ahura Mazda answered: 'It is the dog who goes a Hâthra round about the house, watching for the thief and the wolf.'

19 (53). O Maker of the material world, thou Holy One! Which is the dog that must be called a Vohunazga dog?

Ahura Mazda answered: 'It is the dog who claims none of those talents, and only seeks for his subsistence [2].'

IV.

20 (55). O Maker of the material world, thou Holy One! If a man give bad food to a shepherd's dog, of what sin is he guilty?

Ahura Mazda answered: 'It is the same guilt as though he should serve bad food to a master of a house of the first rank [3].'

---

[1] A measure unknown; it seems to have been the average distance of fourteen houses (see the gloss ad § 17 in the Introd. V, 4, Farg. XV, 45, and Bund. p. 31, 7).

[2] 'He cannot do the same as the shepherd's dog and the house dog do, but he catches Khrafstras and smites the Nasu' (Comm.) It is 'the dog without a master' (gharîb), the vagrant dog; he is held in great esteem (§ 22) and is one of the dogs who can be used for the Sag-dîd (Introd. V, 4).

[3] Invited as a guest.

21 (57). O Maker of the material world, thou Holy One! If a man give bad food to a house dog, of what sin is he guilty?

Ahura Mazda answered: ' It is the same guilt as though he should serve bad food to a master of a house of middle rank.'

22 (59). O Maker of the material world, thou Holy One! If a man give bad food to a Vohunazga dog, of what sin is he guilty?

Ahura Mazda answered: ' It is the same guilt as though he should serve bad food to a holy man, in the character of a priest[1], who should come to his house.'

23 (61). O Maker of the material world, thou Holy One! If a man give bad food to a young dog, of what sin is he guilty?

Ahura Mazda answered: ' It is the same guilt as though he should serve bad food to a young man, born of pious parents, and who can answer for himself[2].'

24 (63). O Maker of the material world, thou Holy One! If a man shall give bad food to a shepherd's dog, what is the penalty that he shall pay?

Ahura Mazda answered: ' He is a Peshôtanu: two hundred stripes with the Aspahê-astra, two hundred stripes with the Sraoshô-karana[3].'

---

[1] The Vohuñazga dog has no domicile, therefore he is not compared with the master of a house; as he smites the Nasu, he is like a holy man, of the wandering class, a sort of begging friar.

[2] Probably, ' Who has performed the nû-zûd, fifteen years old.' The young dog enters the community of the faithful at the age of four months, when he can smite the Nasu.

[3] ' I also saw the soul of a man, whom demons, just like dogs, ever tear. That man gives bread to the dogs, and they eat it not;

25 (66). O Maker of the material world, thou Holy One! If a man shall give bad food to a house dog, what is the penalty that he shall pay?

Ahura Mazda answered: 'Ninety stripes with the Aspahê-astra, ninety stripes with the Sraoshô-karana.'

26 (69). O Maker of the material world, thou Holy One! If a man shall give bad food to a Vohunazga dog, what is the penalty that he shall pay?

Ahura Mazda answered: 'Seventy stripes with the Aspahê-astra, seventy stripes with the Sraoshô-karana.'

27 (72). O Maker of the material world, thou Holy One! If a man shall give bad food to a young dog, what is the penalty that he shall pay?

Ahura Mazda answered: 'Fifty stripes with the Aspahê-astra, fifty stripes with the Sraoshô-karana.

28 (75). 'For it is the dog, of all the creatures of the good spirit, that most quickly decays into age, while not eating near eating people, and watching goods none of which it receives. Bring ye unto him milk and fat with meat; this is the right food for the dog[1].'

---

but they ever devour the breast, legs, belly, and thighs of the man. And I asked thus: What sin was committed by this body, whose soul suffers so severe a punishment? Srôsh the pious and Âtarô the angel said thus: This is the soul of that wicked man who, in the world, kept back the food of the dogs of shepherds and house-holders; or beat and killed them' (Ardai Vîrâf XLVIII, translated by Haug).

[1] 'Whenever one eats bread one must put aside three mouthfuls and give them to the dog . . . for among all the poor there is none poorer than the dog' (Saddar 31; Hyde 35).

V.

29 (80). O Maker of the material world, thou
Holy One! If there be in the house of a worshipper of Mazda a mad dog, or one that bites
without barking, what shall the worshippers of
Mazda do?

30 (82). Ahura Mazda answered: 'They shall put
a wooden collar around his neck, and they shall tie
him to a post, an a*sti*[1] thick if the wood be hard,
two a*stis* thick if it be soft. To that post they shall
tie him; by the two sides[2] of the collar they shall
tie him.

31 (86). 'If they shall not do so, and the mad
dog, or the dog that bites without barking, smite a
sheep or wound a man, the dog shall pay for it as
for wilful murder[3].

32 (88). 'If the dog shall smite a sheep or wound
a man, they shall cut off his right ear. If he shall
smite another sheep or wound another man, they
shall cut off his left ear.

33 (90). 'If he shall smite a third sheep or wound
a third man, they shall cut off his right foot[4]. If he
shall smite a fourth sheep or wound a fourth man,
they shall cut off his left foot.

---

[1] A measure of unknown amount. Aspendiârji reads i*s*ti, 'a
brick' thick.

[2] By the forepart and the back part of it.

[3] As there is no essential difference between man and beast, the
beast must answer for its guilt. According to Solon's law, the dog
who has bitten any one must be delivered to him tied up to a block
four cubits long (Plutarchus, Solon 24); the horse who has killed
a man is put to death (Eusebius, Prep. Evang. 5).

[4] 'They only cut off a piece of flesh from the foot' (Brouillons
d'Anquetil).

34 (92). 'If he shall for the fifth time smite a
sheep or wound a man, they shall cut off his tail.

'Therefore they shall tie him to the post; by the
two sides of the collar they shall tie him. If they
shall not do so, and the mad dog, or the dog that
bites without barking, smite a sheep or wound a
man, he shall pay for it as for wilful murder.'

35 (97). O Maker of the material world, thou
Holy One! If there be in the house of a worshipper of Mazda a scentless dog, or a mad dog,
what shall the worshippers of Mazda do?

Ahura Mazda answered: 'They shall attend him
to heal him, in the same manner as they would do
for one of the faithful.'

36 (100). O Maker of the material world, thou
Holy One! If they try to heal him and fail, what
shall the worshippers of Mazda do?

37 (102). Ahura Mazda answered: 'They shall
put a wooden collar around his neck, and they shall
tie him to a post, an *asti* thick if the wood be hard,
two *asti*s thick if it be soft. To that post they shall
tie him; by the two sides of the collar they shall tie
him.

38 (102). 'If they shall not do so, and the scentless dog fall into a hole, or a well, or a precipice, or
a river, or a canal, and he be wounded and die thereof,
they shall be Peshôtanus.

VI.

39 (106). 'The dog, O Spitama Zarathustra! I,
Ahura Mazda, have made self-clothed and self-shod,
watchful, wakeful, and sharp-toothed, born to take
his food from man and to watch over man's goods.
I, Ahura Mazda, have made the dog strong of body

against the evil-doer, and watchful over your goods, when he is of sound mind.

40 (112). 'And whosoever shall awake at his voice, neither shall the thief nor the wolf steal anything from his house, without his being warned; the wolf shall be smitten and torn to pieces; he is driven away, he flees away.'

VII.

41 (115). O Maker of the material world, thou Holy One! Which of the two wolves deserves more to be killed, the one that is born of a he-dog and of a she-wolf, or the one that is born of a she-dog and of a he-wolf?

Ahura Mazda answered: 'Of these two wolves, the one that is born of a he-dog and of a she-wolf deserves more to be killed than the one that is born of a she-dog and of a he-wolf.

42 (117). 'For there are born of a he-dog and of a she-wolf such dogs as fall on the shepherd's dog, on the house dog, on the Vohunazga dog, on the trained dog, and destroy the folds; such dogs are born as are more murderous, more mischievous, more destructive to the folds than any other dogs.

43 (121). 'And there are born of a he-dog and of a she-wolf such wolves as fall on the shepherd's dog, on the house dog, on the Vohunazga dog, on the trained dog, and destroy the folds; such wolves are born as are more murderous, more mischievous, more destructive to the folds than any other wolves.

VIII.

44 (124). 'A dog has the characters of eight different sorts of people:—

'He has the character of a priest,

[4]   M

'He has the character of a warrior,

'He has the character of a husbandman,

'He has the character of a strolling singer,

'He has the character of a thief,

'He has the character of a wild beast,

'He has the character of a courtezan,

'He has the character of a child.

45 (126). 'He eats broken food, like a priest[1]; he is grateful, like a priest; he is easily satisfied[2], like a priest; he wants only a small piece of bread, like a priest; in these things he is like unto a priest.

'He marches in front, like a warrior; he fights for the beneficent cow, like a warrior[3]; he goes first out of the house, like a warrior[4]; in these things he is like unto a warrior.

46 (135). 'He is watchful and sleeps lightly, like a husbandman; he goes first out of the house, like a husbandman[5]; he returns last into the house, like a husbandman[6]; in these things he is like unto a husbandman.

'He sings like a strolling singer; he is intrusive[7], like a strolling singer; he is meagre, like a strolling singer; he is poor, like a strolling singer; in these things he is like unto a strolling singer.

47 (143). 'He likes darkness, like a thief; he prowls about in darkness, like a thief; he is a shame-

---

[1] A wandering priest (see p. 157, n. 1).

[2] Doubtful.

[3] 'He keeps away the wolf and the thief' (Comm.)

[4] This clause is, as it seems, repeated here by mistake from § 46.

[5] When taking the cattle out of the stables.

[6] When bringing the cattle back to the stables.

[7] Doubtful.

less eater, like a thief; he is an unfaithful keeper, like a thief[1]; in these things he is like unto a thief.

'He likes darkness, like a wild beast[2]; he prowls about in darkness, like a wild beast; he is a shameless eater, like a wild beast; he is an unfaithful keeper, like a wild beast; in these things he is like unto a wild beast.

48 (153). 'He sings, like a courtezan; he is intrusive, like a courtezan; he walks about the roads, like a courtezan; he is meagre, like a courtezan; he is poor, like a courtezan; in these things he is like unto a courtezan.

'He likes sleeping, like a child; he is apt to run away[3], like a child; he is full of tongue, like a child; he goes on all fours[4], like a child; in these things he is like unto a child.

IX.

49 (163). 'If those two dogs of mine, the shepherd's dog and the house dog, pass by the house of any of my faithful people, let them never be kept away from it.

'For no house could subsist on the earth made by Ahura, but for those two dogs of mine, the shepherd's dog and the house dog[5].'

X.

50 (166). O Maker of the material world, thou

---

[1] 'When one trusts him with something, he eats it' (Comm.)

[2] According to Asp.

[3] He is fearful.　　　　　　　　[4] Doubtful.

[5] 'But for the dog not a single head of cattle would remain in existence' (Saddar 31; Hyde 35).

Holy One! When a dog dies, with marrow and seed [1] dried up, whereto does his ghost go?

51 (167). Ahura Mazda answered: 'It passes to the spring of the waters [2], O Spitama Zarathustra! and there out of every thousand dogs and every thousand she-dogs, two water dogs are formed, a water dog and a water she-dog [3].

52 (170). 'He who kills a water dog brings about a drought that dries up pastures. Before that time, O Spitama Zarathustra! sweetness and fatness would flow out from that land and from those fields, with health and healing, with fulness and increase and growth, and a growing of corn and grass.'

53 (171). O Maker of the material world, thou Holy One! When are sweetness and fatness to come back again to that land and to those fields, with health and healing, with fulness and increase and growth, and a growing of corn and grass?

54, 55 (172). Ahura Mazda answered: 'Sweetness and fatness will never come back again to that land and to those fields, with health and healing, with fulness and increase and growth, and a growing of corn and grass, until the murderer of the water dog has been smitten to death and the holy soul of the dog has been offered up a sacrifice, for three days

---

[1] Marrow is the seat of life, the spine is 'the column and the spring of life' (Yt. X, 71); the sperm comes from it (Bundahis XVI). The same theory prevailed in India, where the sperm is called magga-samudbhava, 'what is born from marrow;' it was followed by Plato (Timaeus 74, 91 ; cf. Plut. De Plac. Philos. V, 3, 4), and disproved by Aristotle (De Part. Anim. III, 7).

[2] To the spring of Ardvî Sûra, the goddess of waters.

[3] There is therefore in a single water dog as much life and holiness as in a thousand dogs. This accounts for the following.

and three nights with fire blazing, with baresma tied up, and with Haoma uplifted [1].

56 (174). ['Then sweetness and fatness will come back again to that land and to those fields, with health and healing, with fulness and increase and growth, and a growing of corn and grass [2].']

FARGARD XIV.

This Fargard is nothing more than an appendix to the last clauses in the preceding Fargard (§ 50 seq.) How the murder of a water dog may be atoned for is described in it at full length. As the water dog is the holiest of all dogs [3], and, as it were, a link between the dog and God, the process of atonement must be one of an extraordinary character. It is this chapter, more than any other, which may make it doubtful whether the legislation of the Vendîdâd has ever existed as real and living law. See, however, Introduction V, 20.

1. Zarathustra asked Ahura Mazda: 'O Ahura Mazda, most beneficent Spirit, Maker of the material world, thou Holy One! He who smites one of those water dogs that are born one from a thousand dogs and a thousand she-dogs [4], so that he gives up the ghost and the soul parts from the body, what is the penalty that he shall pay?'

2 (4). Ahura Mazda answered: 'He shall pay ten thousand stripes with the Aspahê-astra, ten thousand stripes with the Sraoshô-karana [5].

---

[1] The zanda ravân, the same sacrifice as is offered up for three days and three nights after the death of a man for the salvation of his soul. Cf. p. 132, n. 4.

[2] Cf. Farg. IX, 53-57.

[3] See preceding page; cf. Introd. IV, 35, and Orm. Ahr. § 230.

[4] See preceding Fargard, § 51.

[5] He shall pay 50 tanâfûhrs (=15000 istîrs=60000 dirhems;

'He shall godly and piously bring unto the fire
of Ahura Mazda [1] ten thousand loads of hard, well
dried, well examined [2] wood, as an atonement unto
the soul (of the water dog).

3 (6). 'He shall godly and piously bring unto the
fire of Ahura Mazda ten thousand loads of soft
wood, of Urvâsna, Vohu-gaona, Vohu-kereti, Hadhâ-
naêpata [3], or any sweet-scented plant, as an atonement unto the soul (of the water dog).

4 (7). 'He shall godly and piously tie and consecrate ten thousand bundles of baresma; he shall
offer up to the good waters ten thousand Zaothra
libations with the Haoma and the sacred meat [4],
cleanly prepared and well strained, cleanly prepared
and well strained by a pious man [5], as an atonement
unto the soul (of the water dog).

5 (9). 'He shall kill ten thousand snakes of those
that go upon the belly; he shall kill ten thousand

---

see Introd. V, 21). 'If he can afford it, he will atone in the manner
stated in the Avesta; if he cannot afford it, it will be sufficient to
perform a complete Izaɼnê (sacrifice),' (Comm.)

[1] To the altar of the Bahrâm fire.

[2] 'It is forbidden to take any ill-smelling thing to the fire and to
kindle it on it; it is forbidden to kindle green wood, and even
though the wood were hard and dry, one must examine it three
times, lest there may be any hair or any unclean matter upon it'
(Gr. Rav.) Although the pious Ardâ Vîrâf had always taken the
utmost care never to put on the fire any wood but such as was
seven years old, yet, when he entered paradise, Atar, the genius of
fire, shewed him reproachfully a large tank full of the water which
that wood had exuded (see Ardâ Vîrâf X).

[3] See above, p. 94, n. 1.

[4] Possibly, milk.

[5] A Mobed called sardâr, 'chief,' who prepares, cleanses, and
disposes everything for the performance of the Yasna (Comm. and
Anquetil, Brouillons ad Farg. XVIII, 72).

snakes of those that have the shape of a dog[1]; he shall kill ten thousand tortoises; he shall kill ten thousand land frogs[2]; he shall kill ten thousand water frogs; he shall kill ten thousand corn-carrying ants[3]; he shall kill ten thousand ants of those that bite and dig holes and work mischief[4].

6 (16). 'He shall kill ten thousand earth worms; he shall kill ten thousand horrid flies[5].

'He shall fill up ten thousand holes for the unclean[6].

---

[1] 'Mâr bânak snakes: they are dog-like, because they sit on their hindparts' (Comm.) The cat seems to be the animal intended by this name. In a paraphrase of this passage in a Parsi Ravâet, the cat is numbered amongst the Khrafstras which it is enjoined to kill to redeem a sin (India Office Library, VIII, 13); cf. G. du Chinon, p. 462: 'Les animaux que les Gaures ont en horreur sont les serpents, les couleuvres, les lezars, et autres de cette espece, les crapaux, les grenouïlles, les écrevisses, les rats et souris, et sur tout le chat.'

[2] 'Those that can go out of water and live on the dry ground' (Comm.) 'Pour les grenouïlles et crapaux, ils disent que ce sont ceux (eux ?) qui sont cause de ce que les hommes meurent, gâtans les eaus où ils habitent continuellement, et que d'autant plus qu'il y en a dans le païs, d'autant plus les eaus causent-elles des maladies et enfin la mort,' G. du Chinon, p. 465.

[3] 'Un jour que j'étois surpris de la guerre qu'ils font aux fourmis, ils me dirent que ces animaux ne faisaient que voler par des amas des grains plus qu'il n'étoit nécessaire pour leur nourriture,' G. du Chinon, p. 464. Firdusi protested against the proscription: 'Do no harm to the corn-carrying ant; a living thing it is, and its life is dear to it.' The celebrated high-priest of the Parsis, the late Moola Firooz, entered those lines into his Pand Nâmah, which may betoken better days for this wise and careful creature.

[4] Doubtful. The Commentary has, 'that is, dârak ants (wood ants; termites ?).'

[5] Corpse flies.

[6] 'The holes at which the unclean are washed' (Comm.; cf. Farg. IX, 6 seq.)

He shall godly and piously give to godly men twice seven sets of implements for the fire, as an atonement unto the soul (of the water dog), namely:

7 (20). 'Two (loads of the) proper materials for fire[1]; a broom[2]; a pair of tongs; a pair of round bellows[3] extended at the bottom, contracted at the top; an adze with a sharp edge and a sharp-pointed handle[4], a saw with sharp teeth and a sharp-pointed handle, by means of which the worshippers of Mazda procure wood for the fire of Ahura Mazda.

8 (26). 'He shall godly and piously give to godly men a set of the priestly instruments of which the priests make use, as an atonement unto the soul (of the water dog), namely: The Astra[5], the meat-vessel[6], the Paitidâna[7], the Khrafstraghna[8], the

---

[1] Doubtful: the intended materials would be two loads of wood, and two loads of incense to burn upon the wood (Asp.)

[2] To cleanse the Atash-dân or fire-vessel (Yasna IX, 1).

[3] Or, a fan.

[4] Asp.; literally, 'sharp-kneed.'

[5] The Aspahê-astra; see Introd. V, 19.

[6] Possibly, the milk-vessel.

[7] As everything that goes out of man is unclean, his breath defiles all that it touches; priests, therefore, while on duty, and even laymen, while praying or eating, must wear a mouth-veil, the Paitidâna (Parsi Penôm), consisting 'of two pieces of white cotton cloth, hanging loosely from the bridge of the nose to, at least, two inches below the mouth, and tied with two strings at the back of the head' (Haug, Essays, 2nd ed. p. 243, n. 1; cf. Comm. ad Farg. XVIII, 1, and Anquetil II, 530). This principle appears not to have been peculiar to the Zoroastrian Aryans, for the Slavonian priest in Arkona was enjoined to go out of the temple, whenever he wanted to draw breath, 'lest the presence of the god should be defiled by contact with mortal breath' (ne dei presentia mortalis spiritus contagio pollueretur, Saxo Grammaticus, ap. Klek, Einleitung in die Slavische Literatur, p. 105). Cf. Introd. V, 8.

[8] The 'Khrafstra-killer;' an instrument for killing snakes, &c.

Sraoshô-*k*arana [1], the cup for the Myazda [2], the cups for the juice [3], the mortar made according to the rules, the Haoma cups [4], and the baresma.

9 (32). 'He shall godly and piously give to godly men a set of all the war implements of which the warriors make use [5], as an atonement unto the soul (of the water dog); the first being a javelin [6], the second a knife [7], the third a club, the fourth a bow [8], the fifth a quiver [9] with shoulder-belt and thirty brass-headed arrows [10], the sixth a sling with arm-string and with thirty sling stones, the seventh a cuirass [11], the eighth a hauberk [12], the ninth a tunic [13], the tenth a helmet, the eleventh a girdle, the twelfth a pair of greaves [14].

---

[1] See Introd. V, 19.

[2] Doubtful.

[3] The cup in which the juice of the hom and of the urvarân (the twigs of hadhâ-naêpata which are pounded together with the hom) is received from the mortar (Comm.)

[4] The cup on which twigs of Haoma are laid before being pounded, the so-called tashtah (Anquetil II, 533); 'some say, the hom-strainer' [a saucer with nine holes], Comm.

[5] The armament detailed in the text agrees partly with that of the Persians and Medians described by Herodotos (VII, 61, 62). It would be desirable for archæologists to ascertain to what time and, if possible, to what province this description refers, as such information might throw some light upon the age of this part of the Avesta at least.

[6] Αἰχμὰς δὲ βραχέας εἶχον.

[7] Ἐγχειρίδια παρὰ τὸν δεξιὸν μηρὸν παραιωρεύμενα ἐκ τῆς ζώνης.

[8] Τόξα δὲ μεγάλα.

[9] Doubtful. Ὑπὸ δὲ φαρετρεῶνες ἐκρέμαντο.

[10] Ὀϊστοὺς δὲ καλαμίνους.

[11] Λεπίδος σιδηρέης ὄψιν ἰχθυοειδέος.

[12] 'Going from the helm to the cuirass' (Comm.)

[13] 'Under the cuirass' (Comm.); περὶ δὲ τὸ σῶμα κιθῶνας χειριδωτοὺς ποικίλους.

[14] Περὶ δὲ τὰ σκέλεα ἀναξυρίδας.

10 (41). 'He shall godly and ·piously give to godly men a set of all the implements of which the husbandmen make use, as an atonement unto the soul (of the water dog), namely: A plough with share and yoke¹, an ox whip², a mortar of stone, a hand-mill for grinding corn,

11 (48). 'A spade for digging and tilling; one measure of silver and one measure of gold.'

O Maker of the material world, thou Holy One! How much silver?

Ahura Mazda answered: 'The price of a stallion.'

O Maker of the material world, thou Holy One! How much gold?

Ahura Mazda answered: 'The price of a camel.

12 (54). 'He shall godly and piously procure a rill of running water for godly husbandmen, as an atonement unto the soul (of the water dog).'

O Maker of the material world, thou Holy One! How large is the rill?

Ahura Mazda answered: 'The depth of a dog, and the breadth of a dog³.

13 (57). 'He shall godly and piously give a piece of arable land to godly men, as an atonement unto the soul (of the water dog).'

O Maker of the material world, thou Holy One! How large is the piece of land?

Ahura Mazda answered: 'As much as can be watered with such a rill on both sides⁴.

14 (60). 'He shall godly and piously procure for godly men a house with ox-stalls, with nine

---

¹ Doubtful.   ² Doubtful.
³ Which is estimated 'a foot deep, a foot broad' (Comm.)
⁴ Doubtful.

hâthras and nine nematas [1], as an atonement unto
the soul (of the water dog) [2].'

O Maker of the material world, thou Holy One!
How large is the house?

Ahura Mazda answered: 'Twelve Vîtâras [3] in the
largest part of the house, nine Vîtâras in the middle
part, six Vîtâras in the smallest part.

'He shall godly and piously give to godly men
goodly beds with cushions, as an atonement unto
the soul (of the water dog).

15 (64). 'He shall godly and piously give to a
godly man a virgin maid, whom no man has known,
as an atonement unto the soul (of the water dog).'

O Maker of the material world, thou Holy One!
What maid?

Ahura Mazda answered: 'A sister or a daughter
of his, at the age of puberty, with ear-rings in her
ears, and past her fifteenth year.

16 (67). 'He shall godly and piously give to
holy men twice seven head of small cattle, as an
atonement unto the soul (of the water dog).

'He shall bring up twice seven whelps.

'He shall throw twice seven bridges over canals.

17 (70). 'He shall put into repair twice nine
stables that are out of repair.

'He shall cleanse twice nine dogs from skin
humours, hair wax, vermin [4], and all the diseases
that are produced on the body of a dog.

---

[1] Meaning unknown.

[2] He shall build a caravansary, which is considered a pious
work (Mainyô-i-khard IV, 6; XXXVII, 36).

[3] A word of unknown meaning; probably a measure, but possibly 'a passage or alley.'

[4] Those three words are doubtful.

'He shall treat twice nine godly men to their fill of meat, bread, strong drink, and wine.

18 (73). 'This is the atonement, this is the penalty that he shall undergo to atone for the deed that he has done.

'If he shall undergo it, he shall enter the world of the holy ones: if he shall not undergo it, he shall fall down into the world of the wicked, into that dark world, made of darkness, the offspring of darkness[1].'

FARGARD XV.

I.

1. How many are the sins that men commit and that, being committed and not confessed, nor atoned for, make their committer a Peshôtanu[2]?

2 (4). Ahura Mazda answered: 'There are five such sins, O holy Zarathustra! It is the first of these sins that men commit when a man teaches one of the faithful a foreign, wrong creed[3], a foreign, wrong law, and he does so with a full knowledge and conscience of the sin: this is a sin that makes him a Peshôtanu.

---

[1] Cf. Farg. V, 62.

[2] See Introd. V, 19.

[3] Literally, 'another wrong creed;' the Commentary has, 'that is, a creed that is not ours.' See Introd. III, 10.

3 (9). 'It is the second of these sins that men commit when a man gives too hard bones or too hot food to a shepherd's dog or to a house dog;

4 (11). 'If the bones stick in the dog's teeth or stop in his throat, or if the hot food burn his mouth or his tongue, so that mischief follows therefrom, and the dog dies, this is a sin that makes the man a Peshôtanu [1].

5 (16). 'It is the third of these sins that men commit when a man smites a bitch big with young or affrights her by running after her, with shouting or with clapping of hands [2];

6 (18). 'If the bitch fall into a hole, or a well, or a precipice, or a river, or a canal, so that mischief follows therefrom, and she dies, this is a sin that makes the man a Peshôtanu [3].

7 (22). 'It is the fourth of these sins that men commit when a man has intercourse with a woman who has an issue of blood, either out of the ordinary course or at the usual period: this is a sin that makes him a Peshôtanu [4].

8 (25). 'It is the fifth of these sins that men commit when a man has intercourse with a woman quick with child [5], whether the milk has already

---

[1] He who gives too hot food to a dog so as to burn his throat is margarzân (guilty of death); he who gives bones to a dog so as to tear his throat is margarzân (Gr. Rav. 639).

[2] Or, 'with stamping on the ground' (? Saddar 31).

[3] If a bitch is big with young and a man shouts or throws stones at her, so that the whelps come to mischief and die, he is margarzân (Gr. Rav. 639).

[4] See Farg. XVI, 14 seq.

[5] When she has been pregnant for four months and ten days, as it is then that the child is formed and a soul is added to its body (Anquetil II, 563).

come to her breasts or has not yet come : if mischief follow therefrom, and she die, this is a sin that makes the man a Peshôtanu [1].

II.

9 (30). 'If a man come near unto a damsel, either dependent on the chief of the family or not dependent, either delivered unto a husband or not delivered [2], and she conceives by him, let her not, from dread of the people, produce in herself the menses, against the course of nature, by means of water and plants [3].

10 (34). 'And if the damsel, from dread of the people, shall produce in herself the menses against the course of nature, by means of water and plants, there is a sin upon her head [4].

11 (36). 'If a man come near unto a damsel, either dependent on the chief of the family or not dependent, either delivered unto a husband or not delivered, and she conceives by him, let her not,

---

[1] Or better, 'if the child die.' 'If a man come to his wife [during her pregnancy] so that she is injured and bring forth a still-born child, he is margarzân' (Old Rav. 115 b).

[2] 'Whether she has a husband in the house of her own parents or has none; whether she has entered from the house of her own parents into the house of a husband [depending on another chief of family] or has not' (Comm.)

[3] By means of drugs.

[4] 'It is a tanâfûhr sin for her: it is sin on sin' (the first sin being to have allowed herself to be seduced), Comm. 'If there has been no sin in her (if she has been forced), and if a man, knowing her shame, wants to take it off her, he shall call together her father, mother, sisters, brothers, husband, the servants, the menials, and the master and the mistress of the house, and he shall say, " This woman is with child by me, and I rejoice in it ;" and they shall answer, "We know it, and we are glad that her shame is taken off her;" and he shall support her as a husband does' (Comm.)

from dread of the people, destroy the fruit in her womb.

12 (38). 'And if the damsel, from dread of the people, shall destroy the fruit in her womb, the sin is on both the father and herself, the murder is on both the father and herself; both the father and herself shall pay the penalty for wilful murder [1].

13 (40). 'If a man come near unto a damsel, either dependent on the chief of the family or not dependent, either delivered unto a husband or not delivered, and she conceives by him, and she says, " I have conceived by thee;" and he replies, " Go then to the old woman [2] and apply to her that she may procure thee miscarriage;"

14 (43). 'And the damsel goes to the old woman and applies to her that she may procure her miscarriage; and the old woman brings her some Banga, or Shaêta, or Ghnâna, or Fraspâta [3], or some other of the drugs that produce miscarriage and [the man says], "Cause thy fruit to perish !" and she causes her fruit to perish; the sin is on the head of all three, the man, the damsel, and the old woman.

III.

15 (49). 'If a man come near unto a damsel, either dependent on the chief of the family or not dependent, either delivered unto a husband or not

---

[1] For baodhô-varsta; see above, p. 84, § 38, and n. 1.

[2] The nurse (Asp.)

[3] Banga is bang or mang, a narcotic made from hempseed; shaêta means literally gold, and must have been some yellow plant or liquor; ghnâna is 'that which kills [the fruit in the womb];' fraspâta is 'that which expels [the fruit] so that it perishes' (Comm.)

delivered, and she conceives by him, so long shall he support her, until the child is born.

16 (51). 'If he shall not support her, so that the child comes to mischief[1], for want of proper support, he shall pay the penalty for wilful murder.'

17 (54). O Maker of the material world, thou Holy One! If she be near her time and be lying on the high road, which is the worshipper of Mazda that shall support her?

18 (56). Ahura Mazda answered: 'If a man come near unto a damsel, either dependent on the chief of the family or not dependent, either delivered unto a husband or not delivered, and she conceives by him, so long shall he support her, until the child is born[2].

19 (58). 'If he shall not support her[3] . . . .

'It lies with the faithful to look in the same way after every pregnant female, either two-footed or four-footed, either woman or bitch.'

20 (61). O Maker of the material world, thou Holy One! If (a bitch[4]) be near her time and be lying on the high road, which is the worshipper of Mazda that shall support her?

21 (63). Ahura Mazda answered: 'He whose house stands nearest, the care of supporting her is

---

[1] And dies.   [2] § 18 = § 15.

[3] The sentence is left unfinished: Aspendiârji fills it with the words in § 16, 'so that the child,' &c. It seems as if §§ 17, 18 were no part of the original text, and as if § 17 were a mere repetition of § 20, which being wrongly interpreted as referring to a woman would have brought about the repetition of § 15 as an answer. See § 20.

[4] The subject is wanting in the text: it is supplied from the Commentary as the sense requires it.

his[1]; so long shall he support her until the whelps are born.

22 (65). 'If he shall not support her, so that the whelps come to mischief, for want of proper support, he shall pay the penalty for wilful murder.'

23 (68). O Maker of the material world, thou Holy One! If a bitch be near her time and be lying in a camel-stall, which is the worshipper of Mazda that shall support her?

24 (70). Ahura Mazda answered: 'He who built the camel-stall or who holds it[2], the care of supporting her is his; so long shall he support her, until the whelps are born.

25 (76). 'If he shall not support her, so that the whelps come to mischief, for want of proper support, he shall pay the penalty for wilful murder.'

26 (77). O Maker of the material world, thou Holy One! If a bitch be near her time and be lying in a horse-stall, which is the worshipper of Mazda that shall support her?

27 (78). Ahura Mazda answered: 'He who built the horse-stall or who holds it, the care of supporting her is his; so long shall he support her, until the whelps are born.

28 (81). 'If he shall not support her, so that the whelps come to mischief, for want of proper support, he shall pay the penalty for wilful murder.'

29 (84). O Maker of the material world, thou

---

[1] 'The bitch is lying on the high road : the man whose house has its door nearest shall take care of her. If she dies, he shall carry her off [to dispose of the body according to the law]. One must support her for at least three nights: if one cannot support her any longer, one intrusts her to a richer man' (Comm. and Asp.)

[2] 'In pledge or for rent' (Asp.; cf. Comm. ad § 42).

[4]   N

Holy One! If a bitch be near her time and be lying in an ox-stall, which is the worshipper of Mazda that shall support her?

30 (86). Ahura Mazda answered: 'He who built the ox-stall or who holds it, the care of supporting her is his; so long shall he support her, until the whelps are born.

31 (89). 'If he shall not support her, so that the whelps come to mischief, for want of proper support, he shall pay the penalty for wilful murder.'

32 (92). O Maker of the material world, thou Holy One! If a bitch be near her time and be lying in a sheep-fold, which is the worshipper of Mazda that shall support her?

33 (94). Ahura Mazda answered : 'He who built the sheep-fold or who holds it, the care of supporting her is his; so long shall he support her, until the whelps are born.

34 (97). 'If he shall not support her so that the whelps come to mischief, for want of proper support, he shall pay the penalty for wilful murder.'

35 (100). O Maker of the material world, thou Holy One! If a bitch be near her time and be lying on the earth-wall[1], which is the worshipper of Mazda that shall support her?

36 (102). Ahura Mazda answered: 'He who erected the wall or who holds it, the care of supporting her is his; so long shall he support her, until the whelps are born.

37 (105). 'If he shall not support her, so that the whelps come to mischief, for want of proper support, he shall pay the penalty for wilful murder.'

---

[1] The wall around the house.

38 (108). O Maker of the material world, thou Holy One! If a bitch be near her time and be lying in the moat[1], which is the worshipper of Mazda that shall support her?

39 (110). Ahura Mazda answered: 'He who dug the moat or who holds it, the care of supporting her is his; so long shall he support her, until the whelps are born.

40 (112). 'If he shall not support her, so that the whelps come to mischief, for want of proper support, he shall pay the penalty for wilful murder.'

41 (113). O Maker of the material world, thou Holy One! If a bitch be near her time and be lying in the middle of a pasture-field, which is the worshipper of Mazda that shall support her?

42 (115). Ahura Mazda answered: 'He who sowed the pasture-field or who holds it, the care of supporting her is his.

43 (117). 'He shall with kind charity[2] take her to rest upon a litter of any foliage fit for a litter; so long shall he support her, until the young dogs are capable of self-defence and self-subsistence.'

44 (122). O Maker of the material world, thou Holy One! When are the dogs capable of self-defence and self-subsistence?

45 (123). Ahura Mazda answered: 'When they are able to run about in a circuit of twice seven houses around[3]. Then they may be let loose, whether it be winter or summer.

'Young dogs ought to be supported for six months, children for seven years.

---

[1] The moat before the earth-wall.

[2] Doubtful.

[3] Probably the distance of one yugyêsti; cf. Farg. XIII, 17.

'Âtar[1], the son of Ahura Mazda, watches as well (over a pregnant bitch) as he does over a woman.'

IV.

46 (127). O Maker of the material world, thou Holy One! If worshippers of Mazda want to have a bitch so covered that the offspring shall be one of a strong nature, what shall they do?

47 (129). Ahura Mazda answered: 'They shall dig a hole in the earth, in the middle of the fold, half a foot deep if the earth be hard, half the height of a man if the earth be soft.

48 (131). 'They shall first tie up the bitch there, far from children and from the Fire, the son of Ahura Mazda[2], and they shall watch by her until a dog comes there from anywhere. They shall afterwards let another dog come near her, and then a third besides[3], each being kept apart from the former, lest they should assail one another.

49 (134)[4]. 'The bitch being thus covered by three dogs, grows big with young, and the milk comes to her teats and she brings forth a young one that is born from (three) dogs.'

50 (135). He who smites a bitch who has been covered by three dogs, and who has already milk, and who shall bring forth a young one born from (three) dogs, what is the penalty that he shall pay?

---

[1] The fire: when a woman is in labour, one lights up a great fire in order to protect her and her child from the fiends (Introd. V, 13).

[2] 'From children, lest she shall bite them; from the fire, lest it shall hurt her' (Comm.)

[3] Cf. Justinus III, 4: maturiorem futuram conceptionem rati, si eam singulae per plures viros experirentur.

[4] The text of this and the following clause is corrupt, and the meaning doubtful.

51 (137). Ahura Mazda answered: 'Seven hundred stripes with the Aspahê-astra, seven hundred stripes with the Sraoshô-karana.'

FARGARD XVI.

I (1–11). On the uncleanness of women during their sickness.
II (11–12). How it can be removed.
III (13–18). Sundry laws relating to the same matter. See Introd. V, 12.

I.

1. O Maker of the material world, thou Holy One! If there be in the house of a worshipper of Mazda a woman who has an issue of blood, either out of the ordinary course or at the usual period, what shall the worshippers of Mazda do?

2 (3). Ahura Mazda answered: 'They shall clear the way[1] of the wood there, both in growing trees and in logs[2]; they shall strew dry dust on the ground[3]; and they shall erect a building there[4], higher than the house by a half, or a third, or a fourth, or a fifth part, lest her look should fall upon the fire[5].'

3 (9). O Maker of the material world, thou Holy One! How far from the fire? How far from the water? How far from the consecrated bundles of baresma? How far from the faithful?

4 (10). Ahura Mazda answered: 'Fifteen paces from the fire, fifteen paces from the water, fifteen

---

[1] The way to the Dashtânistân (see Introd. V, 12).

[2] Lest the wood shall be touched and defiled by the woman on her way to the Dashtânistân.

[3] Lest the earth shall be touched and defiled by her. Cf. Farg. IX, 11, and Introd. V, 10.

[4] The Dashtânistân.   [5] See Introd. V, 12.

paces from the consecrated bundles of baresma, three paces from the faithful.'

5 (11). O Maker of the material world, thou Holy One! How far from her shall he stay, who brings food to a woman who has an issue of blood, either out of the ordinary course or at the usual period?

6 (12). Ahura Mazda answered: 'Three paces [1] from her shall he stay, who brings food to a woman who has an issue of blood, either out of the ordinary course or at the usual period.'

In what kind of vessels shall he bring the food? In what kind of vessels shall he bring the bread?

' In vessels of brass, or of lead, or of any common metal [2].'

7 (15). How much food shall he bring to her? How much bread shall he bring?

'(Only) two danares [3] of long bread, and one danare of milk pap, lest she should gather strength [4].

' If a child has just touched her, they shall first wash his hands and then his body [5].

8 (21). ' If she still see blood after three nights

---

[1] The food is held out to her from a distance in a metal spoon.

[2] Earthen vessels, when defiled, cannot be made clean; but metal vessels can (see Farg. VII, 73 seq.)

[3] A danare is, according to Anquetil, as much as four tolas; a tola is from 105 to 175 grains.

[4] 'Sôshyôs says: For three nights cooked meat is not allowed to her, lest the issue shall grow stronger.' As the fiend is in her, any strength she may gain accrues to Ahriman.

[5] A child whom she suckles. The meaning is, Even a child, if he has touched her, must undergo the rites of cleansing. The general rule is given in the Commentary: 'Whoever has touched a Dashtân woman must wash his body and his clothes with gômêz and water.' The ceremony in question is the simple Ghosel, not the Barashnûm, since the woman herself performs the former only (vide infra, § 11 seq.; cf. Introd. V, 16).

have passed, she shall sit in the place of infirmity until four nights have passed.

'If she still see blood after four nights have passed, she shall sit in the place of infirmity until five nights have passed.

9. 'If she still see blood after five nights have passed, she shall sit in the place of infirmity until six nights have passed.

'If she still see blood after six nights have passed, she shall sit in the place of infirmity until seven nights have passed.

10. 'If she still see blood after seven nights have passed, she shall sit in the place of infirmity until eight nights have passed.

'If she still see blood after eight nights have passed, she shall sit in the place of infirmity until nine nights have passed.

11. 'If she still see blood after nine nights have passed, this is a work of the Daêvas which they have performed for the worship and glorification of the Daêvas [1].

II.

'The worshippers of Mazda shall clear the way [2] of the wood there, both in growing trees and in logs;

12 (26). 'They shall dig three holes in the earth, and they shall wash the woman with gômêz by two of those holes and with water by the third.

'They shall kill Khrafstras, to wit: two hundred corn-carrying ants, if it be summer; two hundred of

---

[1] See Introd. V, 12.

[2] The way to the Barashnûm-gâh, where the cleansing takes place.

any other sort of the Khrafstras made by Angra
Mainyu, if it be winter[1].'

III.

13 (30). If a worshipper of Mazda shall suppress
the issue of a woman who has an issue of blood,
either out of the ordinary course or at the usual
period, what is the penalty that he shall pay?

Ahura Mazda answered: 'He is a Peshôtanu:
two hundred stripes with the Aspahê-astra, two
hundred stripes with the Sraoshô-karana.'

14 (33). O Maker of the material world, thou
Holy One! If a man shall again and again wilfully
touch the body of a woman who has an issue of
blood, either out of the ordinary course or at the
usual period, so that the ordinary issue turns to
the dye of the unusual one, or the unusual issue
to the dye of the ordinary one, what is the penalty
that he shall pay?

15 (36). Ahura Mazda answered: 'For the first
time he comes near unto her, for the first time he
lies by her, thirty stripes with the Aspahê-astra,
thirty stripes with the Sraoshô-karana; for the
second time he comes near unto her, for the second
time he lies by her, fifty stripes with the Aspahê-
astra, fifty stripes with the Sraoshô-karana; for
the third time he comes near unto her, for the
third time he lies by her, seventy stripes with
the Aspahê-astra, seventy stripes with the Sraoshô-
karana.'

16. For the fourth time he comes near unto her,
for the fourth time he lies by her, if he shall press
the body under her clothes, if he shall press the

---

[1] See Introd. IV, 35.

unclean thigh, but without sexual intercourse, what
is the penalty that he shall pay?

Ahura Mazda answered: 'Ninety stripes with
the Aspahê-astra, ninety stripes with the Sraoshô-
*k*arana.

17 (39). 'Whosoever shall lie in sexual intercourse with a woman who has an issue of blood,
either out of the ordinary course or at the usual
period, does no better deed than if he should burn
the corpse of his own son, born of his own body and
dead of naêza[1], and drop its fat into the fire[2].

18 (41). 'All such sinners, embodiments of the
Dru*g*, are scorners of the law: all scorners of the law
are rebels against the Lord: all rebels against the
Lord are ungodly men; and any ungodly man shall
pay for it with his life[3].'

Fargard XVII.

Hair and Nails.

Anything that has been separated from the body of man is considered dead matter (Introd. V, 12), and is accordingly supposed to
fall into the possession of the demon and to become the abode of
death and uncleanness. Therefore, hair and nails, as soon as cut
off, are at once the property of Ahriman, and the demon has to be
driven away from them by spells, in the same way as he is from
the bodies of the dead. They are withdrawn from his power by

---

[1] A disease (Farg. VII, 58). There is another word naêza, 'a
spear,' so that one may translate also 'killed by the spear' (Asp.)

[2] 'Not that the two deeds are equal, but neither is good'
(Comm.) The sin in question is a simple tanâfûhr (Farg. XV, 7),
and therefore can be atoned for by punishment and repentance,
whereas the burning of a corpse is a crime for which there is no
atonement (Farg. I, 17; VIII, 73 seq.; Introd. V, 8).

[3] Literally, 'is a Peshôtanu;' 'he is a tanâfûhr sinner, that is to
say, margarzân (worthy of death),' Comm.

the recital of certain prayers, and by being deposited in the earth inside consecrated circles, which are drawn around them as an intrenchment against the fiend (see above, p. 122, n. 1).

This chapter, which has given full scope to the ironical humour of many, is an invaluable document in the eyes of the mythologist, as he finds in it, if not the origin and explanation, at least the oldest record of world-wide superstitions. Not only in Bombay, but all over the world, people are found who believe that hair and nails are weapons in the hands of the evil one. The Esthonians, on the shores of the Baltic, take the utmost care not to drop the parings of their nails on the ground, lest the devil should pick them up, to make a visor to his cap, which will give him full power to injure men, unless the sign of the cross has been made over them[1]. The Gauchos in the Chilian pampas fear to throw their hair to the winds, but deposit it in holes dug in a wall[2]. In Liége good people are advised not to throw away their hair, nor to leave it in the teeth of the comb, lest a witch take hold of it and cast a spell over them[3].

I.

1. Zarathustra asked Ahura Mazda: 'O Ahura Mazda, most beneficent Spirit, Maker of the material world, thou Holy One! Which is the most deadly deed whereby a man increases most the baleful strength of the Daêvas, as he would do by offering them a sacrifice?'

2 (3). Ahura Mazda answered: 'It is when a man here below combing his hair or shaving it off, or paring off his nails drops them[4] in a hole or in a crack[5].

[1] Cf. infra, 'Thou shalt chant the Ahuna-Vairya,' &c., §§ 6, 8, 9.
[2] Cf. infra, §§ 5, 7.
[3] Mélusine, Recueil de Mythologie populaire, publié par H. Gaidoz et E. Rolland, Paris, 1878; pp. 79, 549, 583. To the same train of ideas seems to belong the Eddic myth of Naglfar, the fatal ship wrought out of the nails of the dead, which is to take the crew of the demon to the shore of the earth when the last day of the world is come (Gylfaginning, 51).
[4] Without performing the requisite ceremonies.
[5] Doubtful.

3 (6). 'Then for want of the lawful rites being observed, Daêvas are produced in the earth; for want of the lawful rites being observed, those Khrafstras are produced in the earth which men call lice, and which eat up the corn in the corn-field and the clothes in the wardrobe.

4 (10). 'Therefore, O Zarathustra! whenever here below thou shalt comb thy hair or shave it off, or pare off thy nails, thou shalt take them away ten paces from the faithful, twenty paces from the fire, thirty paces from the water, fifty paces from the consecrated bundles of baresma.

5 (13). 'Then thou shalt dig a hole, a disti¹ deep if the earth be hard, a vîtasti deep if it be soft; thou shalt take the hair down there and thou shalt say aloud these fiend-smiting words: "Out of him by his piety Mazda made the plants grow up²."

6 (17). 'Thereupon thou shalt draw three furrows with a knife of metal around the hole, or six furrows or nine, and thou shall chant the Ahuna-Vairya three times, or six, or nine.

II.

7 (19). 'For the nails, thou shalt dig a hole, out

---

¹ A disti = ten fingers.   A vîtasti = twelve fingers.

² See above, XI, 6; the choice of this line was determined by the presence of the word plants in it: man was considered a microcosm, and every element in him was supposed to come from a similar element in nature, to which it was to return after death, and whence it was to come back again at the time of the resurrection: his bones from the earth, his blood from the water, his hair from the trees, his life from the fire (Bundahis XXXI, Ulamâi Islâm); an old Aryan theory, traces of which are also to be found in India (Rig-veda X, 16, 3), in Greece (Ilias VII. 99; Empedocles, fr. 378; cf. Epicharmus ap. Plut. Consol. ad Apoll. 15), and in Scandinavia (Edda, Grimnismal 40).

of the house, as deep as the top joint of the little finger; thou shalt take the nails down there and thou shalt say aloud these fiend-smiting words: "The words that are heard from the pious in holiness and good thought[1]."

8 (24). 'Then thou shalt draw three furrows with a knife of metal around the hole, or six furrows or nine, and thou shalt chant the Ahuna-Vairya three times, or six, or nine.

9 (26). 'And then: "Look here, O Ashô-zusta bird[2]! here are the nails for thee: look at the nails here! May they be for thee so many spears, knives, bows, falcon-winged arrows, and sling-stones against the Mâzainya Daêvas[3]!"

10 (29). 'If those nails have not been dedicated (to the bird), they shall be in the hands of the Mâzainya Daêvas so many spears, knives, bows, falcon-winged arrows, and sling stones (against the Mâzainya Daêvas)[4].

---

[1] Yasna XXXIII, 7. There is here only a play upon the word sruyê, 'is heard,' which chances to be homonymous with the dual of srva, 'nails of both hands.'

[2] 'The owl,' according to modern tradition. The word literally means 'friend of holiness.' 'For the bird Ashôzusta they recite the Avesta formula; if they recite it, the fiends tremble and do not take up the nails; but if the nails have had no spell uttered over them, the fiends and wizards use them as arrows against the bird Ashôzusta and kill him. Therefore, when the nails have had a spell uttered over them, the bird takes and eats them up, that the fiends may not do any harm by their means' (Bundahis XIX).

[3] See above, p. 137, n. 1. The nails are cut in two and the fragments are put in the hole with the point directed towards the north, that is to say, against the breasts of the Dêvs (see above, p. 75, n. 2). See Anquetil, Zend-Avesta II, 117; India Office Library, VIII, 80.

[4] Repeated by mistake from § 10.

11 (30). 'All such sinners, embodiments of the
Drug, are scorners of the law: all scorners of the
law are rebels against the Lord: all rebels against
the Lord are ungodly men; and any ungodly man
shall pay for it with his life [1].'

FARGARD XVIII.

I (1–13). On the unworthy priest and enticers to heresy.
II (14–29). The holiness of the cock.
III (30–60). The four paramours of the Drug.
IV (61–71). On unlawful lusts.
The text and the Pahlavi commentary of this Fargard are trans-
lated in Haug's Essays, pp. 243 seq., 364 seq.

I.

1. 'There is many a one, O holy Zarathustra!'
said Ahura Mazda, 'who wears a Paitidâna [2], but
who has not girded his loins with the law [3]; when
such a man says, "I am an Âthravan," he lies; do
not call him an Âthravan, O holy Zarathustra!' thus
said Ahura Mazda.

2 (5). 'He holds a Khrafstraghna [4] in his hand,
but he has not girded his loins with the law; when
he says, "I am an Âthravan," he lies; do not call
him an Âthravan, O holy Zarathustra!' thus said
Ahura Mazda.

---

[1] See preceding Fargard, § 18.

[2] See above, p. 168, n. 7.

[3] The word translated girded is the word used of the Kôstî, the
sacred girdle which the Parsi must never part with (see § 54); the
full meaning, therefore, is, 'girded with the law as with a Kôstî'
(cf. Yasna IX, 26 [81]), that is to say, 'never forsaking the law,' or,
as the Commentary expresses it, 'one whose thought is all on the
law' (cf. § 5).

[4] See above, p. 168, n. 8.

3 (7). 'He holds a twig[1] in his hand, but he has not girded his loins with the law; when he says, "I am an Âthravan," he lies; do not call him an Âthravan, O holy Zarathustra!' thus said Ahura Mazda.

4 (9). 'He wields the Astra mairya[2], but he has not girded his loins with the law; when he says, "I am an Âthravan," he lies; do not call him an Âthravan, O holy Zarathustra!' thus said Ahura Mazda.

5 (11). 'He who sleeps on throughout the night, who does not perform the Yasna nor chant the hymns, who does not worship by word or by deed, who does neither learn nor teach, with a longing for (everlasting) life, he lies when he says, "I am an Âthravan," do not call him an Âthravan, O holy Zarathustra!' thus said Ahura Mazda.

6 (14). 'Him thou shalt call an Âthravan, O holy Zarathustra! who throughout the night sits up and demands of the holy Wisdom[3], which makes man free from anxiety, with dilated heart, and cheerful at the head of the Kinvat bridge[4], and which makes him reach that world, that holy world, that excellent world, the world of paradise.

7 (18). '(Therefore) demand of me, thou upright one! of me, who am the Maker, the best of all beings, the most knowing, the most pleased in answering what is asked of me; demand of me, that

---

[1] The bundles of baresma or the urvarân (see p. 22, n. 2; p. 169, n. 3).

[2] The Aspahê-astra; see Introd. V, 19.

[3] That is to say, studies the law and learns from those who know it (cf. Introd. V, 2).

[4] See Farg. XIX, 30. 'It gives him a stout heart, when standing before the Kinvat bridge' (Comm.)

thou mayst be the better, that thou mayst be the happier [1].'

8 (21). Zarathustra asked Ahura Mazda: 'O Maker of the material world, thou Holy One! What is it that makes the unseen power of Death increase?'

9 (22). Ahura Mazda answered: 'It is the man that teaches a wrong law [2]; it is the man who continues for three years [3] without wearing the sacred girdle [4], without chanting the Gâthas, without worshipping the good waters.

10 (25). 'And he who should set that man at

---

[1] See Introd. V, 2.

[2] 'The deceiver Ashemaogha' (Comm.); the heretic. Cf. Farg. XV, 2, and Introd. III, 10.

[3] Doubtful.

[4] The Kôstî, which must be worn by every Parsi, man or woman, from their fifteenth year of age (see below, § 54 seq.); it is the badge of the faithful, the girdle by which he is united both with Ormazd and with his fellow believers. He who does not wear it must be refused water and bread by the members of the community; he who wears it becomes a participator in the merit of all the good deeds performed all over the Zarathustrian world (Saddar 10 and 46; Hyde 10 and 50). The Kôstî consists 'of seventy-two interwoven filaments, and should three times circumvent the waist. . . . Each of the threads is equal in value to one of the seventy-two Hâhs of the Izashnê; each of the twelve threads in the six lesser cords is equal in value to the dawâzdih hamâist . . .; each of the lesser cords is equal in value to one of the six Gahanbârs; each of the three circumventions of the loins is equal in value to humat, good thought, hukhat, good speech, huaresta, good work; the binding of each of the four knots upon it confers pleasure on each of the four elements, fire, air, water, and the earth' (Edal Daru, apud Wilson, The Parsi Religion Unfolded, p. 163). In the Brahmanical system also the faithful are bound to their god by means of a sacred girdle, the Mekhalâ.

Another piece of clothing which every Parsi is enjoined to wear is the Sadarah, or sacred shirt, a muslin shirt with short sleeves, that does not reach lower than the hips, with a small pocket at the opening in front of the shirt (see § 54 seq.)

liberty, when bound in prison[1], does no better deed than if he should flay a man alive and cut off his head[2].

11 (27). 'The blessing uttered on a wicked, ungodly Ashemaogha does not go past the mouth (of the blesser); the blessing for two Ashemaoghas does not go past his tongue; the blessing for three is no word at all; the blessing for four is a curse against himself.

12 (29). 'Whosoever should give some Haoma juice to a wicked, ungodly Ashemaogha, or some Myazda consecrated with blessings, does no better deed than if he should lead a thousand horse against the cities of the worshippers of Mazda, and should slaughter the men thereof, and drive off the cattle as plunder.

II.

13 (32). 'Demand of me, thou upright one! of me, who am the Maker, the best of all beings, the most knowing, the most pleased in answering what is asked of me; demand of me, that thou mayst be the better, that thou mayst be the happier.'

14 (33). Zarathustra asked Ahura Mazda: 'Who is the Sraoshâ-varez[3] of Sraosha[4]? the holy, strong Sraosha, who is the incarnate Word, a mighty-speared and lordly god.'

---

[1] See Introd. III, 10. Cf. § 12.

[2] Doubtful. The Commentary seems to understand the sentence as follows: 'He who should free him from hell would thus perform no less a feat than if he should cut off the head of a man and then make him alive again.'

[3] 'Who is he who sets the world in motion?' (Comm.) See above, p. 56, n. 2.

[4] See Introd. IV, 31.

15 (34). Ahura Mazda answered : 'It is the bird named Parôdar*s*¹, which ill-speaking people call Kahrkatâs², O holy Zarathu*s*tra! the bird that lifts up his voice against the mighty dawn :

16 (37). ' "Arise, O men! recite the Ashem ya*d* vahi*s*tem that smites down the Daêvas³. Lo! here is Bûshyãsta, the long-handed⁴, coming upon you, who lulls to sleep again the whole living world, as soon as it has awoke : ' Sleep!' she says, ' sleep on, O man! the time⁵ is not yet come.' "

17 (41). ' For the three excellent things be never slack, namely, good thoughts, good words, and good deeds ; for the three abominable things be ever slack, namely, bad thoughts, bad words, and bad deeds."

18 (43). ' In the first part of the night, Fire, the son of Ahura Mazda, calls the master of the house for help, saying :

19 (43). ' " Up! arise, thou master of the house! put on thy girdle on thy clothes, wash thy hands, take wood, bring it unto me, and let me burn bright

---

¹ ' He who foresees ' the coming dawn ; the cock.

² 'When he is not called so, he is powerful' (Comm.) Cf. XIII, 2, 6.

³ The cock is called ' the drum of the world.' As crowing in the dawn that dazzles away the fiends, he shared with it the honour of the victory, and was believed to crow away the demons : ' The cock was created to fight against the fiends and wizards ; . . . he is with the dog an ally of Srôsh against demons' (Bundahi*s* XIX). ' No demon can enter a house in which there is a cock ; and, above all, should this bird come to the residence of a demon, and move his tongue to chaunt the praises of the glorious and exalted Creator, that instant the evil spirit takes to flight' (Mirkhond, History of the Early Kings of Persia, translated by Shea, p. 57 ; cf. Saddar 32, Hyde 35, and J. Ovington, A Voyage to Suratt, 1696, p. 371).

⁴ See Introd. IV, 24.

⁵ ' To perform thy religious duties ' (Comm.)

[4]   O

with the clean wood, carried by thy well-washed
hands[1]. Here comes Âzi[2], made by the Daêvas,
who is about to strive against me, and wants to put
out my life."

20 (46). 'In the second part of the night, Fire,
the son of Ahura Mazda, calls the husbandman for
help, saying :

21 (46). '"Up! arise, thou husbandman! Put
on thy girdle on thy clothes, wash thy hands, take
wood, bring it unto me, and let me burn bright with
the clean wood, carried by thy well-washed hands.
Here comes Âzi, made by the Daêvas, who is about
to strive against me, and wants to put out my life."

22 (48). 'In the third part of the night, Fire,
the son of Ahura Mazda, calls the holy Sraosha
for help, saying : "Come thou, holy, tall-formed
Sraosha, [then he brings unto me some clean wood
with his well-washed hands][3]: here comes Âzi, made
by the Daêvas, who is about to strive against me,
and wants to put out my life."

23 (51). 'And then the holy Sraosha wakes up
the bird named Parôdars, which ill-speaking people
call Kahrkatâs, and the bird lifts up his voice
against the mighty dawn :

24 (52). '"Arise, O men! recite the Ashem yad
vahistem that smites down the Daêvas. Lo! here
is Bûshyãsta, the long-handed, coming upon you,
who lulls to sleep again the whole living world as.

---

[1] The Parsi, as soon as he has risen, must put on the Kôstî,
wash his hands, and put wood on the fire.

[2] See Introd. IV, 19.

[3] The text seems to be corrupt: it must probably be emendated
into 'bring into me . . .'

soon as it has awoke: 'Sleep!' she says, 'sleep on, O man! the time is not yet come.'"

25 (52). '"For the three excellent things be never slack, namely, good thoughts, good words, and good deeds; for the three abominable things be ever slack, namely, bad thoughts, bad words, and bad deeds."

26 (53). 'And then bed-fellows address one another: "Rise up, here is the cock calling me up." Whichever of the two first gets up shall first enter paradise: whichever of the two shall first, with well-washed hands, bring clean wood unto the Fire, the son of Ahura Mazda, the Fire, well pleased with him and not angry, and fed as it required, will thus bless him:

27 (58). '" May herds of oxen grow for thee, and increase of sons: may thy mind be master of its vow, may thy soul be master of its vow, and mayst thou live on in the joy of the soul all the nights of thy life."

'This is the blessing which the Fire speaks unto him who brings him dry wood, well examined by the light of the day, well cleansed with godly intent.

28 (64). 'And whosoever will kindly and piously present one of the faithful with a pair of these my Parôdars birds, a male and a female, it is as though he had given[1] a house with a hundred columns, a thousand beams, ten thousand large windows, ten thousand small windows.

29 (67). 'And whosoever shall give to my Parô-dars bird his fill of meat, I, Ahura Mazda, need not

---

[1] 'In the day of recompense' (Comm.)'; he shall be rewarded as though he had given a house, &c. . . . he shall receive such a house in paradise.

interrogate him any longer; he shall directly go to paradise.'

III.

30 (70). The holy Sraosha asked the Druǵ, with his club uplifted against her: 'O thou wretched and wicked Druǵ! Thou then, alone in the material world, dost bear offspring without any male coming unto thee?'

31 (74). Then the Druǵ demon, the guileful one, answered: 'O holy, tall-formed Sraosha! It is not so, nor do I, alone in the material world, bear offspring without any male coming unto me.

32 (77). 'There are four males who are mine.

'And they make me conceive progeny as other males make their females.'

33 (78). The holy Sraosha asked the Druǵ, with his club uplifted against her: 'O thou wretched and wicked Druǵ! Who is the first of those males of thine?'

34 (79). Then the Druǵ demon, the guileful one, answered: 'O holy, tall-formed Sraosha! He is the first of my males who, being entreated by one of the faithful, does not give him anything, be it ever so little, of the riches he has treasured up[1].

35 (82). 'That man makes me conceive progeny as other males make their females.'

36 (83). The holy Sraosha asked the Druǵ, with his club uplifted against her: 'O thou wretched and wicked Druǵ! What is the thing that can counteract that?'

37 (84). Then the Druǵ demon, the guileful one, answered: 'O holy, tall-formed Sraosha! This is

---

[1] Cf. Farg. III, 34.

the thing that counteracts it, namely, when a man unasked, kindly and piously, gives to one of the faithful something, be it ever so little, of the riches he has treasured up.

38 (87). 'He does thereby as thoroughly destroy the fruit of my womb as a four-footed wolf does, who tears the child out of a mother's womb.'

39 (88). The holy Sraosha asked the Drug, with his club uplifted against her: 'O thou wretched and wicked Drug! Who is the second of those males of thine?'

40 (89). Then the Drug demon, the guileful one, answered: 'O holy, tall-formed Sraosha! He is the second of my males who, making water, lets it fall along the upper forepart of his foot.

41 (92). 'That man makes me conceive progeny as other males make their females.'

42 (93). The holy Sraosha asked the Drug, with his club uplifted against her: 'O thou wretched and wicked Drug! What is the thing that can counter-act that?'

43 (94). Then the Drug demon, the guileful one, answered: 'O holy, tall-formed Sraosha! This is the thing that counteracts it, namely, when the man rising up[1] and stepping three steps further off, shall say three Ahuna-Vairya, two humatanãm, three hukhshathrôtemãm, and then chant the Ahuna-Vairya and offer up one Yênhê hâtãm.

---

[1] 'Nec stando mingens . . . facile visitur Persa' (Amm. Marc. XXIII, 6); Ardâ Vîrâf XXIV; Mainyô-i-khard II, 39 ; Saddar 56, Hyde 60. Cf. Manu IV, 47 seq., and Polack, Persien I, 67: 'Von einem in Paris weilenden Perser hinterbrachte man dem König, um seine Emancipation und Abtrünnigkeit vom Gesetz zu beweisen, dass er Schweinefleisch esse und stehend die Function verrichte.'

44 (98). 'He does thereby as thoroughly destroy the fruit of my womb as a four-footed wolf does, who tears the child out of a mother's womb.'

45 (99). The holy Sraosha asked the Drug, with his club uplifted against her: 'O thou wretched and wicked Drug! Who is the third of those males of thine?'

46 (100). Then the Drug demon, the guileful one, answered: 'O holy, tall-formed Sraosha! He is the third of my males who during his sleep emits seed.

47 (102). 'That man makes me conceive progeny as other males make their females.'

48 (103). The holy Sraosha asked the Drug, with his club uplifted against her: 'O thou wretched and wicked Drug! What is the thing that can counteract that?'

49 (104). Then the Drug demon, the guileful one, answered: 'O holy, tall-formed Sraosha! this is the thing that counteracts it, namely, if the man, when he has risen from sleep, shall say three Ahuna-Vairya, two humatanãm, three hukhshathrô-temãm, and then chant the Ahuna-Vairya and offer up one Yênhê hâtãm.

50 (107). 'He does thereby as thoroughly destroy the fruit of my womb as a four-footed wolf does who tears the child out of a mother's womb.'

51 (108). Then he shall speak unto Spenta Âr-maiti[1], saying: 'O Spenta Ârmaiti, this man do I deliver unto thee; this man deliver thou back unto me, against the mighty day of resurrection; deliver him back as one who knows the Gâthas, who

---

[1] The genius of the earth (cf. Farg. II, 10).

knows the Yasna, and the revealed law [1], a wise and clever man, who is the Word incarnate.

52 (112). 'Then thou shalt call his name "Fire-creature, Fire-seed, Fire-offspring, Fire-land," or any name wherein is the word Fire [2].'

53 (113). The holy Sraosha asked the Druǵ, with his club uplifted against her: ' O thou wretched and wicked Druǵ! Who is the fourth of those males of thine ?'

54 (114). Then the Druǵ demon, the guileful one, answered : ' O holy, tall-formed Sraosha ! This one is my fourth male who, either man or woman, being more than fifteen years of age, walks without wearing the sacred girdle and the sacred shirt [3].

55 (115). 'At the fourth step [4] we Daêvas, at once, wither him even to the tongue and the marrow, and he goes thenceforth with power to destroy the world of the holy spirit, and he destroys it like the Yâtus and the Zandas [5].'

56 (117). The holy Sraosha asked the Druǵ, with his club uplifted against her : ' O thou wretched and wicked Druǵ, what is the thing that can counteract that ?'

57 (118). Then the Druǵ demon, the guileful one, answered : ' O holy, tall-formed Sraosha ! There is no means of counteracting it ;

---

[1] Literally, 'the answers made to the questions (of Zarathustra).'

[2] Cf. Introd. IV, 30, and Orm. Ahr. § 205.

[3] The Kôstî and the Sadarah ; see above, p. 191, n. 4. It is the sin known as kushâd duvârisnî (Mainyô-i-khard II, 35 ; Ardâ Vîrâf XXV, 6).

[4] 'Going three steps without Kôstî is only a three Sraoshô-karana sin ; from the fourth step, it is a tanâfûhr sin' (Comm.)

[5] For the Yâtus, see Introd. IV, 20 ; the zanda is a hobgoblin.

58 (120). 'When a man or a woman, being more than fifteen years of age, walks without wearing the sacred girdle or the sacred shirt.

59 (120). 'At the fourth step we Daêvas, at once, wither him even to the tongue and the marrow, and he goes thenceforth with power to destroy the world of the holy spirit, and he destroys it like the Yâtus and the Za*n*das.'

IV.

60 (122). Demand of me, thou upright one! of me who am the Maker, the best of all beings, the most knowing, the most pleased in answering what is asked of me; demand of me that thou mayst be the better, that thou mayst be the happier.

61 (123). Zarathustra asked Ahura Mazda: 'Who grieves thee with the sorest grief? Who pains thee with the sorest pain?'

62 (124). Ahura Mazda answered: 'It is the *G*ahi [1], O Spitama Zarathustra! who goes a-whoring after the faithful and the unfaithful, after the worshippers of Mazda and the worshippers of the Daêvas, after the wicked and the righteous [2].

63 (125). 'Her look dries up one third of the mighty floods that run from the mountains; her look withers one third of the beautiful, golden hued, growing plants;

64 (127). 'Her look withers one third of the grass

---

[1] The courtezan, as an incarnation of the female demon *G*ahi (see Introd. IV, 15).

[2] '[Whether she gives up her body to the faithful or to the unfaithful], there is no difference; when she has been with three men, she is guilty of death' (Comm.)

wherewith Spe*n*ta Ârmaiti [1] is clad [2], and her touch
withers in the faithful one third of his good thoughts,
of his good words, of his good deeds, one third of
his strength, of his fiend-killing power, and of his
holiness [3].

65 (129). 'Verily I say unto thee, O Spitama
Zarathu*s*tra! such creatures ought to be killed even
more than gliding snakes [4], than howling wolves,
than the wild she-wolf that falls upon the fold, or
than the she-frog that falls upon the waters with her
thousandfold brood.'

66 (133). Demand of me, thou upright one! of
me who am the Maker, the best of all beings, the
most knowing, the most pleased in answering what
is asked of me; demand of me that thou mayst be
the better, that thou mayst be the happier.

67–68 (133). Zarathu*s*tra asked Ahura Mazda: 'If
a man shall come unto a woman who has an issue
of blood, either out of the ordinary course or at the
usual period, and he does so wittingly and knowingly [5], and she allows it wilfully, wittingly, and

---

[1] The earth.

[2] Doubtful. The Pahlavi translation has, 'One third of the
strength of Spe*n*ta Ârmaiti.'

[3] 'If a *G*ahi (courtezan) look at running waters, they fall; if at
trees, they are stunted; if she converse with a pious man, his intelligence and his holiness are withered by it' (Saddar 67; Hyde 74).
Cf. Manu IV, 40 seq.

[4] It is written in the law (the Avesta): 'O Zartu*s*t Isfitamân! with
regard to woman, I say to thee that any woman that has given up
her body to two men in one day is sooner to be killed than a wolf,
a lion, or a snake: any one who kills such a woman will gain as
much merit by it as if he had provided with wood a thousand fire-
temples, or destroyed the dens of adders, scorpions, lions, wolves,
or snakes' (Old Rav. 59 b).

[5] 'Knowing her state and knowing that it is a sin' (Comm.)

knowingly, what is the atonement for it, what is the penalty that he shall pay to atone for the deed they have done?'

69 (136). Ahura Mazda answered : 'If a man shall come unto a woman who has an issue of blood, either out of the ordinary course or at the usual period, and he does so wittingly and knowingly, and she allows it wilfully, wittingly, and knowingly;

70 (137). 'He shall slay a thousand head of small cattle; he shall godly and piously offer up to the fire [1] the entrails [2] thereof together with Zaothra-libations; he shall bring the shoulder bones to the good waters [3].

71 (140). 'He shall godly and piously bring unto the fire a thousand loads of soft wood, of Urvâsna, Vohu-gaona, Vohu-kereti, Hadhâ-naêpata, or of any sweet-scented plant [4].

72 (142). 'He shall tie and consecrate a thousand bundles of baresma; he shall godly and piously offer up to the good waters a thousand Zaothra-libations, together with the Haoma and the meat, cleanly prepared and well strained by a pious man, together with the roots of the tree known as Hadhâ-naêpata [5].

73 (144). 'He shall kill a thousand snakes of

---

[1] To the Bahrâm fire.

[2] The ōmentum (afsman) or epipleon. Strabo XV, 13 : τοῦ ἐπίπλου τι μικρὸν τιθέασι, ὡς λέγουσί τινες, ἐπὶ τὸ πῦρ. 'Ascending six steps they showed me in a Room adjoining to the temple, their Fire which they fed with Wood, and sometimes Burn on it the Fat of the Sheep's Tail.' A Voyage Round the World, Dr. J. F. Gemelli, 1698.

[3] The meat is eaten by the faithful (Asp.); cf. Herod. I, 132.

[4] Cf. Farg. XIV, 3 seq.

[5] See above, p. 94, n. 1.

those that go upon the belly, two thousand of the other kind[1] : he shall kill a thousand land frogs and two thousand water frogs; he shall kill a thousand corn-carrying ants and two thousand of the other kind[2].

74 (147). 'He shall throw thirty bridges over canals; he shall undergo a thousand stripes with the Aspahê-a*s*tra, a thousand stripes with the Sraoshô-*k*arana[3].

75 (149). 'This is the atonement, this is the penalty that he shall pay to atone for the deed that he has done.

76 (150). 'If he shall pay it, he shall enter the world of the holy ones; if he shall not pay it, he shall fall down into the world of the wicked, into that dark world, made of darkness, the offspring of darkness[4].'

FARGARD XIX.

I (1-11). Angra Mainyu attempts to kill Zarathu*s*tra, and, when he fails, tempts him. Zarathu*s*tra withstands both assaults with weapons both material and spiritual.

II (11-43). Zarathu*s*tra applies to Ahura Mazda for a revelation of the law. He is taught how the fiend may be repelled, how the creation of Mazda is to be worshipped, how uncleanness is to be washed away, and what becomes of the soul after death.

III (43-47). Angra Mainyu and his host, driven to despair, and feeling themselves powerless, flee down into hell.

This chapter may be entitled 'The Revelation,' and considered as the frame-work of the Vendîdâd, the remainder of which should have its place between the first and the third part; as the first part

---

[1] 'Two thousand mâr bânak' (Comm.) See above, p. 157, n. 1.

[2] 'Two thousand dârak' (Comm.) See above, p. 157, n. 4.

[3] Five tanâfûhrs, that is six thousand dirhems.

[4] §§ 75, 76 = Farg. XIV, 18.

shows the fiend's struggles to prevent the revelation, and the third
shows the effects of it; the second being, as it were, an abstract of
the law, an abridged Vendîdâd.

The text and the Pahlavi commentary of this Fargard are translated
in Haug's Essays, p. 253 seq., p. 333 seq., and p. 379 seq.

I.

1. From the region of the north, from the regions
of the north [1], forth rushed Angra Mainyu, the
deadly, the Daêva of the Daêvas [2]. And thus spake
the guileful one, he the evil-doer Angra Mainyu,
the deadly: 'Drug, rush down upon him! destroy
the holy Zarathustra!' The Drug came rushing
along, the demon Bûiti [3], the unseen death, the
hell-born.

2 (5). Zarathustra chanted aloud the Ahuna-
Vairya [4]: 'The will of the Lord is the law of
holiness; the riches of Vohu-manô shall be given
to him who works in this world for Mazda, and
wields according to the will of Ahura the power he
gave to him to relieve the poor.'

(He added): 'Offer up prayers to the good waters
of the good Dâitya [5]!

' Profess the law of the worshippers of Mazda!'

The Drug dismayed, rushed away, the demon
Bûiti, the unseen death, the hell-born.

---

[1] From hell; cf. p. 75, n. 2.

[2] 'The fiend of fiends,' the arch-fiend.

[3] 'How does death enter the body of man? There are several
Druges from Ahriman, who come into the body and the soul of
man: one of whom is a Drug known as Bût; she is the forerunner
of death; when the time of the end is at hand, she produces in the
body of man such excessive heat that he falls ill' (Dâdâr i Dâdûkht,
British Museum, Add. 8994, 130 a).

[4] See above, p. 98, n. 2.

[5] The river in Airyana Vaêgô; see Farg. I, 3, and Introd. III, 15.

3 (7). And the Dru*g*, the guileful one, said unto
Angra Mainyu: 'O baneful Angra Mainyu! I see no
way to kill him, so great is the glory of the holy
Zarathu*s*tra.'

Zarathu*s*tra saw (all this) from within his soul:
'The evil-doing Daêvas and Drva*n*ts[1] (thought he)
take counsel together for my death.'

4 (11). Up started Zarathu*s*tra, forward went
Zarathu*s*tra, unshaken by the evil spirit, by the
hardness of his malignant riddles[2], swinging stones
in his hand, stones as big as a house[3], which he
obtained from the Maker, Ahura Mazda, he the
holy Zarathu*s*tra.

'At what on this wide, round earth, whose ends
lie afar, at what dost thou swing (those stones),
thou who standest by the river Dare*g*a[4], upon the
mountains, in the mansion of Pouru*s*aspa[5]?'

5 (16). Thus Zarathu*s*tra answered Angra Mainyu:
'O evil-doer, Angra Mainyu! I will smite the creation of the Daêva; I will smite the Nasu, a creature
of the Daêva; I will smite the Pairika Knãthaiti[6],
till the fiend-smiter Saoshya*n*t come up to life out

---

[1] See Introd. IV, 22.

[2] This is a fragment of an old myth in which Zarathu*s*tra and
Angra Mainyu played respectively the parts of Oedipus and the
Sphinx. See, for further explanation, Orm. Ahr. §§ 163–165.

[3] See Introd. IV, 40. The Commentary has, 'Some say, those
stones are the Ahuna-Vairya.' In another attempt to account for a
mythical expression, which was no longer understood, those thunder-
bolts were turned into the nine-knotted stick used in the Barashnûm
(see Farg. IX, 14; Comm. and Asp.)

[4] See Introd. III, 15.

[5] The father of Zarathu*s*tra.

[6] Cf. Farg. I, 10, and Introd. IV, 21.

of the lake Kăsava, from the region of the dawn, from the regions of the dawn[1].'

6 (20). Again to him said the guileful one, the Maker of the evil world, Angra Mainyu : 'Do not destroy my creatures, O holy Zarathustra! Thou art the son of Pourusaspa[2], just born of thy mother[3]. Renounce the good law of the worshippers of Mazda, and thou shalt gain such a boon as the murderer[4] gained, the ruler of the nations.'

7 (24). Thus in answer to him said Spitama Zarathustra : ' No! never will I renounce the good law of the worshippers of Mazda, though my body, my life, my soul should burst !'

8 (27). Again to him said the guileful one, the Maker of the evil world, Angra Mainyu : ' By whose Word wilt thou strike, by whose Word wilt thou repel, by whose weapon will the good creatures (strike and repel) my creation who am Angra Mainyu ?'

9 (29). Thus in answer to him said Spitama Zarathustra : ' The sacred mortar, the sacred cup, the Haoma, the Words taught by Mazda, these are my weapons, my best weapons! By this Word will I strike, by this Word will I repel, by this weapon the good creatures (will strike and repel thee), O evil-doer, Angra Mainyu! To me Spenta Mainyu gave it, he gave it to me in the boundless Time[5];

---

[1] See Introd. IV, 39–40.　　　　[2] ' I know thee' (Comm.)

[3] Doubtful (cf. § 46); possibly, ' I was invoked by thy mother.' The Commentary has, ' Some explain thus : Thy forefathers worshipped me : worship me also.'

[4] Ajis Dahâka or Zohâk, who, as a legendary king, is said to have ruled the world for a thousand years (Introd. IV, 11).

[5] See Introd. IV, 42. The Ahuna-Vairya was revealed before

to me the Amesha Spentas, the all-ruling, the all-beneficent, gave it.'

10 (35). Zarathustra chanted aloud the Ahuna-Vairya. The holy Zarathustra said aloud: 'This I ask thee: teach me the truth, O Lord[1]!...'

II.

11 (37). Zarathustra asked Ahura Mazda: 'O Ahura Mazda, most beneficent spirit, Maker of the material world, thou Holy One! [he was sitting by the Darega, on the mountain[2], praying to Ahura Mazda, to the good Vohu-manô, to Asha Vahista, Khshathra Vairya, and Spenta Ârmaiti;]

12 (39). 'How shall I make the world free from that Drug, from the evil-doer Angra Mainyu? How shall I drive away direct defilement? How indirect defilement? How shall I drive the Nasu from the house of the worshippers of Mazda? How shall I cleanse the faithful man? How shall I cleanse the faithful woman?'

13 (42). Ahura Mazda answered: 'Invoke, O Zarathustra! the good law of Mazda.

'Invoke, O Zarathustra! the Amesha Spentas who rule over the seven Karshvares of the earth[3].

'Invoke, O Zarathustra! the sovereign Heaven, the boundless Time[4], and Vayu[5], whose action is most high.

---

the creation of the world (Yasna XIX), and consequently in the boundless Time.

[1] This verse is the beginning of a Gâtha (Yasna XLIV), in which Zarathustra applies to Ahura Mazda to be taught the mysteries of the world and of the law.

[2] See § 4 and Introd. III, 15.   [3] See Introd. IV, 7.
[4] See Introd. IV, 42.   [5] See Introd. IV, 15.

'Invoke, O Zarathustra! the powerful Wind, made by Mazda, and Spenta [Ârmaiti][1], the fair daughter of Ahura Mazda.

14 (46). 'Invoke, O Zarathustra! my Fravashi[2], who am Ahura Mazda, the greatest, the best, the fairest of all beings, the most solid[3], the most intelligent, the best shapen, the highest in holiness, and whose soul is the holy Word[4]!

'Invoke, O Zarathustra! this creation of mine, who am Ahura Mazda.'

15 (50). Zarathustra took those words from me, (and said): 'I invoke the holy creation of Ahura Mazda.

'I invoke Mithra[5], the lord of wide pastures, a god armed with beautiful weapons, with the most glorious of all weapons, with the most fiend-smiting of all weapons.

'I invoke the holy, tall-formed Sraosha[6], who wields a club in his hand, to bear upon the heads of the fiends.

16 (54). 'I invoke the most glorious holy Word.

'I invoke the sovereign Heaven, the boundless Time, and Vayu, whose action is most high.

'I invoke the mighty Wind, made by Mazda, and Spenta (Ârmaiti), the fair daughter of Ahura Mazda.

'I invoke the good law of Mazda, the fiend-destroying law of Zarathustra.'

17 (58). Zarathustra asked Ahura Mazda: 'O Maker of the good world, Ahura Mazda! With

[1] See Introd. IV, 30.   [2] See Introd. IV, 37.
[3] See Introd. IV, 5.   [4] Mâthra Spenta; see Introd. IV, 40.
[5] See Introd. IV, 8.
[6] See Introd. IV, 31, and cf. Farg. XVIII, 22 seq.

what manner of sacrifice shall I worship, with what manner of sacrifice shall I worship and forward this creation of Ahura Mazda?'

18 (60). Ahura Mazda answered: 'Go, O Spitama Zarathustra! towards that tree[1] that is beautiful, high-growing, and mighty amongst the high-growing trees, and say thou these words: "Hail to thee! O good, holy tree, made by Mazda! Ashem vohu[2]!"

19 (63). 'Let the faithful man cut off a twig of baresma, long as a ploughshare, thick as a barley-corn[3]. The faithful one, holding it in his left hand, shall not leave off keeping his eyes upon it[4], whilst he is offering up the sacrifice to Ahura Mazda and to the Amesha-Spentas, and to the high and beautiful golden Haomas, and to Vohu-manô[5] and to the good Râta[6], made by Mazda, holy and excellent[7].'

20 (67). Zarathustra asked Ahura Mazda: 'O thou, all-knowing Ahura Mazda! thou art never asleep, never intoxicated, thou Ahura Mazda! Vohu-manô[8] gets directly defiled: Vohu-manô gets indirectly de-

---

[1] The tree, whatever it is, from which the baresma is taken. See p. 22, n. 2.

[2] See § 22.   [3] Doubtful.

[4] The Parsis are recommended to keep their eyes on the baresma during the sacrifice: 'A man is offering the Darûn, he has said all the required Avesta, but he has not looked at the baresma: what is the rule? It would have been better if he had looked at it: however he may proceed to the meal' (Old Rav. 97 b).

[5] See Introd. IV, 7.   [6] See Introd. IV, 30.

[7] Doubtful. Possibly, 'While he is offering up the high and beautiful Haomas, and Vohu-manô (good thoughts) and the good Râta (sacrificial presents).'

[8] Vohu-manô is often used as a designation of the faithful one, literally, 'the good-minded;' this is the meaning which is given to it in this passage by the Commentary, and it certainly belongs

[4]   P

filed; the Daêvas defile him from the bodies smitten by the Daêvas[1]: let Vohu-manô be made clean.'

21 (70). Ahura Mazda answered: 'Thou shalt take some gômêz from a bull ungelded and such as the law requires it[2]; thou shalt take the man who is to be cleansed[3] to the field made by Ahura[4], and the man that is to cleanse him shall draw the furrows[5].

22 (73). 'He shall recite a hundred Ashem vohu: "Holiness is the best of all good. Happy, happy the man who is holy with perfect holiness!"

'He shall chant two hundred Ahuna-Vairya: "The will of the Lord is the law of holiness; the riches of Vohu-manô shall be given to him who works in this world for Mazda, and wields according to the will of Ahura the power he gave to him to relieve the poor."

'He shall wash Vohu-manô four times with the gômêz from the ox, and twice with the water made by Mazda[6].

---

to it in the second part of § 25; but in the first part of the same clause it is translated 'clothes,' a meaning which is not unlikely in itself, as Vohu-manô, being the Amshaspand of cattle, may designate, and in fact did designate, the skins of cattle and leather (Comm. ad Farg. XVIII, 2). On the whole the description in the text applies to the cleansing both of the man and of the clothes, and Vohu-manô sometimes means the one, and sometimes the other.

[1] From dead bodies.

[2] The so-called Varasiô; 'it must be of a white colour; if a single hair on its body be found other than white, the animal is rejected as unfit for the purpose' (Sorâbji Kâvasji Khambâtâ, in the Indian Antiquary, VII, 180).

[3] Or better, 'the things that are to be cleansed.'

[4] The place of the cleansing, the Barashnûm-gâh (see Farg. IX, 3).

[5] See Farg. IX, 10.

[6] This can hardly refer to the cleansing of the man, as the man

23 (76). 'Thus Vohu-manô shall be made clean, and clean shall be the man. Then he shall take up Vohu-manô[1] with his left arm and his right, with his right arm and his left: and thou shalt lay down Vohu-manô under the mighty structure of the bright heavens, by the light of the stars made by the gods, until nine nights have passed away[2].

24 (80). 'When nine nights have passed away, thou shalt bring libations unto the fire, thou shalt bring hard wood unto the fire, thou shalt bring incense of Vohu-gaona unto the fire, and thou shalt perfume Vohu-manô therewith.

25 (82). "Thus shall Vohu-manô become clean, thus shall the man be clean[3]: he shall take up Vohu-manô with the right arm and the left, with the left arm and the right, and Vohu-manô[4] shall say aloud: "Glory be to Ahura Mazda! Glory be to the Amesha-Spentas! Glory be to all the other holy beings."'

26 (85). Zarathustra asked Ahura Mazda: 'O thou all-knowing Ahura Mazda: Should I urge upon the godly man, should I urge upon the godly woman, should I urge upon the wicked Daêva-worshipper who lives in sin, that they have once to leave behind them the earth made by Ahura,

---

ought to be washed six times with gômêz and three times with water (see Farg. VIII, 37 seq.; IX, 28 seq.)

[1] 'The clothes' (Comm.)

[2] The clothes of the unclean shall be exposed to the air for nine nights, all the time while he himself is confined in the Armêst-gâh. The rules for the cleansing of clothes that have been worn by the dead himself are different (see Farg. VII, 12 seq.)

[3] 'Thus Vohu-manô shall be clean—the clothes; thus the man shall be clean—he who wears those clothes' (Comm.)

[4] The faithful one.

P 2

that they have to leave the water that runs, the corn
that grows, and all the rest of their wealth [1]?'

Ahura Mazda answered : 'Thou shouldst, O holy
Zarathustra.'

27 (89). O Maker of the material world, thou
Holy One! Where are the rewards given? Where
does the rewarding take place? Where is the
rewarding fulfilled? Whereto do men come to
take the reward that, in their life in the material
world, they have won for their souls?

28 (90). Ahura Mazda answered: 'When the
man is dead, when his time is over, then the hellish,
evil-doing Daêvas assail him; and when the third
night is gone, when the dawn appears and
brightens up, and makes Mithra, the god with
beautiful weapons, reach the all-happy mountains,
and the sun is rising:

29 (94). 'Then the fiend, named Vîzaresha,
carries off in bonds [2] the souls of the wicked
Daêva-worshippers who live in sin. The soul
enters the way made by Time, and open both to
the wicked and to the righteous. At the head of
the *K*inva*d* bridge, the holy bridge made by
Mazda [3], they ask for their spirits and souls the

---

[1]   'Linquenda tellus, et domus et placens

      Uxor, nec harum, quas colis arborum. . . .'

The translation is doubtful in its details; yet there is little doubt
that the sentence refers to future life (cf. § 27). Aspendiârji translates, 'Shall the godly man . . . arise (from the dead) . . .?' which
seems to be the meaning of the Pahlavi Commentary too.

[2] 'Every one has a noose cast around his neck: when a man
dies, if he has been a righteous man, the noose falls from his neck ;
if a wicked, they drag him with that noose down into hell' (Comm.;
cf. Farg. V, 8, and Introd. IV, 26).

[3] The *K*inva*d* bridge extends over hell and leads to paradise:
for the souls of the righteous it widens to the length of nine javelins;

reward for the worldly goods which they gave away here below [1].

30 (98). 'Then comes the well-shapen, strong and tall-formed maid [2], with the dogs at her sides [3], one who can distinguish [4], who is graceful [5], who does what she wants, and is of high understanding.

'She makes the soul of the righteous one go up above the Hara-berezaiti [6]; above the *K*invad bridge she places it in the presence of the heavenly gods themselves.

31 (102). 'Up rises Vohu-manô [7] from his golden seat; Vohu-manô exclaims: "How hast thou come to us, thou holy one, from that decaying world into this undecaying one [8]?"

---

for the souls of the wicked it narrows to a thread, and they fall down into hell (cf. Ard*â* Vîrâf V, 1). This bridge is known in many mythologies; it is the Sirath bridge of the Musulmans; not long ago they sang in Yorkshire of 'the Brig o' Dread, na brader than a thread' (Thoms, Anecdotes, 89), and even nowadays the peasant in Nièvre tells of a little board—

'Pas pu longue, pas pu large
Qu'un ch'veu de la Sainte Viarge,'

which was put by Saint Jean d'Archange between the earth and paradise:

'Ceux qu'saront la raison (=l'oraison?) d'Dieu
Par dessus passeront.
Ceux qu'la sauront pas
Au bout mourront.' (Mélusine, p. 70.)

[1] Cf. Farg. III, 34, 35; XVIII, 33 seq.

[2] The soul of the dead, on the fourth day, finds itself in the presence of a maid, of divine beauty or fiendish ugliness, according as he himself was good or bad, and she leads him into heaven or hell: this maid is his own conscience (Yasht XXII).

[3] The dogs that keep the *K*invad bridge (see Farg. XIII, 9).

[4] The good from the wicked. [5] Doubtful.

[6] The heavenly mountain, whence the sun rises, and upon which the abode of the gods rests.

[7] The door-keeper of paradise; a Zoroastrian Saint-Pierre.

[8] Cf. Farg. VII, 52.

32 (105). 'Gladly pass the souls of the righteous
to the golden seat of Ahura Mazda, to the golden
seat of the Amesha-Spentas, to the Garô-nmânem¹,
the abode of Ahura Mazda, the abode of the
Amesha-Spentas, the abode of all the other holy
beings.

33 (108). 'As to the godly man that has been
cleansed², the wicked evil-doing Daêvas tremble at
the perfume of his soul after death, as a sheep does
on which a wolf is falling³.

34 (110). 'The souls of the righteous are gathered
together there: Nairyô-sangha⁴ is with them; a friend
of Ahura Mazda is Nairyô-sangha.

'Do thou thyself invoke, O Zarathustra! this
world of Ahura Mazda.'

35 (114). Zarathustra took those words from
Ahura Mazda: 'I invoke the holy world, made by
Ahura Mazda.

'I invoke the earth made by Ahura, the water
made by Mazda, the holy trees.

'I invoke the sea Vouru-kasha⁵.

'I invoke the shining sky.

'I invoke the eternal and sovereign luminous
space⁶.

---

¹ The Garothmân of the Parsis; literally, 'the house of
songs.'

² That has performed the Barashnûm.

³ Ormazd is all perfume, Ahriman is infection and stench (Bundahis I; Eznig, Refutatio Haeresiarum II); the souls of their followers partake of the same qualities, and by the performance of
the Barashnûm both the body and the soul are perfumed and
sweetened.

⁴ The messenger of Ahura Mazda (cf. Farg. XXII, 7).

⁵ See Introd. IV, 11.

⁶ See Introd. IV, 42.

36 (120). 'I invoke the bright, all glorious, blissful abode of the holy ones.

'I invoke the Garô-nmânem, the abode of Ahura Mazda, the abode of the Amesha-Spentas, the abode of all the other holy beings.

'I invoke the sovereign place of eternal weal[1], and the *K*inva*d* bridge made by Mazda.

37 (123). 'I invoke the good Saoka[2], whose looks go far and wide.

'I invoke the mighty Fravashis[3] of the righteous.

'I invoke the whole creation of weal.

'I invoke Verethraghna[4], made by Ahura, who wears the glory made by Mazda[5].

'I invoke Ti*s*trya[6], the bright and glorious star, in the shape of a golden-horned bull.

38 (127). 'I invoke the holy, beneficent Gâthas[7], who rule over the ratus[8]:

'I invoke the Ahunavaiti Gâtha;

'I invoke the U*s*tavaiti Gâtha;

'I invoke the Spe*n*ta-mainyu Gâtha;

'I invoke the Vohu-khshathra Gâtha;

---

[1] Misvâna gâtva, another name of the heavenly spaces; it designates heaven as the abode and source of all blessings, of all savah, or saoka.

[2] A personification of the Ormazdean weal.

[3] See Introd. IV, 37.

[4] See Introd. IV, 14, and Yasht XIV.

[5] The *h*varenô or light of sovereignty (Introd. IV, 11).

[6] See Introd. IV, 13, and Yasht VIII.

[7] The five collections of hymns which form the oldest and holiest part of the Yasna and of the Avesta (Yasna XXVIII–XXXIV; XLIII–XLVI; XLVII–L; LI; LIII); they are named after their first words.

[8] The chiefs of creation (Introd. IV, 35); 'they rule over the ratus insomuch as it is by their means that other beings are invoked' (Comm.)

'I invoke the Vahistôisti Gâtha.

39 (129). 'I invoke the Karshvares of Arzahê and Savahê;

'I invoke the Karshvares of Fradadhafshu and Vidadhafshu;

'I invoke the Karshvares of Vourubaresti and Vouruzaresti;

'I invoke the bright *Hv*aniratha[1];

'I invoke the bright, glorious Haêtuma*nt*[2];

'I invoke the good Ashi[3];

['I invoke the good *K*isti[4];]

'I invoke the most right *K*ista[5];

'I invoke the glory of the Aryan regions[6];

'I invoke the glory of the bright Yima, the great shepherd[7].

40 (133). 'Let him be worshipped with sacrifice, let him be gladdened, gratified, and satisfied, the holy Sraosha, the tall-formed, fiend-smiting, holy Sraosha[8].

'Bring libations unto the Fire, bring hard wood unto the Fire, bring incense of Vohu-gaona unto the Fire.

'Offer up the sacrifice to the Vâzista fire, which

---

[1] See Introd. IV, 7.   [2] See Farg. I, 14.

[3] See Introd. IV, 30.

[4] An angel of knowledge; the clause is found only in the Vendîdâd Sâdah.

[5] Religious knowledge.

[6] The light of sovereignty, *hv*arenô, which if secured by the Aryans makes them rule over their enemies (cf. Introd. IV, 11).

[7] See Introd. IV, 18, and Farg. II.

[8] This praise of Sraosha was probably introduced here with reference to the great part he plays in the fate of the soul after death, and to the performance of the sadis ritual (see above, p. 87, n. 4).

smites the fiend Spen*g*aghra¹ : bring unto it the
cooked meat and the offerings of boiling milk ².

41 (137). 'Offer up the sacrifice to the holy
Sraosha, that the holy Sraosha may smite down
the fiend Ku*n*da³, who is drunken without drinking. He will fall upon the men of the Dru*g*, the
slothful ones⁴, the wicked Daêva-worshippers, who
live in sin.

[42⁵. 'I invoke the Kara fish⁶, who lives beneath
waters in the bottom of the deep lakes.

'I invoke the ancient and sovereign Merezu⁷, the
greatest seat of battle in the creation of the two
spirits⁸.

'I invoke the seven bright Sravah⁹ with their
sons and their flocks.

III.

43. 'They run about to and fro, their minds
waver to and fro¹⁰, Angra Mainyu the deadly, the

---

¹ See Introd. IV, 13.   ² Doubtful.
³ The same as Ku*n*di; see Farg. XI, 9.
⁴ Those who neglect their religious duties. The translation is
doubtful.
⁵ From the Vendîdâd Sâdah. The clause may have belonged
to the original text; it is preceded by another clause which certainly
did not belong to it, and part of which is cited in the Commentary ad Farg. VIII, 103, where it would have been more suitably
placed : 'When he has been cleansed in the next inhabited place,
he may then sow and till the pasture fields, as food for the sheep
and as food for the ox.'
⁶ The Kar-mâhî (see above, p. 59, n. 4).
⁷ According to Professor Justi, 'the milky way' (Handbuch der
Zendsprache s. v.), an Iranian representative of the Eddic Bifrost.
There is much probability in that translation.
⁸ Doubtful.
⁹ A word of unknown meaning.
¹⁰ Up and down, in hope and despair.

Daêva of the Daêvas; I*n*dra the Daêva, Sâuru the
Daêva, N*au*nghaithya the Daêva, Taurvi and Zairi[1],
Aêshma of the wounding spear[2], Akatasha the
Daêva[3], Zaurva[4], baneful to the fathers, Bûiti the
Daêva[5], Driwi[6] the Daêva, Daiwi[7] the Daêva,
Kasvi[8] the Daêva, Paitisha[9] the most Daêva-like
amongst the Daêvas.]

44 (140). 'And he said, the guileful, the evil-
doing Daêva, An*g*ra Mainyu the deadly: "What!
let the wicked, evil-doing Daêvas gather together
at the head of Arezûra[10]."

45 (141). 'They rush, they run away, the wicked,
evil-doing Daêvas; they run away with shouts, the
wicked, evil-doing Daêvas; they run away casting
the evil eye, the wicked, evil-doing Daêvas: "Let
us gather together at the head of Arezûra!

46 (143). '"For he is just born the holy Zarathustra, in the house of Pourushaspa. How can we
procure his death? He is the stroke that fells the
fiends: he is a counter-fiend to the fiends; he is a
Dru*g* to the Dru*g*. Down are the Daêva-worshippers, the Nasu made by the Daêva, the false-
speaking Lie!"

47 (147). 'They run away, they rush away, the
wicked, evil-doing Daêvas, into the depths of the
dark, horrid world of hell.

---

[1] See Introd. IV, 34.   [2] See Introd. IV, 22.
[3] See above, p. 136, n. 5.   [4] Old age.
[5] See above, p. 204, n. 3.
[6] Poverty; see above, Farg. II, 29.
[7] Lying; see above, Farg. II, 29.
[8] Meanness; see above, Farg. II, 29.
[9] 'Opposition, or counter-action,' a personification of the doings
of Ahriman and of his marring power.
[10] At the gate of hell; see above, p. 24, n. 1.

'Ashem·vohu: Holiness is the best of all good.'

FARGARD XX.

Thrita, the First Healer.

Thrita was the first who drove back death and disease, as Ahura Mazda had brought to him down from hea‥ ꝺ ten thousand healing plants that had been growing up around the tree of eternal life, the white Hôm or Gaokerena.

This Thrita is mentioned only once again in the Avesta, in Yasna IX, 7, where he appears to have been one of the first priests of Haoma. This accounts for his medical skill; as Haoma is a source of life and health, his first priests must have been the first healers.

Thrita was originally the same as Thraêtaona[1]. On one hand, we see that in the Rig-veda the great feat of Thraêtaona is ascribed to Trita as well as to Traitâna, and Trita Âptya, 'the son of the waters,' was as well the celestial priest who pours Haoma into rain as the celestial hero who kills the snake in storms. On the other hand, we see that Thraêtaona fulfilled the same functions as Thrita: according to Hamza he was the inventor of medicine[2]; the Tavids[3] against sickness are inscribed with his name, and we find in the Avesta itself the Fravashi of Thraêtaona invoked 'against itch, hot fever, humours, cold fever[4], vâvareshi, against the plagues created by the serpent[5].' We see from this passage that disease was understood as coming from the serpent; in other words, that it was considered a sort of poisoning[6], and this is the reason why the

---

[1] See Introd. IV, 14.

[2] Ed. Gottwaldt, p. 23; cf. Mirkhond, Early Kings of Persia, Shea, p. 152.

[3] Formules of exorcism.

[4] Cf. Farg. VII, 58.

[5] Yasht XIII, 131.

[6] This theory, which modern science would not utterly reject, accounts for the great part which the serpent plays in the worship of Asklepios; as sickness comes from him, from him too must or may come the healing.

killer of the serpent was invoked to act against it. Thus Thrita-Thraêtaona had a double right to the title of the first of the healers, both as a priest of Haoma and as the conqueror of the serpent [1].

1. Zarathustra asked Ahura Mazda: 'Ahura Mazda, most beneficent Spirit, Maker of the material world, thou Holy One! Who was he who first of the healthful [2], the wise, the happy, the wealthy, the glorious, the strong men of yore [3], drove back sickness to sickness, drove back death to death [4], and first turned away the point of the poniard and the fire of fever from the bodies of mortals.'

2 (11). Ahura Mazda answered: 'Thrita it was who first of the healthful, the wise, the happy, the wealthy, the glorious, the strong man of yore, drove back sickness to sickness, drove back death to death, and first turned away the point of the poniard and the fire of fever from the bodies of mortals.

3 (12). 'He asked for a source of remedies [5]; he obtained it from Khshathra-Vairya [6], to withstand sickness and to withstand death, to withstand pain and fever, to withstand the disease [7], rottenness and

---

[1] It seems as if in the Vedas, too, Trita had been a healing god (Rig-veda VIII, 47, 13 seq.)

[2] Whom no weapon could wound, like Isfendiâr (Comm.)

[3] Or better, Paradhâta (or Pêshdâd), 'the kings of yore,' which became the name of the first Iranian dynasty.

[4] 'That is to say, who kept sickness in bonds, who kept death in bonds' (Comm.)

[5] Doubtful.

[6] As Khshathra-Vairya presides over metals, it was a knife he received, 'of which the point and the base were set in gold.' He was therefore the first who healed with the knife (cf. Farg. VII, 44); and it appears from § 4 that he was also the first who healed with herbs. As for the healing with the holy word, see Farg. XXII.

[7] Doubtful.

infection which Angra Mainyu had created by his witchcraft against the bodies of mortals [1].

4 (15). 'And I Ahura Mazda brought down the healing plants that, by many hundreds, by many thousands, by many myriads, grow up all around the one Gaokerena [2].

5 (18). 'All this (health) do we call by our blessing-spells, by our prayers, by our praises, upon the bodies of mortals [3].

7 (19) [4]. 'To thee, O Sickness, I say avaunt! to thee, O Death, I say avaunt! to thee, O Pain, I say avaunt! to thee, O Fever, I say avaunt! to thee, O Disease, I say avaunt [5]!

---

[1] The Vendîdâd Sâdah has here eight names of diseases: to withstand Sârana (head-ache), to withstand Sârastya (cold fever), to withstand Azana, to withstand Azahva, to withstand Kurugha, to withstand Azivâka, to withstand Duruka, and to withstand Astairya.

[2] The white Hôm, which is the king of healing plants (see Introd. IV, 28). The healing plants are said to have been created ten thousand in number, in order to oppose so many diseases that had been created by Ahriman (Bundahis IX; cf. Farg. XXII, 2). In India also, healing plants are said to have Soma for their king, and to have come down from heaven : ' Whilst coming down from heaven, the plants said; He will never suffer any wound, the mortal whom we touch' (Rig-veda X, 97, 17 ; cf. Haurvatâṭ et Ameretâṭ, §§ 46–47).

[3] Or possibly, All those (plants) do we bless, all those (plants) do we pray, all those (plants) do we praise, for (the weal of) the bodies of mortals.

[4] Vendîdâd Sâdah : 6. To withstand sickness, to withstand death, to withstand pain, to withstand fever, to withstand Sârana, to withstand Sârastya, to withstand Azana, to withstand Azahva, to withstand Kurugha, to withstand Azivâka, to withstand Duruka, to withstand Astairya, to withstand the disease, rottenness, and infection which Angra Mainyu has created by his witchcraft against the bodies of mortals.

[5] Vendîdâd Sâdah: To thee, O Sârana, I say avaunt ! to thee,

8 (21). 'By their might may we smite down the Drug! By their might may we smite the Drug! May they give to us strength and power, O Ahura[1]!

9[2] (23). 'I drive away sickness, I drive away death, I drive away pain and fever[3], I drive away the disease, rottenness, and infection which Angra Mainyu has created by his witchcraft against the bodies of mortals.

10 (25). 'I drive away all manner of diseases and deaths, all the Yâtus and Pairikas[4], and all the wicked Gainis[5].

11 (26). ' May the much-desired Airyaman[6] come here, for the men and women of Zarathustra to rejoice, for the faithful to rejoice; with the desirable reward that is won by means of the law, and with that boon for holiness that is vouchsafed by Ahura!

12 (29). 'May the much-desired Airyaman smite

O Sârastya, I say avaunt! to thee, O Asana, I say avaunt! to thee, O Asahva, I say avaunt! to thee, O Kurugha, I say avaunt! to thee, O Asivâka, I say avaunt! to thee, O Duruka, I say avaunt! to thee, O Astairya, I say avaunt!

[1] This clause is borrowed, with some alteration, from Yasna XXXI, 4; the original text is, 'May the strong power come to me, by the might of which we may smite down the Drug!'

[2] The Vendîdâd Sâdah has, 'I drive away Ishirê, I drive away Aghûirê, I drive away Aghra, I drive away Ughra.'

[3] The Vendîdâd Sâdah has, 'I drive away Sârana, I drive away Sârastya, I drive away Asana, I drive away Asahva, I drive away Kurugha, I drive away Asivâka, I drive away Duruka, I drive away Astairya.'

[4] See Introd. IV, 20-21.

[5] ' Gai' (Comm.), that is Gahi (see Introd. IV, 5); cf. p. 89, note 1, and Farg. XXII, 2, note.

[6] Or better, ' Airyaman, the bestower of good.' On Airyaman, see Farg. XXII. Clauses 11-12 are borrowed from Yasna LIV, 1, and form the prayer known as Airyama-ishyô.

all manner of diseases and deaths, all the Yâtus and
Pairikas, and all the wicked *G*ainis.'

13. Yathâ ahû vairyô :—the will of the Lord
is the law of holiness; the riches of Vohu-manô
shall be given to him who works in this world for
Mazda, and wields according to the will of Ahura
the power he gave to him to relieve the poor.

K*e*m nâ mazdâ :—whom hast thou placed to
protect me, O Mazda! while the hate of the fiend is
grasping me ? Whom but thy Âtar and Vohu-
manô, by whose work the holy world goes on ?
Reveal to me the rules of thy law!

K*e* verethrem *g*â :—who is he who will smite
the fiend in order to maintain thy ordinances ?
Teach me clearly thy rules for this world and for
the next, that Sraosha may come with Vohu-manô
and help whomsoever thou pleasest.

Keep us from our hater, O Mazda and Ârmaiti
Spe*n*ta! Perish, O fiendish Dru*g*! Perish, O brood
of the fiend! Perish, O world of the fiend! Perish
away, O Dru*g*! Perish away to the regions of the
north, never more to give unto death the living
world of the holy spirit!][1]

FARGARD XXI.
Waters and Light.

I (1). Praise of the holy bull.

II (2–3). Invocation addressed to rain as a healing power.

III a (4–7). Joint invocation addressed to the waters and to the
light of the sun.

III b (8–11). Joint invocation addressed to the waters and to the
light of the moon.

[1] From the Vendîdâd Sâdah.

III c (12–17). Joint invocation addressed to the waters and to the light of the stars.

IV (18–21). Spells against disease.

I.

1. Hail, holy bull[1]! Hail to thee, beneficent bull! Hail to thee, who makest increase! Hail to thee, who makest growth! Hail to thee, who dost bestow thy gifts upon the excellent faithful, and who wilt bestow them on the faithful yet unborn! Hail to thee, whom the *G*ahi kills[2], and the ungodly Ashemaogha, and the wicked tyrant.

II.

2 (3). 'Come, come on, O clouds, along the sky, through the air, down on the earth, by thousands of drops, by myriads of drops:' thus say, O holy Zarathustra! 'to destroy sickness altogether, to destroy death altogether, to destroy altogether the sickness made by the *G*aini[3], to destroy altogether the death made by the *G*aini, to destroy altogether Gadha and Apagadha[4].

3 (9). 'If death come at eve, may healing come at daybreak!

'If death come at daybreak, may healing come at night!

---

[1] The primeval bull who was created by Ormazd and killed by Ahriman with the help of the *G*ahi. The praise of the holy bull serves as an introduction to the praise of the waters. There were old myths in which a cloud was compared to a bull in the atmosphere, from whom rain was supposed to come. (See Orm. Ahr. § 122 seq.; cf. Introd. V, 5. Clause 1 is to be recited when one meets an ox or any kind of cattle, Gr. Rav. 386.)

[2] Possibly, 'who dost kill the *G*ahi' (by means of gômêz).

[3] The *G*ahi (see Farg. XX, 10) as bringing sickness (cf. Farg. VII, 59).

[4] Names of diseases.

'If death come at night, may healing come at dawn!

'Let showers shower down new waters, new earth, new trees, new health, and new healing powers.

III a.

4 (15). 'As the sea Vouru-kasha is the gathering place of waters [1], rise up, go up the aerial way and go down on the earth; go down on the earth and go up the aerial way [2]. Rise up and roll along! thou in whose rising and growing Ahura Mazda made the aerial way [3].

5 (20). 'Up! rise up and roll along! thou swift-horsed sun, above Hara Berezaiti, and produce light for the world (and mayst thou [O man!] rise up there, if thou art to abide in Garô-nmânem [4]) [5], along the path made by Mazda, along the way made by the gods, the watery way they opened.

---

[1] Waters and light are believed to flow from the same spring and in the same bed: 'As light rises up from Hara Berezaiti [Alborz, the mountain by which the earth is surrounded], so waters spring up from it and come back to it' (Bund. XX); every day the sun, moon, and stars rise up from Alborz, and every day all the waters on the earth come back together to the sea Vouru-kasha, and there collected come down again to the earth from the peaks of Alborz (Bund. VII, Gr. Rav. 431; cf. Farg. V, 15 seq.) As light comes from three different sources, the sun, the moon, and the stars, the waters are invoked three times, first in company with the sun, then with the moon, lastly with the stars, as if there should be three different movements of the rain connected with the three movements of light.

[2] Waters come down from the sky to the earth and come up back from the earth to the sky (see Farg. V, 15 seq.)

[3] Doubtful.

[4] 'If thou art a righteous man' (Comm.)

[5] The translation of this clause is doubtful.

[4]   Q

6 (23). 'And thou shalt keep away the evil by this holy spell[1]: Of thee [O child!] I will cleanse the birth and growth; of thee [O woman!] I will make the body and the strength pure; I make thee a woman rich in children and rich in milk;

7 (27). 'A woman[2] rich in seed, in milk, in fat, in marrow, and in offspring. I shall make for thee a thousand springs flow and run towards the pastures that will give food to the child.

III b.

8 (30). 'As the sea Vouru-kasha is the gathering place of waters, rise up, go up the aerial way, and go down on the earth; go down on the earth and go up the aerial way. Rise up and roll along! thou in whose rising and growing Ahura Mazda made the earth[3].

9 (31). 'Up! rise up, thou moon, that dost keep in thee the seed of the bull[4], rise up above Hara Berezaiti, and produce light for the world (and mayst thou [O man!] rise up there, if thou art to

---

[1] Doubtful; the text is corrupt. The spell refers to the cleansing and generative power of the waters; cf. the invocation to Ardvî Sûra, Farg. VII, 16: the waters are supposed to make females fertile as they make the earth. This spell was probably pronounced to facilitate childbirth.

[2] Or better, 'a female;' there are, in the text, two words for 'milk,' the one referring to the milk of women, the other to the milk of cows.

[3] Doubtful.

[4] When the bull died, 'what was bright and strong in his seed was brought to the sphere of the moon, and when it was cleansed there in the light of the astre, two creatures were shaped with it, a male and a female, from which came two hundred and seventy-two kinds of animals' (Bund. IV, X; cf. Orm. Ahr. §§ 125 and 127).

abide in Garô-nmânem), along the path made by Mazda, along the way made by the gods, the watery way they opened.

10 (32). 'And thou shalt keep away the evil by this holy spell: Of thee [O child!] I will cleanse the birth and growth; of thee [O woman!] I will make the body and the strength pure; I make thee a woman rich in children and rich in milk;

11 (32). 'A woman rich in seed, in milk, in fat, in marrow, and in offspring. I shall make for thee a thousand springs flow and run towards the pastures that will give food to the child.

III c.

12 (32). 'As the sea Vouru-kasha is the gathering place of waters, rise up, go up the aerial way, and go down on the earth; go down on the earth and go up the aerial way. Rise up and roll along! thou in whose rising and growing Ahura Mazda made everything grow [1].

13 (33). 'Up! rise up, ye stars, that have in you the seed of waters [2], rise up above Hara Berezaiti, and produce light for the world (and mayst thou [O man!] rise up there, if thou art to abide in Garô-nmânem), along the path made by Mazda, along the way made by the gods, the watery way they opened.

14 (34). 'And thou shalt keep away the evil by this holy spell: Of thee [O child!] I will cleanse the birth and growth; of thee [O woman!] I will make

---

[1] Doubtful.

[2] When Tistrya, the storm god who gives rain, became a star (see Introd. IV, 36), it was thought that there was a relation between the stars and rain.

the body and the strength pure; I make thee a
woman rich in children and rich in milk;

15 (34). 'A woman rich in seed, in milk, in fat, in
marrow, and in offspring. I shall make for thee a
thousand springs flow and run towards the pastures
that will give food to the child.

16 (34). 'As the sea Vouru-kasha is the gathering
place of waters, rise up and gather together, go up
the aerial way and go down on the earth; go down
on the earth and go up the aerial way. Rise up
and roll along!

17 (35). 'Up! rise up! away will the Ka*hvu*zi[1]
fly and cry, away will Ayêhi[2] fly and cry, away will
the *G*ahi, who is addicted to the Yâtu, fly and cry.

IV.

[18. 'I drive away Ishirê, I drive away Aghûirê,
I drive away Aghra, I drive away Ughra; I drive
away sickness, I drive away death, I drive away
pain and fever; I drive away Sârana, I drive away
Sârasti, I drive away A*z*ana, I drive away A*z*ahva,
I drive away Kurugha, I drive away A*z*ivâka, I drive
away Duruka, I drive away Astairya; I drive away
the disease, rottenness, and infection which Angra
Mainyu has created by his witchcraft against the
bodies of mortals.

19. 'I drive away all manner of diseases and
deaths, all the Yâtus and Pairikas, and all the
wicked *G*ainis.

20. 'May the much-desired Airyaman come here,
for the men and women of Zarathu*s*tra to rejoice, for
the faithful to rejoice; with the desirable reward

---

[1] 'He who diminishes light, Ahriman' (Comm.)
[2] 'Sterility, Ahriman' (Comm.)

that is won by means of the law, and with that boon
for holiness that is vouchsafed by Ahura!

21. 'May the much-desired Airyaman smite all
manner of diseases and deaths, all the Yâtus and
Pairikas, and all the wicked Gainis.

22. 'Yathâ ahû vairyô:—the will of the
Lord . . .[1].

'Kem nâ mazdâ:—whom hast thou placed to
protect me . . .[1]?

'Ke verethrem gâ:—who is he who will smite
the fiend . . .[1]?

23. 'Keep us from our hater, O Mazda and
Ârmaiti Spenta! Perish, O fiendish Drug! Perish,
O brood of the fiend! Perish, O world of the fiend!
Perish away, O Drug! Perish, away to the regions
of the north, never more to give unto death the
living world of the holy spirit!'

FARGARD XXII.

Angra Mainyu creates 99,999 diseases: Ahura Mazda applies
for healing to the holy word and to Airyaman.

Airyaman is an old Indo-Iranian god: in the Rig-veda he is an
Âditya (Aryaman), who is seldom invoked alone, but nearly always
in company with Mitra and Varuna. His name, like Mitra's,
means, 'the friend,' and, like Mitra, he is the god of heavenly light,
kind, beneficent, and helpful to man.

In the Avesta the word Airyaman has the same meaning as in
the Veda; but the character of the god is more fully developed,
and whereas he has no distinct personality in the Vedic hymns,
he appears here in the character of a healing god, which is derived
in a very natural manner from his primitive and general character.

Airyaman abides in a mansion called the mansion of Airyaman
(Airyamnô nmânem), which is the same as ' the bright mansion in

---

[1] As in preceding Fargard, § 13.

which Mitra, Aryaman, Varu*n*a abide,' according to the Vedas, that is to say, the sky. In later Parsism, Airyaman appears as 'the Ized of Heaven[1].'

This Fargard is unfinished or, more correctly, the end of it is understood. Airyaman, called out from his mansion, comes and digs nine furrows. It is no doubt in order to perform the Barashnûm[2] or some ceremony of that kind, in order to cleanse the unclean, that is to say, the sick man[3], and to restore him to health by virtue of the Nirang and of the holy word. The Fargard ends therefore with spells against sickness and against death.

I.

1. Ahura Mazda spake unto Spitama Zarathu*s*tra, saying: 'I, Ahura Mazda, the Maker of all good things, when I made this mansion[4], the beautiful, the shining, seen afar (there may I go up, there may I pass!)

2 (5). 'Then the ruffian looked at me[5]; the ruffian Angra Mainyu, the deadly, wrought by his witchcraft nine diseases, and ninety, and nine hundred, and nine thousand, and nine times ten thousand diseases. So mayst thou heal me, O Mâthra Spe*n*ta[6], thou most glorious one!

3 (8). 'Unto thee will I give in return a thousand fleet, swift-running steeds; offer them up[7] as a sacrifice unto the good Saoka[8], made by Mazda and holy.

'Unto thee will I give in return a thousand fleet,

---

[1] Aspendiârji.   [2] See Farg. IX; cf. infra, § 20, n.

[3] See Introd. V, 14.

[4] 'The Garotman' (Comm.), paradise.

[5] And cast on me the evil eye; 'it was by casting the evil eye on the good creatures of Ormazd that Ahriman corrupted them' (Eznig, Refutatio Haeresiarum II).

[6] The holy word.

[7] Possibly, 'I offer them up as a sacrifice.'

[8] An incarnation of weal; here invoked as procuring health.

high-humped camels ; offer them up as a sacrifice unto the good Saoka, made by Mazda and holy.

4 (12). 'Unto thee will I give in return a thousand brown oxen that do not push [1]; offer them up as a sacrifice unto the good Saoka, made by Mazda and holy.

'Unto thee will I give in return a thousand young of all species of small cattle; offer them up as a sacrifice unto the good Saoka, made by Mazda and holy.

5 (16). 'And I will bless thee with the fair, holy blessing-spell, the friendly, holy blessing-spell, that makes the empty swell to fulness and the full to overflowing, that comes to help him who was sickening, and makes the sick man sound again.

6 (20). 'Mãthra Spenta, the all-glorious, replied unto me : " How shall I heal thee ? How shall I drive away from thee those nine diseases, and those ninety, those nine hundred, those nine thousand, and those nine times ten thousand diseases?"'

II.

7 (22). The Maker Ahura Mazda called for Nairyô-sangha [2]: Go thou, Nairyô-sangha, the herald, and drive towards the mansion of Airyaman, and speak thus unto him :

8 (23). Thus speaks Ahura Mazda, the Holy One, unto thee: 'I, Ahura Mazda, the Maker of all good things, when I made this mansion, the

---

[1] Possibly, ' in which there is no blemish.'

[2] The messenger of Ahura Mazda. He was originally the same as the Vedic Narâ-sansa, a name of Agni, chiefly as the sacrificial fire, that is, as the messenger that goes from the heavens to the earth, and from the earth to the heavens. Mazdeism still knows that he is a form of Âtar, the Fire (Yasna XVII, 11 [68]).

beautiful, the shining, seen afar (there may I go up, there may I pass!)

9 (24). 'Then the ruffian looked at me; the ruffian Angra Mainyu, the deadly, wrought by his witchcraft nine diseases, and ninety, and nine hundred, and nine thousand, and nine times ten thousand diseases. So mayst thou heal me, O Airyaman, the much-desired!

10 (26). 'Unto thee will I give in return a thousand fleet, swift-running steeds; offer them up as a sacrifice unto the good Saoka, made by Mazda and holy.

'Unto thee will I give in return a thousand fleet, high-humped camels; offer them up as a sacrifice unto the good Saoka, made by Mazda and holy.

11 (30). 'Unto thee will I give in return a thousand brown oxen that do not push; offer them up as a sacrifice unto the good Saoka, made by Mazda and holy.

'Unto thee will I give in return a thousand young of all species of small cattle; offer them up as a sacrifice unto the good Saoka, made by Mazda and holy.

12 (34). 'And I will bless thee with the fair, holy blessing-spell, the friendly, holy blessing-spell, that makes the empty swell to fulness and the full to overflowing, that comes to help him who was sickening, and makes the sick man sound again.'

III.

13 (38). In obedience to Ahura's words he went, Nairyô-sangha, the herald; he drove towards the mansion of Airyaman, he spake unto Airyaman, saying:

14 (38). Thus speaks Ahura Mazda, the Holy One, unto thee: 'I, Ahura Mazda, the Maker of all good things, when I made this mansion, the beautiful, the shining, seen afar (there may I go up, there may I pass!)

15 (39). 'Then the ruffian looked at me; the ruffian Angra Mainyu, the deadly, wrought by his witchcraft nine diseases, and ninety, and nine hundred, and nine thousand, and nine times ten thousand diseases. So mayst thou heal me, O Airyaman, the much-desired!

16 (40). 'Unto thee will I give in return a thousand fleet, swift-running steeds; offer them up as a sacrifice unto the good Saoka, made by Mazda and holy.

'Unto thee will I give in return a thousand fleet, high-humped camels; offer them up as a sacrifice unto the good Saoka, made by Mazda and holy.

17 (44). 'Unto thee will I give in return a thousand brown oxen that do not push; offer them up as a sacrifice unto the good Saoka, made by Mazda and holy.

'Unto thee will I give in return a thousand young of all species of small cattle; offer them up as a sacrifice unto the good Saoka, made by Mazda and holy.

18 (48). 'And I will bless thee with the fair, holy blessing-spell, the friendly, holy blessing-spell, that makes the empty swell to fulness and the full to overflowing, that comes to help him who was sickening, and makes the sick man sound again.'

IV.

19 (52). Quickly was it done, nor was it long, eagerly set off the much-desired Airyaman, towards

the mountain of the holy questions [1], towards the forest of the holy questions.

20 (54). Nine stallions brought he with him, the much-desired Airyaman [2].

Nine camels brought he with him, the much-desired Airyaman.

Nine bulls brought he with him, the much-desired Airyaman.

Nine head of small cattle brought he with him, the much-desired Airyaman.

He brought with him the nine twigs [3]; he drew along nine furrows [4].

[21 [5]. 'I drive away Ishirê, I drive away Aghûirê, I drive away Aghra, I drive away Ughra; I drive away sickness, I drive away death, I drive away pain and fever; I drive away Sârana, I drive away Sârastya, I drive away Azana, I drive away Azahva, I drive away Kurugha, I drive away Azivâka, I drive away Duruka, I drive away Astairya; I drive away the disease, rottenness, and infection which Angra Mainyu has created by his witchcraft against the bodies of mortals.

22. 'I drive away all manner of diseases and deaths, all the Yâtus and Pairikas, and all the wicked Gainis.

---

[1] The mountain where 'the holy conversations' between Ormazd and Zoroaster took place (cf. Farg. XIX, 11, and Introd. 40).

[2] According to Aspendiârji, 'He brought with him the strength of nine stallions,' to infuse it into the sick man (cf. Yasht VIII, 24).

[3] That is to say, 'the nine-knotted stick' (Asp.; cf. Farg. IX, 14).

[4] To perform the Barashnûm, 'the great service of the Nirang-Dîn, through which all evil, moral and natural, including evil passions, disease, and death will be removed' (Wilson, The Parsi Religion, p. 341).

[5] From the Vendîdâd Sâdah.

23. 'May the much-desired Airyaman come here for the men and women of Zarathustra to rejoice, for the faithful to rejoice; with the desirable reward that is won by means of the law, and with that boon for holiness that is vouchsafed by Ahura.

24. 'May the much-desired Airyaman smite all manner of diseases and deaths, all the Yâtus and Pairikas, and all the wicked Gainis.

25. 'Yathâ ahû vairyô:—the will of the Lord is the law of holiness; the riches of Vohu-manô shall be given to him who works in this world for Mazda, and wields according to the will of Ahura the power he gave him to relieve the poor.

'Kem nâ mazdâ:—whom hast thou placed to protect me, O Mazda! while the hate of the fiend is grasping me? Whom but thy Âtar and Vohu-manô, by whose work the holy world goes on? Reveal to me the rules of thy law!

'Ke verethrem gâ:—who is he who will smite the fiend in order to maintain thy ordinances? Teach me clearly thy rules for this world and for the next, that Sraosha may come with Vohu-manô and help whomsoever thou pleasest.

'Keep us from our hater, O Mazda and Ârmaiti Spenta! Perish, O fiendish Drug! Perish, O brood of the fiend! Perish, O world of the fiend! Perish away, O Drug! Perish away to the regions of the north, never more to give unto death the living world of the holy spirit!']

CONSONANTS.	MISSIONARY ALPHABET. I Class.	II Class.	III Class.	Sanskrit.	Zend.	Pehlevi.	Persian.	Arabic.	Hebrew.	Chinese.
Gutturales.										
1 Tenuis	k			क	ꭓ	ꝑ	ک	ک	ם ה	k
2 „ aspirata	kh			ख	ꭓ	ꝑ	ک		ם ה	kh
3 Media	g			ग	ꝑ	ꝑ	ݩ		ꝑ ꝑ	
4 „ aspirata	gh			घ	ꝑ	ꝑ	ݩ	ݩ	ꝑ ꝑ	
5 Gutturo-labialis	q									
6 Nasalis	ñ (ng)			ङ	$\{$ ʒ (ng) $\}$ ʒ (ɴ)					ḥ, hs
7 Spiritus asper	h			ह	ʒ (ʜ hu)	ʒ	-	-	ᚷ	
8 „ lenis	'						-	-	ᚷ	
9 „ asper faucalis	'h						ש	ש	ᚷ	
10 „ lenis faucalis	,h						ע ﻭ	ע ﻭ	ᚷ	
11 „ asper fricatus		'h								
12 „ lenis fricatus		,h								
Gutturales modificatae (palatales, &c.)										
13 Tenuis		k		च		ꝑ				k
14 „ aspirata		kh		छ			ع			kh
15 Media		g		ज						
16 „ aspirata	ā	gh		झ				ו ﻉ		ʔ
17 „ Nasalis	ñ			ञ	ʒ	ꝑ	ב ﻉ	ב ﻉ		

CONSONANTS (continued)	I Class	II Class	III Class	Sanskrit	Zend	Pehlevi	Persian	Arabic	Hebrew	Chinese
18 Semivocalis	y									y
19 Spiritus asper		(y)								
20 " lenis		(y)								
21 " asper assibilatus		s								
22 " lenis assibilatus		z								
Dentales.										
23 Tenuis	t									t
24 " aspirata	th		TH							th
25 " assibilata										
26 Media	d									
27 " aspirata	dh		DH							
28 " assibilata										
29 Nasalis	n									n
30 Semivocalis	l	i								l
31 " mollis 1										
32 " mollis 2			L							
33 Spiritus asper 1	s	s	S							s
34 " asper 2	z									z
35 " lenis										
36 " asperrimus 1			z (ṣ)							
37 " asperrimus 2			z (ŝ)							ḥ, ḵh

		Transliteration
Dentales modificatae (linguales, &c.)		
38	Tenuis	
39	„ aspirata	
40	Media	
41	„ aspirata	
42	Nasalis	
43	Semivocalis	r
44	„ fricata	
45	„ diacritica	
46	Spiritus asper	sh
47	„ lenis	zh
Labiales.		
48	Tenuis	p
49	„ aspirata	ph
50	Media	b
51	„ aspirata	bh
52	Tenuissima	
53	Nasalis	m
54	Semivocalis	w
55	„ aspirata	hw
56	Spiritus asper	f
57	„ lenis	v
58	Anusvâra	
59	Visarga	

VOWELS.	MISSIONARY ALPHABET. I Class	II Class	III Class	Sanskrit.	Zend.	Pehlevi.	Persian.	Arabic.	Hebrew.	Chinese.
1 Neutralis	e	.	.	.	.	.	.	.	׀	ă
2 Laryngo-palatalis .	æ	.	.	.	.	) fin.	.	.	.	.
3 „ labialis .	ŏ	.	.	.	.	و init.	.	.	.	.
4 Gutturalis brevis .	a	(a)	.	स	و	ع	ا	ا	׀ ·	a
5 „ longa .	ā	.	.	स	ش	.	ل	ل	· ׀ ·	ā
6 Palatalis brevis .	i	(i)	.	ॲ	ج	.	ا	ا	· ׀	—
7 „ longa .	ī	.	.	ॵ	t	)	ک	ک	· ׀ ·	—
8 Dentalis brevis .	ụ	.	.	.	.	.	.	.	.	.
9 „ longa .	.	.	.	.	.	.	.	.	.	.
10 Lingualis brevis .	r̥	.	.	ऋ	.	.	.	.	.	.
11 „ longa .	r̄	.	.	ॠ	.	.	.	.	.	.
12 Labialis brevis .	u	(u)	.	उ	↗	.	و	و	׀ ·	u
13 „ longa .	ū	.	.	ऊ	و	.	و	و	·	e
14 Gutturo-palatalis brevis	e	(e)	.	ए	E(e) ξ(e)	.	.	.	.	è
15 „ longa .	ê (ai)	(ai)	.	ऐ	ϗ, ϗ	)	ی	ی	׀ ·	äi
16 Diphthongus gutturo-palatalis	ái	.	.	.	.	.	.	.	.	.
17 „	ei (ẽi)	.	.	.	.	.	.	.	.	ei, ĕi
18 „	oi (ŏu)	.	.	.	.	.	.	.	.	.
19 Gutturo-labialis brevis .	o	(o)	.	ओ	↘	.	و	و	׀	o
20 „ longa .	ŏ (au)	(au)	.	औ	ϗus (au)	.	و	و	' ·	.
21 Diphthongus gutturo-labialis	áu	.	.	.	.	.	.	.	.	áu
22 „	eu (ẽu)	.	.	.	.	.	.	.	.	.
23 „	ou (ŏu)	.	.	.	.	.	.	.	.	.
24 Gutturalis fracta . .	ä	.	.	.	.	.	.	.	.	.
25 Palatalis fracta . .	ï	.	.	.	.	.	.	.	.	.
26 Labialis fracta . .	ü	.	.	.	.	.	.	.	.	ü
27 Gutturo-labialis fracta .	ö	.	.	.	.	.	.	.	.	.

April, 1880.

𝕮𝖑𝖆𝖗𝖊𝖓𝖉𝖔𝖓 𝕻𝖗𝖊𝖘𝖘, 𝕺𝖝𝖋𝖔𝖗𝖉.

BOOKS

PUBLISHED FOR THE UNIVERSITY BY

MACMILLAN AND CO., LONDON;

ALSO TO BE HAD AT THE

CLARENDON PRESS DEPOSITORY, OXFORD.

———————— ◆•◉•◆ ————————

LEXICONS, GRAMMARS, &c.

(See also Clarendon Press Series pp. 24, 26.)

A Greek-English Lexicon, by Henry George Liddell, D.D.,
and Robert Scott, D.D. *Sixth Edition, Revised and Augmented.*
1870. 4to. *cloth,* 1*l.* 16*s.*

A copious Greek-English Vocabulary, compiled from the
best authorities. 1850. 24mo. *bound,* 3*s.*

A Practical Introduction to Greek Accentuation, by H. W.
Chandler, M.A. 1862. 8vo. *cloth,* 10*s.* 6*d.*

Etymologicon Magnum. Ad Codd. MSS. recensuit et notis
variorum instruxit Thomas Gaisford, S.T.P. 1848. fol. *cloth,* 1*l.* 12*s.*

Suidae Lexicon. Ad Codd. MSS. recensuit Thomas Gaisford,
S.T.P. Tomi III. 1834. fol. *cloth,* 2*l.* 2*s.*

Scheller's Lexicon of the Latin Tongue, with the German ex-
planations translated into English by J. E. Riddle, M.A. 1835. fol.
cloth, 1*l.* 1*s.*

A Latin Dictionary, founded on Andrews' edition of Freund's
Latin Dictionary, revised, enlarged, and in great part rewritten by
Charlton T. Lewis, Ph.D., and Charles Short, LL.D., Professor of
Latin in Columbia College, New York. 1879. 4to. *cloth,* 1*l.* 11*s.* 6*d.*

Scriptores Rei Metricae. Edidit Thomas Gaisford, S.T.P.
Tomi III. 8vo. *cloth,* 15*s.*

Sold separately:

Hephaestion, Terentianus Maurus, Proclus, cum annotationibus, etc.
Tomi II. 10*s.*   Scriptores Latini. 5*s.*

The Book of Hebrew Roots, by Abu 'L-Walîd Marwân ibn
Janâh. otherwise called Rabbî Yônâh. Now first edited, with an
Appendix, by Ad. Neubauer. 1875. 4to. *cloth*, 2*l.* 7*s.* 6*d.*

A Treatise on the use of the Tenses in Hebrew. By S. R.
Driver, M.A. Extra fcap. 8vo. *cloth*, 6*s.* 6*d.*

Thesaurus Syriacus : collegerunt Quatremère, Bernstein, Lors-
bach, Arnoldi, Field : edidit R. Payne Smith, S.T.P.R.
Fasc. I–V. 1868–80. sm. fol. *each*, 1*l.* 1*s.*
Vol. I, containing Fasc. I–V. sm. fol. *cloth*, 5*l.* 5*s.* *Just Published.*

A Practical Grammar of the Sanskrit Language, arranged
with reference to the Classical Languages of Europe, for the use of
English Students, by Monier Williams, M.A., Boden Professor of Sanskrit. *Fourth Edition*, 1877. 8vo. *cloth*, 15*s.*

A Sanskrit-English Dictionary, Etymologically and Philo-
logically arranged, with special reference to Greek, Latin, German,
Anglo-Saxon, English, and other cognate Indo-European Languages.
By Monier Williams, M.A., Boden Professor of Sanskrit. 1872. 4to.
cloth, 4*l.* 14*s.* 6*d.*

Nalopákhyánam. Story of Nala, an Episode of the Mahá-
Bhárata : the Sanskrit text, with a copious Vocabulary, and an im-
proved version of Dean Milman's Translation. By Monier Williams, M.A.
Second Edition, Revised and Improved. 1879. 8vo. *cloth*, 15*s.*

Sakuntalá. A Sanskrit Drama, in seven Acts. Edited by
Monier Williams, M.A. *Second Edition*, 1876. 8vo. *cloth*, 21*s.*

An Anglo-Saxon Dictionary, by Joseph Bosworth, D.D., Professor of Anglo-Saxon, Oxford. *New edition. In the Press.*

An Icelandic-English Dictionary, based on the MS. collections of the late Richard Cleasby. Enlarged and completed by
G. Vigfússon. With an Introduction, and Life of Richard Cleasby,
by G. Webbe Dasent, D.C.L. 1874. 4to. *cloth*, 3*l.* 7*s.*

A List of English Words the Etymology of which is
illustrated by comparison with Icelandic. Prepared in the form
of an APPENDIX to the above. By W. W. Skeat, M.A., *stitched*, 2*s.*

A Handbook of the Chinese Language. Parts I and II,
Grammar and Chrestomathy. By James Summers. 1863. 8vo. *half
bound*, 1*l.* 8*s.*

Cornish Drama (The Ancient). Edited and translated by E.
Norris, Esq., with a Sketch of Cornish Grammar, an Ancient Cornish
Vocabulary, etc. 2 vols. 1859. 8vo. *cloth*, 1*l.* 1*s.*
The Sketch of Cornish Grammar separately, *stitched*, 2*s.* 6*d.*

An Etymological Dictionary of the English Language,
arranged on an Historical Basis. By W. W. Skeat, M.A., Elrington
and Bosworth Professor of Anglo-Saxon in the University of Cambridge.
To be completed in Four Parts. Parts I and II 4to. 10*s.* 6*d.* each.
Part III will be published July 1, 1880.

GREEK CLASSICS, &c.

Aeschylus: quae supersunt in Codice Laurentiano typis descript. Edidit R. Merkel. 1861. Small folio, *cloth, 1l. 1s.*

Aeschylus: **Tragoediae** et Fragmenta, ex recensione Guil. Dindorfii. *Second Edition,* 1851. 8vo. *cloth,* 5*s.* 6*d.*

Aeschylus: Annotationes Guil. Dindorfii. Partes II. 1841. 8vo. *cloth,* 10*s.*

Aeschylus: Scholia Graeca, ex Codicibus aucta et emendata a Guil. Dindorfio. 1851. 8vo. *cloth,* 5*s.*

Sophocles: **Tragoediae** et Fragmenta, ex recensione et cum commentariis Guil. Dindorfii. *Third Edition,* 2 vols. 1860. fcap. 8vo. *cloth, 1l. 1s.*

Each Play separately, *limp,* 2*s.* 6*d.*

The Text alone, printed on writing paper, with large margin, royal 16mo. *cloth,* 8*s.*

The Text alone, square 16mo. *cloth,* 3*s.* 6*d.*

Each Play separately, *limp,* 6*d.* (See also p. 26.)

Sophocles: **Tragoediae** et Fragmenta cum Annotatt. Guil. Dindorfii. Tomi II. 1849. 8vo. *cloth,* 10*s.*

The Text, Vol. I. 5*s.* 6*d.* The Notes, Vol. II. 4*s.* 6*d.*

Sophocles: Scholia Graeca:

Vol. I. ed. P. Elmsley, A.M. 1825. 8vo. *cloth,* 4*s.* 6*d.*

Vol. II. ed. Guil. Dindorfius. 1852. 8vo. *cloth,* 4*s.* 6*d.*

Euripides: **Tragoediae** et Fragmenta, ex recensione Guil. Dindorfii. Tomi II. 1834. 8vo. *cloth,* 10*s.*

Euripides: Annotationes Guil. Dindorfii. Partes II. 1840. 8vo. *cloth,* 10*s.*

Euripides: Scholia Graeca, ex Codicibus aucta et emendata a Guil. Dindorfio. Tomi IV. 1863. 8vo. *cloth, 1l. 16s.*

Euripides: **Alcestis,** ex recensione Guil. Dindorfii. 1834. 8vo. *sewed,* 2*s.* 6*d.*

Aristophanes: **Comoediae** et Fragmenta, ex recensione Guil. Dindorfii. Tomi II. 1835. 8vo. *cloth,* 11*s.*

Aristophanes: Annotationes Guil. Dindorfii. Partes II. 1837. 8vo. *cloth,* 11*s.*

Aristophanes: Scholia Graeca, ex Codicibus aucta et emendata a Guil. Dindorfio. Partes III. 1839. 8vo. *cloth, 1l.*

B 2

Aristophanem, Index in: J. Caravellae. 1822. 8vo. *cloth*, 3*s.*

Metra Aeschyli Sophoclis Euripidis et Aristophanis. Descripta a Guil. Dindorfio. Accedit Chronologia Scenica. 1842. 8vo. *cloth*, 5*s.*

Anecdota Graeca Oxoniensia. Edidit J. A. Cramer, S.T.P. Tomi IV. 1835. 8vo. *cloth*, 1*l.* 2*s.*

Anecdota Graeca e Codd. MSS. Bibliothecae Regiae Parisiensis. Edidit J. A. Cramer, S.T.P. Tomi IV. 1839. 8vo. *cloth*, 1*l.* 2*s.*

Apsinis et Longini Rhetorica. E Codicibus MSS. recensuit Joh. Bakius. 1849. 8vo. *cloth*, 3*s.*

Aristoteles; ex recensione Immanuelis Bekkeri. Accedunt Indices Sylburgiani. Tomi XI. 1837. 8vo. *cloth*, 2*l.* 10*s.*
The volumes (except vol. IX.) may be had separately, price 5*s.* 6*d.* each.

Aristotelis Ethica Nicomachea, ex recensione Immanuelis Bekkeri. Crown 8vo. *cloth*, 5*s.*

Choerobosci Dictata in Theodosii Canones, necnon Epimerismi in Psalmos. E Codicibus MSS. edidit Thomas Gaisford, S.T.P. Tomi III. 1842. 8vo. *cloth*, 15*s.*

Demosthenes: ex recensione Guil. Dindorfii. Tomi I. II. III. IV. 1846. 8vo. *cloth*, 1*l.* 1*s.*

Demosthenes: Tomi V. VI. VII. Annotationes Interpretum. 1849. 8vo. *cloth*, 15*s.*

Demosthenes: Tomi VIII. IX. Scholia. 1851. 8vo. *cloth*, 10*s.*

Harpocrationis Lexicon, ex recensione G. Dindorfii. Tomi II. 1854. 8vo. *cloth*, 10*s.* 6*d.*

Heracliti Ephesii Reliquiae. Recensuit I. Bywater, M.A. 1877. 8vo. *cloth*, price 6*s.*

Herculanensium Voluminum Partes II. 1824. 8vo. *cloth*, 10*s.*

Homerus: Ilias, cum brevi Annotatione C. G. Heynii. Accedunt Scholia minora. Tomi II. 1834. 8vo. *cloth*, 15*s.*

Homerus: Ilias, ex rec. Guil. Dindorfii. 1856. 8vo. *cloth*, 5*s.* 6*d.*

Homerus: Scholia Graeca in Iliadem. Edited by Prof. W. Dindorf, after a new collation of the Venetian MSS. by D. B. Monro, M.A., Fellow of Oriel College.
Vols. I. II. 1875. 8vo. *cloth*, 24*s.* Vols. III. IV. 1877. 8vo. *cloth*, 26*s.*

Homerus: Odyssea, ex rec. Guil. Dindorfii. 1855. 8vo. *cloth*, 5*s.* 6*d.*

Homerus: Scholia Graeca in Odysseam. Edidit Guil. Dindorfius. Tomi II. 1855. 8vo. *cloth*, 15*s.* 6*d.*

Homerum, Index in: Seberi. 1780. 8vo. *cloth, 6s. 6d.*

Homer: A Complete Concordance to the Odyssey and Hymns of Homer; to which is added a Concordance to the Parallel Passages in the Iliad, Odyssey, and Hymns. By Henry Dunbar, M.D., Member of the General Council, University of Edinburgh. 4to. *cloth,* 1l. 1s. *Just Published.*

Oratores Attici ex recensione Bekkeri:
  I. Antiphon, Andocides, et Lysias. 1822. 8vo. *cloth, 7s.*
  II. Isocrates. 1822. 8vo. *cloth, 7s.*
  III. Isaeus, Aeschines, Lycurgus, Dinarchus, etc. 1823. 8vo. *cloth, 7s.*

Scholia Graeca in Aeschinem et Isocratem. Edidit G. Dindorfius. 1852. 8vo. *cloth, 4s.*

Paroemiographi Graeci, quorum pars nunc primum ex Codd. MSS. vulgatur. Edidit T. Gaisford, S.T.P. 1836. 8vo. *cloth, 5s. 6d.*

Plato: The Apology, with a revised Text and English Notes, and a Digest of Platonic Idioms, by James Riddell, M.A. 1878. 8vo. *cloth, 8s. 6d.*

Plato: Philebus, with a revised Text and English Notes, by Edward Poste, M.A. 1860. 8vo. *cloth, 7s. 6d.*

Plato: Sophistes and Politicus, with a revised Text and English Notes, by L. Campbell, M.A. 1866. 8vo. *cloth, 18s.*

Plato: Theaetetus, with a revised Text and English Notes, by L. Campbell, M.A. 1861. 8vo. *cloth, 9s.*

Plato: The Dialogues, translated into English, with Analyses and Introductions, by B. Jowett, M.A., Regius Professor of Greek. *A new Edition in 5 volumes,* medium 8vo. 1875. *cloth,* 3l. 10s.

Plato: Index to. Compiled for the Second Edition of Professor Jowett's Translation of the Dialogues. By Evelyn Abbott, M.A. 1875. 8vo. *paper covers,* 2s. 6d.

Plato: The Republic, with a revised Text and English Notes, by B. Jowett, M.A., Regius Professor of Greek. Demy 8vo. *Preparing.*

Plotinus. Edidit F. Creuzer. Tomi III. 1835. 4to. 1l. 8s.

Stobaei Florilegium. Ad MSS. fidem emendavit et supplevit T. Gaisford, S.T.P. Tomi IV. 1822. 8vo. *cloth,* 1l.

Stobaei Eclogarum Physicarum et Ethicarum libri duo. Accedit Hieroclis Commentarius in aurea carmina Pythagoreorum. Ad MSS. Codd. recensuit T. Gaisford, S.T.P. Tomi II. 1850. 8vo. *cloth,* 11s.

Thucydides: History of the Peloponnesian War, translated into English by B. Jowett, M.A., Regius Professor of Greek. *In the Press.*

Xenophon : Historia Graeca, ex recensione et cum annotationibus L. Dindorfii. *Second Edition,* 1852. 8vo. *cloth,* 10s. 6d.

Xenophon : Expeditio Cyri, ex rec. et cum annotatt. L. Dindorfii. *Second Edition,* 1855. 8vo. *cloth,* 10s. 6d.

Xenophon : Institutio Cyri, ex rec. et cum annotatt. L. Dindorfii. 1857. 8vo. *cloth,* 10s. 6d.

Xenophon : Memorabilia Socratis, ex rec. et cum annotatt. L.
Dindorfii. 1862. 8vo. *cloth,* 7s. 6d.

Xenophon : Opuscula Politica Equestria et Venatica cum Arri-
ani Libello de Venatione, ex rec. et cum annotatt. L. Dindorfii. 1866.
8vo. *cloth,* 10s. 6d.

THE HOLY SCRIPTURES, &c.

The Holy Bible in the earliest English Versions, made from the
Latin Vulgate by John Wycliffe and his followers: edited by the Rev.
J. Forshall and Sir F. Madden. 4 vols. 1850. royal 4to. *cloth,* 3l. 3s.

The New Testament in English, according to the Version by
John Wycliffe, about A.D. 1380, and Revised by John Purvey, about
A.D. 1388. *Reprinted from the above.* With Introduction and Glossary
by W. W. Skeat, M.A. 1879. Extra fcap. 8vo. *cloth,* 6s.

The Holy Bible: an exact reprint, page for page, of the Author-
ized Version published in the year 1611. Demy 4to. *half bound,* 1l. 1s.

Vetus Testamentum Graece cum Variis Lectionibus. Edi-
tionem a R. Holmes, S.T.P. inchoatam continuavit J. Parsons, S.T.B.
Tomi V. 1798–1827. folio, 7l.

Vetus Testamentum ex Versione Septuaginta Interpretum
secundum exemplar Vaticanum Romae editum. Accedit potior varietas
Codicis Alexandrini. Tomi III. *Editio Altera.* 18mo. *cloth,* 18s.

Origenis Hexaplorum quae supersunt; sive, Veterum Interpretum Graecorum in totum Vetus Testamentum Fragmenta. Edidit
Fridericus Field, A.M. 2 vols. 1867–1874. 4to. *cloth,* 5l. 5s.

Libri Psalmorum Versio antiqua Latina, cum Paraphrasi
Anglo-Saxonica. Edidit B. Thorpe, F.A.S. 1835. 8vo. *cloth,* 10s. 6d.

Libri Psalmorum Versio antiqua Gallica e Cod. MS. in Bibl.
Bodleiana adservato, una cum Versione Metrica aliisque Monumentis
pervetustis. Nunc primum descripsit et edidit Franciscus Michel, Phil.
Doct. 1860. 8vo. *cloth,* 10s. 6d.

The Psalms in Hebrew without points. 1879. Crown 8vo.
cloth, 3s. 6d.

Libri Prophetarum Majorum, cum Lamentationibus Jere-
miae, in Dialecto Linguae Aegyptiacae Memphitica seu Coptica. Edidit
cum Versione Latina H. Tattam, S.T.P. Tomi II. 1852. 8vo. *cloth,* 17s.

Libri duodecim Prophetarum Minorum in Ling. Aegypt. vulgo Coptica. Edidit H. Tattam, A.M. 1836. 8vo. *cloth*, 8s. 6d.

Novum Testamentum Graece. Antiquissimorum Codicum Textus in ordine parallelo dispositi. Accedit collatio Codicis Sinaitici. Edidit E. H. Hansell, S.T.B. Tomi III. 1864. 8vo. *half morocco*, 2l. 12s. 6d.

Novum Testamentum Graece. Accedunt parallela S. Scripturae loca, necnon vetus capitulorum notatio et canones Eusebii. Edidit Carolus Lloyd, S.T.P.R., necnon Episcopus Oxoniensis. 18mo. *cloth*, 3s.

The same on writing paper, with large margin, cloth, 10s. 6d.

Novum Testamentum Graece juxta Exemplar Millianum. 18mo. *cloth*, 2s. 6d.

The same on writing paper, with large margin, cloth, 9s.

Evangelia Sacra Graece. fcap. 8vo. *limp*, 1s. 6d.

The New Testament in Greek and English. Edited by E. Cardwell, D.D. 2 vols. 1837. crown 8vo. *cloth*, 6s.

Novum Testamentum Coptice, cura D. Wilkins. 1716. 4to. *cloth*, 12s. 6d.

Evangeliorum Versio Gothica, cum Interpr. et Annott. E. Benzelii. Edidit, et Gram. Goth. praemisit, E. Lye, A.M. 1759. 4to. *cloth*, 12s. 6d.

Diatessaron; sive Historia Jesu Christi ex ipsis Evangelistarum verbis apte dispositis confecta. Ed. J. White. 1856. 12mo. *cloth*, 3s. 6d.

Canon Muratorianus. The earliest Catalogue of the Books of the New Testament. Edited with Notes and a Facsimile of the MS. in the Ambrosian Library at Milan, by S. P. Tregelles, LL.D. 1868. 4to. *cloth*, 10s. 6d.

The Five Books of Maccabees, in English, with Notes and Illustrations by Henry Cotton, D.C.L. 1833. 8vo. *cloth*, 10s. 6d.

Horae Hebraicae et Talmudicae, a J. Lightfoot. *A new Edition*, by R. Gandell, M.A. 4 vols. 1859. 8vo. *cloth*, 1l. 1s.

FATHERS OF THE CHURCH, &c.

Liturgies, Eastern and Western. Edited, with Introduction, Notes, and a Liturgical Glossary, by C. E. Hammond, M.A. 1878. Crown 8vo. *cloth*, 10s. 6d.

An Appendix to the above. 1879. Crown 8vo. *paper covers*, 1s. 6d.

St. Athanasius: Orations against the Arians. With an Account of his Life by William Bright, D.D., Regius Professor of Ecclesiastical History, Oxford. 1873. Crown 8vo. *cloth*, 9s.

St. Augustine: Select Anti-Pelagian Treatises, with the Acts of the Second Council of Orange. With an Introduction by William Bright, D.D. Crown 8vo. *cloth*, 9s.

The Canons of the First Four General Councils of Nicaea, Constantinople, Ephesus, and Chalcedon. 1877. Crown 8vo. *cloth*, 2s. 6d.

Catenae Graecorum Patrum in Novum Testamentum. Edidit J. A. Cramer, S.T.P. Tomi VIII. 1838–1844. 8vo. *cloth*, 2l. 4s.

Clementis Alexandrini Opera, ex recensione Guil. Dindorfii. Tomi IV. 1869. 8vo. *cloth*, 3l.

Cyrilli Archiepiscopi Alexandrini in XII Prophetas. Edidit P. E. Pusey, A.M. Tomi II. 1868. 8vo. *cloth*, 2l. 2s.

Cyrilli Archiepiscopi Alexandrini in D. Joannis Evangelium. Accedunt Fragmenta Varia necnon Tractatus ad Tiberium Diaconum Duo. Edidit post Aubertum P. E. Pusey, A.M. Tomi III. 1872. 8vo. 2l. 5s.

Cyrilli Archiepiscopi Alexandrini Commentarii in Lucae Evangelium quae supersunt Syriace. E MSS. apud Mus. Britan. edidit R. Payne Smith, A.M. 1858. 4to. *cloth*, 1l. 2s.

The same, translated by R. Payne Smith, M.A. 2 vols. 1859. 8vo. *cloth*, 14s.

Ephraemi Syri, Rabulae Episcopi Edesseni, Balaei, aliorumque Opera Selecta. E Codd. Syriacis MSS. in Museo Britannico et Bibliotheca Bodleiana asservatis primus edidit J. J. Overbeck. 1865. 8vo. *cloth*, 1l. 1s.

Eusebii Pamphili Evangelicae Praeparationis Libri XV. Ad Codd. MSS. recensuit T. Gaisford, S.T.P. Tomi IV. 1843. 8vo. *cloth*, 1l. 10s.

Eusebii Pamphili Evangelicae Demonstrationis Libri X. Recensuit T. Gaisford, S.T.P. Tomi II. 1852. 8vo. *cloth*, 15s.

Eusebii Pamphili contra Hieroclem et Marcellum Libri. Recensuit T. Gaisford, S.T.P. 1852. 8vo. *cloth*, 7s.

Eusebius' Ecclesiastical History, according to the text of Burton, with an Introduction by William Bright, D.D. 1872. Crown 8vo. *cloth*, 8s. 6d.

Eusebii Pamphili Hist. Eccl.: **Annotationes Variorum.** Tomi II. 1842. 8vo. *cloth*, 17s.

Evagrii Historia Ecclesiastica, ex recensione H. Valesii. 1844. 8vo. *cloth*, 4s.

Irenaeus: The Third Book of St. Irenaeus, Bishop of Lyons, against Heresies. With short Notes and a Glossary by H. Deane, B.D., Fellow of St. John's College, Oxford. 1874. Crown 8vo. *cloth*, 5s. 6d.

Origenis Philosophumena; sive omnium Haeresium Refutatio.
E Codice Parisino nunc primum edidit Emmanuel Miller. 1851. 8vo.
cloth, 10s.

Patrum Apostolicorum, S. Clementis Romani, S. Ignatii, S.
Polycarpi, quae supersunt. Edidit Guil. Jacobson, S.T.P.R. Tomi II.
Fourth Edition, 1863. 8vo. *cloth*, 1l. 1s.

Reliquiae Sacrae secundi tertiique saeculi. Recensuit M. J.
Routh, S.T.P. Tomi V. *Second Edition*, 1846–1848. 8vo. *cloth*, 1l. 5s.

Scriptorum Ecclesiasticorum Opuscula. Recensuit M. J.
Routh, S.T.P. Tomi II. *Third Edition*, 1858. 8vo. *cloth*, 10s.

Socratis Scholastici Historia Ecclesiastica. Gr. et Lat. Edidit
R. Hussey, S.T.B. Tomi III. 1853. 8vo. *cloth*, 15s.

Socrates' Ecclesiastical History, according to the Text of
Hussey, with an Introduction by William Bright, D.D. 1878. Crown
8vo. *cloth*, 7s. 6d.

Sozomeni Historia Ecclesiastica. Edidit R. Hussey, S.T.B.
Tomi III. 1859. 8vo. *cloth*, 15s.

Theodoreti Ecclesiasticae Historiae Libri V. Recensuit T.
Gaisford, S.T.P. 1854. 8vo. *cloth*, 7s. 6d.

Theodoreti Graecarum Affectionum Curatio. Ad Codices MSS.
recensuit T. Gaisford, S.T.P. 1839. 8vo. *cloth*, 7s. 6d.

Dowling (J. G.) Notitia Scriptorum SS. Patrum aliorumque vet.
Eccles. Mon. quae in Collectionibus Anecdotorum post annum Christi
MDCC. in lucem editis continentur. 1839. 8vo. *cloth*, 4s. 6d.

ECCLESIASTICAL HISTORY, BIOGRAPHY, &c.

Baedae Historia Ecclesiastica. Edited, with English Notes
by G. H. Moberly, M.A. 1869. crown 8vo. *cloth*, 10s. 6d.

Bingham's Antiquities of the Christian Church, and other
Works. 10 vols. 1855. 8vo. *cloth*, 3l. 3s.

Bright (W., D.D.). Chapters of Early English Church History.
1878. 8vo. *cloth*, 12s.

Burnet's History of the Reformation of the Church of England. *A new Edition.* Carefully revised, and the Records collated
with the originals, by N. Pocock, M.A. 7 vols. 1865. 8vo. *4l. 4s.*

Burnet's Life of Sir M. Hale, and Fell's Life of Dr. Hammond.
1856. small 8vo. *cloth*, 2s. 6d.

Cardwell's Two Books of Common Prayer, set forth by
authority in the Reign of King Edward VI, compared with each other.
Third Edition, 1852. 8vo. *cloth*, 7s.

Cardwell's Documentary Annals of the Reformed Church of England; being a Collection of Injunctions, Declarations, Orders, Articles of Inquiry, &c. from 1546 to 1716. 2 vols. 1843. 8vo. *cloth*, 18s.

Cardwell's History of Conferences on the Book of Common Prayer from 1551 to 1690. *Third Edition*, 1849. 8vo. *cloth*, 7s. 6d.

Councils and Ecclesiastical Documents relating to Great Britain and Ireland. Edited, after Spelman and Wilkins, by A. W. Haddan, B.D., and W. Stubbs, M.A., Regius Professor of Modern History, Oxford. Vols. I. and III. 1869-71. Medium 8vo. *cloth*, each 1l. 1s.

> Vol. II. Part I. 1873. Medium 8vo. *cloth*, 10s. 6d.
>
> Vol. II. Part II. 1878. Church of Ireland; Memorials of St. Patrick. *stiff covers*, 3s. 6d.

Formularies of Faith set forth by the King's Authority during the Reign of Henry VIII. 1856. 8vo. *cloth*, 7s.

Fuller's Church History of Britain. Edited by J. S. Brewer, M.A. 6 vols. 1845. 8vo. *cloth*, 1l. 19s.

Gibson's Synodus Anglicana. Edited by E. Cardwell, D.D. 1854. 8vo. *cloth*, 6s.

Hussey's Rise of the Papal Power traced in three Lectures. *Second Edition*, 1863. fcap. 8vo. *cloth*, 4s. 6d.

Inett's Origines Anglicanae (in continuation of Stillingfleet). Edited by J. Griffiths, M.A. 3 vols. 1855. 8vo. *cloth*, 15s.

John, Bishop of Ephesus. The Third Part of his Ecclesiastical History. [In Syriac.] Now first edited by William Cureton, M.A. 1853. 4to. *cloth*, 1l. 12s.

The same, translated by R. Payne Smith, M.A. 1860. 8vo. *cloth*, 10s.

Knight's Life of Dean Colet. 1823. 8vo. *cloth*, 7s. 6d.

Le Neve's Fasti Ecclesiae Anglicanae. *Corrected and continued from 1715 to 1853* by T. Duffus Hardy. 3 vols. 1854. 8vo. *cloth*, 1l. 1s.

Noelli (A.) Catechismus sive prima institutio disciplinaque Pietatis Christianae Latine explicata. Editio nova cura Guil. Jacobson, A.M. 1844. 8vo. *cloth*, 5s. 6d.

Prideaux's Connection of Sacred and Profane History. 2 vols. 1851. 8vo. *cloth*, 10s.

Primers put forth in the Reign of Henry VIII. 1848. 8vo. *cloth*, 5s.

Records of the Reformation. The Divorce, 1527—1533. Mostly now for the first time printed from MSS. in the British Museum and other Libraries. Collected and arranged by N. Pocock, M.A. 1870. 2 vols. 8vo. *cloth*, 1l. 16s.

Reformatio Legum Ecclesiasticarum. The Reformation of Ecclesiastical Laws, as attempted in the reigns of Henry VIII, Edward VI, and Elizabeth. Edited by E. Cardwell, D.D. 1850. 8vo. *cloth*, 6*s.* 6*d.*

Shirley's (W. W.) Some Account of the Church in the Apostolic Age. *Second Edition*, 1874. fcap. 8vo. *cloth*, 3*s.* 6*d.*

Shuckford's Sacred and Profane History connected (in continuation of Prideaux). 2 vols. 1848. 8vo. *cloth*, 10*s.*

Stillingfleet's Origines Britannicae, with Lloyd's Historical Account of Church Government. Edited by T. P. Pantin, M.A. 2 vols. 1842. 8vo. *cloth*, 10*s.*

Stubbs (W.). Registrum Sacrum Anglicanum. An attempt to exhibit the course of Episcopal Succession in England. 1858. small 4to. *cloth*, 8*s.* 6*d.*

Strype's Works Complete, with a General Index. 27 vols. 1821–1843. 8vo. *cloth*, 7*l.* 13*s.* 6*d.* Sold separately as follows:—

Memorials of Cranmer. 2 vols. 1840. 8vo. *cloth*, 11*s.*
Life of Parker. 3 vols. 1828. 8vo. *cloth*, 16*s.* 6*d.*
Life of Grindal. 1821. 8vo. *cloth*, 5*s.* 6*d.*
Life of Whitgift. 3 vols. 1822. 8vo. *cloth*, 16*s.* 6*d.*
Life of Aylmer. 1820. 8vo. *cloth*, 5*s.* 6*d.*
Life of Cheke. 1821. 8vo. *cloth*, 5*s.* 6*d.*
Life of Smith. 1820. 8vo. *cloth*, 5*s.* 6*d.*
Ecclesiastical Memorials. 6 vols. 1822. 8vo. *cloth*, 1*l.* 13*s.*
Annals of the Reformation. 7 vols. 8vo. *cloth*, 2*l.* 3*s.* 6*d.*
General Index. 2 vols. 1828. 8vo. *cloth*, 11*s.*

Sylloge Confessionum sub tempus Reformandae Ecclesiae editarum. Subjiciuntur Catechismus Heidelbergensis et Canones Synodi Dordrechtanae. 1827. 8vo. *cloth*, 8*s.*

ENGLISH THEOLOGY.

Beveridge's Discourse upon the XXXIX Articles. *The third complete Edition*, 1847. 8vo. *cloth*, 8*s.*

Bilson on the Perpetual Government of Christ's Church, with a Biographical Notice by R. Eden, M.A. 1842. 8vo. *cloth*, 4*s.*

Biscoe's Boyle Lectures on the Acts of the Apostles. 1840. 8vo. *cloth*, 9*s.* 6*d.*

Bull's Works, with Nelson's Life. Edited by E. Burton, D.D. *A new Edition*, 1846. 8 vols. 8vo. *cloth*, 2*l.* 9*s.*

Burnet's Exposition of the XXXIX Articles. 1845. 8vo. *cloth*, 7*s.*

Burton's (Edward) Testimonies of the Ante-Nicene Fathers to the Divinity of Christ. *Second Edition*, 1829. 8vo. *cloth*, 7*s.*

B 3

Burton's (Edward) Testimonies of the Ante-Nicene Fathers to the Doctrine of the Trinity and of the Divinity of the Holy Ghost. 1831. 8vo. *cloth*, 3*s.* 6*d.*

Butler's Works, with an Index to the Analogy. 2 vols. 1874. 8vo. *cloth*, 11*s.*

Butler's Sermons. 8vo. *cloth*, 5*s.* 6*d.*

Butler's Analogy of Religion. 8vo. *cloth*, 5*s.* 6*d.*

Chandler's Critical History of the Life of David. 1853. 8vo. *cloth*, 8*s.* 6*d.*

Chillingworth's Works. 3 vols. 1838. 8vo. *cloth*, 1*l.* 1*s.* 6*d.*

Clergyman's Instructor. *Sixth Edition*, 1855. 8vo. *cloth*, 6*s.* 6*d.*

Comber's Companion to the Temple; or a Help to Devotion in the use of the Common Prayer. 7 vols. 1841. 8vo. *cloth*, 1*l.* 11*s.* 6*d.*

Cranmer's Works. Collected and arranged by H. Jenkyns, M.A., Fellow of Oriel College. 4 vols. 1834. 8vo. *cloth*, 1*l.* 10*s.*

Enchiridion Theologicum Anti-Romanum.

    Vol. I.   Jeremy Taylor's Dissuasive from Popery, and Treatise on the Real Presence. 1852. 8vo. *cloth*, 8*s.*

    Vol. II. Barrow on the Supremacy of the Pope, with his Discourse on the Unity of the Church. 1852. 8vo. *cloth*, 7*s.* 6*d.*

    Vol. III. Tracts selected from Wake, Patrick, Stillingfleet, Clagett, and others. 1837. 8vo. *cloth*, 11*s.*

[Fell's] Paraphrase and Annotations on the Epistles of St. Paul. 1852. 8vo. *cloth*, 7*s.*

Greswell's Harmonia Evangelica. *Fifth Edition*, 1856. 8vo. *cloth*, 9*s.* 6*d.*

Greswell's Prolegomena ad Harmoniam Evangelicam. 1840. 8vo. *cloth*, 9*s.* 6*d.*

Greswell's Dissertations on the Principles and Arrangement of a Harmony of the Gospels. 5 vols. 1837. 8vo. *cloth*, 3*l.* 3*s.*

Hall's (Bp.) Works. *A new Edition*, by Philip Wynter, D.D. 10 vols. 1863. 8vo. *cloth*, 3*l.* 3*s.*

Hammond's Paraphrase and Annotations on the New Testament. 4 vols. 1845. 8vo. *cloth*, 1*l.*

Hammond's Paraphrase on the Book of Psalms. 2 vols. 1850. 8vo. *cloth*, 10*s.*

Heurtley's Collection of Creeds. 1858. 8vo. *cloth*, 6*s.* 6*d.*

Homilies appointed to be read in Churches. Edited by J. Griffiths, M.A. 1859. 8vo. *cloth*, 7*s.* 6*d.*

Hooker's Works, with his Life by Walton, arranged by John Keble, M.A. *Sixth Edition,* 1874. 3 vols. 8vo. *cloth,* 1*l.* 11*s.* 6*d.*

Hooker's Works; the text as arranged by John Keble, M.A. 2 vols. 1875. 8vo. *cloth,* 11*s.*

Hooper's (Bp. George) Works. 2 vols. 1855. 8vo. *cloth,* 8*s.*

Jackson's (Dr. Thomas) Works. 12 vols. 1844. 8vo. *cloth,* 3*l.* 6*s.*

Jewel's Works. Edited by R. W. Jelf, D.D. 8 vols. 1847. 8vo. *cloth,* 1*l.* 10*s.*

Patrick's Theological Works. 9 vols. 1859. 8vo. *cloth,* 1*l.* 1*s.*

Pearson's Exposition of the Creed. Revised and corrected by E. Burton, D.D. *Sixth Edition,* 1877. 8vo. *cloth,* 10*s.* 6*d.*

Pearson's Minor Theological Works. Now first collected, with a Memoir of the Author, Notes, and Index, by Edward Churton, M.A. 2 vols. 1844. 8vo. *cloth,* 10*s.*

Sanderson's Works. Edited by W. Jacobson, D.D. 6 vols. 1854. 8vo. *cloth,* 1*l.* 10*s.*

Stanhope's Paraphrase and Comment upon the Epistles and Gospels. *A new Edition.* 2 vols. 1851. 8vo. *cloth,* 10*s.*

Stillingfleet's Origines Sacrae. 2 vols. 1837. 8vo. *cloth,* 9*s.*

Stillingfleet's Rational Account of the Grounds of Protestant Religion; being a vindication of Abp. Laud's Relation of a Conference, &c. 2 vols. 1844. 8vo. *cloth,* 10*s.*

Wall's History of Infant Baptism, with Gale's Reflections, and Wall's Defence. *A new Edition,* by Henry Cotton, D.C.L. 2 vols. 1862. 8vo. *cloth,* 1*l.* 1*s.*

Waterland's Works, with Life, by Bp. Van Mildert. *A new Edition,* with copious Indexes. 6 vols. 1857. 8vo. *cloth,* 2*l.* 11*s.*

Waterland's Review of the Doctrine of the Eucharist, with a Preface by the present Bishop of London. 1868. crown 8vo. *cloth,* 6*s.* 6*d.*

Wheatly's Illustration of the Book of Common Prayer. *A new Edition,* 1846. 8vo. *cloth,* 5*s.*

Wyclif. A Catalogue of the Original Works of John Wyclif, by W. W. Shirley, D.D. 1865. 8vo. *cloth,* 3*s.* 6*d.*

Wyclif. Select English Works. By T. Arnold, M.A. 3 vols. 1871. 8vo. *cloth,* 2*l.* 2*s.*

Wyclif. Trialogus. *With the Supplement now first edited.* By Gotthard Lechler. 1869. 8vo. *cloth,* 14*s.*

ENGLISH HISTORICAL AND DOCUMENTARY WORKS.

British Barrows, a Record of the Examination of Sepulchral Mounds in various parts of England. By William Greenwell, M.A., F.S.A. Together with Description of Figures of Skulls, General Remarks on Prehistoric Crania, and an Appendix by George Rolleston, M.D., F.R.S. 1877. Medium 8vo. *cloth*, 25s.

Two of the Saxon Chronicles parallel, with Supplementary Extracts from the Others. Edited, with Introduction, Notes, and a Glossarial Index, by J. Earle, M.A. 1865. 8vo. *cloth*, 16s.

Magna Carta, a careful Reprint. Edited by W. Stubbs, M.A., Regius Professor of Modern History. 1879. 4to. *stitched*, 1s.

Britton, a Treatise upon the Common Law of England, composed by order of King Edward I. The French Text carefully revised, with an English Translation, Introduction, and Notes, by F. M. Nichols, M.A. 2 vols. 1865. royal 8vo. *cloth*, 1l. 16s.

Burnet's History of His Own Time, with the suppressed Passages and Notes. 6 vols. 1833. 8vo. *cloth*, 2l. 10s.

Burnet's History of James II, with additional Notes. 1852. 8vo. *cloth*, 9s. 6d.

Carte's Life of James Duke of Ormond. *A new Edition*, carefully compared with the original MSS. 6 vols. 1851. 8vo. *cloth*, 1l. 5s.

Casauboni Ephemerides, cum praefatione et notis J. Russell, S.T.P. Tomi II. 1850. 8vo. *cloth*, 15s.

Clarendon's (Edw. Earl of) History of the Rebellion and Civil Wars in England. To which are subjoined the Notes of Bishop Warburton. 7 vols. 1849. medium 8vo. *cloth*, 2l. 10s.

Clarendon's (Edw. Earl of) History of the Rebellion and Civil Wars in England. 7 vols. 1839. 18mo. *cloth*, 1l. 1s.

Clarendon's (Edw. Earl of) History of the Rebellion and Civil Wars in England. Also His Life, written by Himself, in which is included a Continuation of his History of the Grand Rebellion. With copious Indexes. In one volume, royal 8vo. 1842. *cloth*, 1l. 2s.

Clarendon's (Edw. Earl of) Life, including a Continuation of his History. 2 vols. 1857. medium 8vo. *cloth*, 1l. 2s.

Clarendon's (Edw. Earl of) Life, and Continuation of his History. 3 vols. 1827. 8vo. *cloth*, 16s. 6d.

Calendar of the Clarendon State Papers, preserved in the Bodleian Library. *In three volumes*. 1869-76.

 Vol. I. From 1523 to January 1649. 8vo. *cloth*, 18s.
 Vol. II. From 1649 to 1654. 8vo. *cloth*, 16s.
 Vol. III. From 1655 to 1657. 8vo. *cloth*, 14s.

Calendar of Charters and Rolls preserved in the Bodleian Library. 1878. 8vo. *cloth*, 1*l*. 11*s*. 6*d*.

Freeman's (E. A.) History of the Norman Conquest of England; its Causes and Results. *In Six Volumes.* 8vo. *cloth*, 5*l*. 9*s*. 6*d*.

> Vols. I–II together, 3rd edition, 1877. 1*l*. 16*s*.
> Vol. III, 2nd edition, 1874. 1*l*. 1*s*.
> Vol. IV, 2nd edition, 1875. 1*l*. 1*s*.
> Vol. V, 1876. 1*l*. 1*s*.
> Vol. VI. Index. 1879. 8vo. *cloth*, 10*s*. 6*d*.

Lloyd's Prices of Corn in Oxford, 1583–1830. 8vo. *sewed*, 1*s*.

Luttrell's (Narcissus) Diary. A Brief Historical Relation of State Affairs, 1678–1714. 6 vols. 1857. 8vo. *cloth*, 1*l*. 4*s*.

May's History of the Long Parliament. 1854. 8vo. *cloth*, 6*s*. 6*d*.

Rogers's History of Agriculture and Prices in England, A.D. 1259–1793. Vols. I and II (1259–1400). 8vo. *cloth*, 2*l*. 2*s*. Vols. III and IV *in the Press*.

Sprigg's England's Recovery; being the History of the Army under Sir Thomas Fairfax. 1854. 8vo. *cloth*, 6*s*.

Whitelock's Memorials of English Affairs from 1625 to 1660. 4 vols. 1853. 8vo. *cloth*, 1*l*. 10*s*.

Protests of the Lords, including those which have been expunged, from 1624 to 1874; with Historical Introductions. Edited by James E. Thorold Rogers, M.A. 1875. 3 vols. 8vo. *cloth*, 2*l*. 2*s*.

Enactments in Parliament, specially concerning the Universities of Oxford and Cambridge. Collected and arranged by J. Griffiths, M.A. 1869. 8vo. *cloth*, 12*s*.

Ordinances and Statutes [for Colleges and Halls] framed or approved by the Oxford University Commissioners. 1863. 8vo. *cloth*, 12*s*.—Sold separately (except for Exeter, All Souls, Brasenose, and Corpus), at 1*s*. each.

Statuta Universitatis Oxoniensis. 1879. 8vo. *cloth*, 5*s*.

The Student's Handbook to the University and Colleges of Oxford. *Fifth Edition.* 1879. Extra fcap. 8vo. *cloth*, 2*s*. 6*d*.

Index to Wills proved in the Court of the Chancellor of the University of Oxford, &c. Compiled by J. Griffiths, M.A. 1862. royal 8vo. *cloth*, 3*s*. 6*d*.

Catalogue of Oxford Graduates from 1659 to 1850. 1851. 8vo. *cloth*, 7*s*. 6*d*.

CHRONOLOGY, GEOGRAPHY, &c.

Clinton's Fasti Hellenici. The Civil and Literary Chronology of Greece, from the LVIth to the CXXIIIrd Olympiad. *Third edition,* 1841. 4to. *cloth,* 1*l.* 14*s.* 6*d.*

Clinton's Fasti Hellenici. The Civil and Literary Chronology of Greece, from the CXXIVth Olympiad to the Death of Augustus. *Second edition,* 1851. 4to. *cloth,* 1*l.* 12*s.*

Clinton's Epitome of the Fasti Hellenici. 1851. 8vo. *cloth,* 6*s.* 6*d.*

Clinton's Fasti Romani. The Civil and Literary Chronology of Rome and Constantinople, from the Death of Augustus to the Death of Heraclius. 2 vols. 1845, 1850. 4to. *cloth,* 3*l.* 9*s.*

Clinton's Epitome of the Fasti Romani. 1854. 8vo. *cloth,* 7*s.*

Cramer's Geographical and Historical Description of Asia Minor. 2 vols. 1832. 8vo. *cloth,* 11*s.*

Cramer's Map of Asia Minor, 15*s.*

Cramer's Map of Ancient and Modern Italy, on two sheets, 15*s.*

Cramer's Description of Ancient Greece. 3 vols. 1828. 8vo. *cloth,* 16*s.* 6*d.*

Cramer's Map of Ancient and Modern Greece, on two sheets, 15*s.*

Greswell's Fasti Temporis Catholici. 1852. 4 vols. 8vo. *cloth,* 2*l.* 10*s.*

Greswell's Tables to Fasti, 4to., and Introduction to Tables, 1852. 8vo. *cloth,* 15*s.*

Greswell's Origines Kalendariæ Italicæ. 1854. 4 vols. 8vo. *cloth,* 2*l.* 2*s.*

Greswell's Origines Kalendariæ Hellenicæ. 6 vols. 1862. 8vo. *cloth,* 4*l.* 4*s.*

MATHEMATICS, PHYSICAL SCIENCE, &c.

Archimedis quae supersunt omnia cum Eutocii commentariis ex recensione Josephi Torelli, cum novâ versione Latinâ. 1792. fol. *cloth,* 1*l.* 5*s.*

Bradley's Miscellaneous Works and Correspondence. With an Account of Harriot's Astronomical Papers. 1832. 4to. *cloth,* 17*s.*

   Reduction of Bradley's Observations by Dr. Busch. 1838. 4to. *cloth,* 3*s.*

Astronomical Observations made at the University Observatory, Oxford, under the direction of C. Pritchard, M.A., Savilian Professor of Astronomy. No. 1. 1878. Royal 8vo. *paper covers*, 3s. 6d.

Treatise on Infinitesimal Calculus. By Bartholomew Price, M.A., F.R.S., Professor of Natural Philosophy, Oxford.

> Vol. I. Differential Calculus. *Second Edition*, 8vo. *cloth*, 14s. 6d.

> Vol. II. Integral Calculus, Calculus of Variations, and Differential Equations. *Second Edition*, 1865. 8vo. *cloth*, 18s.

> Vol. III. Statics, including Attractions; Dynamics of a Material Particle. *Second Edition*, 1868. 8vo. *cloth*, 16s.

> Vol. IV. Dynamics of Material Systems; together with a Chapter on Theoretical Dynamics, by W. F. Donkin, M.A., F.R.S. 1862. 8vo. *cloth*, 16s.

Rigaud's Correspondence of Scientific Men of the 17th Century, with Table of Contents by A. de Morgan, and Index by the Rev. J. Rigaud, M.A., Fellow of Magdalen College, Oxford. 2 vols. 1841–1862. 8vo. *cloth*, 18s. 6d.

Daubeny's Introduction to the Atomic Theory. 1850. 16mo. *cloth*, 6s.

Vesuvius. By John Phillips, M.A., F.R.S., Professor of Geology, Oxford. 1869. Crown 8vo. *cloth*, 10s. 6d.

Geology of Oxford and the Valley of the Thames. By the same Author. 1871. 8vo. *cloth*, 21s.

Synopsis of the Pathological Series in the Oxford Museum. By H. W. Acland, M.D., F.R.S., 1867. 8vo. *cloth*, 2s. 6d.

Thesaurus Entomologicus Hopeianus, or a Description of the rarest Insects in the Collection given to the University by the Rev. William Hope. By J. O. Westwood, M.A., F.L.S. With 40 Plates. 1874. Small folio, *half morocco*, 7l. 10s.

Text-Book of Botany, Morphological and Physiological. By Dr. Julius Sachs, Professor of Botany in the University of Würzburg. Translated by A. W. Bennett, M.A. and S. H. Vines, M.A., and edited by W. T. Thiselton Dyer, M.A. Royal 8vo. *Second Edition, in the Press.*

Johannes Müller on Certain Variations in the Vocal Organs of the Passeres that have hitherto escaped notice. Translated by F. J. Bell, B.A., and edited with an Appendix, by A. H. Garrod, M.A., F.R.S. With Plates. 4to. *paper covers*, 7s. 6d.

BIBLIOGRAPHY.

Ebert's Bibliographical Dictionary, translated from the German. 4 vols. 1837. 8vo. *cloth,* 1l. 10s.

Cotton's List of Editions of the Bible in English. *Second Edition,* corrected and enlarged. 1852. 8vo. *cloth,* 8s. 6d.

Cotton's Typographical Gazetteer. 1831. 8vo. *cloth,* 12s. 6d.

Cotton's Typographical Gazetteer, Second Series. 1866. 8vo. *cloth,* 12s. 6d.

Cotton's Rhemes and Doway. An attempt to shew what has been done by Roman Catholics for the diffusion of the Holy Scriptures in English. 1855. 8vo. *cloth,* 9s.

MISCELLANEOUS.

The Logic of Hegel; translated from the Encyclopaedia of the Philosophical Sciences. With Prolegomena by William Wallace, M.A. 1874. 8vo. *cloth,* 14s.

Bacon's Novum Organum. Edited, with English notes, by G. W. Kitchin, M.A. 1855. 8vo. *cloth,* 9s. 6d.

Bacon's Novum Organum. Translated by G. W. Kitchin, M.A. 1855. 8vo. *cloth,* 9s. 6d. (See also p. 35.)

The Works of George Berkeley, D.D., formerly Bishop of Cloyne; including many of his writings hitherto unpublished. With Prefaces, Annotations, and an Account of his Life and Philosophy, by Alexander Campbell Fraser, M.A. 4 vols. 1871. 8vo. *cloth,* 2l. 18s.

The Life, Letters, &c. 1 vol. *cloth,* 16s. *See also* p. 35.

Smith's Wealth of Nations. A new Edition, with Notes, by J. E. Thorold Rogers, M.A. 2 vols. 1870. *cloth,* 21s.

A Course of Lectures on Art, delivered before the University of Oxford in Hilary Term, 1870, by John Ruskin, M.A., Slade Professor of Fine Art. 8vo. *cloth,* 6s.

A Critical Account of the Drawings by Michel Angelo and Raffaello in the University Galleries, Oxford. By J. C. Robinson, F.S.A. 1870. Crown 8vo. *cloth,* 4s.

Sturlunga Saga, including the Islendinga Saga of Lawman Sturla Thordsson and other works. Edited with Prolegomena, Appendices, Tables, Indices, and Maps, by Dr. Gudbrand Vigfusson. In 2 vols. 1878. 8vo. *cloth,* 2l. 2s.

The Ormulum; with the Notes and Glossary of Dr. R. M. White. Edited by Rev. R. Holt, M.A. 1878. 2 vols. Extra fcap. 8vo. *cloth,* 21*s.*

The Sacred Books of the East. Translated by various, Oriental Scholars, and edited by F. Max Müller.

Vol. I. **The Upanishads.** Part I. The *Kh*andogya-upanishad, The Talavakara-upanishad, The Aitareya-ara*n*yaka, The Kaushitaki-brahma*n*a-upanishad, and The Va*g*asaneyi-sa*m*hita-upanishad. Translated by F. Max Müller. 8vo. *cloth,* 10*s.* 6*d.*

Vol. II. **The Sacred Laws of the Aryas,** as taught in the Schools of Apastamba and Gautama. Translated by Georg Bühler. 8vo. *cloth,* 10*s.* 6*d.*

Vol. III. **The Sacred Books of China.** The Texts of Confucianism. Part I. The Shu King, The Shih King, and The Hsiao King. Translated by James Legge. 8vo. *cloth,* 12*s.* 6*d.*

Vol. IV. **The Zend-Avesta.** Part I. The Vendîdâd. Translated by James Darmesteter. 8vo. *cloth,* 10*s.* 6*d.*

Vol. V. **Pahlavi Texts.** Part I. The Bundahi*s*, Bahman Yast, and Shâyast-lâ-Shâyast. Translated by E. W. West. 8vo. *cloth,* 12*s.* 6*d.*

Vol. VII. **The Institutes of Vishnu.** Translated by Julius Jolly. 8vo. *cloth,* 10*s.* 6*d.*

The following Volumes are also in the Press :—

Vol. VI. **The Qur'ân.** Part I. Translated by Professor E. H. Palmer.

Vol. VIII. **The Bhagavadgîtâ** with other extracts from the Mahâbhârata. Translated by Kashinath Trimbak Telang.

Vol. IX. **The Qur'ân.** Part II. Translated by Professor E. H. Palmer.

Vol. X. **The Suttanipâta,** etc. Translated by Professor Fausböll.

Vol. XI. **The Mahâparinibbâna Sutta, The Tevi*gg*a** Sutta, The Mahâsudassana Sutta, The Dhamma-*K*akkappavattana Sutta. Translated by T. W. Rhys Davids.

𝕮𝖑𝖆𝖗𝖊𝖓𝖉𝖔𝖓 𝕻𝖗𝖊𝖘𝖘 𝕾𝖊𝖗𝖎𝖊𝖘.

The Delegates of the Clarendon Press having undertaken the publication of a series of works, chiefly educational, and entitled the 𝕮𝖑𝖆𝖗𝖊𝖓𝖉𝖔𝖓 𝕻𝖗𝖊𝖘𝖘 𝕾𝖊𝖗𝖎𝖊𝖘, have published, or have in preparation, the following.

Those to which prices are attached are already published; the others are in preparation.

I. ENGLISH.

A First Reading Book. By Marie Eichens of Berlin; and edited by Anne J. Clough. Extra fcap. 8vo. *stiff covers*, 4*d.*

Oxford Reading Book, Part I. For Little Children. Extra fcap. 8vo. *stiff covers*, 6*d.*

Oxford Reading Book, Part II. For Junior Classes. Extra fcap. 8vo. *stiff covers*, 6*d.*

An Elementary English Grammar and Exercise Book. By O. W. Tancock, M.A., Assistant Master of Sherborne School. Extra fcap. 8vo. *cloth*, 1*s.* 6*d.*

An English Grammar and Reading Book, for Lower Forms in Classical Schools. By O. W. Tancock, M.A., Assistant Master of Sherborne School. *Third Edition.* Extra fcap. 8vo. *cloth*, 3*s.* 6*d.*

Typical Selections from the best English Writers, with Introductory Notices. *Second Edition.* In Two Volumes. Extra fcap. 8vo. *cloth*, 3*s.* 6*d.* each.
  Vol. I. Latimer to Berkeley.   Vol. II. Pope to Macaulay.

The Philology of the English Tongue. By J. Earle, M.A. formerly Fellow of Oriel College, and sometime Professor of Anglo-Saxon Oxford. *Third Edition.* Extra fcap. 8vo. *cloth*, 7*s.* 6*d.*

A Book for the Beginner in Anglo-Saxon. By John Earle, M.A., Professor of Anglo-Saxon, Oxford. *Second Edition.* Extra fcap. 8vo. *cloth*, 2*s.* 6*d.*

An Anglo-Saxon Reader. In Prose and Verse. With Grammatical Introduction, Notes, and Glossary. By Henry Sweet, M.A. *Second Edition.* Extra fcap. 8vo. *cloth,* 8s. 6d.

Specimens of Early English. A New and Revised Edition. With Introduction, Notes, and Glossarial Index. By R. Morris, LL.D., and W. W. Skeat, M.A.

    Part I. *In the Press.*

    Part II. From Robert of Gloucester to Gower (A.D. 1298 to A.D. 1393). *Second Edition.* Extra fcap. 8vo. *cloth,* 7s. 6d.

Specimens of English Literature, from the 'Ploughmans Crede' to the 'Shepheardes Calender' (A.D. 1394 to A.D. 1579). With Introduction, Notes, and Glossarial Index. By W. W. Skeat, M.A. Extra fcap. 8vo. *cloth.* 7s. 6d.

The Vision of William concerning Piers the Plowman, by William Langland. Edited, with Notes, by W. W. Skeat, M.A. Extra fcap. 8vo. *cloth,* 4s. 6d.

Chaucer. The Prioresses Tale; Sir Thopas; The Monkes Tale; The Clerkes Tale; The Squieres Tale, &c. Edited by W. W. Skeat, M.A. *Second Edition.* Extra fcap. 8vo. *cloth,* 4s. 6d.

Chaucer. The Tale of the Man of Lawe; The Pardoneres Tale; The Second Nonnes Tale; The Chanouns Yemannes Tale. By the same Editor. Extra fcap. 8vo. *cloth,* 4s. 6d. (See also p. 22.)

Old English Drama. Marlowe's Tragical History of Dr. Faustus, and **Greene's** Honourable History of Friar Bacon and Friar Bungay. Edited by A. W. Ward, M.A., Professor of History and English Literature in Owens College, Manchester. 1878. Extra fcap. 8vo. *cloth,* 5s. 6d.

Marlowe. Edward II. With Introduction, Notes, &c. By O. W. Tancock, M.A., Assistant Master of Sherborne School. Extra fcap. 8vo. *cloth,* 3s.

Shakespeare. Hamlet. Edited by W. G. Clark, M.A., and W. Aldis Wright, M.A. Extra fcap. 8vo. *stiff covers,* 2s.

Shakespeare. Select Plays. Edited by W. Aldis Wright, M.A. Extra fcap. 8vo. *stiff covers.*

The Tempest, 1s. 6d.	King Lear, 1s. 6d.
As You Like It, 1s. 6d.	A Midsummer Night's Dream, 1s. 6d.
Julius Cæsar, 2s.	Coriolanus. 2s. 6d.

            Richard the Third. *In the Press.*

          (For other Plays, see p. 23.)

Milton. Areopagitica. With Introduction and Notes. By J. W. Hales, M.A., late Fellow of Christ's College, Cambridge. *Second Edition.* Extra fcap. 8vo. *cloth*, 3*s.*

Addison. Selections from Papers in the Spectator. With Notes. By T. Arnold, M.A., University College. *Second Edition.* Extra fcap. 8vo. *cloth*, 4*s.* 6*d.*

Burke. Four Letters on the Proposals for Peace with the Regicide Directory of France. Edited, with Introduction and Notes, by E. J. Payne, M.A. Extra fcap. 8vo. *cloth*, 5*s.* (See also p. 23.)

Also the following in paper covers :—

Goldsmith. The Deserted Village. 2*d.*

Gray. Elegy, and Ode on Eton College. 2*d.*

Johnson. Vanity of Human Wishes. With Notes by E. J. Payne, M.A. 4*d.*

Keats. Hyperion, Book I. With Notes by W. T. Arnold, B.A. 4*d.*

Milton. With Notes by R. C. Browne, M.A.

Lycidas, 3*d.*   L'Allegro, 3*d.*   Il Penseroso, 4*d.*   Comus, 6*d.*
Samson Agonistes, 6*d.*

Parnell. The Hermit. 2*d.*

A SERIES OF ENGLISH CLASSICS,

Designed to meet the wants of Students in English Literature, by the late Rev. J. S. BREWER, M.A., *of Queen's College, Oxford, and Professor of English Literature at King's College, London.*

1. **Chaucer.** The Prologue to the Canterbury Tales; The Knightes Tale; The Nonne Prestes Tale. Edited by R. Morris, Editor of Specimens of Early English, &c., &c. *Sixth Edition.* Extra fcap. 8vo. *cloth*, 2*s.* 6*d.* (See also p. 21.)

2. **Spenser's Faery Queene.** Books I and II. Designed chiefly for the use of Schools. With Introduction, Notes, and Glossary. By G. W. Kitchin, M.A.

    Book I. *Eighth Edition.* Extra fcap. 8vo. *cloth*, 2*s.* 6*d.*

    Book II. *Third Edition.* Extra fcap. 8vo. *cloth*, 2*s.* 6*d.*

3. **Hooker.** Ecclesiastical Polity, Book I. Edited by R. W. Church, M.A., Dean of St. Paul's; formerly Fellow of Oriel College, Oxford. *Second Edition.* Extra fcap. 8vo. *cloth*, 2*s.*

4. **Shakespeare.** Select Plays. Edited by W. G. Clark, M.A., Fellow of Trinity College, Cambridge; and W. Aldis Wright, M.A., Trinity College, Cambridge. Extra fcap. 8vo. *stiff covers.*

    I. The Merchant of Venice. 1s.

    II. Richard the Second. 1s. 6d.

    III. Macbeth. 1s. 6d. (For other Plays, see p. 21.)

5. **Bacon.**

    I. Advancement of Learning. Edited by W. Aldis Wright, M.A. *Second Edition.* Extra fcap. 8vo, *cloth*, 4s. 6d.

    II. The Essays. With Introduction and Notes. By J. R. Thursfield, M.A., Fellow and formerly Tutor of Jesus College, Oxford.

6. **Milton.** Poems. Edited by R. C. Browne, M.A. 2 vols. *Fourth Edition.* Extra fcap. 8vo. *cloth*, 6s. 6d.

    Sold separately, Vol. I. 4s.; Vol. II. 3s. (See also p. 22.)

7. **Dryden.** Select Poems. Stanzas on the Death of Oliver Cromwell; Astræa Redux; Annus Mirabilis; Absalom and Achitophel; Religio Laici; The Hind and the Panther. Edited by W. D. Christie, M.A. *Second Edition.* Ext. fcap. 8vo. *cloth*, 3s. 6d.

8. **Bunyan.** The Pilgrim's Progress, Grace Abounding. Edited, with Biographical Introduction and Notes, by E. Venables, M.A. 1879. Extra fcap. 8vo. *cloth*, 5s.

9. **Pope.** With Introduction and Notes. By Mark Pattison, B.D., Rector of Lincoln College, Oxford.

    I. Essay on Man. *Sixth Edition.* Extra fcap. 8vo. 1s. 6d.

    II. Satires and Epistles. *Third Edition.* Extra fcap. 8vo. 2s.

10. **Johnson.** Rasselas; Lives of Pope and Dryden. Edited by Alfred Milnes, B.A. (London), late Scholar of Lincoln College, Oxford. Extra fcap. 8vo. *cloth*, 4s. 6d.

11. **Burke.** Select Works. Edited, with Introduction and Notes, by E. J. Payne, M.A., of Lincoln's Inn, Barrister-at-Law, and Fellow of University College, Oxford.

    I. Thoughts on the Present Discontents; the two Speeches on America. *Second Edition.* Extra fcap. 8vo. *cloth*, 4s. 6d.

    II. Reflections on the French Revolution. *Second Edition.* Extra fcap. 8vo. *cloth*, 5s. (See also p. 22.)

12. **Cowper.** Edited, with Life, Introductions, and Notes, by H. T. Griffith, B.A., formerly Scholar of Pembroke College, Oxford.

    I. The Didactic Poems of 1782, with Selections from the Minor Pieces, A.D. 1779–1783. Extra fcap. 8vo. *cloth*, 3s.

    II. The Task, with Tirocinium, and Selections from the Minor Poems, A.D. 1784–1799. Extra fcap. 8vo. *cloth*, 3s.

II. LATIN.

An Elementary Latin Grammar. By John B. Allen, M.A., Head Master of Perse Grammar School, Cambridge. *Third Edition, Revised and Corrected.* Extra fcap. 8vo. *cloth*, 2s. 6d.

A First Latin Exercise Book. By the same Author. *Second Edition.* Extra fcap. 8vo. *cloth*, 2s. 6d.

Anglice Reddenda, or Easy Extracts, Latin and Greek, for Unseen Translation. By C. S. Jerram, M.A. Extra fcap. 8vo. *cloth*, 2s.

Passages for Translation into Latin. For the use of Passmen and others. Selected by J. Y. Sargent, M.A., Fellow and Tutor of Magdalen College, Oxford. *Fifth Edition.* Ext. fcap. 8vo. *cloth*, 2s. 6d.

First Latin Reader. By T. J. Nunns, M.A. *Third Edition.* Extra fcap. 8vo. *cloth*, 2s.

Second Latin Reader. *In Preparation.*

Caesar. The Commentaries (for Schools). With Notes and Maps. By Charles E. Moberly, M.A.
    Part I. The Gallic War. *Third Edition.* Extra fcap. 8vo. *cloth*, 4s. 6d.
    Part II. The Civil War. Extra fcap. 8vo. *cloth*, 3s. 6d.
    The Civil War. Book I. Extra fcap. 8vo. *cloth*, 2s.

Cicero. Selection of interesting and descriptive passages. With Notes. By Henry Walford, M.A. In three Parts. *Second Edition.* Extra fcap. 8vo. *cloth*, 4s. 6d. *Each Part separately, limp,* 1s. 6d.
    Part I. Anecdotes from Grecian and Roman History.
    Part II. Omens and Dreams: Beauties of Nature.
    Part III. Rome's Rule of her Provinces.

Cicero. Selected Letters (for Schools). With Notes. By the late C. E. Prichard, M.A., and E. R. Bernard, M.A. *Second Edition.* Extra fcap. 8vo. *cloth*, 3s.

Cicero. Select Orations (for Schools). With Notes. By J. R. King, M.A. Extra fcap. 8vo. *cloth*, 2s. 6d. *Just Published.*

Cornelius Nepos. With Notes. By Oscar Browning, M.A. *Second Edition.* Extra fcap. 8vo. *cloth*, 2s. 6d.

Livy. Selections (for Schools). With Notes and Maps. By H. Lee-Warner, M.A. Extra fcap. 8vo. *In Parts, limp, each* 1s. 6d.
    Part I. The Caudine Disaster.
    Part II. Hannibal's Campaign in Italy.
    Part III. The Macedonian War.

Ovid. Selections for the use of Schools. With Introductions and Notes, and an Appendix on the Roman Calendar. By W. Ramsay, M.A. Edited by G. G. Ramsay, M.A., Professor of Humanity, Glasgow. *Second Edition.* Ext. fcap. 8vo. *cloth,* 5s. 6d.

Pliny. Selected Letters (for Schools). With Notes. By the late C. E. Prichard, M.A., and E. R. Bernard, M.A. *Second Edition.* Extra fcap. 8vo. *cloth,* 3s.

Catulli Veronensis Liber. Iterum recognovit, apparatum criticum prolegomena appendices addidit, Robinson Ellis, A.M. 1878. Demy 8vo. *cloth,* 16s.

A Commentary on Catullus. By Robinson Ellis, M.A. 1876. Demy 8vo. *cloth,* 16s.

Catulli Veronensis Carmina Selecta, secundum recognitionem Robinson Ellis, A.M. Extra fcap. 8vo. *cloth,* 3s. 6d.

Cicero de Oratore. Book I. With Introduction and Notes. By A. S. Wilkins, M.A., Professor of Latin, Owens College, Manchester. 1879. 8vo. *cloth,* 6s.

Cicero's Philippic Orations. With Notes. By J. R. King, M.A. *Second Edition.* 1879. 8vo. *cloth,* 10s. 6d.

Cicero. Select Letters. With English Introductions, Notes, and Appendices. By Albert Watson, M.A. *Second Edition.* 1874. Demy 8vo. *cloth,* 18s.

Cicero. Select Letters. *Text.* By the same Editor. Extra fcap. 8vo. *cloth,* 4s.

Cicero pro Cluentio. With Introduction and Notes. By W. Ramsay, M.A. Edited by G. G. Ramsay, M.A. Extra fcap. 8vo. *cloth,* 3s. 6d.

Horace. With a Commentary. Volume I. The Odes, Carmen Seculare, and Epodes. By Edward C. Wickham, M.A., Head Master of Wellington College. *Second Edition.* 1877. 8vo. *cloth,* 12s.
Also a small edition for Schools.

Livy, Books I-X. By J. R. Seeley, M.A., Regius Professor of Modern History, Cambridge. Book I. *Second Edition.* 1874. 8vo. *cloth,* 6s.
Also a small edition for Schools.

Persius. The Satires. With a Translation and Commentary. By John Conington, M.A. Edited by Henry Nettleship, M.A. *Second Edition.* 1874. 8vo. *cloth,* 7s. 6d.

Selections from the less known Latin Poets. By North
Pinder, M.A. 1869. Demy 8vo. *cloth*, 15s.

Fragments and Specimens of Early Latin. With Introductions and Notes. 1874. By John Wordsworth, M.A. 8vo. *cloth*, 18s.

Tacitus. The Annals. Books I–VI. With Essays and Notes.
By T. F. Dallin, M.A., Tutor of Queen's College, Oxford. *Preparing*.

Vergil : Suggestions Introductory to a Study of the Aeneid.
By H. Nettleship, M.A. 8vo. *sewed*, 1s. 6d.

Ancient Lives of Vergil ; with an Essay on the Poems of Vergil,
in connection with his Life and Times. By H. Nettleship, M.A. 8vo.
sewed, 2s.

The Roman Satura : its original form in connection with its
literary development. By H. Nettleship, M.A. 8vo. *sewed*, 1s.

A Manual of Comparative Philology. By T. L. Papillon,
M.A., Fellow and Lecturer of New College. *Second Edition.* Crown
8vo. *cloth*, 6s.

The Roman Poets of the Augustan Age. By William
Young Sellar, M.A., Professor of Humanity in the University of
Edinburgh. VIRGIL. 1877. 8vo. *cloth*, 14s.

The Roman Poets of the Republic. By the same Editor.
Preparing.

III. GREEK.

A Greek Primer, for the use of beginners in that Language.
By the Right Rev. Charles Wordsworth, D.C.L., Bishop of St. Andrews.
Sixth Edition, Revised and Enlarged. Extra fcap. 8vo. *cloth*, 1s. 6d.

Graecae Grammaticae Rudimenta in usum Scholarum. Auctore
Carolo Wordsworth, D.C.L. *Nineteenth Edition*, 1877. 12mo. *bound*, 4s.

A Greek-English Lexicon, abridged from Liddell and Scott's
4to. edition, chiefly for the use of Schools. *Eighteenth Edition. Carefully Revised throughout.* 1879. Square 12mo. *cloth*, 7s. 6d.

Greek Verbs, Irregular and Defective; their forms, meaning, and quantity; embracing all the Tenses used by Greek writers,
with reference to the passages in which they are found. By W. Veitch.
Third Edition. Crown 8vo. *cloth*, 10s. 6d.

The Elements of Greek Accentuation (for Schools): abridged
from his larger work by H. W. Chandler, M.A., Waynflete Professor of
Moral and Metaphysical Philosophy, Oxford. Ext. fcap. 8vo. *cloth*, 2s. 6d.

A Series of Graduated Greek Readers;—

First Greek Reader. By W. G. Rushbrooke, M.L., formerly Fellow of St. John's College, Cambridge, Second Classical Master at the City of London School. Extra fcap. 8vo. *cloth*, 2*s.* 6*d.*

Second Greek Reader. By A. M. Bell, M.A. Extra fcap. 8vo. *cloth*, 3*s.* 6*d. Just Published.*

Third Greek Reader. *In Preparation.*

Fourth Greek Reader; being Specimens of Greek. Dialects. With Introductions and Notes. By W. W. Merry, M.A., Fellow and Lecturer of Lincoln College. Extra fcap. 8vo. *cloth*, 4*s.* 6*d.*

Fifth Greek Reader. Part I. Selections from Greek Epic and Dramatic Poetry, with Introductions and Notes. By Evelyn Abbott, M.A., Fellow of Balliol College. Ext. fcap. 8vo. *cloth*, 4*s.* 6*d.*

Part II. By the same Editor. *In Preparation.*

The Golden Treasury of Ancient Greek Poetry; being a Collection of the finest passages in the Greek Classic Poets, with Introductory Notices and Notes. By R. S. Wright, M.A., Fellow of Oriel College, Oxford. Ext. fcap. 8vo. *cloth*, 8*s.* 6*d.*

A Golden Treasury of Greek Prose, being a collection of the finest passages in the principal Greek Prose Writers, with Introductory Notices and Notes. By R. S. Wright, M.A., and J. E. L. Shadwell, M.A. Ext. fcap. 8vo. *cloth*, 4*s.* 6*d.*

Aeschylus. Prometheus Bound (for Schools). With Introduction and Notes, by A. O. Prickard, M.A., Fellow of New College. Extra fcap. 8vo. *cloth*, 2*s.*

Aeschylus. Agamemnon (for Schools), with Introduction and Notes by Arthur Sidgwick, M.A., Lecturer at Corpus Christi College, Oxford; late Assistant Master at Rugby School, and Fellow of Trinity College, Cambridge.

Aristophanes. In Single Plays, edited, with English Notes, Introductions, etc., by W. W. Merry, M.A. Extra fcap. 8vo.

The Clouds, 2*s.*   The Acharnians. *In Preparation.*

Other Plays will follow.

Arrian. Selections (for Schools). With Notes. By J. S. Phillpotts, B.C.L., Head Master of Bedford School.

Cebes. Tabula. With Introduction and Notes by C. S. Jerram, M.A. Extra fcap. 8vo. *cloth*, 2*s.* 6*d.*

Euripides. Alcestis (for Schools). By C. S. Jerram, M.A. Extra fcap. 8vo. *cloth*, 2*s.* 6*d. Just Published.*

Herodotus. Selections from. Edited, with Introduction, Notes, and a Map, by W. W. Merry, M.A., Fellow and Lecturer of Lincoln College. *cloth,* 2s. 6d.

Homer. Odyssey, Books I—XII (for Schools). By W. W. Merry, M.A. *Nineteenth Thousand.* Extra fcap. 8vo. *cloth,* 4s. 6d. Book II, *separately,* 1s. 6d.

Homer. Odyssey, Books XIII–XXIV (for Schools). By the same Editor. Extra fcap. 8vo. *cloth,* 5s.

Homer. Iliad, Book I (for Schools). By D. B. Monro, M.A. Extra fcap. 8vo. *cloth,* 2s.

Lucian. Vera Historia (for Schools). By C. S. Jerram, M.A. Extra fcap. 8vo. *cloth,* 1s. 6d.

Plato. Selections (for Schools). With Notes. By B. Jowett, M.A., Regius Professor of Greek; and J. Purves, M.A., Fellow and Lecturer of Balliol College, Oxford. *In the Press.*

Sophocles. In Single Plays, with English Notes, &c. By Lewis Campbell, M.A., and Evelyn Abbott, M.A. Extra fcap. 8vo. *limp.*

Oedipus Rex,   Oedipus Coloneus,   Antigone, 1s. 9d. each.

Ajax,   Electra,   Trachiniae,   Philoctetes, 2s. each.

Sophocles. Oedipus Rex: Dindorf's Text, with Notes by the present Bishop of St. David's. Ext. fcap. 8vo. *limp,* 1s. 6d.

Theocritus (for Schools). With Notes. By H. Kynaston, M.A. (late Snow), Head Master of Cheltenham College. *Second Edition.* Extra fcap. 8vo. *cloth,* 4s. 6d.

Xenophon. Easy Selections (for Junior Classes). With a Vocabulary, Notes, and Map. By J. S. Phillpotts, B.C.L., and C. S. Jerram, M.A. Extra fcap. 8vo. *cloth,* 3s. 6d.

Xenophon. Selections (for Schools). With Notes and Maps. By J. S. Phillpotts, B.C.L., Head Master of Bedford School. *Fourth Edition.* Ext. fcap. 8vo. *cloth,* 3s. 6d.

Xenophon. Anabasis, Book II. With Notes and Map. By C. S. Jerram, M.A. Extra fcap. 8vo. *cloth,* 2s.

Aristotle's Politics. By W. L. Newman, M.A., Fellow of Balliol College, Oxford.

Aristotelian Studies. I. On the Structure of the Seventh Book of the Nicomachean Ethics. By J. C. Wilson, M.A., Fellow of Oriel College, Oxford. 1879. Medium 8vo. *stiff,* 5s.

Demosthenes and Aeschines. The Orations of Demosthenes and Æschines on the Crown. With Introductory Essays and Notes. By G. A. Simcox, M.A., and W. H. Simcox, M.A. 1872. 8vo. *cloth,* 12s.

Homer. Odyssey, Books I–XII. Edited with English Notes, Appendices, etc. By W. W. Merry, M.A., and the late James Riddell, M.A. 1876. Demy 8vo. *cloth,* 16s.

Homer. Odyssey, Books XIII–XXIV. With Introduction and Notes. By S. H. Butcher, M.A., Fellow of University College.

Homer. Iliad. With Introduction and Notes. By D. B. Monro, M.A., Vice-Provost of Oriel College, Oxford. *Preparing.*

A Homeric Grammar. By D. B. Monro, M.A. *In the Press.*

Sophocles. The Plays and Fragments. With English Notes and Introductions. By Lewis Campbell, M.A., Professor of Greek, St. Andrews, formerly Fellow of Queen's College, Oxford. 2 vols.

Vol. I. Oedipus Tyrannus. Oedipus Coloneus. Antigone. *Second Edition.* 1879. 8vo. *cloth,* 16s. Vol. II. *In the Press.*

Sophocles. The Text of the Seven Plays. By the same Editor. Ext. fcap. 8vo. *cloth,* 4s. 6d.

A Handbook of Greek Inscriptions, illustrative of Greek History. By E. L. Hicks, M.A., formerly Fellow of Corpus Christi College, Oxford. *In Preparation.*

IV. FRENCH.

An Etymological Dictionary of the French Language, with a Preface on the Principles of French Etymology. By A. Brachet. Translated into English by G. W. Kitchin, M.A. *Second Edition.* Crown 8vo. *cloth,* 7s. 6d.

Brachet's Historical Grammar of the French Language. Translated into English by G. W. Kitchin, M.A. *Fourth Edition.* Extra fcap. 8vo. *cloth,* 3s. 6d.

French Classics, Edited by GUSTAVE MASSON, B.A.

Corneille's Cinna, and **Molière's** Les Femmes Savantes. With Introduction and Notes. Extra fcap. 8vo. *cloth,* 2s. 6d.

Racine's Andromaque, and **Corneille's** Le Menteur. With Louis Racine's Life of his Father. Extra fcap. 8vo. *cloth,* 2s. 6d.

Molière's Les Fourberies de Scapin, and **Racine's** Athalie. With Voltaire's Life of Molière. Extra fcap. 8vo. *cloth,* 2s. 6d.

Selections from the Correspondence of **Madame de Sévigné** and her chief Contemporaries. Intended more especially for Girls' Schools. Extra fcap. 8vo. *cloth,* 3s.

Voyage autour de ma Chambre, by **Xavier de Maistre**; Ourika, by **Madame de Duras**; La Dot de Suzette, by **Fievée**; Les Jumeaux de l'Hôtel Corneille, by **Edmond About**; Mésaventures d'un Écolier, by **Rodolphe Töpffer**. Extra fcap. 8vo. *cloth,* 2s. 6d.

Regnard's Le Joueur, and **Brueys** and **Palaprat's** Le Grondeur. By Gustave Masson, B.A. Extra fcap. 8vo. *cloth*, 2s. 6d.

Louis XIV and his Contemporaries; as described in Extracts from the best Memoirs of the Seventeenth Century. With English Notes, Genealogical Tables, &c. By the same Editor. Extra fcap. 8vo. *cloth*, 2s. 6d.

V. GERMAN.

LANGE'S *German Course. By* HERMANN LANGE, *Teacher of Modern Languages, Manchester:*

The Germans at Home; a Practical Introduction to German Conversation, with an Appendix containing the Essentials of German Grammar. *Second Edition.* 8vo. *cloth*, 2s. 6d.

The German Manual; a German Grammar, a Reading Book, and a Handbook of German Conversation. 8vo. *cloth*, 7s. 6d.

A Grammar of the German Language. 8vo. *cloth*, 3s. 6d.

This 'Grammar' is a reprint of the Grammar contained in 'The German Manual,' and, in this separate form, is intended for the use of students who wish to make themselves acquainted with German Grammar chiefly for the purpose of being able to read German books.

German Composition; Extracts from English and American writers for Translation into German, with Hints for Translation in footnotes. *In the Press.*

Lessing's Laokoon. With Introduction, English Notes, etc. By A. HAMANN, Phil. Doc., M.A., Taylorian Teacher of German in the University of Oxford. Extra fcap. 8vo. *cloth*, 4s. 6d.

Wilhelm Tell. A Drama. By Schiller. Translated into English Verse by E. Massie, M.A. Extra fcap. 8vo. *cloth*, 5s.

Also, *Edited by* C. A. BUCHHEIM, *Phil. Doc., Professor in King's College, London:*

Goethe's Egmont. With a Life of Goethe, &c. *Second Edition.* Extra fcap. 8vo. *cloth*, 3s.

Schiller's Wilhelm Tell. With a Life of Schiller; an historical and critical Introduction, Arguments, and a complete Commentary. *Third Edition.* Extra fcap. 8vo. *cloth*, 3s. 6d.

Lessing's Minna von Barnhelm. A Comedy. With a Life of Lessing, Critical Analysis, Complete Commentary, &c. *Third Edition.* Extra fcap. 8vo. *cloth*, 3s. 6d.

Schiller's Historische Skizzen; Egmont's Leben und Tod, and Belagerung von Antwerpen. Extra fcap. 8vo. *cloth*, 2s. 6d.

Goethe's Iphigenie auf Tauris. A Drama. With a Critical Introduction and Notes. Extra fcap. 8vo. *cloth*, 3s.

In Preparation.

Schiller's Maria Stuart. With Notes, Introduction, &c.

Selections from the Poems of **Schiller** and **Goethe.**

Becker's (K. F.) Friedrich der Grosse.

VI. MATHEMATICS, &c.

Figures Made Easy: a first Arithmetic Book. (Introductory to 'The Scholar's Arithmetic.') By Lewis Hensley, M.A., formerly Fellow and Assistant Tutor of Trinity College, Cambridge. Crown 8vo. *cloth*, 6d.

Answers to the **Examples in Figures made Easy,** together with two thousand additional Examples formed from the Tables in the same, with Answers. By the same Author. Crown 8vo. *cloth*, 1s.

The Scholar's Arithmetic; with Answers to the Examples. By the same Author. Crown 8vo. *cloth*, 4s. 6d.

The Scholar's Algebra. An Introductory work on Algebra. By the same Author. Crown 8vo. *cloth*, 4s. 6d.

Book-keeping. By R. G. C. Hamilton, Financial Assistant Secretary to the Board of Trade, and John Ball (of the Firm of Quilter, Ball, & Co.), Co-Examiners in Book-keeping for the Society of Arts. *New and enlarged Edition.* Extra fcap. 8vo. *limp cloth*, 2s.

A Course of Lectures on Pure Geometry. By Henry J. Stephen Smith, M.A., F.R.S., Fellow of Corpus Christi College, and Savilian Professor of Geometry in the University of Oxford.

Acoustics. By W. F. Donkin, M.A., F.R.S., Savilian Professor of Astronomy, Oxford. 1870. Crown 8vo. *cloth*, 7s. 6d.

A Treatise on Electricity and Magnetism. By J. Clerk Maxwell, M.A., F.R.S., Professor of Experimental Physics in the University of Cambridge. 1873. 2 vols. 8vo. *cloth*, 1l. 11s. 6d.

An Elementary Treatise on the same subject. By the same Author. *Preparing.*

A Treatise on Statics. By G. M. Minchin, M.A., Professor of Applied Mathematics in the Indian Engineering College, Cooper's Hill. *Second Edition, Revised and Enlarged.* 1879. 8vo. *cloth*, 14s.

A Treatise on the Kinetic Theory of Gases. By Henry William Watson, M.A., formerly Fellow of Trinity College, Cambridge. 1876. 8vo. *cloth,* 3s. 6d.

A Treatise on the Application of Generalised Coordinates to the Kinetics of a Material System. By H. W. Watson, M.A., and S. H. Burbury, M.A., formerly Fellow of St. John's College, Cambridge. 1879. 8vo. *cloth,* 6s.

Geodesy. By Colonel Alexander Ross Clarke, C.B., R.E. 8vo. *cloth,* 12s. 6d. *Just Published.*

VII. PHYSICAL SCIENCE.

A Handbook of Descriptive Astronomy. By G. F. Chambers, F.R.A.S. *Third Edition.* 1877. Demy 8vo. *cloth,* 28s.

Chemistry for Students. By A. W. Williamson, Phil. Doc., F.R.S., Professor of Chemistry, University College, London. *A new Edition, with Solutions.* 1873. Extra fcap. 8vo. *cloth,* 8s. 6d.

A Treatise on Heat, with numerous Woodcuts and Diagrams. By Balfour Stewart, LL.D., F.R.S., Professor of Natural Philosophy in Owens College, Manchester. *Third Edition.* 1876. Extra fcap. 8vo. *cloth,* 7s. 6d.

Lessons on Thermodynamics. By R. E. Baynes, M.A., Senior Student of Christ Church, Oxford, and Lee's Reader in Physics. 1878. Crown 8vo. *cloth,* 7s. 6d.

Forms of Animal Life. By G. Rolleston, M.D., F.R.S., Linacre Professor of Physiology, Oxford. Illustrated by Descriptions and Drawings of Dissections. Demy 8vo. *cloth,* 16s.

Exercises in Practical Chemistry (Laboratory Practice). By A. G. Vernon Harcourt, M.A., F.R.S., Senior Student of Christ Church, and Lee's Reader in Chemistry; and H. G. Madan, M.A., Fellow of Queen's College, Oxford. *Second Edition.* Crown 8vo. *cloth,* 7s. 6d.

Crystallography. By M. H. N. Story-Maskelyne, M.A., Professor of Mineralogy, Oxford; and Deputy Keeper in the Department of Minerals, British Museum. *In the Press.*

VIII. HISTORY.

The Constitutional History of England, in its Origin and Development. By William Stubbs, M.A., Regius Professor of Modern History. *Library Edition.* Three vols. demy 8vo. *cloth,* 2l. 8s. *Just Published.*

Also in crown 8vo. vols. II and III, price 12s. each. Vol. I *Reprinting.*

Select Charters and other Illustrations of English Constitutional History, from the Earliest Times to the Reign of Edward I. Arranged and Edited by W. Stubbs, M.A. *Third Edition.* 1876. Crown 8vo. *cloth,* 8s. 6d.

A History of England, principally in the Seventeenth Century. By Leopold Von Ranke. Translated by Resident Members of the University of Oxford, under the superintendence of G. W. Kitchin, M.A., and C. W. Boase, M.A. 1875. 6 vols. 8vo. *cloth,* 3l. 3s.

Genealogical Tables illustrative of Modern History. By H. B. George, M.A. *Second Edition.* Small 4to. *cloth,* 12s.

A History of France. With numerous Maps, Plans, and Tables. By G. W. Kitchin, M.A. *In Three Volumes.* 1873–77. Crown 8vo. *cloth,* each 10s. 6d.

Vol. 1. Down to the Year 1453. Vol. 2. From 1453–1624.
Vol. 3. From 1624–1793.

A History of the United States of America. By E. J. Payne, M.A., Barrister-at-Law, and Fellow of University College, Oxford. *In the Press.*

A Manual of Ancient History. By George Rawlinson, M.A., Camden Professor of Ancient History, formerly Fellow of Exeter College, Oxford. Demy 8vo. *cloth,* 14s.

A History of Germany and of the Empire, down to the close of the Middle Ages. By J. Bryce, D.C.L., Regius Professor of Civil Law in the University of Oxford.

Italy and her Invaders, A.D. 376–476. By T. Hodgkin, Fellow of University College, London. Illustrated with Plates and Maps. 2 vols. 8vo. *cloth,* 1l. 12s. *Just Published.*

A History of British India. By S. J. Owen, M.A., Reader in Indian History in the University of Oxford.

A History of Greece. By E. A. Freeman, M.A., formerly Fellow of Trinity College, Oxford.

A History of Greece from its Conquest by the Romans to the present time, B.C. 146 to A.D. 1864. By George Finlay, LL. D. A new Edition, revised throughout, and in part re-written, with considerable additions, by the Author, and Edited by H. F. Tozer, M.A., Tutor and late Fellow of Exeter College, Oxford. 1877. 7 vols. 8vo. *cloth,* 3l. 10s.

A Selection from the Despatches, Treaties, and other Papers of the Marquess Wellesley, K.G., during his Government of India. Edited by S. J. Owen, M.A., formerly Professor of History in the Elphinstone College, Bombay. 1877. 8vo. *cloth,* 1l. 4s.

A Selection from the Wellington Despatches. By the same Editor. *In the Press.*

IX. LAW.

Elements of Law considered with reference to Principles of General Jurisprudence. By William Markby, M.A., Judge of the High Court of Judicature, Calcutta. *Second Edition, with Supplement.* 1874. Crown 8vo. *cloth,* 7s. 6d. Supplement *separately,* 2s.

An Introduction to the History of the Law of Real Property, with original Authorities. By Kenelm E. Digby, M.A., of Lincoln's Inn, Barrister-at-Law. *Second Edition.* 1876. Crown 8vo. *cloth,* 7s. 6d.

The Elements of Jurisprudence. By Thomas Erskine Holland, D.C.L., Chichele Professor of International Law and Diplomacy, and Fellow of All Souls College, Oxford. *cloth,* 10s. 6d.

The Institutes of Justinian, edited as a recension of the Institutes of Gaius. By the same Editor. 1873. Extra fcap. 8vo. *cloth,* 5s.

Alberici Gentilis, I. C. D., I. C. Professoris Regii, De Iure Belli Libri Tres. Edidit Thomas Erskine Holland I. C. D., Iuris Gentium Professor Chicheleianus, Coll. Omn. Anim. Socius, necnon in Univ. Perusin. Iuris Professor Honorarius. 1877. Small 4to. *half morocco,* 21s.

Gaii Institutionum Juris Civilis Commentarii Quatuor; or, Elements of Roman Law by Gaius. With a Translation and Commentary by Edward Poste, M.A., Barrister-at-Law, and Fellow of Oriel College, Oxford. *Second Edition.* 1875. 8vo. *cloth,* 18s.

Select Titles from the Digest of Justinian. By T. E. Holland, D.C.L., Chichele Professor of International Law and Diplomacy, and Fellow of All Souls' College, Oxford, and C. L. Shadwell, B.C.L., Fellow of Oriel College, Oxford. *In Parts.*

Part I.   Introductory Titles. 8vo. *sewed,* 2s. 6d.

Part II. Family Law. 8vo. *sewed,* 1s.

Part III. Property Law. 8vo. *sewed,* 2s. 6d.

Part IV. (No. 1.) Law of Obligations. 8vo. *sewed,* 3s. 6d.

Principles of the English Law of Contract. By Sir William R. Anson, Bart., B.C.L., Vinerian Reader of English Law, and Fellow of All Souls College, Oxford. 1879. Crown 8vo. *cloth,* 9s.

A Treatise on International Law. By W. E. Hall, M.A., University College, Oxford. *In the Press.*

X. MENTAL AND MORAL PHILOSOPHY.

Bacon. Novum Organum. Edited, with Introduction, Notes, &c., by T. Fowler, M.A., Professor of Logic in the University of Oxford. 1878. 8vo. *cloth*, 14*s.*

Selections from Berkeley, with an Introduction and Notes. For the use of Students in the Universities. By Alexander Campbell Fraser, LL.D. *Second Edition.* Crown 8vo. *cloth*, 7*s.* 6*d.* (*See also* p. 18.)

The Elements of Deductive Logic, designed mainly for the use of Junior Students in the Universities. By T. Fowler, M.A., Professor of Logic in the University of Oxford. *Seventh Edition*, with a Collection of Examples. Extra fcap. 8vo. *cloth*, 3*s.* 6*d.*

The Elements of Inductive Logic, designed mainly for the use of Students in the Universities. By the same Author. *Third Edition.* Extra fcap. 8vo. *cloth*, 6*s.*

A Manual of Political Economy, for the use of Schools. By J. E. Thorold Rogers, M.A., formerly Professor of Political Economy, Oxford. *Third Edition.* Extra fcap. 8vo. *cloth*, 4*s.* 6*d.*

An Introduction to the Principles of Morals and Legislation. By Jeremy Bentham. Crown 8vo. *cloth*, 6*s.* 6*d.*

XI. ART, &c.

A Handbook of Pictorial Art. By R. St. J. Tyrwhitt, M.A., formerly Student and Tutor of Christ Church, Oxford. With coloured Illustrations, Photographs, and a chapter on Perspective by A. Macdonald. *Second Edition.* 1875. 8vo. *half morocco*, 18*s.*

A Music Primer for Schools. By J. Troutbeck, M.A., Music Master in Westminster School, and R. F. Dale, M.A., B. Mus., Assistant Master in Westminster School. Crown 8vo. *cloth*, 1*s.* 6*d.*

A Treatise on Harmony. By Sir F. A. Gore Ouseley, Bart., Professor of Music in the University of Oxford. *Second Edition.* 4to. *cloth*, 10*s.*

A Treatise on Counterpoint, Canon, and Fugue, based upon that of Cherubini. By the same Author. 4to. *cloth*, 16*s.*

A Treatise on Musical Form and General Composition. By the same Author. 4to. *cloth*, 10*s.*

The Cultivation of the Speaking Voice. By John Hullah. *Second Edition.* Extra fcap. 8vo. *cloth*, 2*s.* 6*d.*

XII. MISCELLANEOUS.

Houses, Cottages, Barracks, and Hospitals; the Conditions and Arrangements necessary for their healthy Construction. By Captain Douglas Galton, C.B., D.C.L., F.R.S. *In the Press.*

Specimens of Lowland Scotch and Northern English. By Dr. J. A. H. Murray. *Preparing.*

Dante. Selections from the Inferno. With Introduction and Notes. By H. B. Cotterill, B.A. Extra fcap. 8vo. *cloth,* 4s. 6d.

Tasso. La Gerusalemme Liberata. Cantos i, ii. With Introduction and Notes. By the same Editor. Extra fcap. 8vo. *cloth,* 2s. 6d.

An Icelandic Prose Reader, with Notes, Grammar, and Glossary by Dr. Gudbrand Vigfusson and F. York Powell, M.A. 1879. Extra fcap. 8vo. *cloth,* 10s. 6d.

The Book of Tobit. A Chaldee Text, from a unique MS. in the Bodleian Library; with other Rabbinical Texts, English Translations, and the Itala. Edited by Ad. Neubauer, M.A. 1878. Crown 8vo. *cloth,* 6s.

Outlines of Textual Criticism applied to the New Testament. By C. E. Hammond, M.A., Fellow and Tutor of Exeter College, Oxford. *Third Edition.* Extra fcap. 8vo. *cloth,* 3s. 6d.

The Modern Greek Language in its relation to Ancient Greek. By E. M. Geldart, B.A. Extra fcap. 8vo. *cloth,* 4s. 6d.

A Handbook of Phonetics, including a Popular Exposition of the Principles of Spelling Reform. By Henry Sweet, President of the Philological Society, Author of a 'History of English Sounds,' &c. Extra fcap. 8vo. *cloth,* 4s. 6d.

A System of Physical Education: Theoretical and Practical. By Archibald Maclaren. Extra fcap. 8vo. *cloth,* 7s. 6d.

Published for the University by
MACMILLAN AND CO., LONDON.

Also to be had at the
CLARENDON PRESS DEPOSITORY, OXFORD.

The DELEGATES OF THE PRESS *invite suggestions and advice from all persons interested in education; and will be thankful for hints, &c. addressed to the* SECRETARY TO THE DELEGATES, *Clarendon Press, Oxford.*